Accounting Principles
Ninth Edition
Weygandt, Kieso, and Kimmel

Peachtree Complete Accounting for Accounting Principles
by
Mel Coe, Jr. and Rex A. Schildhouse

WILEY

John Wiley & Sons, Inc.

COVER PHOTO: OJO Images/SuperStock

ISBN-13   978-0-470-38667-5

10 9 8 7 6 5 4 3 2 1

Printed and bound by Bind-Rite, Inc.

Table of Contents

CHAPTER 3   **85**

CHAPTER 4   **103**

CHAPTER 5   **139**

CHAPTER 6   181

CHAPTER 7   199

CHAPTER 8   217

CHAPTER 1A

Peachtree Installation and Setup

OBJECTIVES
- Explanation of Chapter 1A and Chapter 1B.
- Explanation and walk-through the installation of Peachtree Complete Accounting.

- Installing the Student Data Set.

EXPLANATION OF CHAPTER 1A AND CHAPTER 1B

This text is written to accompany Accounting Principles, Ninth Edition by Weygandt, Kieso, and Kimmel. To keep in synchronization with the main textbook Chapter 1 of this text had been divided into to significant parts – Chapter 1A and Chapter 1B. Chapter 1A deals with the installation issues of Peachtree Complete Accounting by Sage and the Windows by Microsoft interactions necessary to work with Peachtree Complete Accounting. Chapter 1B relates to the first chapter of the Accounting Principles textbook.

EXPLANATION AND WALK-THROUGH OF THE INSTALLATION OF PEACHTREE COMPLETE ACCOUNTING

Peachtree Complete Accounting is commonly referred to as "Peachtree" and will frequently be called Peachtree in this text. The installation of Peachtree is compliant with Windows by Microsoft design specifications. If you have previously installed any other Windows compliant software you will see the similarities and appreciate the simplicity of this installation.

When the installation disk is first installed it should self-start unless that feature is disabled on your system and you will see the screen shown in Figure 1A. 1. If not, utilize Windows Explorer and select the drive which contains the installation disk and double-click on the "SETUP.EXE" to initiate installation.

NOTE: Some screens have been trimmed for presentation and fit to the page.

Figure 1A. 1 Top portion of Peachtree installation screen

On the setup screen for Peachtree, shown in Figure 1A. 1, double-click on the "Install Peachtree Accounting" option to continue the installation. And Peachtree will provide you Figure 1A. 2, a standard advisory screen recommending you close all other applications and programs during installation. It is recommended that you follow this advice as your operating system and storage disk will be busy with installation tasks for a while and any interference or improper interaction could result in a faulty installation. Viewing the installation instructions is recommended as it may contain current information about your specific installation not addressed where.

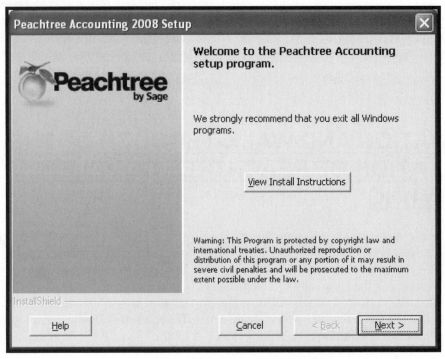

Figure 1A. 2 Peachtree advisory screen about other applications and programs

When ready, click on "Next >" in the bottom right corner to proceed with the installation. Peachtree is going to ask that you read the licensing agreement, also recommended as it explains the privileges and restrictions of this educational software package.

You must select the "Agree" radio button to accept the terms of the educational software license and that will enable you to click on "Next >" which is grayed out until Agree is selected. If Disagree is selected the installation process is cancelled. The license agreement screen is shown in Figure 1A. 3. Once "Agree" is selected and

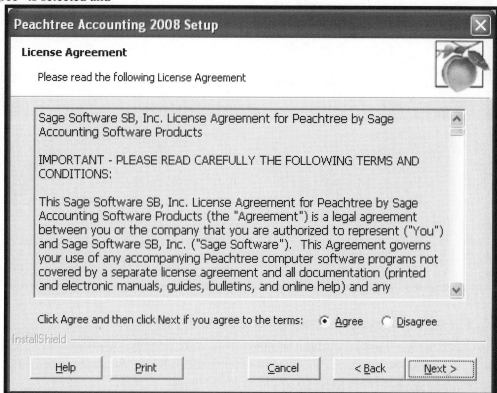

Figure 1A. 3 Peachtree license agreement screen with "Agree" already selected and "Next >" available

The next several screens presented by Peachtree is optional as controlled by your system configuration. If Peachtree's installation process is blocked by the Windows configurations you have set it, Windows will advise you of this protection and ask what you want to do. If presented with a "Firewall Detected," "Installation Blocked," "Antivirus Software Detected" dialog boxes, installation will only proceed if you "Approve," "Allow," or "OK" it.

With permission from you to disable firewall and antivirus protection for the installation of Peachtree, Peachtree will proceed with the installation and present you with a "progress" screen such as that shown in Figure 1A. 4. During installation Peachtree may provide you with "information" screens about Peachtree Complete Accounting.

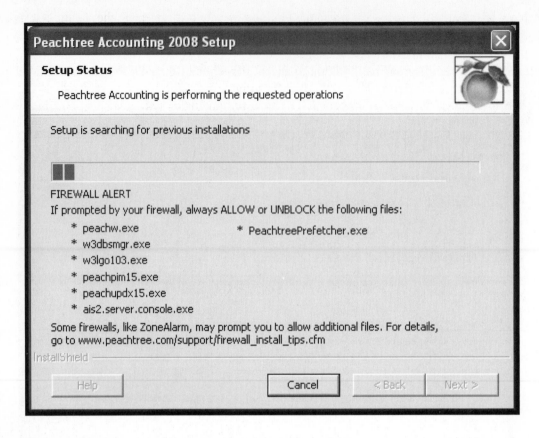

Figure 1A. 4   Peachtree setup and installation progress screen

Peachtree requires an installation serial number. This number is provided on your installation disk envelope within the textbook. You are required to enter that number in the screen represented in Figure 1A. 5. When the number is entered, click on "Next >" to continue.

Figure 1A. 5   Peachtree installation serial number input screen

Peachtree will ask if this installation is a stand-alone or network system in the dialog box shown in Figure 1A. 6. With the typical installation on a desktop or laptop system, select "Yes" followed by "Next >" to continue.

**Note:** The bottom of the screen print has been trimmed and does not show the "Next >" buttons. This area will trimmed in future screen prints unless it shows other information.

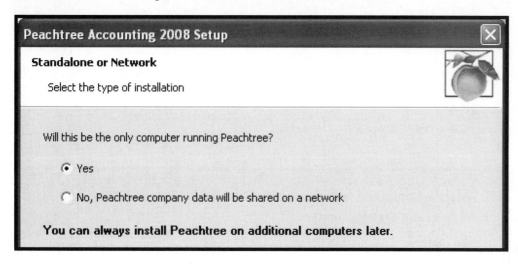

Figure 1A. 6   Peachtree installation stand-alone or network system input screen

The next screen, Figure 1A. 7, presented by Peachtree establishes where the data directories are to be installed. The default answer of "Yes" (Stored on this computer) is correct for any general desktop or laptop system installation. Click on the radio button to the left of "Yes" and click on "Next >" at the bottom of the dialog box.

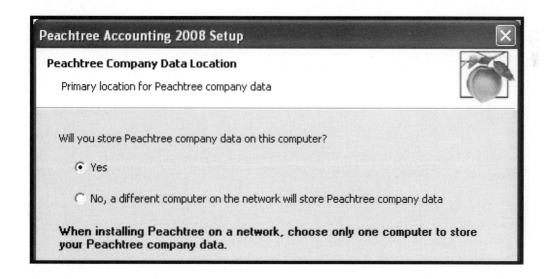

Figure 1A. 7   Peachtree data location screen

The following is a single screen print, Figure 1A. 8, of two installation screens Peachtree offers you to change the directories where Peachtree installs the program and where Peachtree will look for the company data files. Accept both defaults and click on "Next >" in both screens.

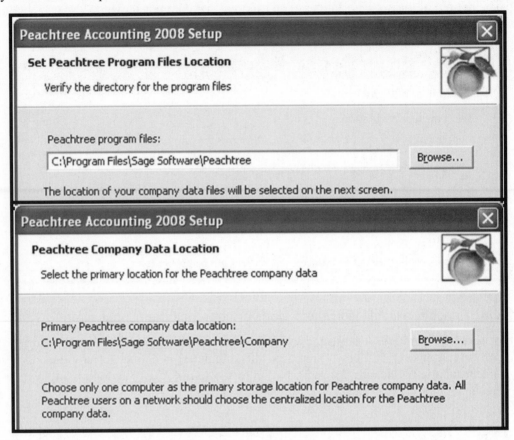

Figure 1A. 8 Peachtree program installation directory selection and data directory location selection

The next screen, shown in Figure 1A. 9, contains critical information you need to make note of. In this example Peachtree is telling you that it expects to locate the data directories in a subdirectory called "Company." You need to know where that subdirectory is – C:\Program Files\Sage Software\Peachtree. You will need to install the student data sets to this same directory in a late step. This screen also asks for permission to put a shortcut to Peachtree on the desktop and an icon on the quick launch toolbar. It is recommend you select both icon options before clicking "Install" to continue.

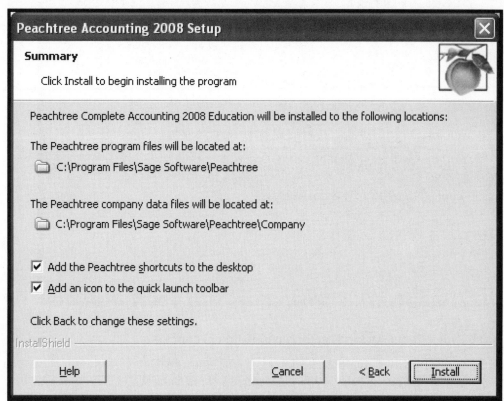

Figure 1A. 9 Peachtree data location confirmation.

And Peachtree will continue with its installation cycle. If your particular installation presents you with other options Peachtree is set to provide the best solution under most situation by accepting the defaults presented. When installation is complete, which may take fifteen or more minutes depending on many issues, Peachtree will present the screen shown in Figure 1A. 10.

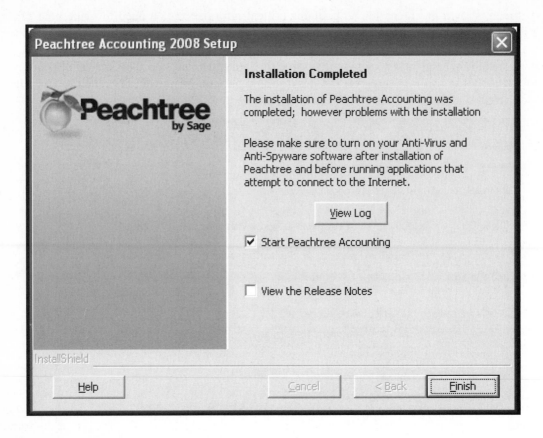

Figure 1A. 10 Peachtree's declaration that installation is complete

It is recommended you remove the checkmark from "Start Peachtree Accounting" as you need to install the student data sets into a directory that Peachtree will be using while it is open. Click on "Finish" to acknowledge that installation is complete.

INSTALLING THE STUDENT DATA SET

The student data set is the set of directories containing the information for each challenge of the textbook identified with the Peach icon of Peachtree. When you want to open a Microsoft Word document you can simply find the file and double-click on it. Then Word will open and the file will be opened and displayed. Peachtree does not work that way. Its data for a company is kept in a specific directory and subdirectory structure and within those directories there are many files which provide Peachtree with all of the information for the specific company. As such you cannot go into a company's directory or subdirectories and click on any specific file to open Peachtree or the specific company. And trying to open Peachtree or a Peachtree company in this manner may actually damage the integrity of the data files. With these restrictions you have been provided a self-extracting program on the Peachtree installation disk titled "Student Data Set." This file, shown in Figure 1A. 11, will self-execute when double-clicked.

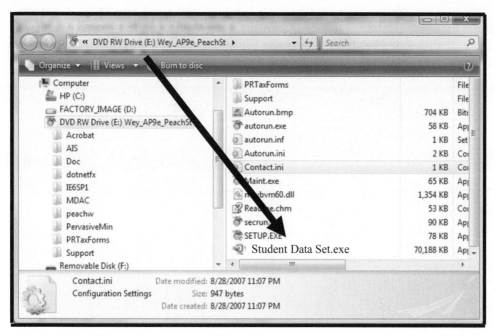

Figure 1A. 11 Peachtree's student data set file

From the start menu, open Windows Explorer and locate this file. Double-click on it or right-click on it and select "Open" from the pop-up menu. The dialog box presented by your system may vary from that presented here. Set the preferences as close as possible to those presented here. The "Unzip to folder" needs to be the same directory you identified in Figure 1A. 8 and 9. By design this is "C:\Program Files\Sage Software\Peachtree\Company." This default will allow the easiest access to company files from within Peachtree through the normal "open a company" path. Any selection other than this will required actions not addressed in this book. And this default It is important that no check mark appears in the "Overwrite files without prompting" option, shown in Figure 1A. 12. Click on "Unzip" to start the process, which may take several minutes.

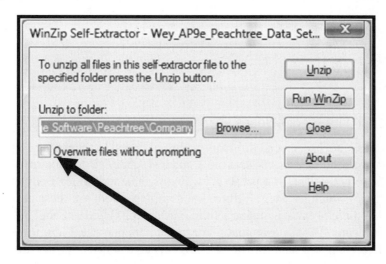

Figure 1A. 12 WinZip Self-Extractor dialog box

When the extraction of the student data sets is complete the unzip operation may close or report its success. Close the dialog boxes open as appropriate and utilize Windows Explorer to examine the contents of the C:\Program Files\Sage Software\Peachtree\Company directory contents. Figure 1A. 13 shows a partial listing of the newly installed student data sets.

Figure 1A. 13 Student data set directories within the "Company" subdirectory of Peachtree

The student data sets have had special directory names assigned to them after Peachtree created them. Figure 1A. 13 shows two subdirectories within the company subdirectory. Both of these were created by Peachtree in its normal process. The first is "BCS" which is the data file for Bellwether Garden Supply . The second is "!_PDG" which is Stone Arbor Landscaping. Both of these are Peachtree example companies. And neither directory title contains a solid clue as to its contents. Since students may be asked to submit Peachtree company files for examination or instructors may want to transport selected company data files, all Peachtree company data directories have been renamed for easy identification. And this identification is given with each challenge.

CHAPTER 1B

Accounting in Action

OBJECTIVES

- Explain what accounting is.
- Identify the users and uses of accounting.
- Understand why ethics is a fundamental business concept.
- Explain generally accepted accounting principles and the cost principle.
- Explain the monetary unit assumption and the economic entity assumption.
- State the accounting equation, and define its components.
- Analyze the effects of business transactions on the accounting equation.
- Be able to launch the Peachtree Complete Accounting application.
- Be able to open a previously set up business.
- Be able to understand the basic accounting equation and relate it to entries made in Peachtree Complete Accounting.

- Be able to enter transactions into Peachtree's general journal system.
- Be able to check for errors in entries made into the general journal.
- Be able to edit a general journal entry
- Be able to understand how to view and print the four basic financial statements in Peachtree Complete Accounting.
- Be able to identify your work.
- Be able to label your disk.
- Be able to identify a folder.
- Be able to identify your work directly on a Peachtree report.
- Be able to place your name in the header of the report.
- Be able to add your name to the company's name.

BASIC ACCOUNTING

Before you start entering data into the Peachtree software, there are several simple basic principles of accounting you must learn first. Specifically, you must be aware that there are two groupings in which fiscal events are classified: 1) what a business owns and 2) what a business owes. Assets are the resources a company owns. They will generally provide a value or a service in the future. Cash, as asset will allow a business to pay its employees and its creditors. Accounts receivable will generally provide cash in the future. A computer recorded as office equipment will allow the company to record its accounting events into Peachtree. The second group, liabilities and owner's equity, are the rights or claims against these resources. The claims by creditors are called liabilities and they will generally be resolved by providing a value or a service in the future. Accounts payable will be resolved by paying cash. Unearned magazine subscriptions will be resolved by providing the appropriate issues. Unearned service fees will be resolved by providing the contracted service at a later date. Claims by the owners are called owner's equity. You use these groupings, assets, liabilities, and owner's equity, whether you're using a computerized or a manual accounting system.

The relationship between the assets, the liabilities, and owner's equity is referred to as the Accounting Equation. The total assets of a business must be equal to the sum of liabilities and owner's equity. The Accounting Equation as a mathematical formula:

Assets = Liabilities + Owner's Equity

The accounting equation applies to all economic and business entities regardless of size, nature of the business, or how the organization is formed and operated.

Let's look in detail at the categories that make up the accounting equation.

- **Assets** – Assets are all of the resources owned by a business that are used in carrying out the company's activities such as production, consumption of goods, and exchange.

- **Liabilities** – Liabilities are the company's existing debts and obligations. They are the claims against the assets by creditors. For example, businesses usually borrow money from banks and purchase merchandise on credit. This transaction results in the business *owing* money and is recorded in the accounting records as liabilities.

- **Owner's Equity** - The ownership claim on the assets is known as owner's equity. It is equal to total assets minus total liabilities. Here's why: The assets of a business are supplied or claimed by either creditors or owner(s). To find out what belongs to owners, you subtract the creditors' claims, the liabilities, from the assets. The remainder is the owner's claim on the assets, the owner's equity. Because the claims of creditors must be paid before ownership claims, the owner's equity is sometimes referred to as residual equity. There are subcomponents of owner's equity. They are 1) investments by owner, 2) drawings or withdrawals by owner, 3) revenues, 4) expenses, and 5) retained earnings.

  - *Investments by the Owner* – Investments by the owner are the assets that the owner puts into the business. These investments increase owner's equity. The investments may be cash or material items.

  - *Drawings or Withdrawals* – An owner may take cash or other assets from the business for personal use. Drawings or Withdrawals are **_NOT_** expenses of the company and they decrease owner's equity.

  - *Revenues* – Revenues are the gross increase in owner's equity resulting from business activities that have been entered into for the purpose of earning income. Generally, revenues result from the sale of merchandise (a retail establishment), the sale of finished goods (a manufacturing company), or the performance of services (a service related company). A business may also earn money by other means including the rental of its property or the lending of money.

  - *Expenses* – Expenses decrease owner's equity. A business incurs expenses as a result of the operation of the business. The cost of assets purchased and consumed or services that are used in the process of earning revenue are considered expenses.

  - *Retained Earnings* – While generally not considered part of a sole proprietorship or partnership, retained earnings is an element of computerized accounting systems and corporations. Retained earnings is the value of net income reduced by drawings, withdrawals, or dividends, depending on the form of the company.

THE TRANSACTION PROCESS

A transaction is often referred to as an external or internal economic event of an enterprise. Transactions are recorded. An external transaction involves economic events between the company and some outside enterprise. For example, the purchase of equipment from a supplier or the payments of rent to a landlord are external transactions. Sales and purchases of merchandise are also external transactions.

An internal transaction is an economic event that occurs entirely within a company; for example, when office supplies are utilized by the staff to prepare notes for a meeting.

A company may also carry on activities that do not in themselves represent business transactions. Hiring employees, answering the phone, and taking a sales order are examples. Some of those activities will eventually lead to a business transaction. You will soon have to pay wages to workers you hired and merchandise must be delivered to customers.

Before you enter any transaction, you must install (if needed) and launch Peachtree, then open the company in which you wish to work. Only then can any data can be entered.

LAUNCHING PEACHTREE COMPLETE ACCOUNTING 2008 SOFTWARE

Step 1: Follow the instructions given to you by your instructor or lab administrator in opening the Peachtree Complete Accounting software package.

Step 2: Once Peachtree is open, you will see the Peachtree screen.

Step 3: This screen will change to Peachtree's start screen as shown in Figure 1B.1.

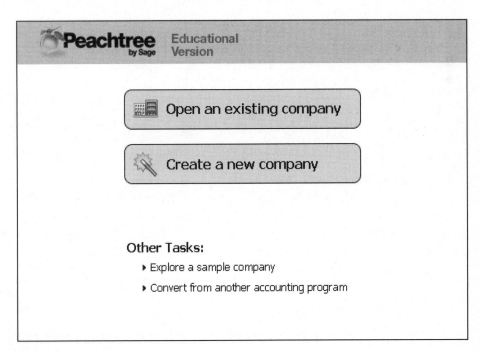

Figure 1B. 1 Peachtree start screen

Step 4: Click on "Open an existing company" to open an existing company and advance to the screen shown in Figure 1B. 2. Your screens may vary depending on installation, version, and update options. For example, you may need to click on a "browse" button to advance to this screen.

Step 5: Click on "Softbyte" which should appear if the student data sets were correctly loaded from the CD-ROM. (Reload the student data sets if "Softbyte" does not appear.) Depending on your system, your screen may or may not have the exact same companies listed.

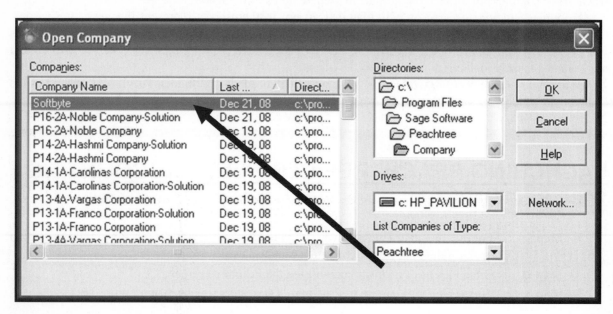

Figure 1B. 2 Open Company menu screen

Step 6: Check to make sure "Softbyte" appears in the Title bar above the main window of Peachtree. The upper left corner of the screen is shown in Figure 1B. 3.

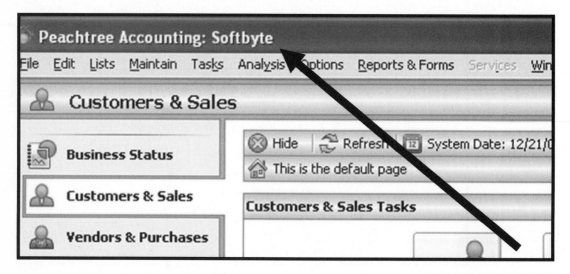

Figure 1B. 3 The upper left corner of the main window of Peachtree Complete Accounting

Even though your text does not cover general journal entries or debits and credits in the first chapter, you can get a little ahead by working in Peachtree and start to understand how the computerized accounting process works.

With that in mind, now you may enter transactions into Peachtree Complete Accounting by following these step-by-step instructions. You will be working with the Softbyte which can be found within your student data set and in the first chapter of your text. You will build on this file for the next several chapters. So, be sure to back up your data on a regular basis. Good luck and have fun.

ENTERING GENERAL JOURNAL TRANSACTIONS

Transaction (1) Investment by Owner. Ray Neal decides to open a computer programming service. On September 1, 2010, he invests $15,000 cash in the business, which he names Softbyte. This transaction results in an equal increase in assets and owner's equity. The asset cash increases by $15,000 and the owner's equity, R. Neal, Capital, increases by the same amount. Using Peachtree Complete Accounting, step through this initial entry.

Step 1: Using the menu bar from the main Peachtree window, click on "Tasks."

Step 2: On the pull down menu, as shown in Figure 1B. 4, click on "General Journal Entry."

Figure 1B. 4   Pull down menu from Tasks on menu bar

Step 3: Make sure that your window looks like that shown in Figure 1B. 5.

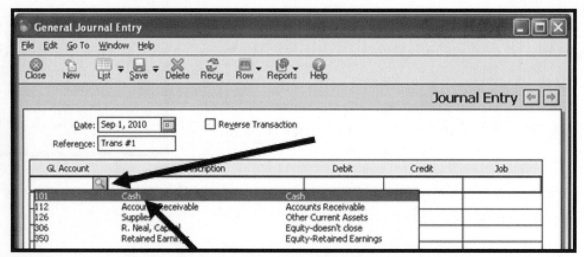

Figure 1B. 5   Blank screen for general journal entry

Note: The actual color scheme of your presentation may vary from that presented here. The color scheme is selectable by the system and is controlled through Options > Global > General.

Step 4:   As a reference, type in "Trans #1" in the blank "Reference" window, just under the date which is preset for September 1, 2010. Keep pressing the Tab key until the cursor is in the GL (General Ledger) account column.

Step 5:   Click on the magnifying glass that appears next to the GL (General Ledger) account column to get a pull down menu that lists the available accounts for Softbyte, the chart of accounts, as shown in Figure 1B. 6.

Figure 1B. 6   Journal Entry with Chart of Accounts Drop Down shown

Step 6:   Click on GL (General Ledger) account "101" (Cash). In the description column type in "Owner's investment in business" And, in the debit column, type in "1-5-0-0-0-decimal point-0-0." (Don't type in the dashes; they represent the separation of each numeral.)

> Be careful in Peachtree Complete Accounting how you enter numbers. The "system" may *automatically* insert a decimal point two places within the entered number. For example, if you entered "1-5-0-0-0" Peachtree may recognize it as $150.00 not $15,000.00. Make sure your screen looks like Figure 1B. 7.

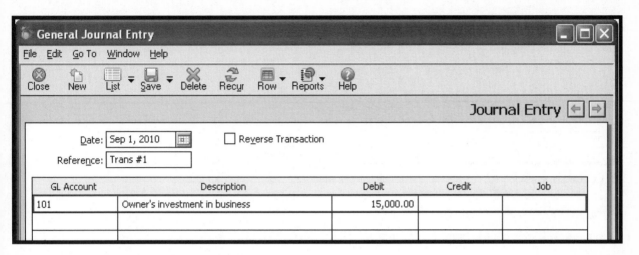

Figure 1B. 7   First entry line of Transaction 1

Step 7:   Press the enter key (or tab key) three times to get your insertion point to the next line, as shown in Figure 1B. 8.

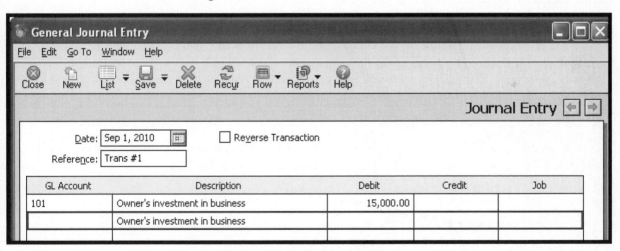

Figure 1B. 8   Beginning the second entry line for Transaction 1

Using the illustrated examples above, enter the amount for owner's equity by:

Step 8:   Click on the magnifying glass in the GL (General Ledger) account column.

Step 9:   Click the GL (General Ledger) account "306" for R. Neal, Capital.

Step 10:   In the credit column, entering the amount, 15000 – the dollar sign should not be entered. The decimal point may have to be entered manually. Your entry should look like Figure 1B. 9.

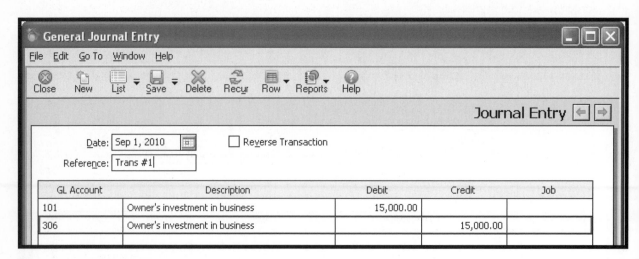

Figure 1B. 9   Entry for owner's investment of cash in the business

BEFORE YOU CONTINUE

Look at the window in Figure 1B. 10. Notice the amounts at the bottom of the window, in the gray area outside the entry area. They indicate whether or not your entry is in balance. In Figure 1B. 10, $15,000 appears under the debit column and under the credit column. The figure next to "Out of Balance" is zero. Therefore, your entry is in balance. (Note: This screen has been reduced in size by eliminating unneeded rows; your presentation will show more rows.)

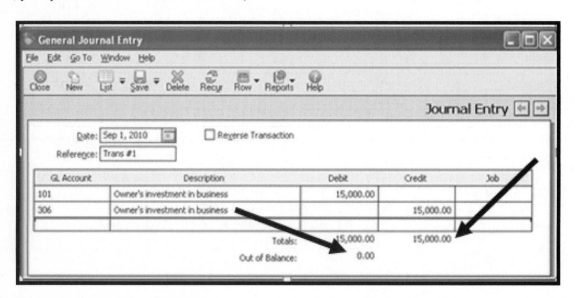

Figure 1B. 10 In balance journal entry

If you had mistakenly entered both amounts in the debit column as shown in Figure 1B. 11 (or even both amounts in the credit column), you would be "Out of Balance."

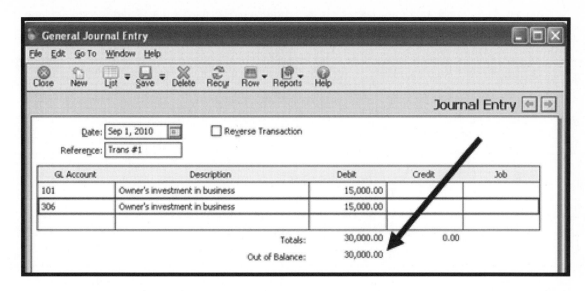

Figure 1B. 11 Entry error as shown by out of balance tally

Always double-check your entries before continuing. Just because the system indicates you are "In Balance" does not necessarily mean your transaction is correct. It just means what you have entered is "In Balance." However, as shown in Figure 1B. 12, the system will not let you continue if you are "Out of Balance" and will return an error message.

Figure 1B. 12 The system will not let you continue if you are "Out of Balance" on your entry

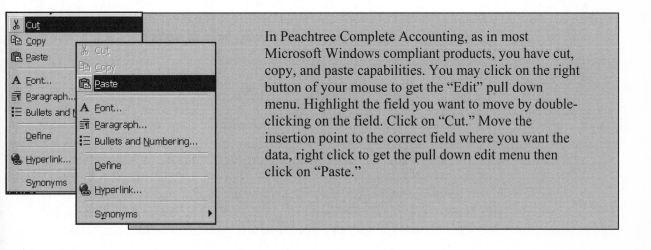

In Peachtree Complete Accounting, as in most Microsoft Windows compliant products, you have cut, copy, and paste capabilities. You may click on the right button of your mouse to get the "Edit" pull down menu. Highlight the field you want to move by double-clicking on the field. Click on "Cut." Move the insertion point to the correct field where you want the data, right click to get the pull down edit menu then click on "Paste."

POSTING THE TRANSACTION

Step 1: To post the transaction (enter it into the system) click on the "Save" icon (see Figure 1B. 13) in the tool bar section toward the top of the window.

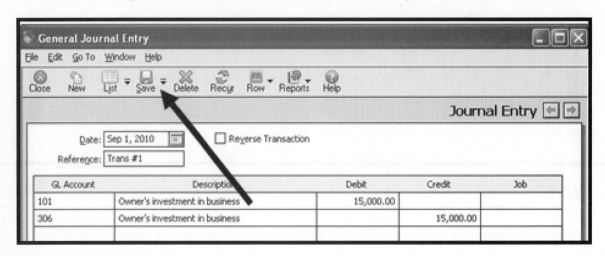

Figure 1B. 13 Click on the "Save" icon to post your transaction

Step 2: The general journal window clears all that has been previously entered and is now ready for the second transaction. Notice that the general journal window's reference window has now automatically advanced to "Trans #2."

You are now ready for the next transaction.

Transaction (2). Purchase of Equipment for Cash. On September 1, 2010, Softbyte purchases computer equipment for $7,000 cash. This transaction will result in an equal increase and decrease in total assets. Cash is decreased by $7,000 whereas the asset equipment is increased by $7,000.

Using the process you learned in Transaction 1 make this general journal entry.

Step 1: Type in "Trans #2" in the reference box, if it is different. Leave the date as it is, September 1, 2010.

Step 2: Click on the magnifying glass to get the pull down menu of the chart of accounts. Highlight "Equipment" and click (you may also press the <TAB> key).

Step 3: Press the <TAB> key to move your insertion point over to the description column and type in "Paid cash for equipment."

Step 4: Press the <TAB> key to move your insertion point to the next column, the debit column and enter, in error, the amount 8000. This amount is in error because in the second part of this exercise you will learn how to edit a general journal entry, after it has been posted. Remember you do not enter the "$" but you may have to enter the decimal point.

Step 5: Press the <ENTER> key three times so that your insertion point is in the GL (General Ledger) account column of the next line. Click on the magnifying glass to get the pull down menu of the chart of accounts. Highlight "Cash" and double-click (you may also press the <ENTER> key).

Step 6: Press the <TAB> key to move your insertion point over to the description column and type in "Paid cash for equipment." (The system may have already generated this for you.)

Step 7: Press the <TAB> key twice to move your insertion point to the credit column and enter the amount, purposely in error, 8000. You enter this amount in error for your books to balance. This will be edited in the next part of this exercise. Again, remember you should not enter the "$."

Step 8: Make sure your screen looks like Figure 1B. 14 before continuing. If there are no errors (besides the intentional ones you typed in) go ahead and post your transaction. Notice that even though you know there is an error, the system will let you post because technically your books are in balance.

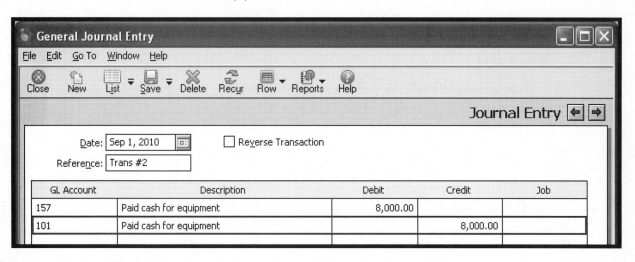

Figure 1B. 14 General journal Entry # 2 shown with amount in error

EDITING A GENERAL JOURNAL ENTRY

Editing a general journal entry is just as simple as making the original entry.

Step 1: Make sure you have a blank general journal screen. If not, create one by clicking on "Tasks" then "General Journal Entry."

Step 2: On the Menu bar, illustrated in Figure 1B. 15, click on "Go To" and then "Find Transaction" from the drop-down menu.

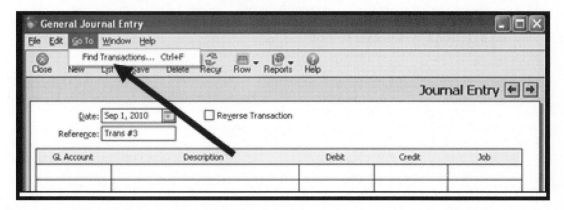

Figure 1B. 15 General journal entry screen tool bar

Step 3:   The find transaction dialog box, shown in Figure 1B. 16, will fill in most fields with acceptable default values. You know the journal entry is in the date range of September 1 to September 30, 2010, and the search tool is set to all types of transactions within the timeframe so click on the "Find" icon shown by the arrow.

Note: As an option, you could use the left and right arrows near the right side, upper portion of the general journal entry screen. With each mouse click on the arrows you will move one journal entry earlier (left arrow) or one journal entry later (right arrow). Since there are only two journal entries in Softbyte at this time this is the fastest way to locate Trans #2, which should be one click on the left arrow. For an active company this could be thousands of mouse clicks to locate the one journal entry.

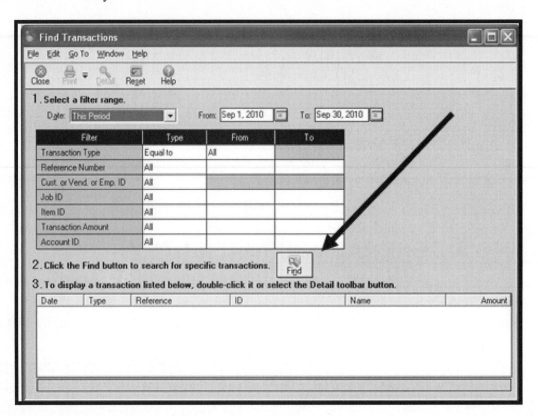

Figure 1B. 16 Find Transactions entry menu

Step 4:   And the dialog box will show the two general journal entries, Figure 1B. 17, recorded so far by Softbyte. Double-click on Trans #2 or click on it once and then click on "Details" in the dialog box's task bar.

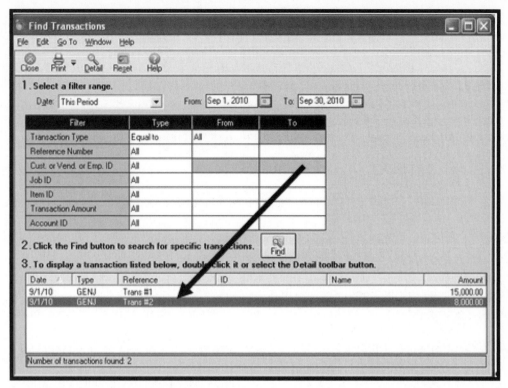

Figure 1B. 17 Find Transaction dialog box

Step 5: And you will be returned to the general journal entry screen like the one you had when you made the earlier entry. Your screen should look like Figure 1B 14, shown earlier.

Step 5: Any field on the screen can be changed and reposted (saved). However, you are only interested in changing the amounts, 8000 to 7000. Place the insertion point in the first amount field, highlight the 8000, and change it to 7000.

Step 6: Do the same with the second amount. Your screen should match the one shown in Figure 1B. 18.

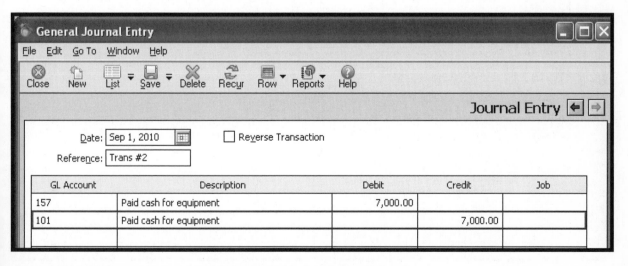

Figure 1B. 18 Corrected general journal entry for Transaction 2

Now click on "Save" on the general journal entry task bar to save the corrected journal entry.

Transaction (3). Purchase of Supplies on Credit. On September 1, 2010, Softbyte purchases computer paper and other supplies expected to last several months for $1,600 from Acme Supply Company. Acme will allow Softbyte to pay this bill next month. This transaction is referred to as a purchase on account or a credit purchase. Assets will be increased (a debit – remember a debit entry will increase an asset account) because the expected future benefits of using the paper and supplies. Liabilities will also be increased (a credit – a credit entry will increase a liability account) by the amount due to Acme Company. With an equal debit and credit entry, your accounting equation will remain in balance.

Using the process you learned in Transaction 1 make this general journal entry on your own.

Step 1:	Type in "Trans #3" in the reference window if required. Leave the date as it is, September 1, 2010.
Step 2:	Click on the magnifying glass to get the pull down menu of the chart of accounts. Highlight "Supplies" and double-click (you may also press the <ENTER> key).
Step 3:	Press the <TAB> key to move your insertion point over to the description column and type in "Purchased supplies on account."
Step 4:	Press the <TAB> key to move your insertion point to the next column, the debit column and enter 1600.
Step 5:	Press the <ENTER> key three times so that your insertion point is in the GL (General Ledger) account column of the next line. Click on the magnifying glass to get the pull-down menu of the chart of accounts. Highlight "Accounts Payable" and click (you may also press the <ENTER> key).
Step 6:	Press the <TAB> key to move your insertion point over to the description column "Purchased supplies on account" should have automatically been generated for you; if not go ahead and enter it.
Step 7:	Press the <TAB> key twice to move your insertion point to the credit column and enter the amount 1600.
Step 8:	Make sure your screen looks like Figure 1B. 18 and correct any errors before continuing.

Before you post your entry, double-check what you have entered. Make sure your entries match Figure 1B. 19.

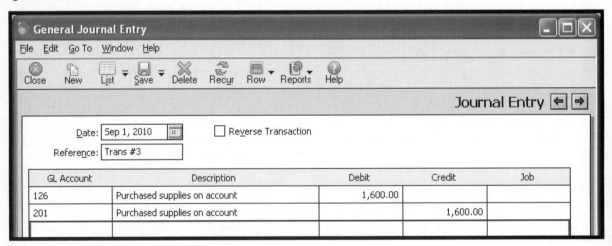

Figure 1B. 19 Journal entry for a credit (on account) purchase

Before you "save" Transaction 3, appreciate that both accounts, Supplies and Accounts Payable, are going to be increased by this entry. You have added $1,600 worth of supplies to the company (an asset) and you have also incurred a liability of $1,600 (money owed to the seller of the supplies).

Looking at the "big picture," total assets are now $16,600 ($15,000 + $7,000 - $7,000 + $1,600). This total is matched by a $1,600 creditor's claim (the supplies just purchased on account)) and a $15,000 ownership claim (the initial cash the owner put into the business).

Now click on the "Save" icon on the task bar to post your transaction into the general journal.

Transaction (4). Services Provided for Cash. On September 1, 2010, Softbyte receives $1,200 cash from customers for programming services it has provided. This transaction represents the company's principal revenue producing activity. Remember that revenue will increase owner's equity. However, revenue does have its own account, "Service Revenue", an income account.

Make the general journal entry:

Step 1: Change the reference to "Trans #4", if required.

Step 2: The GL (General Ledger) account number 101, Cash, enter the text "Services rendered for cash" as the description, and cash should be increased by $1,200 (a debit entry).

Step 3: The GL (General Ledger) account number 401, Service Revenue, should be increased by $1,200 (a credit entry).

Remember that an asset is increased by a debit entry and that revenue is increased by a credit entry.

Step 4: Before posting, make sure your entry matches the one below in Figure 1B. 20, on the next page.

Before posting, make sure your entry matches the one below in Figure 1B. 20, on the next page.

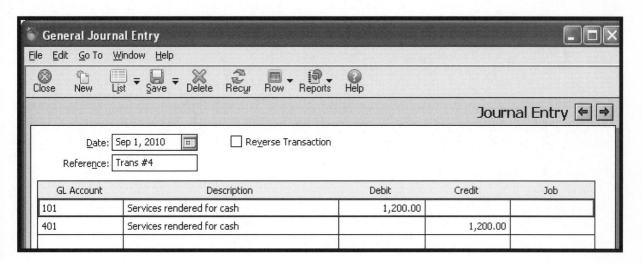

Figure 1B. 20 General journal entry for service revenue

Step 5: If there are no errors, post (save) the entry.

Transaction (5). Purchase of Advertising on Credit. On September 1, 2010, Softbyte receives a bill for $250 from the *Daily News* for advertising. Softbyte decides to postpone payment of the bill until a later date. This transaction results in an increase in liabilities and an increase in expenses (or a decrease in equity).

Step 1: Change the reference to "Trans #5" if required.

Step 2: Utilize the GL (General Ledger) account number 610 – Advertising Expense, enter "Daily News ad on account" as description, is increased (debited) by $250.

Step 3: The Accounts Payable account number is 201 which is also increased (credited) by $250.

As a rule of thumb, it is rare that any expense account would be credited. So it is relatively safe to say that all expense accounts will only be debited. The entry is shown in Figure 1B. 21 below.

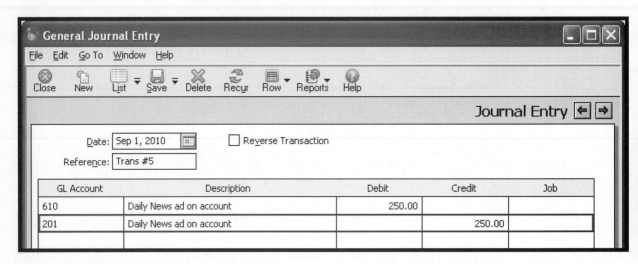

Figure 1B. 21 Advertising expense to be paid later

Step 4: If your entries are correct, post (save) the general journal entry.

The two sides of the accounting equation still balance at $17,800. Owner's equity will be decreased when the expense (Advertising Expense) is incurred and is noted. Expenses do not have to be paid in cash at the time they are incurred. When payment is made at a later date, the liability, accounts payable, will be decreased and the asset, cash, will be decreased. You will see how that works in Transaction 8. The cost of advertising is considered an expense.

Transaction (6). Services Provided for Cash and Credit. On September 7, 2010, Softbyte provides $3,500 of programming services for customers. Cash, $1,500 is received from customers and the balance of $2,000 is billed on account. This transaction results in an equal increase in assets and owner's equity.

Three specific accounts are affected:
- Cash is increased by $1,500
- Accounts Receivable is increased by $2,000
- The Service Revenue account is increased by $3,500.

Cash and Accounts Receivable, both assets, will be increased (debited). Cash increases by $1,500, Accounts Receivable increases by $2,000, and revenues increase by $3,500 (credited).

Step 1: Change the date from September 1 to September 7. You may enter the date directly in the date box or by clicking on the calendar icon, you will be able to click the appropriate date for entry directly from a pull-down calendar as shown in Figure 1B. 22.

The "double – double" arrows on either side of the year allow you choose a different year.

The double arrows on either side of the month allow you to choose a different month.

Figure 1B. 22 Pull down calendar

Step 2: Change the reference to "Trans #6" as required.

Step 3: Using the magnifying glass, find the account number (#101) for Cash and press <ENTER>. In the description column type in "Received cash from customers for services rendered" and enter the amount, 1500 in the debit column.

Step 4: Using the magnifying glass, find the account number (#112) for Accounts Receivable and press <ENTER>. In the description column type in "Services On Account" and enter the amount, 2000, in the debit column.

Step 5: And again, using the magnifying glass, find the account number (#401) for Service Revenue and press <ENTER>. In the description column type in "Service revenue." Tab over to the credit column and enter the amount, 3500.

Step 6: Notice that all three entries will increase the appropriate accounts and that glancing at the bottom of the window, you should be in balance at $3,500.

Step 7: Your entry should match Figure 1B. 23. Make any necessary changes before posting your entry.

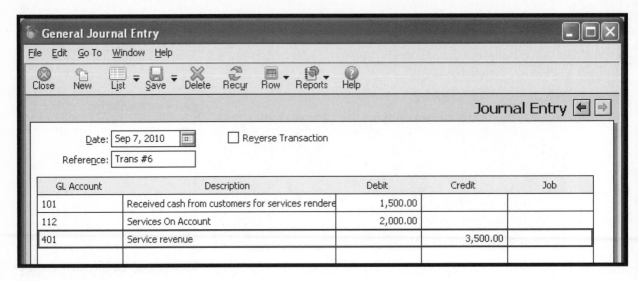

Figure 1B. 23 General journal entry showing date change and account entries

Transaction (7). Payment of Expenses. Expenses paid in cash on September 15 include the store rent $600; salaries of employees $900; and utilities $200. These payments will result in an equal decrease in assets (cash) and owner's equity (the individual expense items).

Step 1:	Change the date to September 15, 2010.
Step 2:	Change the reference to "Trans #7".
Step 3:	Identify the Store Rent Expense account, #729, highlight it and press <ENTER> (or click) to place it the GL (General Ledger) account window. Type in "Paid store rent" in the description column and 600 in the debit column.
Step 4:	On the next line, identify the Salaries Expense account number, #726 making sure it appears in the GL (General Ledger) account window on the second line. Type in "Paid employee's salaries" on the description line and type in 900 in the debit column. (You'll worry about payroll tax in a later chapter.)
Step 5:	On the third line, identify and place account #732, the Utilities Expense account, in the appropriate column. In the description column, type in "Paid utilities expense" and in the debit column, type in 200.
Step 6:	Cash will be decreased by the total amount of the above expenses, $1,700. By now you should know that the account number for Cash is 101. You may type that in directly or search for it using the magnifying glass. Type in "Paid various expenses." The total amount, $1,700, is credited to cash (you're decreasing an asset).
Step 7:	Check to see that your entries are in balance before posting. Your entry should match the one in Figure 1B. 24.

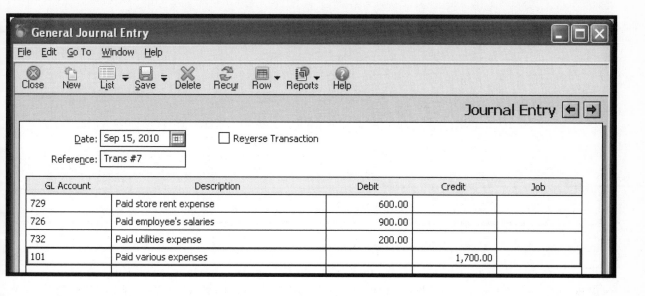

Figure 1B. 24 Paid monthly expenses with cash

Transaction (8). Payment of Accounts Payable. Softbyte pays its *Daily News* advertising bill of $250 in cash. The bill had been previously recorded in Transaction (5) as an increase in accounts payable and an increase in expenses (a decrease in owner's equity). This payment "on account" will decrease the asset cash (a credit) and will also decrease the liability accounts payable (a debit) – both by $250.

Step 1:	Keep the date, September 15, 2010 as is, but change the reference to "Trans #8" as required.
Step 2:	Entering the debit amount first, the account number is 201 for Accounts Payable.
Step 3:	Type in "Paid Daily News for ads on account" in the description column. And, type in 250 in the debit column to complete the first line.
Step 4:	Account number 101 is the number for the cash account which goes in the first column of the second line.
Step 5:	"Paid Daily News for ads on account." This should have been automatically generated by the system. If so, press the <TAB> key twice to move to the credit column and enter 250.
Step 6:	Check to make sure your entry is in balance and matches Figure 1B. 25.

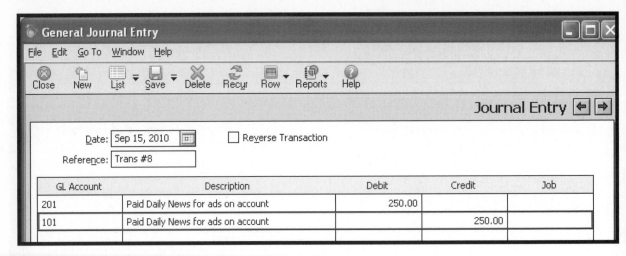

Figure 1B. 25 Paid Daily News account due

Transaction (9). Receipt of Cash on Account. The sum of $600 in cash is received from those customers who have previously been billed for services in Transaction 6. This transaction does not change any of the totals in assets, but it will change the composition of those accounts. Cash is increased by $600 and Accounts Receivable is decreased by $600.

Step 1: If you went directly to Transaction 9 from Transaction 8, you will notice that the reference has automatically changed to "Trans #9." If that change did not occur, enter "Trans #9" in the reference box. Leave the date at September 15.

Step 2: Enter GL (General Ledger) account number 101 for the Cash account. And, in the description column type in "Received cash from customers." In the debit column, enter 600.

Step 3: On the second line, enter GL (General Ledger) account number 112 for the Accounts Receivable account. "Received cash from customers" should have been automatically entered by the system. However, you need to enter 600 in the credit column so that your entry will balance.

Step 4: Check your entry with the one in Figure 1B. 26 before posting. Make any necessary changes.

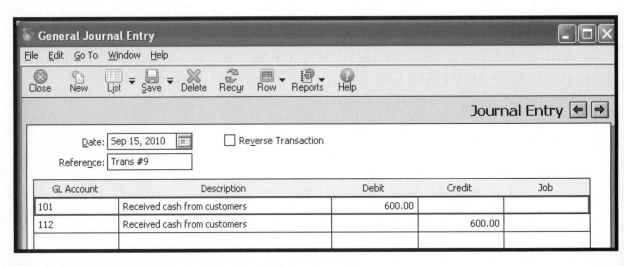

Figure 1B. 26 Received cash from customers on account

Transaction (10). Withdrawal of Cash by Owner. On September 30, 2010, Ray Neal withdraws $1,300 in cash from the business for his personal use. This transaction results in an equal decrease in assets (Cash) and owner's equity (Drawing).

Step 1: Change the date to September 30. Also, make sure that "Trans #10" is in the reference window.

Step 2: GL (General Ledger) account number 308 is the Drawing account that will be debited. Enter 308 as the GL (General Ledger) account number. In the description column, type in "Ray Neal, Drawing" and in the debit column (a decrease to capital), enter 1300.

Step 3: Because Neal wants cash for his withdrawal, the asset cash must be decreased (a credit). Enter GL (General Ledger) account number 101 for the Cash account. "Ray Neal, Drawing" will most likely have been defaulted in the description column; if not, make the appropriate entry. And, in the credit column enter 1300.

Step 4: Check your entry with Figure 1B. 27 and make any corrections before posting your entry.

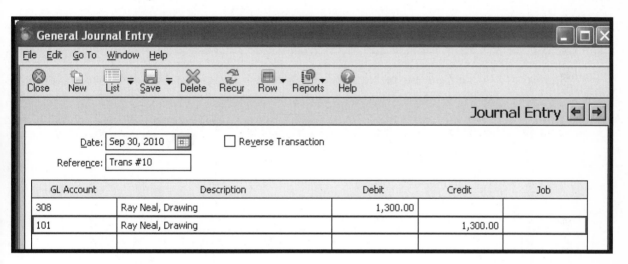

Figure 1B. 27 Owner withdraws cash from the business for personal use

You can close the general journal entry dialog box at this time to expose the full Peachtree desktop.

FINANCIAL STATEMENTS

After transactions have been identified, analyzed, and entered into the computer, four financial statements can be prepared from your data. In fact, when you made your first entry each of the statements was updated, and kept up to date as you went along.

Those statements are:

- An income statement - presents the revenues and expenses and resulting net income or net loss for a specific period of time.
- A statement of retained earnings (very similar to statement of owner's equity) - summarizes the changes in owner's equity for a specific period of time due to earnings and withdrawals.
- A balance sheet - a company's report of the assets, liabilities, and owner's equity at a specific date.

- A statement of cash flow - a summary of information about the cash inflows (receipts) and outflows (payments) for a specific period of time.

Each Peachtree financial statement provides management, owners, and other interested parties with relevant financial data. The statements are interrelated. For example, Net income of $2,750 shown on the income statement is added to the beginning balance of retained earnings (equity). Owner's capital of $16,450 at the end of the reporting period shown in the balance sheet. Cash of $8,050 on the balance sheet is reported on the statement of cash flows.

The reports used throughout this workbook are already preset for each of your assignments. The assignments in Peachtree that appear in Accounting Principles by Weygandt, Kieso, and Kimmel are noted by the Peachtree logo - a peach, in the margin.

In addition to the four statements mentioned previously, several other reports also deserve attention. They are included, under the general ledger heading:

- Chart of Accounts
- General Journal
- General Ledger

GENERATING THE INCOME STATEMENT

Step 1: On the main menu bar click on "Reports" to get the drop down menu shown in Figure 1B. 28.

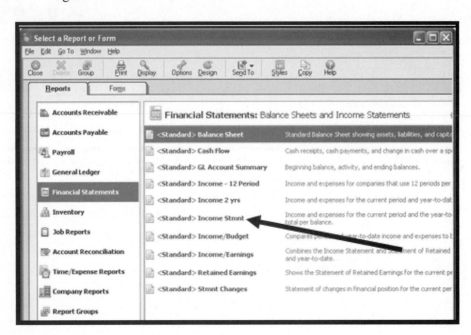

Figure 1B. 28 Main Menu Bar and Reports List

Step 2: Click on "Financial Statements" to get the "Select a Report or Form" menu.

Step 3: Double-click on "<Standard> Income Stmnt" (Statement) toward the middle of the list. You can also click on "Display" on the task bar but this will take you past the Options dialog box.

Step 4: The "Options" dialog box, shown in Figure 1B. 29, gives several option choices including the choice of financial periods, the margins for the report, whether or not you want to show accounts that have a zero balance, whether or not you want page numbers, and so on.

Note: One of the important, and often overlooked, options available to the accountant is the ability to "Show Zero Amounts" in the lower left corner of the dialog box. It is recommended that this option be selected, as shown in Figure 1B. 29 on all reports. Often it is what is not shown – zero – that makes you aware of an error or omission.

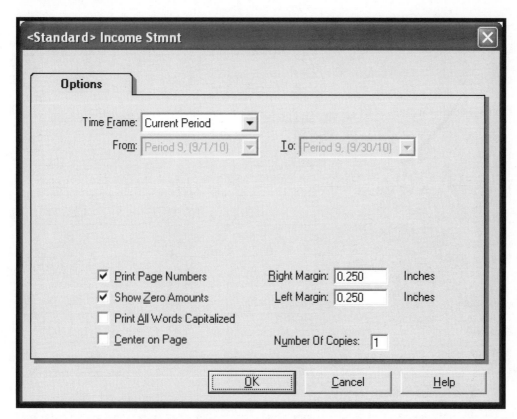

Figure 1B. 29 Dialog box to prepare income statement for display

Step 5: Click "OK" to show the income statement, Figure 1B. 30, on your computer screen.

The <Standard> Income Statement is a complete income statement already set up by the Peachtree system during the original company set up.

<Standard> Income Stmnt

File Edit Go To Window Help

Close | Save | Print | Options | Setup | E-mail | Excel | PDF | Preview | Design | Find | Help

Softbyte
Income Statement
For the Nine Months Ending September 30, 2010

	Current Month			Year to Date	
Revenues					
Service Revenue	$ 4,700.00	100.00	$	4,700.00	100.00
Total Revenues	4,700.00	100.00		4,700.00	100.00
Cost of Sales					
Total Cost of Sales	0.00	0.00		0.00	0.00
Gross Profit	4,700.00	100.00		4,700.00	100.00
Expenses					
Advertising Expense	250.00	5.32		250.00	5.32
Salaries Expense	900.00	19.15		900.00	19.15
Store Rent Expense	600.00	12.77		600.00	12.77
Utilities Expense	200.00	4.26		200.00	4.26
Total Expenses	1,950.00	41.49		1,950.00	41.49
Net Income	$ 2,750.00	58.51	$	2,750.00	58.51

Figure 1B. 30 Display of the income statement for Softbyte

The revenues and expenses are reported for a specific period of time, the month ending on September 30, 2010. The statement was generated from all of the data you entered since the beginning of the chapter. Make sure your data matches what is shown in Figure 1B. 30. Go back and verify your entries if your figures do not match.

On the income statement the revenues are listed first, followed by expenses. Finally net income (or net loss) is determined. A difference that you will see between your textbook and Peachtree is that textbooks and financial reports released as company results generally list expenses in decreasing order of magnitude while Peachtree lists them in ascending GL (General Ledger) account number order. Also notice that financial analysis, the percentage of the expenses in relation to total revenues, is provided for you.

Note: Investment and withdrawal transactions between the owner and the business are not included in the measurement of net income.

Close the income statement to view the full Peachtree desktop.

GENERATING THE RETAINED EARNINGS STATEMENT

Peachtree Complete Accounting utilizes a "retained earnings statement" to record the period changes in owner's equity. This statement is very similar to a statement of owner's equity. Both show the changes caused by revenues and expenses summarized as "net income" and withdrawals by the owner. The main difference between the two is that the owner's equity statement includes the owner's investments in the business; the retained earnings statement does not. In Peachtree, owner's investments are included in the capital section of the balance sheet.

Note: When learning accounting principles, retained earnings, is usually covered as a part of corporate accounting and not while learning about sole proprietorships. You will look at retained earnings more in depth in the section on corporate accounting. However Peachtree Complete Accounting application requires the creation of a retained earnings account in the set up procedure.

By definition, retained earnings are the net income retained in a corporation. Net income is recorded and added to retained earnings by a closing entry in which income summary is debited and retained earnings is credited. Closing entries will be covered later.

To generate the retained earnings statement:

Step 1:   On the main menu bar, click on "Reports" to get the pull down menu as required.

Step 2:   Click on "Financial Statements" to get the "Select a Report or Form" menu of shown in Figure 1B. 31 as required.

Figure 1B. 31 Select a Report or Form menu

Step 3:	Double-click on "<Standard> Retained Earnings" toward the bottom of the list.
Step 4:	Again, the dialog box, as shown in Figure 1B. 32, gives you several choices including the choice of financial periods, the margins for the report, whether or not you want to show accounts that have a zero balance, whether or not you want page numbers, etc.
Step 5:	Click "OK" to show the retained earnings statement, Figure 1B.32, on your computer screen.

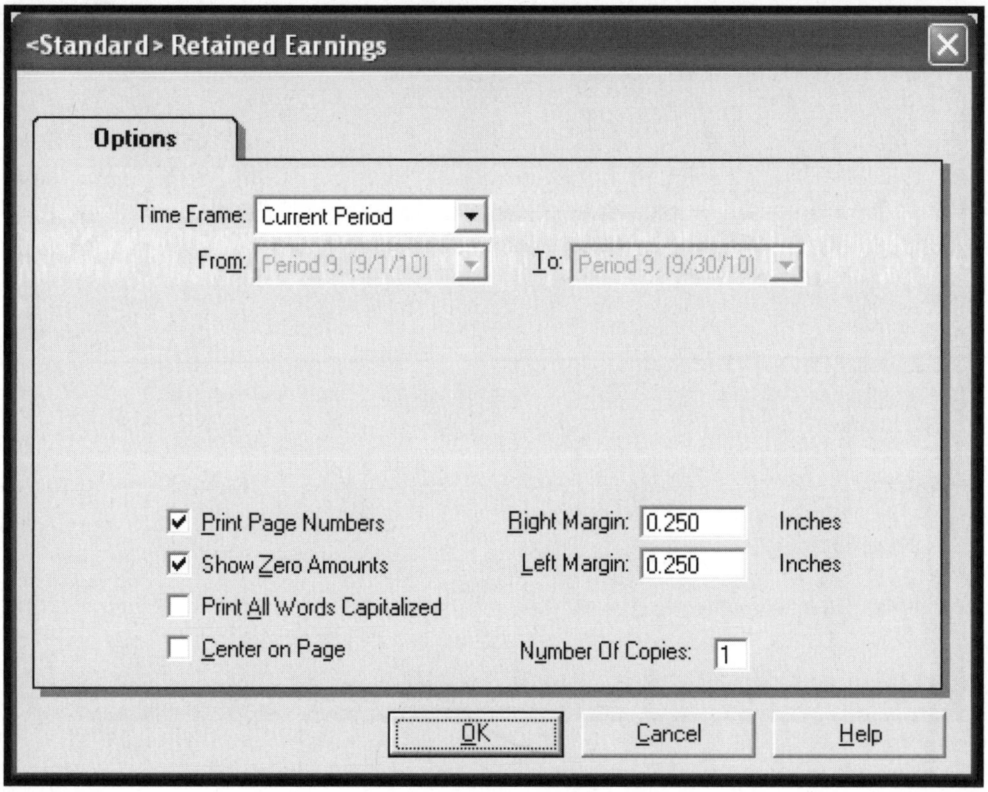

Figure 1B. 32 Dialog box to prepare retained earnings statement for display

Softbyte
Statement of Retained Earnings
For the Nine Months Ending September 30, 2010

Beginning Retained Earnings	$	0.00
Adjustments To Date		0.00
Net Income		2,750.00
Subtotal		2,750.00
R. Neal, Drawing		(1,300.00)
Ending Retained Earnings	$	1,450.00

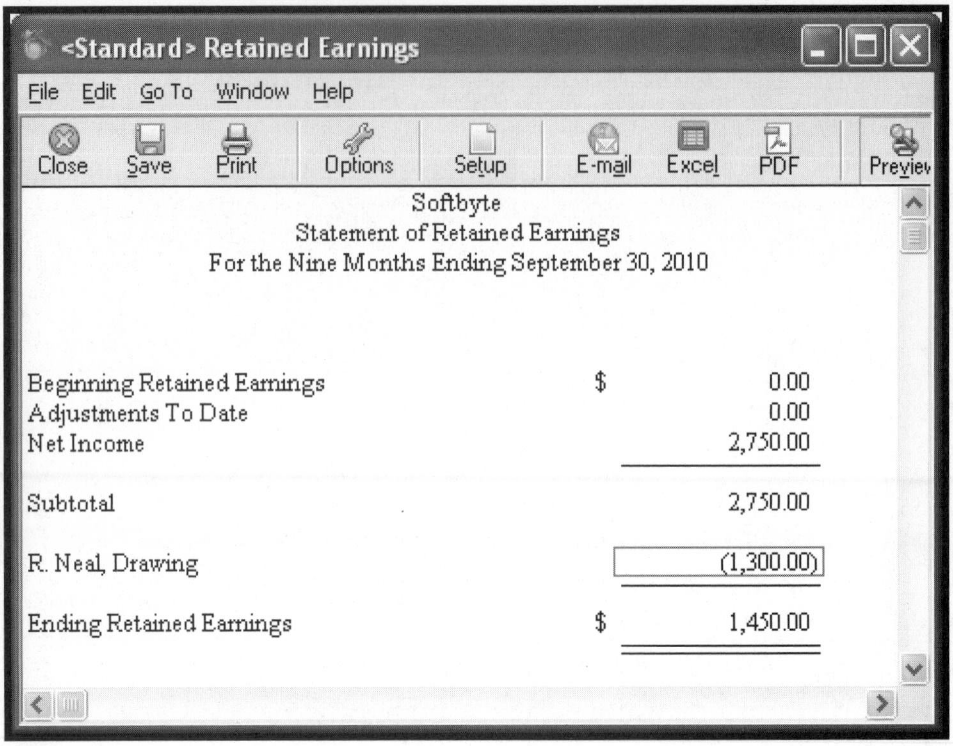

Figure 1B. 33 The retained earnings statement

The beginning retained earnings is shown on the first line of the statement. The balance is zero since this is a startup company with no previous earned income. Next month, the amount should equal (for the beginning balance) the ending balance, $1,450 as of September 30, 2010.

The next line shows the amount of net income of $2,750. This figure was acquired by subtracting all of this period's expenses from all of this period's revenue (See Figure 1B. 30).

The amount Ray took out or withdrew from the company, $1,300, is shown next as a subtraction from retained earnings. And, the final figure is the ending balance, ending retained earnings of $1,450 which will be the beginning balance for the next accounting period.

GENERATING THE BALANCE SHEET

The balance sheet also is prepared from all of the data you previously entered. The assets will appear at the top of the balance sheet, followed by liabilities, then owner's equity. Recall from the beginning of the chapter that assets must equal the total of the liabilities plus (in addition to) the owner's equity. Peachtree Complete Accounting will make sure this balances for you. The system will let you know if it does not balance.

The balance sheet is obtained in the same way the income statement and retained earnings statement were obtained.

Step 1: On the main menu bar click on "Reports" to get the pull-down menu as required.

Step 2: Click on "Financial Statements" to get the "Select a Report or Form" menu as required.

Step 3: Double-click on "<Standard> Balance Sheet."

Step 4: Again, the dialog box gives us several choices including the choice of financial periods, the margins for the printer; whether or not you want to show accounts that have a zero balance, whether or not you want page numbers, and so on.

Step 5: Click "OK" to show the Softbyte balance sheet on your computer screen. It is shown in Figure 1B. 34.

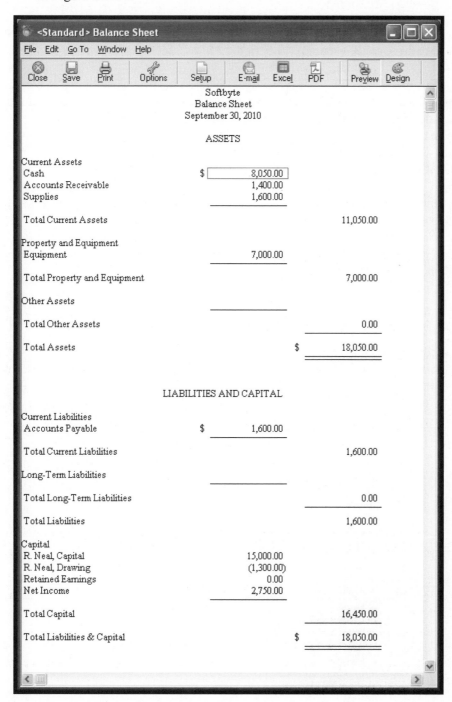

Figure 1B. 34 Balance sheet for Softbyte

GENERATING THE STATEMENT OF CASH FLOWS

The statement of cash flows reports:
1. The cash effects of a company's operations during a period.
2. Its investing transactions.
3. Its financing transactions.
4. The net increase or decrease in cash during the period.
5. The cash amount at the end of the period.

Reporting the sources, uses, and net increase or decrease in cash is useful because investors, creditors, and others want to know what is happening to a company's most liquid resource. Thus the statement of cash flows provides answers to the following simple but important questions:
1. Where did the cash come from during the period?
2. What was the cash used for during the period?
3. What was the change in the cash balance during the period?

The statement of cash flows for Softbyte is shown in Figure 1B. 35. Cash increased by $8,050 during the period (September). Net Cash provided by operations increased cash $1,350. Cash flow from investing activities decreased cash by $7,000 and cash flow from financing activities increased cash $13,700. Do not be concerned at this point with how these amounts were determined, but, be aware that they are based on your earlier entries.

Step 1: On the main menu bar click on "Reports" to get the pull down menu as required. Click on "Financial Statements" to access the "Select a Report or Form" menu as required.

Step 2: Double-click on "<Standard> Cash Flow."

Step 3: Again, the dialog box gives you several choices including the choice of financial periods, the margins for the printer; whether or not you want to show accounts that have a zero balance, whether or not you want page numbers, etc. If you wish to print the statement of cash flows, make sure the printer at the bottom of the dialog box matches the printer you are using on your computer system.

Step 4: Click "OK" to show the statement of cash flows for Softbyte, Figure 1B. 35, on your computer screen. It is shown full screen below.

```
 <Standard> Cash Flow                                    [_][□][X]
 File  Edit  Go To  Window  Help
 ┌──────┬──────┬──────┬──────────┬───────┬──────┬──────┬──────┬────────┬────────┐
 │  ⊗   │  💾  │  🖨  │    🔧    │  📄   │ 📧   │ ▦   │ 📄  │   🖼   │   🎨   │
 │ Close│ Save │ Print│  Options │ Setup │E-mail│ Excel│ PDF │ Preview│ Design │
```

Softbyte
Statement of Cash Flow
For the nine Months Ended September 30, 2010

		Current Month		Year to Date
Cash Flows from operating activities				
Net Income	$	2,750.00	$	2,750.00
Adjustments to reconcile net income to net cash provided by operating activities				
Accounts Receivable		(1,400.00)		(1,400.00)
Supplies		(1,600.00)		(1,600.00)
Accounts Payable		1,600.00		1,600.00
Total Adjustments		(1,400.00)		(1,400.00)
Net Cash provided by Operations		1,350.00		1,350.00
Cash Flows from investing activities				
Used For				
Equipment		(7,000.00)		(7,000.00)
Net cash used in investing		(7,000.00)		(7,000.00)
Cash Flows from financing activities				
Proceeds From				
R. Neal, Capital		15,000.00		15,000.00
R. Neal, Drawing		0.00		0.00
Used For				
R. Neal, Capital		0.00		0.00
R. Neal, Drawing		(1,300.00)		(1,300.00)
Net cash used in financing		13,700.00		13,700.00
Net increase <decrease> in cash	$	8,050.00	$	8,050.00
Summary				
Cash Balance at End of Period	$	8,050.00	$	8,050.00
Cash Balance at Beg of Period		0.00		0.00
Net Increase <Decrease> in Cash	$	8,050.00	$	8,050.00

Figure 1B. 35 Statement of cash flows

IDENTIFYING YOUR WORK

Peachtree Complete Accounting is designed to operate in a "real world" environment. With that being so, the only identifying tools built into Peachtree are the company names. That does not help your professor in identifying the work you turn in to them since there could be 40 "Softbyte" income statements received by the professor.

Let's look at some of the popular ways to identify your work. It will be up to your professor to decide which he/she would like you to identify your work with.

LABELING YOUR DISK

All disks (and disk drives) used in a Microsoft Windows® environment can be labeled. In other words, they can specifically be identified.

First, to check the label on a disk:

Step 1: Click on "My Computer." This is shown below in Figure 1B. 36. The My Computer icon may be found on your desktop.

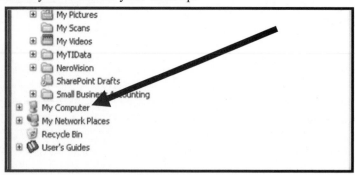

Figure 1B. 36 The My Computer selection

Step 2: Scroll up until your screen looks similar to the one partially shown in Figure A. 2. Your screen may be a little different because of how everyone sets their computer up different.

Step 3: Click on the drive in which your student data set is in. The right side of the screen will indicate the title of the files that are in that directory or folder.

NOTE: You will get an error message if there is not a in the selected drive.

Figure A. 2 My Computer showing the folders in the "A" drive, example.

Step 1:   Right click your mouse button to get a pull down menu.

Step 2:   Click "Properties" to get a screen similar to that in Figure 1B. 37.

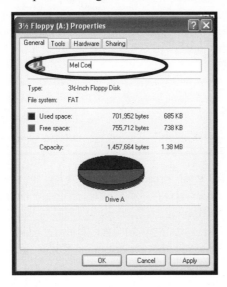

Figure 1B. 37 The properties box of Diskette "A"

The label text box, shown in Figure 1B. 37 above, shows how the current disk is labeled. For example, the author's name is used. Anything could be used as a label as long as it fits within Microsoft labeling guidelines. The system will send back an error message if the label chosen is "illegal."

Since the current label shown "Mel Coe" is highlighted you may change it (or whatever is in the text box) to reflect either your name or student number or whatever your professor would like for you to use to identify the disk.

Step 3:   Click "OK" when you are finished changing the label.

You may follow the steps above again to see the label for identification.

IDENTIFYING A FOLDER

As a professor, I prefer this identification method – Identify the folder with the student's name. This is preferable because I can see the name as soon as the disk is put in my computer.
Open Microsoft Explorer as before:

Step 1:   Again, click "My Computer." The text is shown below in Figure 1B. 38 and may be found on your desktop.

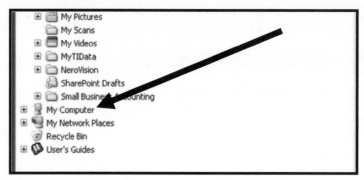

Figure 1B. 38 The "My Computer" text

Step 2:   Again, scroll up until your screen looks similar to the one partially shown in Figure 1B. 39. Your screen should be a little different because of how everyone sets his or her computer up different.

Step 3:   Click on the drive which contains your data. The right side of the screen will indicate the title of the files that are in that directory or folder. In this example the A drive is used.

NOTE: You will get an error message if there is not a disk in the selected drive.

Figure 1B. 39 Directory/Folder structure

Step 4:   Create a new folder by clicking on "File" at the top of window.

Step 5:   Click on "New."

Step 6:   On the "Pull-down menu" click on "Folder." You will be presented with the "New Folder" label shown in Figure 1B. 40, which can be changed.

Step 7:   In the highlighted area type in the Name or ID asked for by your professor.

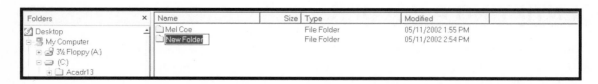

Figure 1B. 40 The "New Folder" shown in the directory structure

IDENTIFYING YOUR WORK DIRECTLY ON A PEACHTREE REPORT

You may identify your work by putting your name on the reports turned in to your professor.

Step 1:   Open the Peachtree company from which you want to individualize a report.

Step 2:   Click on "Reports" to get the reports selection pull down menu.

Step 3:   Select "Financial Statements." In our example we will use the income statement from Softbyte.

Step 4:   Click on the "<Standard>Income Statement." An example is shown below in Figure 1B. 41.

NOTE: Your figures in this statement *may not agree* with the ones shown in the example. That is okay – the format of the statement is what is important in this example. In fact, any <Standard> statement from any company would work.

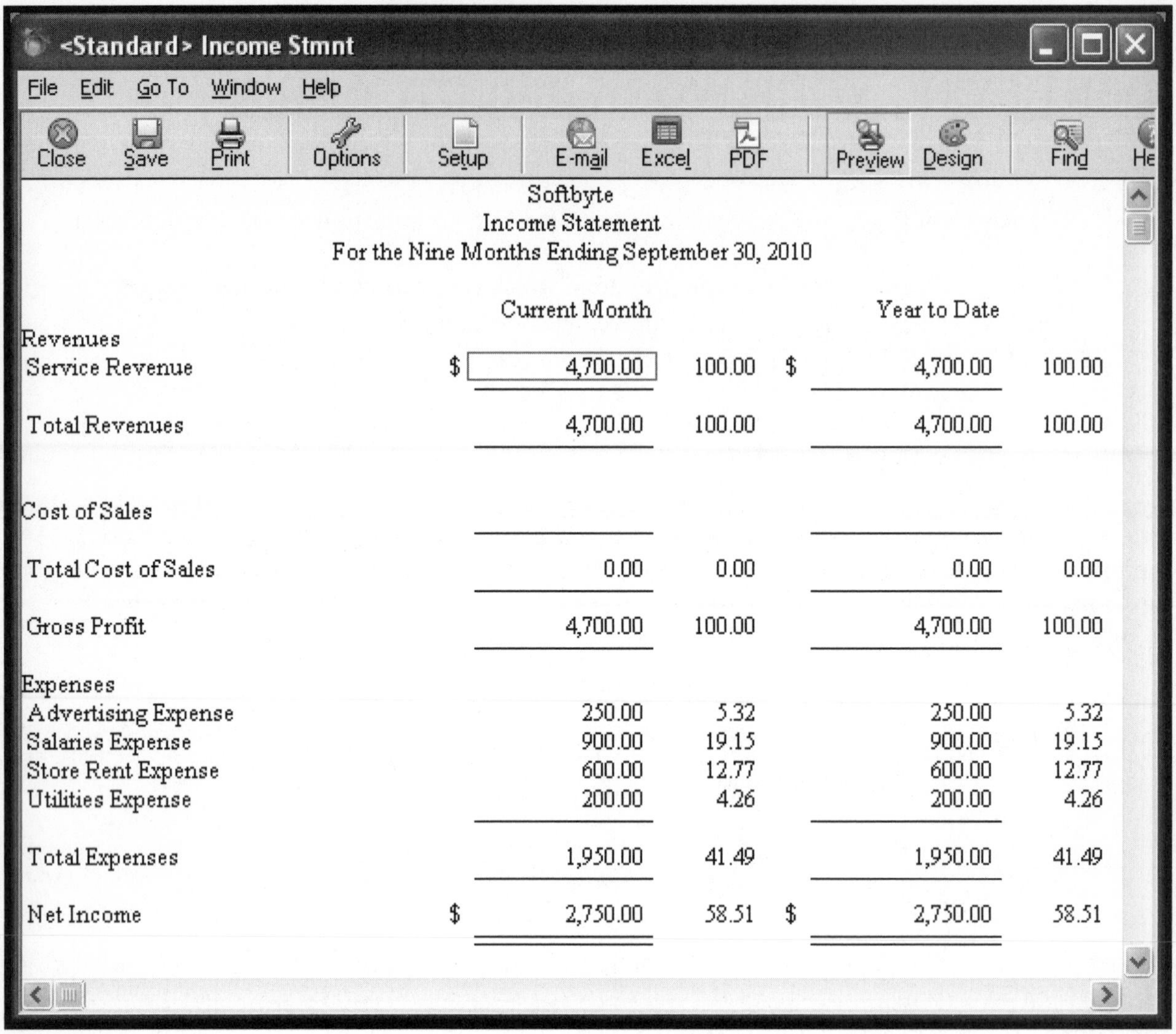

Softbyte
Income Statement
For the Nine Months Ending September 30, 2010

	Current Month		Year to Date	
Revenues				
Service Revenue	$ 4,700.00	100.00	$ 4,700.00	100.00
Total Revenues	4,700.00	100.00	4,700.00	100.00
Cost of Sales				
Total Cost of Sales	0.00	0.00	0.00	0.00
Gross Profit	4,700.00	100.00	4,700.00	100.00
Expenses				
Advertising Expense	250.00	5.32	250.00	5.32
Salaries Expense	900.00	19.15	900.00	19.15
Store Rent Expense	600.00	12.77	600.00	12.77
Utilities Expense	200.00	4.26	200.00	4.26
Total Expenses	1,950.00	41.49	1,950.00	41.49
Net Income	$ 2,750.00	58.51	$ 2,750.00	58.51

Figure 1B. 41 An example of a standard income statement

PLACING YOUR NAME IN THE HEADER OF THE REPORT

Several financial statements under the "Reports" menu are designated <Standard> as the prefix of the title of the report. In Peachtree accounting, the format of those <Standard> reports cannot be changed. However, you may use those reports, make changes and save them as another report as in the example we are about to perform.

Step 1: Click on the "Design" icon on the statement's task bar to get a window similar to the one in Figure 1B. 42.

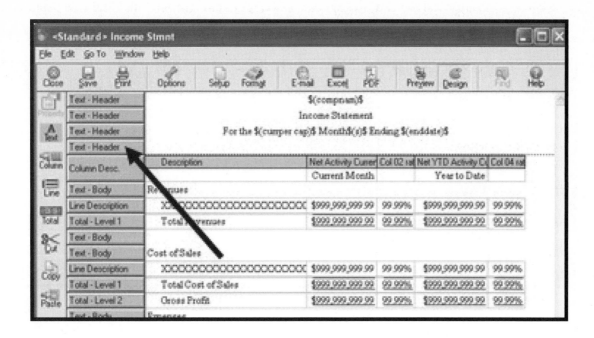

Figure 1B. 42 The design screen for the <Standard> Income Statement

Step 2: To place your name on the right side of the report, click double-click on the "Text" tile immediately below the last line of the title and immediately above the body of the report, as shown in Figure 1B. 42.

Step 3: On the pop-up dialog box, fill in the required information such as your name or other identification your professor, in this exam the name "Mel Coe" has been inserted, Figure 1B. 43.

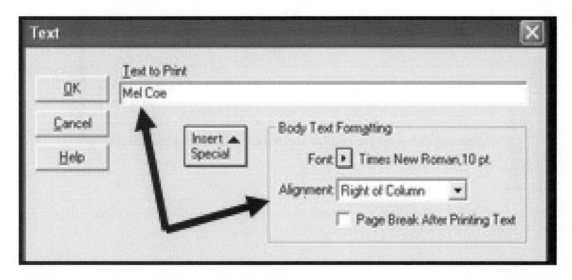

Figure 1B. 43 Header text information input box

Step 4: Make sure the alignment is set where your professor requests. In this example it is set for the "Right of Column." Then click "OK."

Step 5: Verify that the text appears as desired, in Figure 1B. 44 with "Mel Coe" appearing below the title block on the right side of the report.

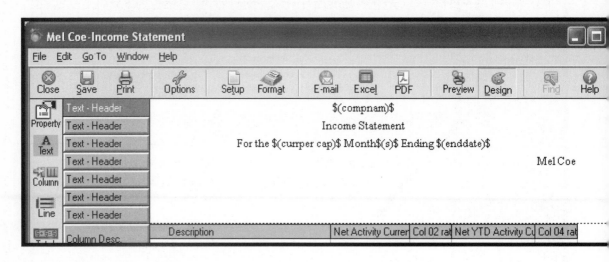

Figure 1B. 44 Header with inserted identification text

Step 6: Click "Save" in the task bar if the report is satisfactory. If it needs to be edited, click on the appropriate tile or task. And Peachtree will present a "Save As" dialog box, as shown in Figure 1B. 45.

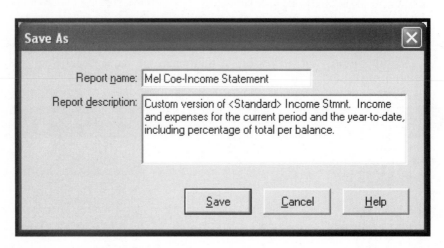

Figure 1B. 45 "Save As" dialog box

Note: A <Standard> financial statement cannot be changed. You first must change the name of the statement to reflect your customization.

When you look at the Select a Report or Form dialog box you will see, as shown in Figure 1B. 46, your customized report, Mel Coe-Income Statement, in this example.

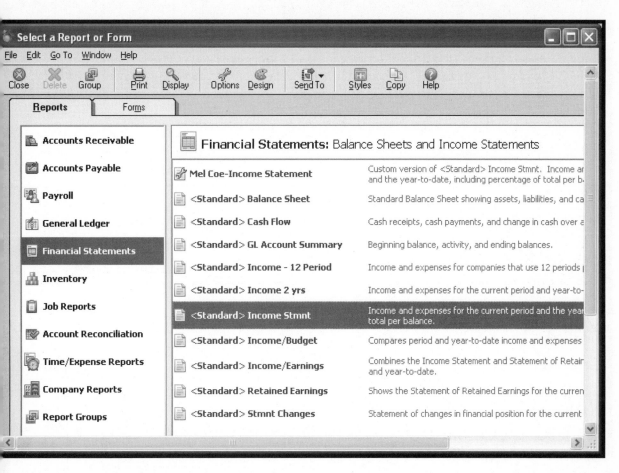

Figure 1B. 46 The Select a Report or Form dialog box with Mel Coe-Income Statement shown

And when this report is opened the name, Mel Coe, appears automatically on the right side of the report, as shown in Figure 1B. 47.

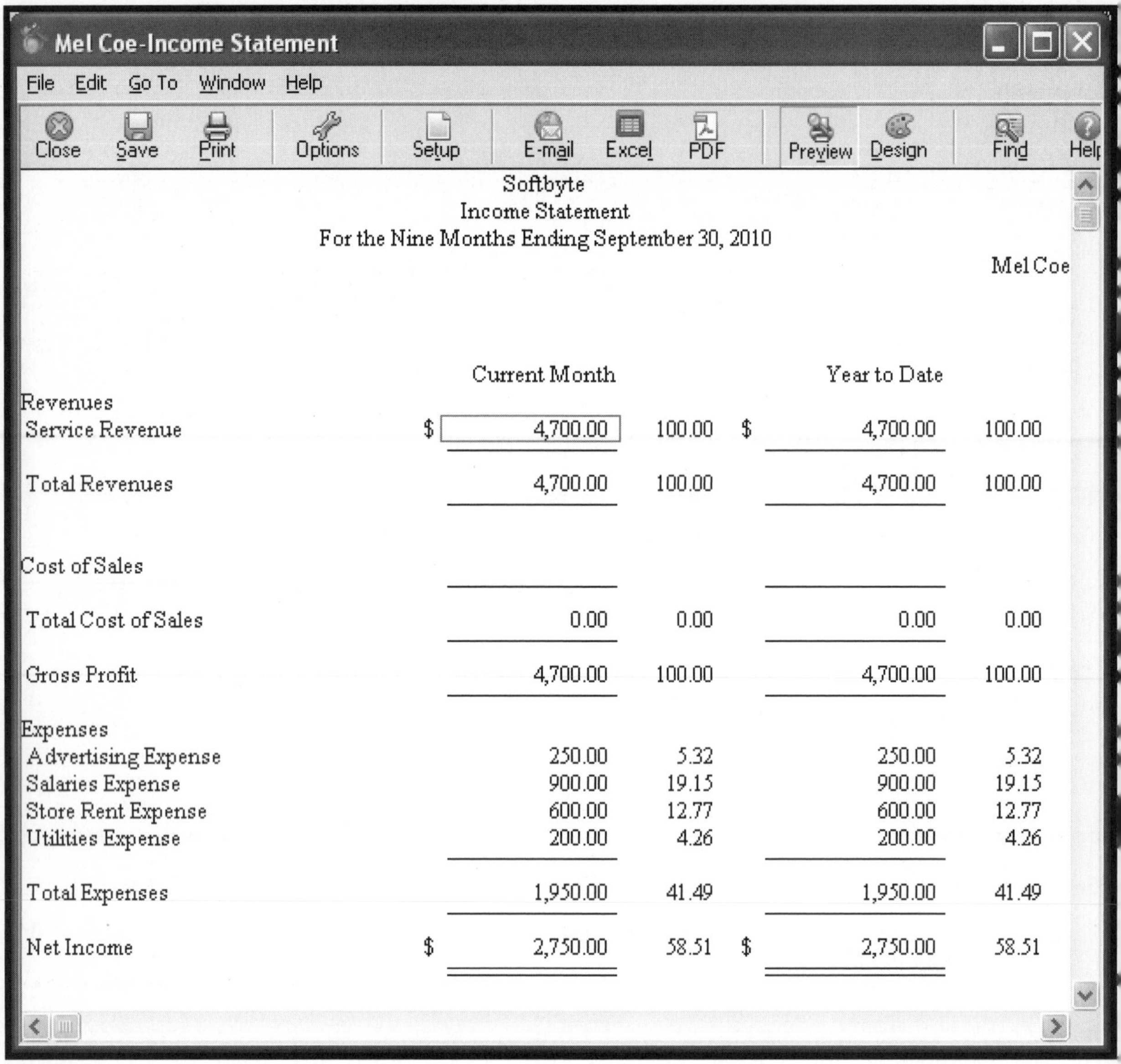

Mel Coe-Income Statement
File Edit Go To Window Help
Close Save Print Options Setup E-mail Excel PDF Preview Design Find Help

Softbyte
Income Statement
For the Nine Months Ending September 30, 2010

Mel Coe

		Current Month			Year to Date	
Revenues						
Service Revenue	$	4,700.00	100.00	$	4,700.00	100.00
Total Revenues		4,700.00	100.00		4,700.00	100.00
Cost of Sales						
Total Cost of Sales		0.00	0.00		0.00	0.00
Gross Profit		4,700.00	100.00		4,700.00	100.00
Expenses						
Advertising Expense		250.00	5.32		250.00	5.32
Salaries Expense		900.00	19.15		900.00	19.15
Store Rent Expense		600.00	12.77		600.00	12.77
Utilities Expense		200.00	4.26		200.00	4.26
Total Expenses		1,950.00	41.49		1,950.00	41.49
Net Income	$	2,750.00	58.51	$	2,750.00	58.51

Figure 1B. 47 The income statement with "Mel Coe" on the right side

ADDING YOUR NAME TO THE NAME OF THE COMPANY

You can modify the company name or replace it with your name if instructed to which will greatly ease the identification of your work. You will be working with Softbyte on this example so ensure that it is open.

Click on "Maintain" on the menu bar. From the drop-down menu, click on "Company Information," as shown in Figure 1B. 48.

Figure 1B. 48 The drop-down menu associated with Maintain showing the company information option

In this example the instructor wants your work identified with the problem number (P1-1A example) and your name (my name in this example - Rex A Schildhouse) separated by a hyphen. And this information replaces the company name, Softbyte. Figure 1B. 49 shows this information inserted into the company name window. When "OK" is clicked, the next report, Figure 1B. 50, will contain this information. Peachtree will not update this information in the title bar of the application until the next time this company is opened. The text will continue to refer to Softbyte as example company.

Maintain Company Information

Cancel | OK | Help

Company Name: P1-1A - Rex A Schildhouse

Address:

Figure 1B. 49 The Maintain Company Information dialog box with the new information entered

\<Standard\> Income Stmnt

File   Edit   Go To   Window   Help

Close   Save   Print   Options   Setup   E-mail   Excel   PDF   Preview   Design   Find   He

P1-1A - Rex A Schildhouse
Income Statement
For the Nine Months Ending September 30, 2010

	Current Month		Year to Date	
Revenues				
Service Revenue	$ 4,700.00	100.00	$ 4,700.00	100.00
Total Revenues	4,700.00	100.00	4,700.00	100.00
Cost of Sales				
Total Cost of Sales	0.00	0.00	0.00	0.00
Gross Profit	4,700.00	100.00	4,700.00	100.00
Expenses				
Advertising Expense	250.00	5.32	250.00	5.32
Salaries Expense	900.00	19.15	900.00	19.15
Store Rent Expense	600.00	12.77	600.00	12.77
Utilities Expense	200.00	4.26	200.00	4.26
Total Expenses	1,950.00	41.49	1,950.00	41.49
Net Income	$ 2,750.00	58.51	$ 2,750.00	58.51

Figure 1B. 50 The income statement viewed with the new identity information entered through the Maintain Company Information dialog box

Comprehensive Do It! Problem, Joan Robinson, Attorney at Law, Directory Wey_AP9e_Joan_Robinson

Joan Robinson opens her own law office on July 1, 2010. During the first month of operations, the following transactions occurred: (Note: Dates have been added as required for journalizing order.)

1.	July 1, 2010	Joan invested $11,000 in cash in the law practice.
2.	July 2, 2010	Paid $800 for July rent on office space.
3.	July 3, 2010	Purchased office equipment on account, $3,000.
4.	July 4, 2010	Provided legal services to clients for cash, $1,500
5.	July 5, 2010	Borrowed $700 cash from a bank on a note payable.
6.	July 6, 2010	Performed legal services for a client on account for $2,000.
7.	July 7, 2010	Paid monthly expenses: salaries $500; utilities $300 and telephone $100.
8.	July 8, 2010	Joan withdraws $1,000 cash for personal use.

Instructions:
(a) Open the company "Joan Robinson, Attorney at Law" found within your student data set and familiarize yourself with the chart of accounts.

(b) Enter and post (save) the above transactions utilizing the general journal entry screen within Peachtree Complete Accounting.

(c) Print the income statement and statement of retained earnings for the month ended July 31, 2010.

(d) Print the balance sheet as of July 31, 2010.

Solution to Comprehensive Do It! Problem

General journal entries of Joan Robinson provided for reference.

General Journal Entry

File Edit Go To Window Help

Close New List Save Delete Recur Row Reports Help

Journal Entry

Date: Jul 1, 2010   ☐ Reverse Transaction

Reference: Trans #1

GL Account	Description	Debit	Credit	Job
101	Owner invested cash in business	11,000.00		
301	Owner invested cash in business		11,000.00	

General Journal Entry

File Edit Go To Window Help

Close New List Save Delete Recur Row Reports Help

Journal Entry

Date: Jul 2, 2010   ☐ Reverse Transaction

Reference: Trans #2

GL Account	Description	Debit	Credit	Job
729	Paid July rent	800.00		
101	Paid July rent		800.00	

General Journal Entry

File Edit Go To Window Help

Close New List Save Delete Recur Row Reports Help

Journal Entry

Date: Jul 3, 2010   ☐ Reverse Transaction

Reference: Trans #3

GL Account	Description	Debit	Credit	Job
157	Purchased office equipment on account	3,000.00		
201	Purchased office equipment on account		3,000.00	

General Journal Entry

File Edit Go To Window Help

Close New List Save Delete Recur Row Reports Help

Journal Entry

Date: Jul 4, 2010   ☐ Reverse Transaction

Reference: Trans #4

GL Account	Description	Debit	Credit	Job
101	Earned service revenue in cash	1,500.00		
401	Earned service revenue in cash		1,500.00	

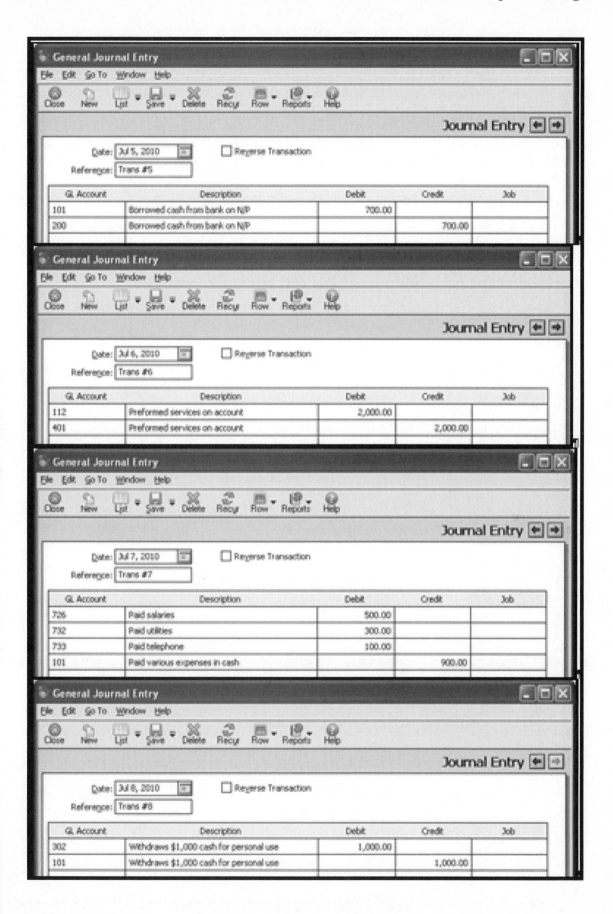

General Journal Entry

File Edit Go To Window Help

Close New List Save Delete Recur Row Reports Help

Journal Entry ← →

Date: Jul 5, 2010 ☐ Reverse Transaction
Reference: Trans #5

GL Account	Description	Debit	Credit	Job
101	Borrowed cash from bank on N/P	700.00		
200	Borrowed cash from bank on N/P		700.00	

General Journal Entry

File Edit Go To Window Help

Close New List Save Delete Recur Row Reports Help

Journal Entry ← →

Date: Jul 6, 2010 ☐ Reverse Transaction
Reference: Trans #6

GL Account	Description	Debit	Credit	Job
112	Preformed services on account	2,000.00		
401	Preformed services on account		2,000.00	

General Journal Entry

File Edit Go To Window Help

Close New List Save Delete Recur Row Reports Help

Journal Entry ← →

Date: Jul 7, 2010 ☐ Reverse Transaction
Reference: Trans #7

GL Account	Description	Debit	Credit	Job
726	Paid salaries	500.00		
732	Paid utilities	300.00		
733	Paid telephone	100.00		
101	Paid various expenses in cash		900.00	

General Journal Entry

File Edit Go To Window Help

Close New List Save Delete Recur Row Reports Help

Journal Entry ← →

Date: Jul 8, 2010 ☐ Reverse Transaction
Reference: Trans #8

GL Account	Description	Debit	Credit	Job
302	Withdraws $1,000 cash for personal use	1,000.00		
101	Withdraws $1,000 cash for personal use		1,000.00	

General journal report of Joan Robinson provided for reference.

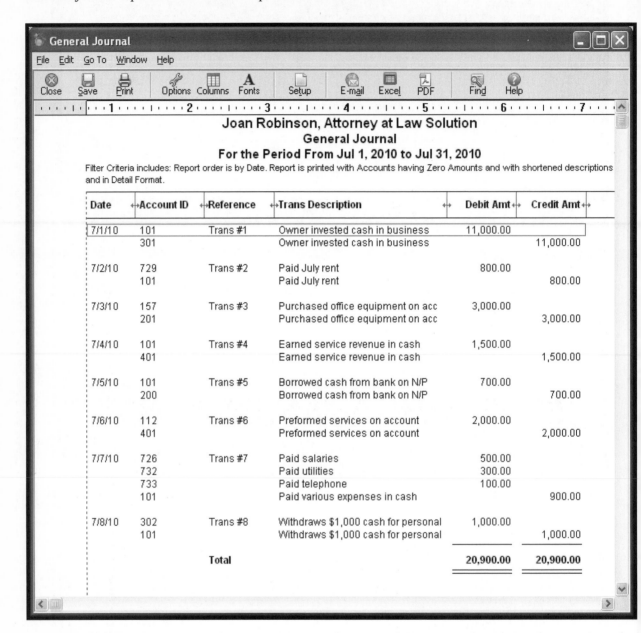

Income statement of Joan Robinson

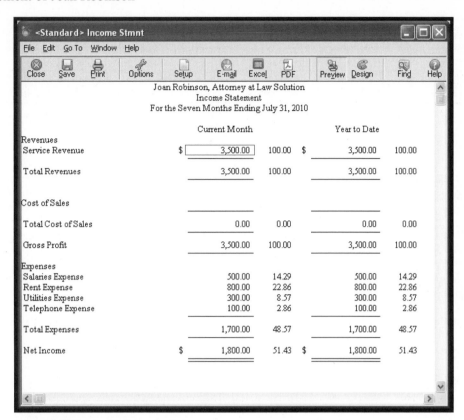

Statement of retained earnings of Joan Robinson

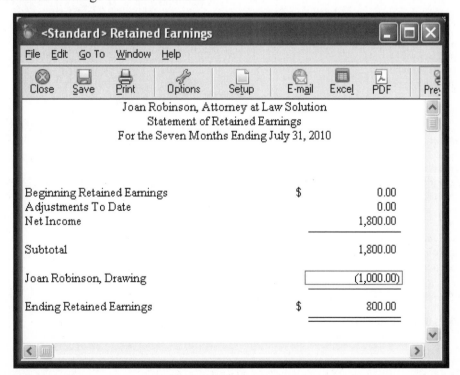

Joan Robinson's balance sheet

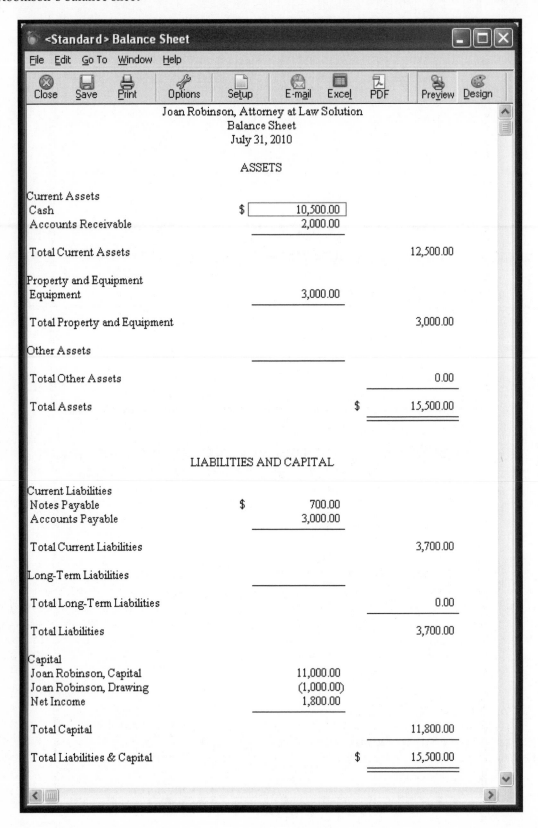

CHAPTER 2

The Recording Process

OBJECTIVES

- Explain what an account is and how it helps in the recording process.
- Define debits and credits and explain how their use in recording business transactions.
- Identify the basic steps in the recording process.
- Explain what a journal is and how it helps in the recording process.
- Explain what a ledger is and how it helps in the recording process.
- Explain what posting is and how it helps in the recording process.
- Prepare a trial balance and explain its purpose.
- Explain the general journal and general ledger in Peachtree Complete Accounting
- Generate the trial balance provided in Peachtree Complete Accounting.

THE ACCOUNT

An account is an individual accounting record of the increases and decreases in a specific asset, liability, or owner's equity item. For example, Softbyte has separate accounts for cash, accounts receivable, accounts payable, service revenue, salaries expense, and so on.

In its simplest form, a "T-account format," an account has three parts:

- The title.
- The left side or debit side.
- A right side or credit side .

The accounting term "*debit*" refers to the left side of a column and "*credit*" refers to the right side. Therefore, entering an amount on the left side is called debiting the account while entering a value on the right side is called crediting the account. The common abbreviations are Dr. for debit and Cr. for credit. In Peachtree reports credits will frequently be shown as negative numbers – in parenthesis – (1,300.00), the drawing amount on Softbyte's balance sheet.

To "balance" your account, add up the debit amounts entered, then add up the credit amounts entered. Subtract the smaller total from the larger total. The difference is called the balance with the identity of the larger total. Peachtree will balance your accounts for you and show credit balances as negative numbers.

In the first chapter, as you made general journal entries for each of the Softbyte transactions, you learned how a transaction affects the basic accounting equation. Each transaction must affect two or more accounts, and for each transaction debits must equal credits. That keeps the accounting equation in balance. This is the basis for the double entry accounting system, which is the heart of Peachtree Complete Accounting.

THE GENERAL JOURNAL

In manual accounting, transactions are recorded in a journal in sequential order as they happen before being transferred to the account in the general ledger. The general journal is referred to as the "Book of Original Entry" by the accounting profession. For each transaction the journal shows the debit and credit effects on the individual accounts. Companies use various kinds of journals but every company uses the most basic form of journal - a general journal.

Peachtree's automated version of the general journal was used when you made your entries for Softbyte in Chapter 1. As you recall, the general journal has spaces for dates, account titles and explanations/references (descriptions) and debit and credit value columns.

Let's look at Softbyte's general journal. From the start screen, click on "Open an Existing company," then "Softbyte." This will be the same file you used during the exercises in Chapter 1.

Step 1:   On the menu bar click on "Reports & Forms."

Step 2:   On the pull down menu, click on "General Ledger."

Step 3:   Double-click on the "General Journal" option from the reports menu.

Part of the general journal report is shown in Figure 2. 1. It shows the initial entry for cash and capital from the first transactions in the previous chapter. Notice the debit entry (increasing) cash and the credit entry (increasing) capital, each for $15,000. Some of the other entries made in September also appear in this general journal report example.

Note that the name of the account does not appear, only the account number. The reference and the trans(action) description columns is the data from the reference window and the description column's information of the journal entry itself. The description is entered for each line of the entry rather than once below the credit account title as shown in your textbook.

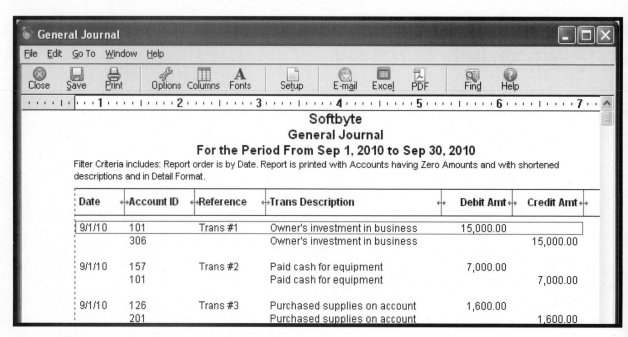

Figure 2. 1   General journal report for Softbyte

While viewing the general journal report in Peachtree, moving your cursor pointer over a data item you may get a magnifying glass with a "Z" in its lens area. When this happens you can "drill down" to the original information by double-clicking with your mouse. So, while the general journal report is not general journal entries, you are two clicks away from the journal entry of interest, if visible.

Another difference of Peachtree – a choice actually taken during the setup of the company, when you click on "Save" on the menu bar of the general journal entry, that entry, if no errors are detected, is automatically posted to the appropriate ledger accounts. As such, when utilizing Peachtree to solve textbook challenges your posting to the general ledger will be accomplished automatically when "Save" is clicked. The option, not frequently in small business, is "Batch Processing" where journal entries are held in a queue until approved by an appropriate authority for recording as a journal entry and posting to the general ledger. Batch processing is not addressed in this text as most small businesses do not use it.

THE GENERAL LEDGER

The entire group of accounts maintained by a company is called the general ledger. The ledger, as it is commonly referred to, keeps in one place all of the information about any changes in individual account balances. Each transaction is entered in the ledger, which was the "posting" process performed in the previous chapter.

Every company has some type of general ledger that contains all of the assets, liabilities, and owner's equity accounts, their related transactions and balances.

The ledger provides management with the balances in various accounts. For example, the Cash account shows the amount of cash that is available to meet current obligations. Amounts due from customers can be found by examining Accounts Receivable and amounts owed to creditors can be found by looking at Accounts Payable.

Let's look at the general ledger for Softbyte. Return to the main menu bar for Softbyte file from within your student data set. This will be the same file you used in Chapter 1.

Step 1: On the menu bar click on "Reports & Forms."

Step 2: On the drop-down menu, click on "General Ledger."

Step 3: Double-click on "General Ledger" from the report selection menu as shown in Figure 2. 2.

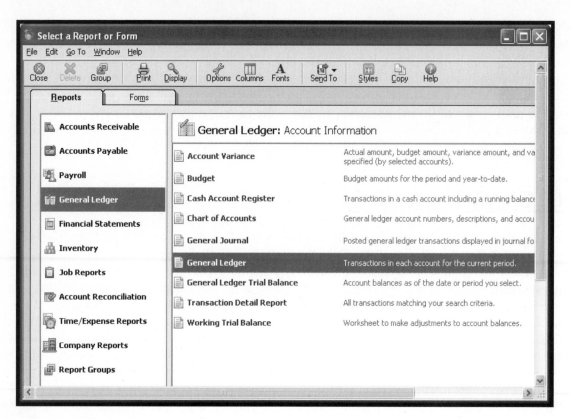

Figure 2. 2   Report a Report or Form menu

Peachtree then presents a complete general ledger report, a portion of which is shown Figure 2. 3. The entire report would list each active account without a zero balance and the associated transactions. However, you have an option to list the accounts with zero balances if you wish, which would make for an even longer report.

Notice that under the balance column, debit balances are positive amounts while credit balances have a negative sign.

General Ledger

File Edit Go To Window Help

Close Save Print Options Columns Fonts Setup E-mail Excel PDF Find Help

Softbyte
General Ledger
For the Period From Sep 1, 2010 to Sep 30, 2010
Filter Criteria includes: Report order is by ID. Report is printed with shortened descriptions and in Detail Format.

Account ID Account Description	Date	Reference	Jrnl	Trans Description	Debit Amt	Credit Amt	Balance
101	9/1/10			Beginning Balance			
Cash	9/1/10	Trans #1	GEN	Owner's investme	15,000.00		
	9/1/10	Trans #2	GEN	Paid cash for equi		7,000.00	
	9/1/10	Trans #4	GEN	Services rendered	1,200.00		
	9/7/10	Trans #6	GEN	Received cash fro	1,500.00		
	9/15/10	Trans #7	GEN	Paid various expen		1,700.00	
	9/15/10	Trans #8	GEN	Paid Daily News fo		250.00	
	9/15/10	Trans #9	GEN	Received cash fro	600.00		
	9/30/10	Trans #10	GEN	Ray Neal, Drawing		1,300.00	
				Current Period Ch	18,300.00	10,250.00	8,050.00
	9/30/10			**Ending Balance**			**8,050.00**
112	9/1/10			Beginning Balance			
Accounts Receivable	9/7/10	Trans #6	GEN	Services On Accou	2,000.00		
	9/15/10	Trans #9	GEN	Received cash fro		600.00	
				Current Period Ch	2,000.00	600.00	1,400.00
	9/30/10			**Ending Balance**			**1,400.00**

Figure 2. 3 Portion of Softbyte's general ledger report

ASSETS AND LIABILITIES

In the Softbyte exercise in Chapter 1, you were shown that increases in cash (an asset) were entered on the left side (debit side) of the journal amount column and decreases in cash were entered on the right side (credit side) of the journal amount column. You also know that both sides of the basic accounting equation (Assets = Liabilities + Owner's Equity) must be equal. It makes sense that increases and decreases in liabilities will be recorded opposite from assets, therefore, increases in liabilities must be entered on the right (credit side), and decreases in liabilities must be entered on the left (debit side).

Knowing the normal balance in an account will help you trace errors. For example, a credit balance in an asset account such as Land or a debit balance in a liability account such as Wages Payable usually indicates an error. Occasionally, however, an abnormal balance may be correct. For example, the Cash account could have a credit balance when a company has overdrawn its bank balance.

OWNER'S EQUITY

Owner's equity is increased either by additional investments by the owner or by revenue earned in the business. For example, when the owner invests cash in the business, (Softbyte's Transaction #1), Cash is debited (increased) and Owner's Capital (R. Neal, Capital for Softbyte) is credited (also increased). An owner may withdraw cash or other assets from the business for personal use, these events are called withdrawals or drawings. Withdrawals are normally debited to a withdrawals or drawing (R. Neal, Drawing for Softbyte) to indicate a decrease in owner's equity. Expenses also decrease the owner's equity.

REVENUES AND EXPENSES

When revenues are earned, owner's equity is increased. That means simply that the effect of debits and credits on revenue accounts is the same as their effect on owner's capital. Revenue accounts are increased by credits (sales). When expenses are incurred, owner's equity is decreased. The recognition of an expense represents a decrease in owner's equity. Therefore, expenses are recorded as debits.

THE CHART OF ACCOUNTS

The number and type of accounts used are likely to differ for each enterprise depending on the amount of detail required by management. Although Softbyte is able to manage and report its activities with just a few accounts, a large corporation such as Robinson-Humphrey, a stock brokerage firm in Atlanta, requires more accounts to keep track of its activities. But too many accounts create problems while attempting to provide data for analysis. If a company has "Office Supplies," "Toner and Ink," and "Printer Supplies" one accountant may put toner values into "Toner and Ink" while another may insert other toner purchases into "Printer Supplies." A third accountant might record toner values to "Office Supplies." And, by title, all three are correct and consistent analysis is ineffective due to this inconsistent use of the chart of accounts.

Companies have a chart of accounts (COA), a master listing of the accounts and the account numbers, which identify their location in the ledger. The numbering system used to identify the accounts usually starts with the balance sheet accounts and ends with the expenses on the income statement.

To examine the chart of accounts for Softbyte.

Step 1: On the menu bar, click on "Reports & Forms."

Step 2: On the pull down menu, click on "General Ledger."

Step 3: Then select "Chart of Accounts" from the Select a Report or Form menu by double-clicking on the title. The general ledger list of reports is shown with chart of accounts selected in Figure 2. 4.

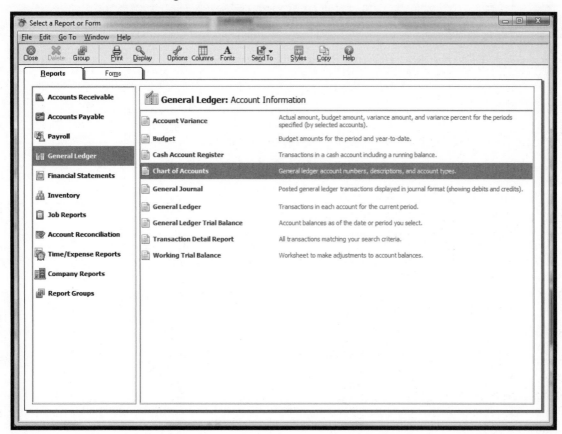

Figure 2. 4   Report select menu for chart of accounts

The chart of accounts used to this point for Softbyte is shown in Figure 2. 5. You may print the chart of accounts by clicking on the "Print" icon.

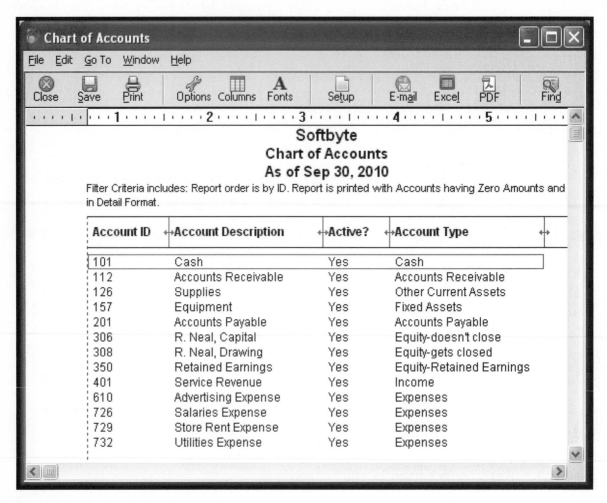

Figure 2. 5   Chart of accounts report for Softbyte

HOW ACCOUNTS ARE ASSIGNED NUMBERS

The numbering system used to identify accounts can be quite sophisticated or as in Softbyte's case, fairly simple. For example, one major company uses an 18-digit account numbering system. The first three digits identify the division or plant; the second set of three digit numbers contains the plant location, and so on. Softbyte uses a three-digit classification.

Softbyte
Account Number Classification

100 – 199	Assets
200 – 299	Liabilities
300 – 399	Equity/Capital
400 – 499	Revenue
500 – 799	Expenses

When setting up a new business, you will discover that Peachtree contains many sample companies and their related charts of accounts. You will be given a choice of setting up your own chart of accounts or you may select one of the sample company's chart of account.

To see the sample companies and their Charts of Accounts, open up either of the two sample companies, Bellwether Garden Supply or Stone Arbor Landscaping. Both of these companies are part of the standard installation of Peachtree Complete Accounting.

You can also access the help screens of Peachtree by:

Step 1: Clicking on the "Help" on the menu bar,

Step 2: Selecting "Peachtree Accounting Help" from the drop-down menu options, Figure 2. 6.

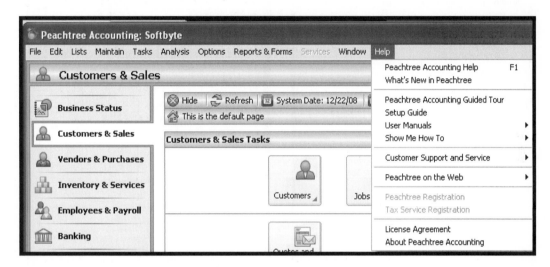

Figure 2. 6 Pull down window for help

Step 3: Then selecting either "Index" or "Contents" tab. The index table and contents table both provide many options on numerous subjects. If one does not provide the answer, try the other or the "Search" option. The index and help dialog boxes are shown in Figure 2. 7.

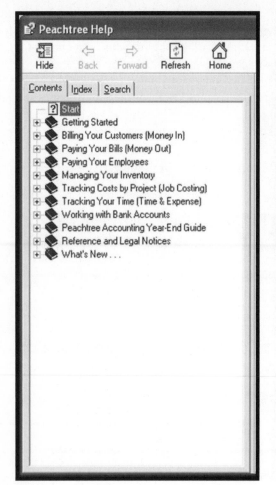 

Figure 2. 7   Contents and index dialog boxes

SETTING UP A NEW ACCOUNT

If you choose to use a company that has accounts already set up, you still may create new accounts, as needed, at any time. For example, let's say the owner of Softbyte would like to set up an account for Telephone Expense. Originally Ray Neal classified the phone bill as part of the Utilities Expenses. But now he wants the Utilities Expense account to reflect only the gas and power bills and would like a separate account, the Telephone Expense account, to reflect payments for regular phone service.

Setting up the new account:

Step 1:   Click on "Maintain" from the main menu bar.

Step 2:   From the pull down menu (Figure 2. 8) click on "Chart of Accounts."

Figure 2. 8   Drop-down menu from Maintain for Chart of Accounts option

The chart of accounts entry screen is displayed on your screen as shown in Figure 2. 9.

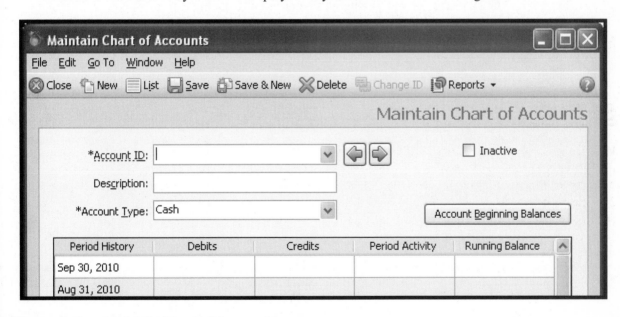

Figure 2. 9   Maintain Chart of Accounts screen

Step 3:   Enter "733" as the Account ID.

Step 4:   In the description window, enter "Telephone Expense."

Step 5:   The account must have a type that is assigned by you. (Account types are discussed in the next section.) In the Account Type window click on the drop-down menu arrow and scroll down until "Expenses" is shown in the window, see Figure 2. 10.

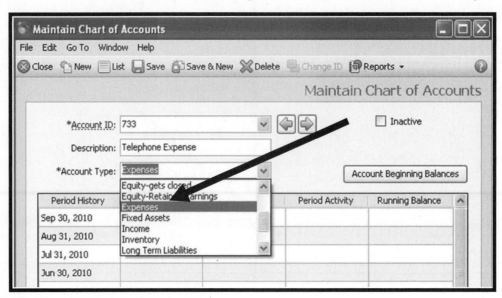

Figure 2. 10   New account entry, assigning account type of "Expense"

Step 6:   Double-click on "Expenses" to classify the account as an expense account within the Peachtree system. You will not enter a beginning balance or any budget items at this time.

Step 7:   Click "Save" on the task bar to save the new account.

Step 8:   To make sure your new account has been entered and saved properly, view the chart of accounts report (Figure 2. 11.)

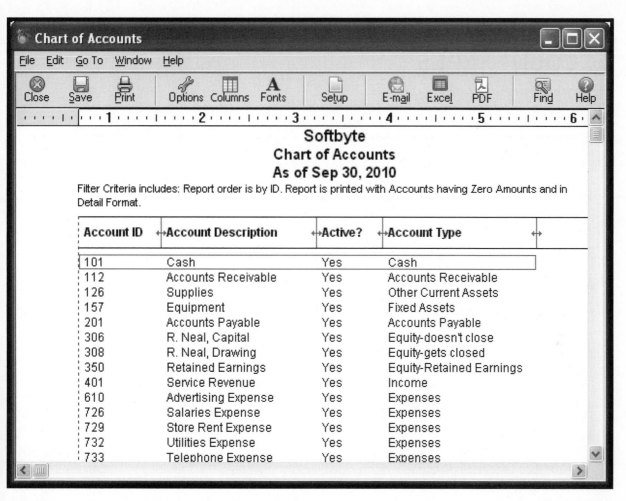

Figure 2. 11   New chart of accounts report reflecting the 733 – Telephone Expense account

ACCOUNT TYPES

When creating new accounts in Peachtree, account types will define how the account will be grouped in reports and financial statements. (Figure 2. 12) They also control what happens during fiscal year-end.

Accounts Payable	Equity – Gets closed	Long-Term Liabilities
Accounts Receivable	Equity – Retained Earnings	Other Assets
Accumulated Depreciation	Expenses	Other Current Assets
Cash	Fixed Assets	Other Current Liabilities
Cost of Sales	Income	
Equity – Doesn't close	Inventory	

Figure 2. 12   Menu of account types in creating new accounts

Accounts Payable - Account balances owed to vendors for goods, supplies, and services purchased on an open account that are generally due in 30 or 60 days, and do not bear interest. Select this account type if you are setting up open vendor accounts or credit card (purchase) accounts.

Accounts Receivable - Account balances owed by customers for items or services sold to them when cash is not received at the time of sale.

Accumulated Depreciation - This is a contra asset account to depreciable (fixed) assets such as buildings, machinery, and equipment. Recording depreciation is a way to indicate that assets have declined in service potential. Accumulated depreciation represents total depreciation taken to date on the assets.

Cash - This represents deposits in banks available for current operations, plus cash on hand consisting of currency, undeposited checks, drafts, and money orders. Select this account type if you are setting up bank checking accounts, petty cash accounts, money market accounts, and certificates of deposit (CDs).

Cost of Sales - This represents the known cost to your business for items or services when sold to customers. Cost of sales is also known as cost of goods sold for inventory items and computed based on inventory costing method (FIFO, LIFO or Average). Select this account type if you are setting up cost-of-goods-sold accounts to be used when selling inventory items.

Equity - Doesn't Close - This represents the paid-in equity or capital that is carried forward from period to period. It is also used for preferred and common stock.

Equity - Gets Closed - This represents equity that is closed or zeroed out at the end of the fiscal year, such as withdrawals, drawings, and dividends, with their amounts moved to the retained earnings account.

Equity - Retained Earnings - This represents the balance of the earned capital or equity of the enterprise. Its balance is the cumulative, lifetime earnings of the company that have not been distributed to owners. Peachtree Complete Accounting requires you to have a retained earnings account and it will post values to this account during the automated closing process.

Expenses - These represent the costs incurred to produce revenues. The assets surrendered or consumed when serving customers are the company's expenses. If revenue exceeds expenses, net income results, if expenses exceed income, the business is operating at a net loss.

Fixed Assets - These represent property, plant, or equipment assets that are acquired for use in a business rather than for resale. They are called fixed assets because they are to be used for long periods of time. Select this account type if you are setting up any of the following fixed assets:

- **Land** - property.
- **Buildings** - structures in which the business is carried out.
- **Machinery** - heavy equipment used to carry out business operations.

In addition, you may want to set up any of the following: store equipment or fixtures, factory equipment of fixtures, office equipment or fixtures (including computers and furniture), and delivery equipment (including autos, trucks, and vans used primarily in making deliveries to customers).

Income - Revenue is the inflow of assets resulting from the sale of products and services to customers. Select this account type if you are setting up sales and service revenue accounts. It is common practice to create different revenue accounts for each category of revenue that you want to track (for example, retail revenue, service revenue, interest revenue, and so on).

Inventory - This represents the value of goods on hand and available for sale at any given time. Inventory is considered to be an asset that is purchased, manufactured (or assembled), and sold to customers for revenue. Select this account type if you are setting up assets that are intended for resale. It is common practice to create different accounts for each category of inventory that you want to track. For example, retail inventory, raw materials inventory, work in process inventory, finished goods inventory, and so on can be tracked through the inventory account.

Long-Term Liabilities - This represents debts that are not due for a relatively long period of time, usually more than one year. Portions of long-term loans due and notes payable with maturity dates at least one year or more beyond the current balance sheet date are considered to be long-term liabilities.

Other Assets - This represents assets that are considered nonworking capital and are not due for a relatively long period of time, usually more than one year. Notes receivable with maturity dates at least one year or more beyond the current balance sheet date are considered to be "noncurrent" assets. Select this account type if you are setting up assets such as long-term investments, intangible assets, noncurrent notes receivable, and so on.

Other Current Assets - This represents those assets that will be used or consumed within a short period of time, usually less than a year. Prepaid expenses, employee advances, and notes receivable with maturity dates of less than one year of the current balance sheet date are considered to be "current" assets. Select this account type if you are setting up assets such as prepaid expenses, employee advances, current notes receivable, and so on.

Other Current Liabilities - This represents debts that are due within a short period of time, usually less than a year. The payment of these debts usually requires the use of current assets. Select this account type if you are setting up accrued expenses from a vendor, extended lines of credit, short-term loans, sales tax payables, payroll tax payables, client escrow accounts, suspense (clearing) accounts, and so on.

THE TRIAL BALANCE AND THE WORKING TRIAL BALANCE

A trial balance is a list of accounts and their balances at a given time. Using a manual accounting system, a trial balance usually would be prepared at the end of an accounting period. However, Peachtree keeps a continual trial balance available for you. In a manual system, the primary purpose of a trial balance is to prove that the debits equal the credits after posting. Because Peachtree will not let you continue an entry unless it is in balance, the trial balance Peachtree generates will always be "in balance." As mentioned earlier, however, that does not mean your accounting record is error free, that all transactions have been recorded, or that the journal entries are correct. In Peachtree, this trial balance is called the general ledger trial balance.

The working trial balance in Peachtree has a somewhat different purpose. In Peachtree, the working trial balance report prints the accounts and their balances, together with spaces to fill in information so you can have a worksheet to help make adjustments to account balances.

To see the working trial balance in Peachtree:

Step 1: On the menu bar, click on "Reports," and then click "General Ledger."

Step 2: On the pull down menu, double-click on "Working Trial Balance."

A portion of the working trial balance for Softbyte is shown in Figure 2. 13.

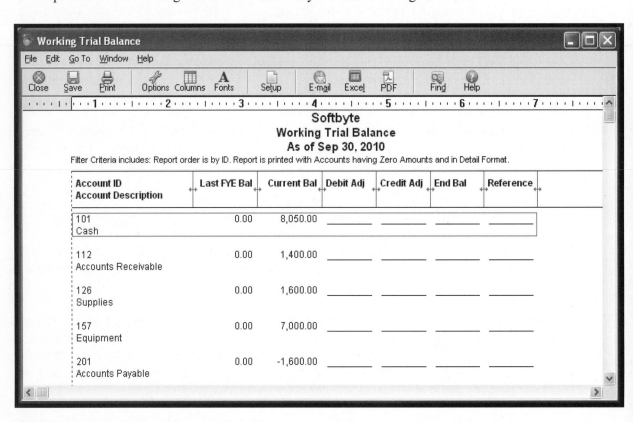

Figure 2. 13 Working trial balance

Notice that under the current balance column, the debit balances are positive amounts while the credit balances have a negative sign.

CHANGING ACCOUNTING PERIODS

Peachtree keeps all information in "accounting periods" organized by dates. All of January 2010 data is in the January 2010 accounting period while all February 2010 data is in the February 2010 accounting period. This isolates nominal or temporary account information within the accounting period. Each accounting period starts with the ending balances of the real account values from the previous accounting period. This may preclude you from making journal entries or viewing other period reports. To change the accounting period,

Step 1: On the menu bar, click on "Tasks."

Step 2: Click on "System."

Step 3: Click on "Change Accounting Periods," as shown below.

Step 4: The Change Accounting Period dialog box, shown in Figure 2. 14, will appear.

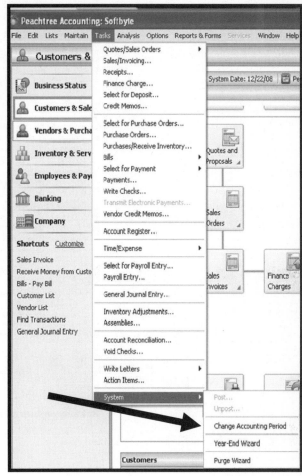

Figure 2. 14 Change Accounting Period option on Tasks drop-down menu

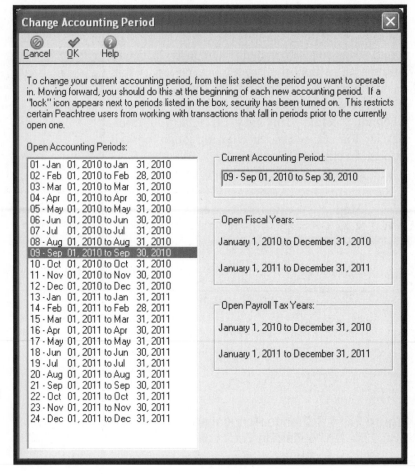

Figure 2. 15 Change
Accounting
Period option on
Tasks drop-
down menu

Step 5:   To change the accounting period from "09 – Sep 01, 2010 to Sep 30, 2010," to another period, such as "03 – Mar 01, 2010 to Mar 31, 2010" double-click on "03 – Mar 01, 2010 to Mar 31, 2010" and the period will change and dialog box will disappear. If you single-click, you will have to click "OK" as well.

Step 6:   Peachtree will respond with another dialog box asking if you would like to print period reports. In most cases you can click "No" to continue.

Step 8:   Peachtree will then ask if you want to run an internal accounting review, as shown below. In most cases you can click "No" to continue.

Step 8:   And Peachtree will complete the change to the new accounting period. The accounting period can be determined by reading the period box in the upper section of the main Peachtree screen, Figure 2. 16.

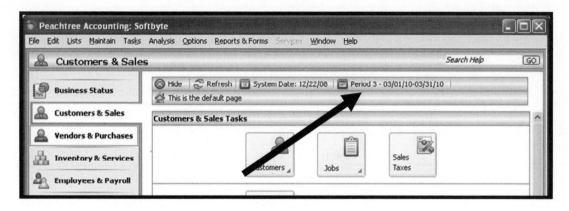

Figure 2. 16 The current accounting period and date range

Comprehensive Do It! Problem, Campus Laundromat, Directory Campus_Laundromat

Bob Sample opened the Campus Laundromat on September 1, 2010. During the first month of operations the following transactions occurred.

Sept. 1   Bob invested $20,000 cash in the business.

2   The company paid $1,000 cash for store rent for September.

3   Purchased washers and dryers for $25,000, paying $10,000 in cash and signing a $15,000, 6-month, 12% note payable.

4   Paid $1,200 for a one-year accident insurance policy.

10   Received a bill from the *Daily News* for advertising the opening of the laundromat, $200.

20   Bob withdrew $700 cash for personal use.

30   The company determined that cash receipts for laundry services for the month were $6,200.

Open Campus Laundromat from within the student data set.

Instructions:

(a) Familiarize yourself with Campus Laundromat's chart of accounts and verify that the beginning balances are zero by previewing the general ledger trial balance report.

(b) Journalize in Peachtree's general journal screen the September transactions. Use "Trans #1", "Trans #2", etc. as the reference number.

(c) Print a copy of the general journal report, general ledger, and the general ledger trial balance report.

Solution to Comprehensive Do It! Problem

General Journal Report

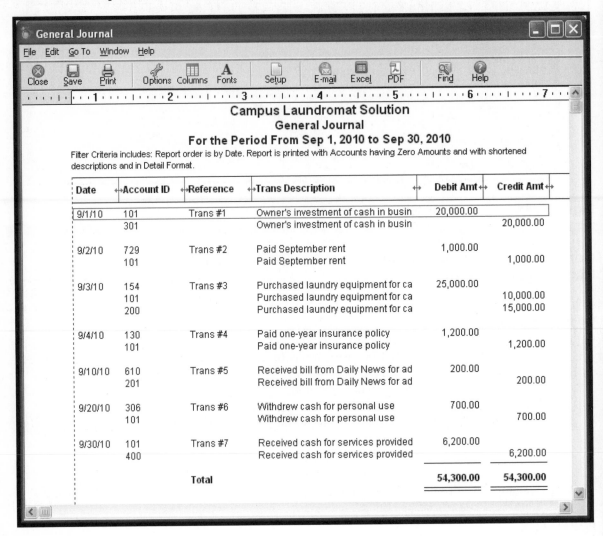

General Ledger

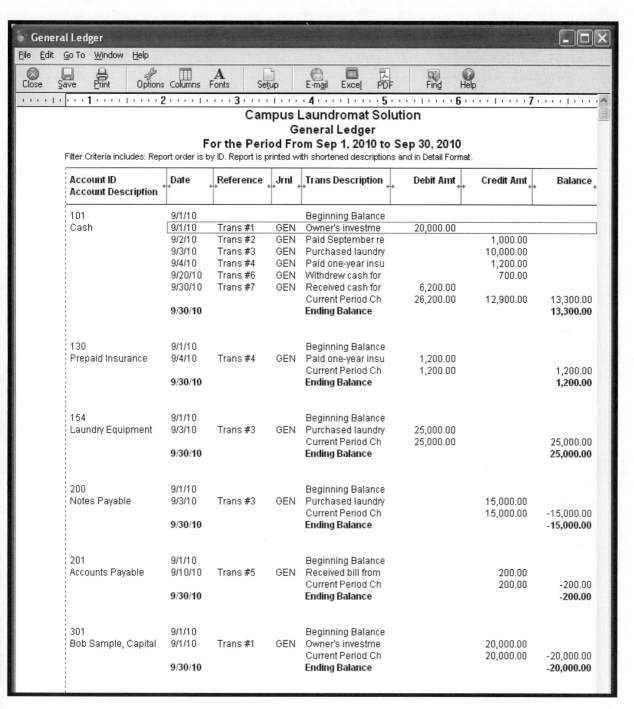

General Ledger

File Edit Go To Window Help

Close Save Print Options Columns Fonts Setup E-mail Excel PDF Find Help

Campus Laundromat Solution
General Ledger
For the Period From Sep 1, 2010 to Sep 30, 2010

Filter Criteria includes: Report order is by ID. Report is printed with shortened descriptions and in Detail Format.

Account ID Account Description	Date	Reference	Jrnl	Trans Description	Debit Amt	Credit Amt	Balance
101	9/1/10			Beginning Balance			
Cash	9/1/10	Trans #1	GEN	Owner's investme	20,000.00		
	9/2/10	Trans #2	GEN	Paid September re		1,000.00	
	9/3/10	Trans #3	GEN	Purchased laundry		10,000.00	
	9/4/10	Trans #4	GEN	Paid one-year insu		1,200.00	
	9/20/10	Trans #6	GEN	Withdrew cash for		700.00	
	9/30/10	Trans #7	GEN	Received cash for	6,200.00		
				Current Period Ch	26,200.00	12,900.00	13,300.00
	9/30/10			**Ending Balance**			**13,300.00**
130	9/1/10			Beginning Balance			
Prepaid Insurance	9/4/10	Trans #4	GEN	Paid one-year insu	1,200.00		
				Current Period Ch	1,200.00		1,200.00
	9/30/10			**Ending Balance**			**1,200.00**
154	9/1/10			Beginning Balance			
Laundry Equipment	9/3/10	Trans #3	GEN	Purchased laundry	25,000.00		
				Current Period Ch	25,000.00		25,000.00
	9/30/10			**Ending Balance**			**25,000.00**
200	9/1/10			Beginning Balance			
Notes Payable	9/3/10	Trans #3	GEN	Purchased laundry		15,000.00	
				Current Period Ch		15,000.00	-15,000.00
	9/30/10			**Ending Balance**			**-15,000.00**
201	9/1/10			Beginning Balance			
Accounts Payable	9/10/10	Trans #5	GEN	Received bill from		200.00	
				Current Period Ch		200.00	-200.00
	9/30/10			**Ending Balance**			**-200.00**
301	9/1/10			Beginning Balance			
Bob Sample, Capital	9/1/10	Trans #1	GEN	Owner's investme		20,000.00	
				Current Period Ch		20,000.00	-20,000.00
	9/30/10			**Ending Balance**			**-20,000.00**

General Ledger

File Edit Go To Window Help

Close Save Print Options Columns Fonts Setup E-mail Excel PDF Find Help

Campus Laundromat Solution
General Ledger
For the Period From Sep 1, 2010 to Sep 30, 2010
Filter Criteria includes: Report order is by ID. Report is printed with shortened descriptions and in Detail Format.

Account ID Account Description	Date	Reference	Jrnl	Trans Description	Debit Amt	Credit Amt	Balance
306 Bob Sample, Drawing	9/1/10 9/20/10	Trans #6	GEN	Beginning Balance Withdrew cash for Current Period Ch	700.00 700.00		700.00
	9/30/10			Ending Balance			**700.00**
400 Service Revenue	9/1/10 9/30/10	Trans #7	GEN	Beginning Balance Received cash for Current Period Ch		6,200.00 6,200.00	-6,200.00
	9/30/10			Ending Balance			**-6,200.00**
610 Advertising Expense	9/1/10 9/10/10	Trans #5	GEN	Beginning Balance Received bill from Current Period Ch	200.00 200.00		200.00
	9/30/10			Ending Balance			**200.00**
729 Rent Expense	9/1/10 9/2/10	Trans #2	GEN	Beginning Balance Paid September re Current Period Ch	1,000.00 1,000.00		1,000.00
	9/30/10			Ending Balance			**1,000.00**

General Ledger Trial Balance

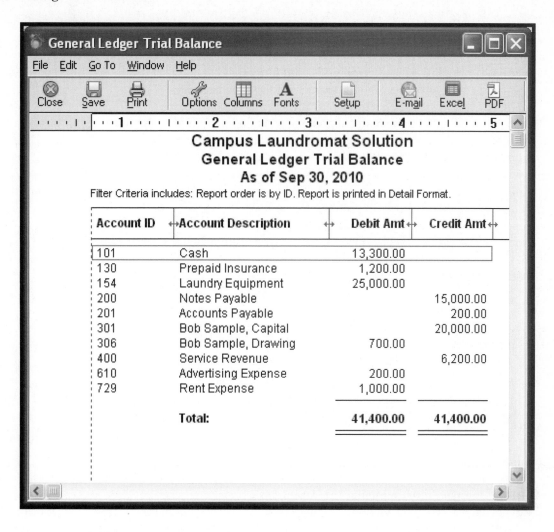

Campus Laundromat Solution
General Ledger Trial Balance
As of Sep 30, 2010

Filter Criteria includes: Report order is by ID. Report is printed in Detail Format.

Account ID	Account Description	Debit Amt	Credit Amt
101	Cash	13,300.00	
130	Prepaid Insurance	1,200.00	
154	Laundry Equipment	25,000.00	
200	Notes Payable		15,000.00
201	Accounts Payable		200.00
301	Bob Sample, Capital		20,000.00
306	Bob Sample, Drawing	700.00	
400	Service Revenue		6,200.00
610	Advertising Expense	200.00	
729	Rent Expense	1,000.00	
	Total:	**41,400.00**	**41,400.00**

P2-1A, Frontier Park, Directory Wey_AP9e_P2_1A_Frontier_Park

Frontier Park was started on April 1 by C. J. Mendez. The following selected events and transactions occurred during April.

April 1	Mendez invested $40,000 cash in the business.
April 4	Purchased land costing $30,000 for cash.
April 8	Incurred advertising expense of $1,800 on account.
April 11	Paid salaries to employees $1,500.
April 12	Hired park manager at a salary of $4,000 per month, effective May 1.
April 13	Paid $1,500 cash for a one-year insurance policy.
April 17	Withdrew $1,000 cash for personal use.
April 20	Received $5,700 in cash for admission fees.
April 25	Sold 100 coupon books for $25 each. Each book contains 10 coupons that entitle the holder to one admission to the park.
April 30	Received $8,900 in cash admission fees.
April 30	Paid $900 on balance owed for advertising incurred on April 8.

Mendez uses the following accounts:

101	Cash	306	C. J. Mendez, Drawing
130	Prepaid Insurance	350	Retained Earnings
140	Land		(Required by Peachtree.)
201	Accounts Payable	405	Admission Revenue
205	Unearned Admission Revenue	610	Advertising Expense
301	C. J. Mendez, Capital	726	Salaries Expense

The chart of accounts, as shown above, has been established within the Peachtree template file, Wey_AP9e_P2_1A_Frontier_Park.

Instructions:

(a) Using the chart of accounts, given, and the general journal, found through the path Tasks > General Journal Entry, journalize the April transactions.

(b) Review your work by following the path Reports & Forms > General Ledger > General Journal

(c) While the general journal report is open, use the "Print" icon to print the general journal report.

P2-5A, Lake Theater, Directory Wey_AP9e_P2_5A_Lake_Theater

The Lake Theater is owned by Tony Carpino. All facilities were completed on March 31. At this time, the
ledger showed:

101	Cash	$6,000	275	Mortgage Payable	$8,000
112	Accounts Receivable	$0	301	Tony Carpino, Capital	$20,000
136	Prepaid Rentals	$0	350	Retained Earnings	$0
140	Land	$10,000		(Required by Peachtree.)	
145	Buildings (concession stand,		405	Admission Revenue	$0
	projection room, ticket		406	Concession Revenue	$0
	booth, and screen)	$8,000	610	Advertising Expense	$0
157	Equipment	$6,000	632	Film Rental Expense	$0
201	Accounts Payable	$2,000	726	Salaries Expense	$0

The chart of accounts and beginning balances, as shown above, has been established within the Peachtree
template file, Wey_AP9e_P2_5A_Lake Theater.

During April, the following events and transactions occurred.

April 2	Paid film rental of $800 on first movie.
April 3	Ordered two additional films at $1,000 each.
April 9	Received $2,800 cash from admissions.
April 10	Made $2,000 payment on mortgage and $1,000 for accounts payable due.
April 11	Lake Theater contracted with R. Wynns Company to operate the concession stand. Wynns is to pay 17% of gross concession receipts (payable monthly) for the right to operate the concession stand.
April 12	Paid advertising expenses $500.
April 20	Received one of the films ordered on April 3 and was billed $1,000. The film will be shown in April.
April 25	Received $5,200 cash from admissions.
April 29	Paid salaries $2,000.
April 30	Received statement from R. Wynns showing gross concession receipts of $1,000 and the balance due to The Lake Theater of $170 ($1,000 × 17%) for April. Wynns paid one-half of the balance due and will remit the remainder on May 5.
April 30	Prepaid $900 rental on special film to be run in May.

Instructions:

(a) Using the chart of accounts, given, and the general journal, found through the path Tasks > General
Journal Entry, journalize the April transactions.

(b) Review your work by following the path Reports & Forms > General Ledger > General Journal

(c) While the general journal report is open, use the "Print" icon to print the general journal.

(d) Print the trial balance by following the path Reports & Forms > General Ledger > General Ledger
Trial Balance and clicking on the "Print" icon when it is viewed.

CHAPTER 3

Adjusting the Accounts

OBJECTIVES
- Explain the time period assumption.
- Explain the accrual basis of accounting.
- Explain the reasons for adjusting entries.
- Identify the major types of adjusting entries.

- Prepare adjusting entries for deferrals.
- Prepare adjusting entries for accruals.
- Describe the nature and purpose of an adjusting entry.

SELECTING AN ACCOUNTING TIME PERIOD

In the previous chapter you worked with the general journal recording process and how Peachtree keeps a running record of the trial balance and balance sheet. Before you can prepare the final set of financial statements there are some additional steps that must be taken.

What portion of your assets' costs, if any, should be recognized as an expense for the current accounting period? Those relevant account balances must be adjusted before you continue.

Because management usually wants monthly financial statements, and the Internal Revenue Service requires all businesses to file annual tax returns, accountants divide the economic life of a business into artificial time periods. This convenient assumption is referred to as the time period assumption.

Many business transactions affect more than one of these arbitrary time periods. For example a milking machine purchased by a farmer four years ago and aircraft purchased by Delta Airlines two years ago most likely are still in use today. You must determine the relevance of each business transaction to specific accounting periods.

FISCAL AND CALENDAR YEARS

All companies prepare financial statements periodically in order to assess their financial condition and results of operations. Accounting time periods are generally a month, a quarter, or a year. Monthly and quarterly time periods are called interim periods. Many large companies are required to prepare both quarterly and annual financial statements.

An accounting time period that is a year in length is referred to as a fiscal year. A fiscal year usually begins with the first day of a month and ends 12 months later on the last day of a month. However, the accounting period used by most businesses coincides with the calendar year, January 1 to December 31. Some companies have a fiscal year that differs from the calendar year. For example, many educational institutions use a July 1 to June 30 fiscal year. The U.S. Government uses October 1 to September 30 as a fiscal year.

INTRODUCING PIONEER ADVERTISING AGENCY

Pioneer Advertising Agency, owned by C. R. Byrd, has the following chart of accounts.

PIONEER ADVERTISING AGENCY
Chart of Accounts

Assets		**Owner's Equity**	
101	Cash	301	C. R. Byrd, Capital
112	Accounts Receivable	306	C. R. Byrd, Drawing
126	Advertising Supplies	340	Income Summary
130	Prepaid Insurance	350	Retained Earnings
157	Office Equipment		**Revenues**
158	Accumulated Depreciation	400	Service Revenue
	—Office Equipment		
Liabilities		**Expenses**	
200	Notes Payable	631	Advertising Supplies Expense
201	Accounts Payable	711	Depreciation Expense
209	Unearned Revenue	722	Insurance Expense
212	Salaries Payable	726	Salaries Expense
230	Interest Payable	729	Rent Expense
		905	Interest Expense

Table 3. 1   Pioneer Advertising Agency chart of accounts.

The following journal entries have been recorded in the Pioneer Advertising Agency's data file. The details of these transactions are in Chapter 2 of the textbook.

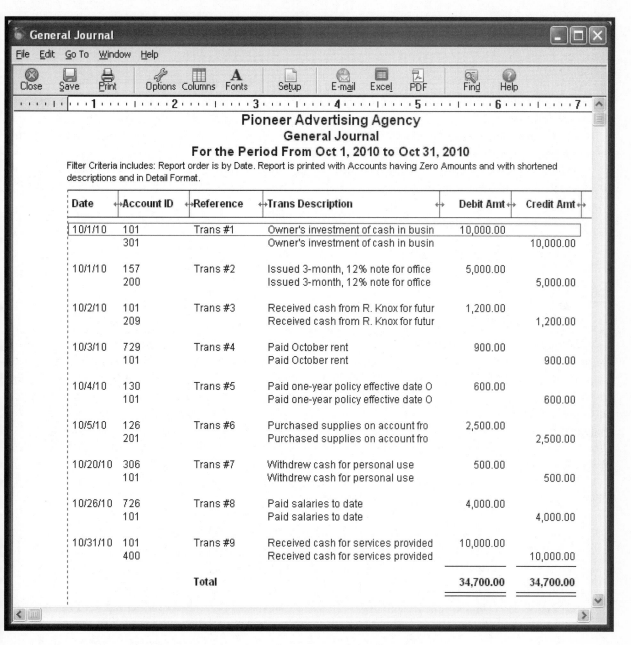

Figure 3. 1   Pioneer Advertising Agency's general journal to date

Pioneer Advertising's accounts will be utilized in this chapter to maintain a parallel to the textbook.

BASICS OF ADJUSTING ENTRIES

In order for revenues to be recorded in the period in which they are earned and for expenses to be recognized in the period in which they are incurred, adjusting entries are made at the end of the accounting period. In short, adjusting entries are needed to ensure that the revenue recognition and matching principles are followed.

Adjusting entries make it possible to report on the balance sheet the appropriate assets, liabilities, and owner's equity at the statement date and to report on the income statement the proper net income (or loss) for the period.

Any prepaid expense account, such as Prepaid Insurance or Prepaid Rent (where more than a month has been paid), and Unearned Revenue account must be adjusted.

Supplies that have been used up will require an adjustment to the Supplies account. Depreciation on productive facilities (fixed assets), will have to be adjusted and expensed. Unearned revenue must be adjusted. Accrued revenues and expenses must be recorded.

These adjustments require general journal entries, just like those you did in the first two chapters.

SUPPLIES

In Chapter 2 of the textbook Pioneer Advertising purchased advertising supplies worth $2,500. It is not relevant to the adjusting process as to how these supplies were purchased – cash or on account. During the month of October Pioneer utilized these supplies to generate revenues. At the end of the month an inspection of the advertising supplies reveals that $1,000 worth of supplies remains available. So the value of available supplies for the month - $2,500 less the remaining value at the end of the month results in the recognition of $1,500 worth of these supplies being consumed to generate revenues in the month. As such Pioneer must recognize the Advertising Supplies Expense of $1,500 to correctly calculate the affect of Advertising Supplies contribution to net income. This journal entry will also reduce the asset Advertising Supplies to it is not overstated on the balance sheet.

The adjusting entry is a debit entry to Supplies Expense, increasing the expense, and a credit entry to Supplies reducing the asset. To make the journal entry:

Step 1: Ensure that Supplies Expense account, Account No. 631, Account Type of "Expense" is available in the chart of accounts of Pioneer Advertising Agency.

Step 2: The date is October 31, 2010. All adjusting entries are recorded the last day of the fiscal period, in Pioneer's case this is October 31, 2010.

Step 3: Set the reference to "Adj Entry #1."

Step 4: The debit GL (General Ledger) account is 631 – Advertising Supplies Expense, the description is "To record supplies used," and the debit value is $1,500.

Step 5: The credit GL (General Ledger) account is 126 – Advertising Supplies, the description should "auto fill" from the first line – To record supplies used.

Note: This is where "Microsoft Windows compliant" plays a labor saving role – If description did not auto fill, cursor to the first line's description window. With the text highlighted, press and hold the Control key on the keyboard then press the "C" key, release both keys, this is the Copy Command. Use the down arrow to move to the second line's description's window. Press and hold the Control key on the keyboard then press the "V" key, release both keys, this is the Paste Command. And the text from Line 1 should be pasted into Line 2. The credit value is $1,500, as computed earlier.

Step 6:   Your adjusting journal entry should match the entry shown in Figure 3. 2. Make sure your work matches Figure 3. 2 before posting (saving) the entry.

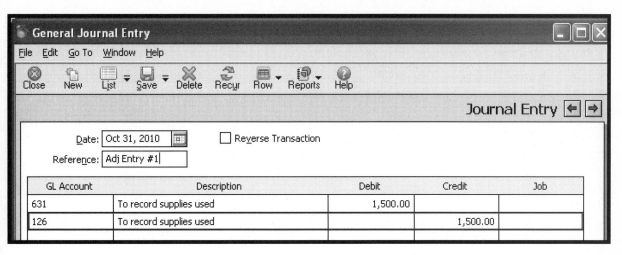

Figure 3. 2   General journal entry adjusting supplies

If you view the income statement at this time you will see that Advertising Supplies Expense has been recognized. Viewing the balance sheet will ensure that only $1,000 worth of Advertising Supplies remains available for future periods.

PREPAID ASSETS (INSURANCE AND RENT)

Many companies prepay their insurance premiums and office rent as part of their contracts for these items. Insurance companies frequently require six or twelve months of premiums while landlords will usually require payment on or before the first of the month for which the rent is paying for. ***Note:*** If the landlord requires the first and last month's rent at the initiation of the contract, the last month's rent is a deposit for a future month, a current or long-term asset depending on the length of the agreement. What prepaid insurance and prepaid rent both have in common is that they "expire" as time passes converting from an asset to an expense. And adjusting entries recognize this passage of time.

Transaction #4 for Pioneer recorded the purchase of an insurance policy with a life of one year for $600 on October 4th with coverage starting October 1st. As such, $600 / 12 months, $50 in value of Prepaid Insurance has expired due to the passage of time (the month of October) and this expense must be recognized is a similar manner as the supplies in the first adjusting entry – increasing expenses with a debit and decreasing the asset with a credit.

To accomplish Adjusting Entry #2 (Adj Entry #2):

Step 1:   With Pioneer Advertising Agency open, verify that Account 722 – Insurance Expense is available in the chart of accounts. If not, construct it as an expense account.

Step 2:   Ensure the date is October 31, 2010.

Step 3:   Enter "Adj Entry #2" in the reference window if Peachtree did not auto fill the entry.

Step 4:   The debit line is GL (General Ledger) account 722 – Insurance Expense with a description of "To record insurance expired" and a debit value of $50.

Step 5:   The credit line is GL (General Ledger) account 130 – Prepaid Insurance. The description window should auto fill from the first line.

Step 6:   Compare your work with Figure 3. 3, and if satisfied, post it to the general ledger by saving it.

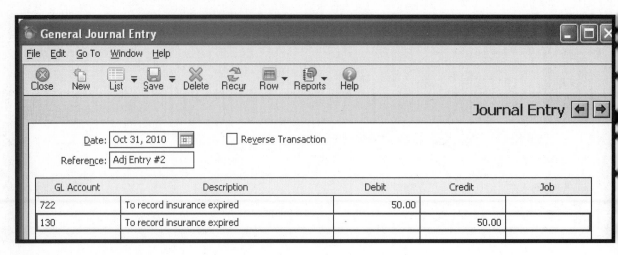

Figure 3. 3   Adjusting journal entry for prepaid assets

DEPRECIATION

Pioneer purchases equipment in Transaction #2 with a note payable. The utilization of this equipment and the mere passage of time results in the loss of value. As an example, a car loses value the moment it is driven off the showroom floor – it has been used. And it loses value the next year as it is now "last year's model." The adjusting entry for this event is referred to as Depreciation and this process will be covered in depth in a later chapter in the textbook. To recognize this loss in value due to time and service the adjusting entry increases depreciation expense and increases a contra account title Accumulated Depreciation – Office Equipment. Pioneer calculates that the depreciation value is $480 per year or ($480 / 12 months) $40 per month. And the $40 value is the appropriate amount for the adjusting journal entry since Pioneer is making monthly adjusting entries.

To the adjusting entry for depreciation:

Step 1:   With Pioneer Advertising Agency open, verify that Account 711 – Depreciation Expense and account 158 – Accumulated Depreciation – Office Equipment (Accum Deprec – Office Equip) are both in the chart of accounts. If not, construct 711 as an expense account and 158 as an Accumulated Depreciation account.

Step 2:   Ensure the date is October 31, 2010.

Step 3:   Enter "Adj Entry #3" in the reference window if Peachtree did not auto fill the entry.

Step 4:   The debit line is GL (General Ledger) account 711 – Depreciation Expense with a description of "To record monthly depreciation" and a debit value of $40.

Step 5:   The credit line is GL (General Ledger) account 158 – Accumulated Depreciation – Office Equipment (Accum Deprec-Office Equip). The description should auto fill from the first line. The credit value is $40, as stated earlier.

Step 6: Compare your work with Figure 3. 4, and if satisfied, post it to the general ledger by saving it.

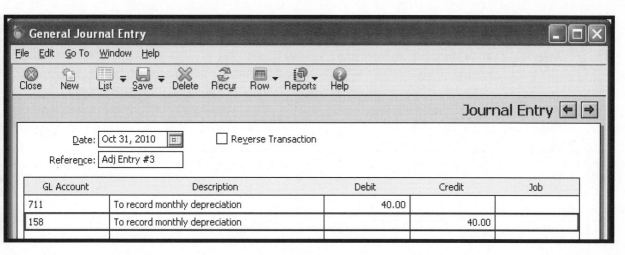

Figure 3. 4 Adjusting entry for depreciation of equipment

As mentioned earlier, Account 158 – Accumulated Depreciation – Office Equipment is a contra account and is established as an Accumulated Depreciation account. This classification and relationship will direct Peachtree to show this account and Office Equipment in the same manner as your textbook shows. A portion of the Peachtree balance sheet shown in Figure 3. 5.

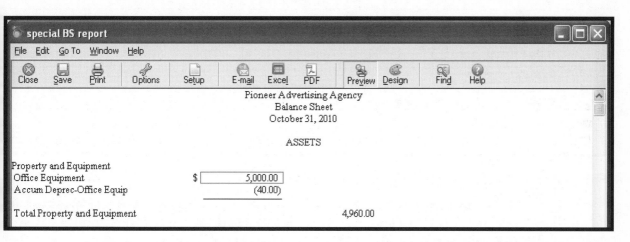

Figure 3. 5 The balance sheet presentation of property, plant, and equipment with accumulated depreciation

The $5,000 for office equipment is cost, the $40 is the contra account value of Accumulated Depreciation – Office Equipment, and the ($5,000 - $40) $4,960 is book value. If you view the income statement at this time you can verify that Depreciation Expense is now shown for $40.

UNEARNED REVENUE

In the normal course of many businesses customers will prepay for services or products. Since the service or product has not yet been provided, this event increases the asset Cash ***AND*** it increases the liability

Unearned Revenues when the money was received. This is reflected in Transaction #3 when R. Knox prepaid $1,200 for services to be provided. During the month of October Pioneer has provided $400 in value of this obligation and can now, with Adjusting Entry #4, reduce the liability by this $400 and increase Service Revenues by $400.

To accomplish this adjusting entry:

Step 1:	With Pioneer Advertising Agency open, verify that Account 209 – Unearned Revenue and Account 400 – Service Revenue are both in the chart of accounts. If not, construct 209 as a current liability account and 400 as an income account.
Step 2:	Ensure the date is October 31, 2010.
Step 3:	Enter "Adj Entry #4" in the reference window if Peachtree did not auto fill the entry.
Step 4:	The debit line is GL (General Ledger) account 209 – Unearned Revenue with a description of "To record revenue for services provided" and a debit value of $400.
Step 5:	The credit line is GL (General Ledger) account 400 – Service Revenue. The description window should auto fill from the first line. The credit value is $400, as stated earlier.
Step 6:	Compare your work with Figure 3. 6, and if satisfied, post it to the general ledger by saving it.

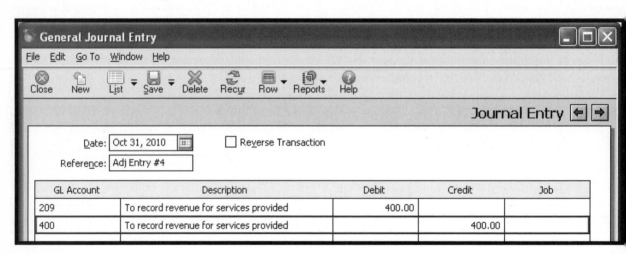

Figure 3. 6   Adjusting entry for Unearned Service Revenue

If you view the income statement at this point you will see that revenues and net income have both increased by $400. A look at the balance sheet will show that the Unearned Revenue account has been reduced by the same value - $400.

ACCRUED REVENUES

Companies and their clients often have relationships based on trust or processes which preclude prepayment. Pioneer may have service contracts with clients which state something like: "If it is the 30th of October and rain is forecast for the 31st of October push our 'Ghosts and Goblins across the United States' feature length film in the theaters on the local radio and television stations." Since this is a contingency contract – no action is taken unless certain events are likely or take place, and no fees are earned until action is taken.

Suppose that at the end of October rain is forecast and Pioneer Advertising Agency runs the ads for the film on the local radio and television stations. Pioneer has earned revenues which have not yet been billed to the customer. This results in revenues being understated and assets (Accounts Receivable) being understated. (*Note:* It may also result in costs of services provided and liabilities being understated as well – the cost of the ads and the payments due for those ads.)

To accomplish this adjusting entry:

Step 1: With Pioneer Advertising Agency open, verify that Account 112 – Accounts Receivable and Account 400 – Service Revenue are both in the chart of accounts. If not, construct 112 as an Accounts Receivable account and 400 as an Income account.

Step 2: Ensure the date is October 31, 2010.

Step 3: Enter "Adj Entry #5" in the reference window if Peachtree did not auto fill the entry.

Step 4: The debit line is GL (General Ledger) account 112 – Accounts Receivable with a description of "To record revenue for services provided" and a debit value of $200.

Step 5: The credit line is GL (General Ledger) account 400 – Service Revenue. The description window should auto fill from the first line. The credit value is $200, as stated earlier.

Step 6: Compare your work with Figure 3. 7, and if satisfied, post it to the general ledger by saving it.

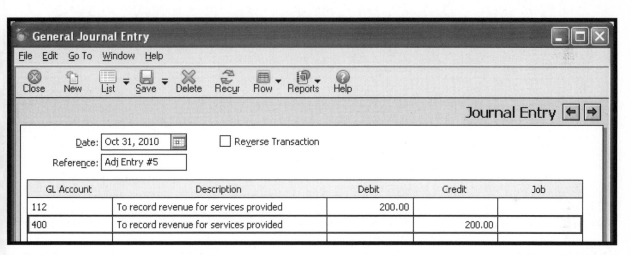

Figure 3. 7   Adjusting entry for unearned service revenue

If you view the income statement at this point you will see that revenues and net income have both increased by $200. A look at the balance sheet will show that the Accounts Receivable account has increased by the same value - $200.

ACCRUED EXPENSES

Numerous expenses can be incurred before the bill associated with those expenses are received or those expenses are paid. For example, in the accrued revenues example the cost of the radio and television ads may not be received for ten or more days after the fiscal period (the month of October) in which they occurred or in the fiscal period they generated revenues in.

Pioneer Advertising purchased office equipment in Transaction #2 by issuing a $5,000, 12%, 3 month note payable. And the interest on this note payable is an expense incurred in October. Without an adjusting entry for the passage of time as related to this note payable expenses will be understated resulting in net income being overstated and liabilities will be understated. The value is Principal × Rate × Time, or $5,000 × 12% × (3/12) or $50.

To accomplish this adjusting entry:

Step 1:   With Pioneer Advertising Agency open, verify that Account 905 – Interest Expense and Account 230 – Interest Payable are both in the chart of accounts. If not, construct 905 as an Expense account and 230 as an Other Current Liability account.

Step 2:   Ensure the date is October 31, 2010.

Step 3:   Enter "Adj Entry #6" in the reference window if Peachtree did not auto fill the entry.

Step 4:   The debit line is GL (General Ledger) account 905 – Interest Expense with a description of "To record interest on notes payable" and a debit value of $50.

Step 5:   The credit line is GL (General Ledger) account 230 – Interest Payable. The description should auto fill from the first line. The credit value is $50, as stated earlier.

Step 6:   Compare your work with Figure 3. 8, and if satisfied, post it to the general ledger by saving it.

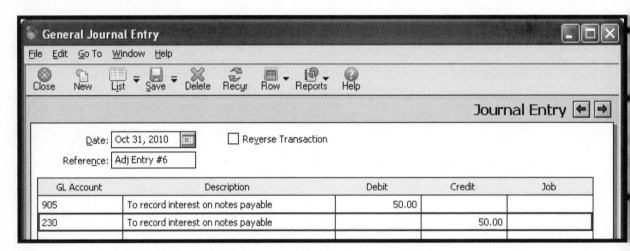

Figure 3. 8   Adjusting entry for accrued interest on notes payable

If you view the income statement at this point you will see that expenses have increased by $50 and net income has decreased by $50. A look at the balance sheet will show that the Interest Payable account has increased by the same value - $50.

Other common accrued expenses are Salaries Expense and Wages Expense which result in Salaries Payable and Wages Payable. For individuals getting paid weekly, pay periods will frequently end on Friday or Sunday with paychecks being distributed the following Friday. But month ends and pay period ends seldom coincide so adjusting entries must be made to ensure that expenses and liabilities are properly stated for the fiscal periods – Months for Pioneer. So adjusting entries for Pioneer's Salaries Expense and Salaries Payable must be made. The calendar for this adjusting entry is shown in Figure 3. 9 and shown in the textbook as Illustration 3-19.

Figure 3. 9   Textbook calendar for salaries expense adjusting entry

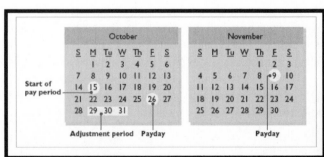

Pioneer, using a two-week pay period, last paid salaries on October 26; the next payday is November 9. Pioneer calculates that the employees receive total salaries of $2,000 for a five-day workweek, or $400 per day. As the calendar in Figure 3. 9 shows, three working days remain in October (October 29–31). Thus, accrued salaries at October 31 are $1,200 ($400 × 3 days).

To accomplish this adjusting entry:

Step 1: With Pioneer Advertising Agency open, verify that Account 726 – Salaries Expense and Account 212 – Salaries Payable are both in the chart of accounts. If not, construct 726 as an Expense account and 212 as an Other Current Liability account.

Step 2: Ensure the date is October 31, 2010.

Step 3: Enter "Adj Entry #7" in the reference window if Peachtree did not auto fill the entry.

Step 4: The debit line is GL (General Ledger) account 726 – Salaries Expense with a description of "To record accrued salaries" and a debit value of $1,200.

Step 5: The credit line is GL (General Ledger) account 212 – Salaries Payable. The description should auto fill from the first line. The credit value is $1,200, as stated earlier.

Step 6: Compare your work with Figure 3. 10, and if satisfied, post it to the general ledger by saving it.

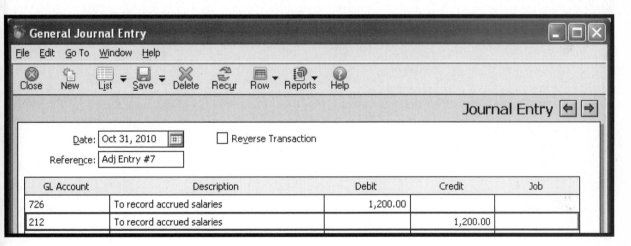

Figure 3. 10 Adjusting entry for accrued salaries

The results of this adjusting entry increases expenses and increases liabilities by $1,200. The increase in expenses results in a decrease in net income. This can be verified by viewing the income statement and the balance sheet after this journal entry is saved.

THE AFFECT OF ADJUSTING ENTRIES

The adjusting journal entries are shown in the following general journal report for Pioneer Advertising Agency.

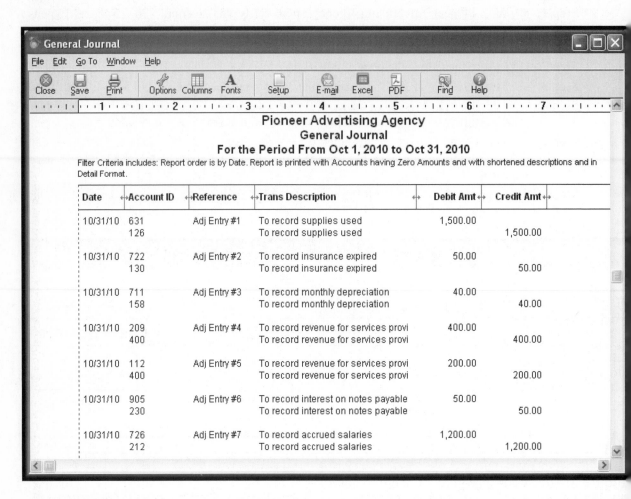

Figure 3. 11   Pioneer Advertising Agency's general journal report for adjusting entries

The income statement for Pioneer for the month ending October 31, 2010, is shown in Figure 3. 12.

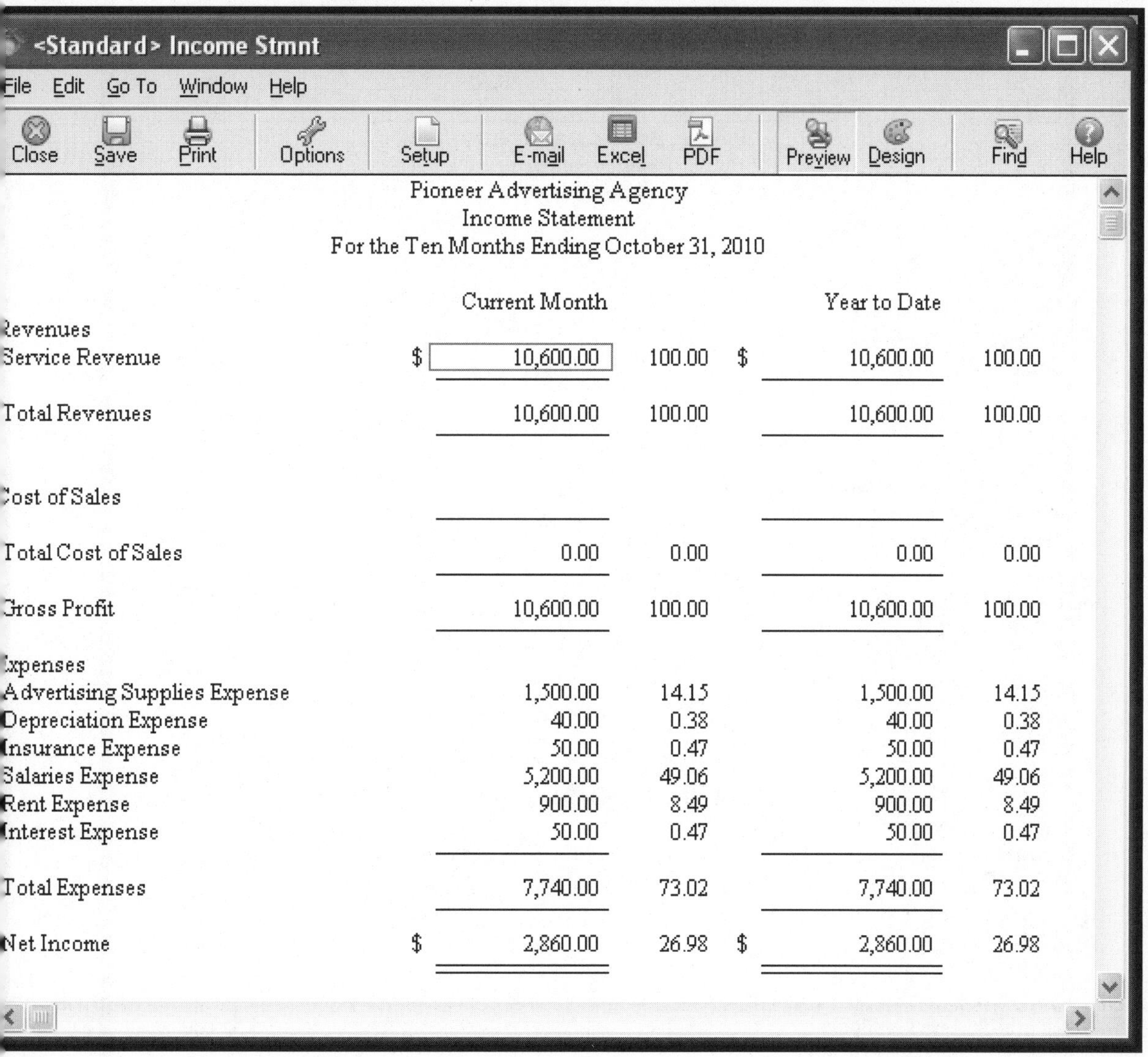

<Standard> Income Stmnt

File   Edit   Go To   Window   Help

Close   Save   Print   Options   Setup   E-mail   Excel   PDF   Preview   Design   Find   Help

Pioneer Advertising Agency
Income Statement
For the Ten Months Ending October 31, 2010

	Current Month			Year to Date	
Revenues					
Service Revenue	$ 10,600.00	100.00	$	10,600.00	100.00
Total Revenues	10,600.00	100.00		10,600.00	100.00
Cost of Sales					
Total Cost of Sales	0.00	0.00		0.00	0.00
Gross Profit	10,600.00	100.00		10,600.00	100.00
Expenses					
Advertising Supplies Expense	1,500.00	14.15		1,500.00	14.15
Depreciation Expense	40.00	0.38		40.00	0.38
Insurance Expense	50.00	0.47		50.00	0.47
Salaries Expense	5,200.00	49.06		5,200.00	49.06
Rent Expense	900.00	8.49		900.00	8.49
Interest Expense	50.00	0.47		50.00	0.47
Total Expenses	7,740.00	73.02		7,740.00	73.02
Net Income	$ 2,860.00	26.98	$	2,860.00	26.98

Figure 3. 12   Pioneer Advertising Agency's income statement for the month ended October 31, 2010

File   Edit   Go To   Window   Help

Close   Save   Print   Options   Setup   E-mail   Excel   PDF   Preview   Desi...

Pioneer Advertising Agency
Balance Sheet
October 31, 2010
ASSETS

Current Assets		
Cash	$ 15,200.00	
Accounts Receivable	200.00	
Advertising Supplies	1,000.00	
Prepaid Insurance	550.00	
Total Current Assets		16,950.00
Property and Equipment		
Office Equipment	5,000.00	
Accum Deprec-Office Equip	(40.00)	
Total Property and Equipment		4,960.00
Other Assets		
Total Other Assets		0.00
Total Assets	$	21,910.00

LIABILITIES AND CAPITAL

Current Liabilities		
Notes Payable	$ 5,000.00	
Accounts Payable	2,500.00	
Unearned Revenue	800.00	
Salaries Payable	1,200.00	
Interest Payable	50.00	
Total Current Liabilities		9,550.00
Long-Term Liabilities		
Total Long-Term Liabilities		0.00
Total Liabilities		9,550.00
Capital		
C. R. Byrd, Capital	10,000.00	
C. R. Byrd, Drawing	(500.00)	
Net Income	2,860.00	
Total Capital		12,360.00
Total Liabilities & Capital	$	21,910.00

Figure 3. 13   Pioneer Advertising Agency's balance sheet as of October 31, 2010

Comprehensive Do It! Problem, Green Thumb Lawn Care Company, Directory Wey_AP9e_Green_Thumb_Lawn_Care

Terry Thomas opened the Green Thumb Lawn Care Company on April 1st. At April 30th, the general ledger trial balance reflected the following balances for selected accounts:

No. 120	Prepaid Insurance	$3,600
No. 157	Equipment	28,000
No. 201	Notes Payable	20,000
No. 209	Unearned Revenue	4,200
No. 301	T. Thomas, Capital	5,600
No. 400	Service Revenue	1,800

All beginning balances and all other accounts have been established in the student data set for Green Thumb Lawn Care Company.

End of the month analysis reveals the following additional data:

(1) Prepaid insurance is the cost of a 2-year insurance policy, effective April 1.

(2) Depreciation on the equipment is $500 per month.

(3) The note payable is dated April 1st. It is a 6-month, 12% note.

(4) Seven customers paid for the company's 6-months' lawn service package of $600 beginning in April. The company performed services for these customers in April.

(5) Lawn services provided other customers but not billed on April 30th totaled $1,500.

Instructions:

(a) Open Green Thumb Lawn Care from within your student data set into Peachtree.

(b) Utilize the general journal entry screen to journalize the adjusting entries for the month of April.

(c) Print the general journal report.

Solution to Comprehensive Do It! Problem

General Journal Report showing adjusting entries #1 through #5:

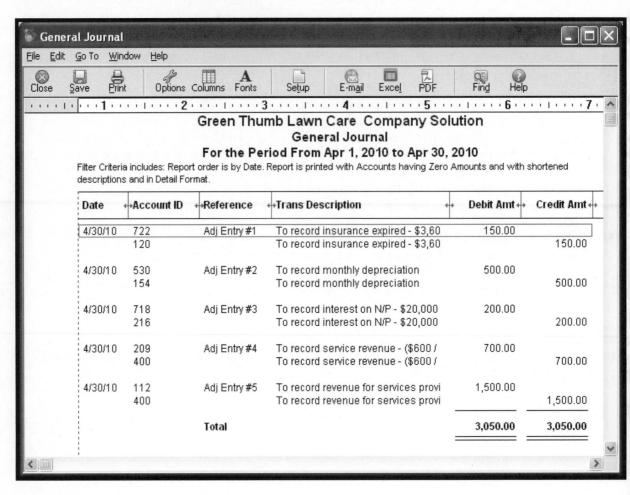

Green Thumb Lawn Care Company Solution
General Journal
For the Period From Apr 1, 2010 to Apr 30, 2010

Filter Criteria includes: Report order is by Date. Report is printed with Accounts having Zero Amounts and with shortened descriptions and in Detail Format.

Date	Account ID	Reference	Trans Description	Debit Amt	Credit Amt
4/30/10	722	Adj Entry #1	To record insurance expired - $3,60	150.00	
	120		To record insurance expired - $3,60		150.00
4/30/10	530	Adj Entry #2	To record monthly depreciation	500.00	
	154		To record monthly depreciation		500.00
4/30/10	718	Adj Entry #3	To record interest on N/P - $20,000	200.00	
	216		To record interest on N/P - $20,000		200.00
4/30/10	209	Adj Entry #4	To record service revenue - ($600 /	700.00	
	400		To record service revenue - ($600 /		700.00
4/30/10	112	Adj Entry #5	To record revenue for services provi	1,500.00	
	400		To record revenue for services provi		1,500.00
			Total	**3,050.00**	**3,050.00**

P3-2A, Neosho River Resort, Directory Wey_AP9e_P3_2A_Neosho_River_Resort

Neosho River Resort opened for business on June 1, 2010, with eight air-conditioned units. Its trial balance as of August 31, 2010, includes accounts with zero balances, is before adjustments are made:

Neosho River Resort
Trial Balance
August 31, 2010

Acct Nbr	Account	Debit	Credit
101	Cash	$19,600	
112	Accounts Receivable		
126	Supplies	3,300	
130	Prepaid Insurance	6,000	
140	Land	25,000	
143	Cottages	125,000	
144	Accumulated Depreciation—Cottages		
149	Furniture	26,000	
150	Accumulated Depreciation—Furniture		
201	Accounts Payable		$6,500
209	Unearned Rent Revenue		7,400
212	Salaries Payable		
230	Interest Payable		
275	Mortgage Payable		80,000
301	P. Harder, Capital		100,000
306	P. Harder, Drawing	5,000	
429	Rent Revenue		80,000
620	Depreciation Expense—Cottages		
621	Depreciation Expense—Furniture		
622	Repair Expense	3,600	
726	Salaries Expense	51,000	
631	Supplies Expense		
718	Interest Expense		
722	Insurance Expense		
732	Utilities Expense	9,400	
		$273,900	$273,900

Other data:
(1) Insurance expires at the rate of $400 per month.
(2) A count on August 31 shows $600 of supplies on hand.
(3) Annual depreciation is $6,000 on cottages and $2,400 on furniture. *1500 / 600*
(4) Unearned rent of $4,100 was earned prior to August 31st.
(5) Salaries of $400 were unpaid at August 31st.
(6) Rentals of $1,000 were due from tenants on August 31st. (Use Accounts Receivable)
(7) The mortgage interest rate is 9% per year. The note was dated August 1, 2010.

100,000 × .09 × 1/12
9,000/12 = 750

Instructions:
(a) Load Neosho River Resort into Peachtree from within your student data set.
(b) Create any accounts that do not appear in the August 31, 2010, trial balance.
(c) Journalize the adjusting entries on August 31 for the 3-month period June 1 – August 31 in the general journal using Peachtree Complete Accounting.
(d) Print the general journal report, general ledger, general ledger trial balance, income statement, a statement of retained earnings for the month ending August 31, 2010, and a balance sheet as of August 31, 2010 after the adjusting entries are made. Peachtree may label the time period differently.

P3-5A, Rand Equipment Repair, Directory
Wey_AP9e_P3_5A_Rand_Equipment_Repair

On September 1, 2010, the account balances of Rand Equipment Repair were as follows:

No.	Debits		No.	Credits	
101	Cash	$ 4,880	154	Accumulated Depreciation	$ 1,500
112	Accounts Receivable	3,520	201	Accounts Payable	3,400
126	Supplies	2,000	209	Unearned Service Revenue	1,400
153	Store Equipment	15,000	212	Salaries Payable	500
			301	J. Rand, Capital	18,600
		$25,400			$25,400

During September the following summary transactions were completed:

Sept	8	Paid $1,400 for salaries due employees, of which $900 is for September.
	10	Received $1,200 cash from customers on account.
	12	Received $3,400 cash for services performed in September.
	15	Purchased store equipment on account $3,000.
	17	Purchased supplies on account $1,200.
	20	Paid creditors $4,500 on account.
	22	Paid September rent $500.
	25	Paid salaries $1,250.
	27	Performed services on account and billed customers for services rendered $1,500.
	29	Received $650 from customers for future service.

Adjustment data consists of:
(1) Supplies on hand $1,200.
(2) Accrued salaries payable $400.
(3) Depreciation is $100 per month.
(4) Unearned service revenue of $1,450 is earned.

Instructions:
(a) Load Rand Equipment Repair into Peachtree from within your student data set.
(b) Verify the beginning balances and the chart of accounts by previewing the general ledger trial balance.
(c) Journalize in Peachtree's general journal the transactions for September.
(d) Journalize in Peachtree's general journal the adjusting entries for September.
(e) Print a general journal report, general ledger, general ledger trial balance, an income statement, a statement of retained earnings for the month of September 2010, and a balance sheet as of September 30, 2010, for Rand Equipment Repair.

CHAPTER 4

Completion of the Accounting Cycle

OBJECTIVES
- Prepare a worksheet.
- Explain the process of closing the books.
- Describe the content and purpose of a post-closing trial balance.
- State the required steps in the accounting cycle.
- Explain the approaches to preparing correcting entries.
- Identify the sections of a classified balance sheet.
- Explain the process of changing the accounting period within Peachtree.
- Explain the process of closing the books within Peachtree.

USING A WORKSHEET

Two somewhat different but similar trial balance reports are available in Peachtree. The general ledger trial balance, Figure 4. 2, shows each account and its balance as of the date or period you select. The working trial balance, Figure 4. 4, provides blank spaces so you can fill in any adjusting trial balance information. These reports are designed to help you make adjustments to account balances. These reports are simply devices used to make it easier to prepare adjusting entries and to guide you in the process of preparing your financial statements.

In the "manual" accounting process, financial statements are prepared directly from the worksheets prepared by the accountant. The account balances of these worksheets are gathered directly from the general ledger and the postings from the general journal. In an automated system, such as Peachtree, the balances of the general ledger accounts are continually updated as entries are made resulting in statement balances being continually updated. At the end of the accounting period however, general journal adjusting entries must be made as you did in the previous chapter.

THE GENERAL LEDGER TRIAL BALANCE

Step 1: Open Pioneer Advertising Agency from within you student data set.

Step 2: Click on "Reports & Forms" on the Menu Bar, then the "General Ledger" option followed by double-clicking the "General Ledger Trial Balance." Figure 4. 1 shows the "Select a Report or Form" dialog box with "General Ledger" and "General Ledger Trial Balance" selected.

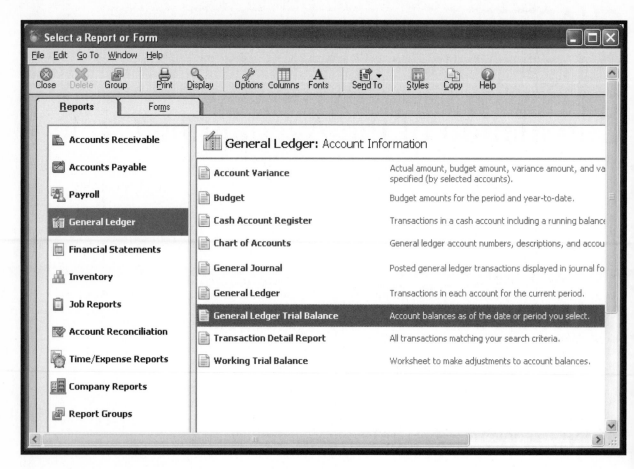

Figure 4. 1   Select a Report or Form menu screen

And Peachtree provides Figure 4. 2, the general ledger trial balance for the current accounting period, as of October 31, 2010.

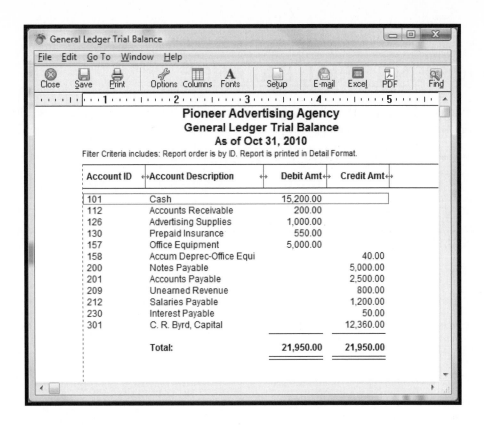

Figure 4. 2   The general ledger trial balance for Pioneer Advertising Agency as of October 31, 2010

THE WORKING TRIAL BALANCE

While in the "Select a Report or Form" dialog box with general ledger option highlighted, double-click on "Working Trial Balance" and Peachtree will present you with a working trial balance suitable for making adjusting entries, a portion of which is shown in Figure 4. 3, below.

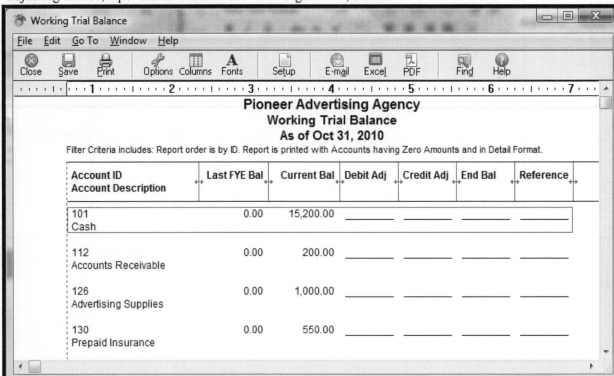

Figure 4. 3   Portion of the working trial balance report for Pioneer Advertising Agency

The obvious difference is the debit adjustment, credit adjustment, end balance, and reference columns which have been inserted to assist in determining the adjustment value. By default all accounts are provided on this report. It, however, does not extend into the income statement and balance sheet as the textbook examples do as these calculations and presentations will be accomplished by Peachtree as the adjusting journal entries are posted (saved).

One of the significant powers built into Peachtree is the ability to download or export screens and reports to Microsoft Excel. By clicking on the Excel icon on the task bar of the working trial balance screen you will initiate this process. The safest option is to select "Create a new Microsoft Excel workbook" from the "Copy Report to Excel" dialog box when presented with the options. Then click "OK" to continue the download or export process. And Peachtree will whiz and whirl as Microsoft Excel is opened and the data is inserted, as shown in Figure 4. 4.

	A	B	C	D	E	F	G	H
1	Account ID	Account Description	Last FYE Bal	Current Bal	Debit Adj	Credit Adj	End Bal	Reference
2	101	Cash	0.00	15,200.00				
3	112	Accounts Receivable	0.00	0.00				
4	126	Advertising Supplies	0.00	2,500.00				
5	130	Prepaid Insurance	0.00	600.00				
6	157	Office Equipment	0.00	5,000.00				
7	158	Accum Deprec-Office Equip	0.00	0.00				
8	200	Notes Payable	0.00	-5,000.00				
9	201	Accounts Payable	0.00	-2,500.00				
10	209	Unearned Revenue	0.00	-1,200.00				
11	212	Salaries Payable	0.00	0.00				
12	230	Interest Payable	0.00	0.00				
13	301	C. R. Byrd, Capital	0.00	-10,000.00				
14	306	C. R. Byrd, Drawing	0.00	500.00				
15	350	Retained Earnings	0.00	0.00				
16	400	Service Revenue	0.00	-10,000.00				
17	631	Advertising Supplies Expens	0.00	0.00				
18	711	Depreciation Expense	0.00	0.00				
19	722	Insurance Expense	0.00	0.00				
20	726	Salaries Expense	0.00	4,000.00				
21	729	Rent Expense	0.00	900.00				
22	905	Interest Expense	0.00	0.00				
23								
24		Total:	0.00	0.00				

Figure 4. 4   The working trial balance for Pioneer Advertising Agency downloaded into Excel

While this worksheet does not have the income statement and balance sheet columns, similar to the textbook worksheet, they can be easily inserted and formatted.

Remember that this worksheet is currently not saved and should be saved before significant time and effort is invested in its modification. The rest of this chapter is going to assume that you downloaded or exported the working trial balance for Pioneer and saved it as Pioneer Working Trial Balance-2010-10-31.xls.

WORKING WITH THE EXCEL WORKING TRIAL BALANCE

The next several steps will be utilizing the Excel download or export of Pioneer's working trial balance rather than the Peachtree printed report.

First, as a matter of preference and convenience the worksheet needs to be formatted for consistency. Highlight all of the columns from C through Z and format them to a format such as Currency – 2 decimals, no symbol, and (1,234.10) presentation, as shown in Figure 4. 5. Then, through the Alignment tab or with the Right Alignment icon on the task bar, right align the cells before removing the highlight.

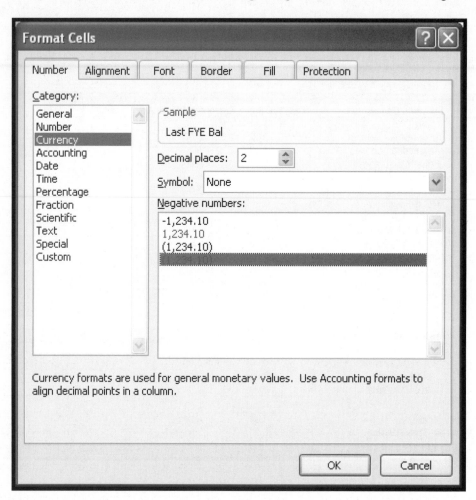

Figure 4. 5   The Microsoft Excel Format Cell dialog box

This will replace any formatting imposed during the download or export process.

NOTE: The adjusting entries for Pioneer Advertising Agency were accomplished in your file in Chapter 3. As such your displayed and downloaded or exported values already have the adjustments incorporated into them. You can continue this exercise by changing the values in the Excel Current Balance worksheet column to match those shown in Figure 4. 6.

	A	B	C	D	E	F	G	H	I
1	Account ID	Account Description	Last FYE Bal	Current Bal	Debit Adj	Credit Adj	End Bal	Reference	
2	101	Cash	0.00	15,200.00			15,200.00		
3	112	Accounts Receivable	0.00	0.00	200.00		200.00	(e-5)	
4	126	Advertising Supplies	0.00	2,500.00		(1,500.00)	1,000.00	(a-1)	
5	130	Prepaid Insurance	0.00	600.00		(50.00)	550.00	(b-2)	
6	157	Office Equipment	0.00	5,000.00			5,000.00		
7	158	Accum Deprec-Office Equip	0.00	0.00		(40.00)	(40.00)	(c-3)	
8	200	Notes Payable	0.00	(5,000.00)			(5,000.00)		
9	201	Accounts Payable	0.00	(2,500.00)			(2,500.00)		
10	209	Unearned Revenue	0.00	(1,200.00)	400.00		(800.00)	(d-4)	
11	212	Salaries Payable	0.00	0.00		(1,200.00)	(1,200.00)	(g-7)	
12	230	Interest Payable	0.00	0.00		(50.00)	(50.00)	(f-6)	
13	301	C. R. Byrd, Capital	0.00	(10,000.00)			(10,000.00)		
14	306	C. R. Byrd, Drawing	0.00	500.00			500.00		
15	350	Retained Earnings	0.00	0.00			0.00		
16	400	Service Revenue	0.00	(10,000.00)		(600.00)	(10,600.00)	(d-4) & (e-5)	
17	631	Advertising Supplies Expens	0.00	0.00	1,500.00		1,500.00	(a-1)	1
18	711	Depreciation Expense	0.00	0.00	40.00		40.00	(c-3)	
19	722	Insurance Expense	0.00	0.00	50.00		50.00	(b-2)	
20	726	Salaries Expense	0.00	4,000.00	1,200.00		5,200.00	(g-7)	5
21	729	Rent Expense	0.00	900.00			900.00		
22	905	Interest Expense	0.00	0.00	50.00		50.00	(f-6)	
23			The # in reference is the Adj Entry #						
24		Total:	0.00	0.00	3,440.00	(3,440.00)	0.00		7

Figure 4. 6   The Microsoft Excel formatted as desired

The values inserted in the debit column, Column E of the display are all positive numbers while the values inserted in the credit column, Column F are all negative numbers. Formulas have been inserted in Line 24 in Columns G and I through L to total the columns. The values in the reference column, Column H are set so that the letter agrees with the textbook reference of Chapter 4 and the Adjusting Entry # of Chapter 3.

After the adjusting values have been inserted into Columns E and F, a formula is inserted into Cell G2 that reads "=D2+E2+F2". Then this formula is dragged down from Row 2 through Row 22 resulting in Ending Balances that are debits being positive numbers while ending balances that are credits are negative numbers. The sum of these numbers, Cell G24, must be zero or debits do not equal credits and something is wrong, recheck your work.

The next step is to merge Cells I1 and J1 and title them "Income Statement." The Merge Cell icon is highlighted in Figure 4. 6 just to the right of the Right Alignment icon on the task bar. To merge Cells I1 and J1, highlight both cells with a single sweep of the mouse. Then click on the "Merge Cells" icon. Now when you enter "Income Statement" in Cell I1 it will appear centered over both Columns I and J. Now merge K1 and L1 and title them "Balance Sheet." Then insert Net Income text in Cell A25.

The next step is to transfer the ending balance values to the appropriate financial statement as positive values. Excel has an absolute value formula which will convert all values to positive, absolute, values and an absolute reference capability and both will be used here. In Cell I2 enter the formula =ABS($G2). This will put the absolute value of Cell G2 in Cell I2. Now drag the formula right into Columns J, K, and L. All of these cells will now reference Cell G2. Highlight all four cells, I1 through L1, in one stroke. As shown in Figure 4. 7.

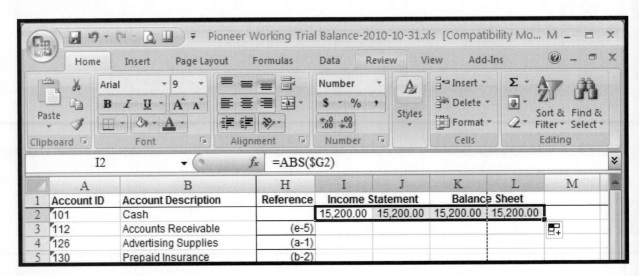

Figure 4. 7   Cells I2 through L2 highlighted and ready to be dragged through Row 22

Then drag the formulas from Row 2 through Row 22 as shown in Figure 4. 8.

Figure 4. 8 The formulas in Row 2 dragged through Row 22

The sum formulas for the columns, =SUM(I2:I22) can be manually entered into Cell I24 and dragged into Cells J24, K24, and L24 the Sum icon (the Sigma – Σ) can be utilized.

The next step is to delete inappropriate values – it is easier to delete MANY formulas than to write specific formulas for each cell. Since cash, accounts receivable, etc are inappropriate to the income statement while service revenue and all expense accounts are in appropriate to the balance sheet columns, click into Cell I2, then hold the Control (CTRL) key down while continuing to select all accounts that present values in inappropriate columns. These cells are shown as selected in Figure 4. 9. When they are all selected, simply press the Delete key on your keyboard.

Excel window — Pioneer Working Trial Balance-2010-10-31.xls [Compatibility Mo...]

Cell L16: =ABS($G16)

#	A — Account ID	B — Account Description	H — Reference	I — Income Statement	J	K — Balance Sheet	L	M
1	Account ID	Account Description	Reference	Income Statement		Balance Sheet		
2	101	Cash		15,200.00	15,200.00	15,200.00	15,200.00	
3	112	Accounts Receivable	(e-5)	200.00	200.00	200.00	200.00	
4	126	Advertising Supplies	(a-1)	1,000.00	1,000.00	1,000.00	1,000.00	
5	130	Prepaid Insurance	(b-2)	550.00	550.00	550.00	550.00	
6	157	Office Equipment		5,000.00	5,000.00	5,000.00	5,000.00	
7	158	Accum Deprec-Office Equip	(c-3)	40.00	40.00	40.00	40.00	
8	200	Notes Payable		5,000.00	5,000.00	5,000.00	5,000.00	
9	201	Accounts Payable		2,500.00	2,500.00	2,500.00	2,500.00	
10	209	Unearned Revenue	(d-4)	800.00	800.00	800.00	800.00	
11	212	Salaries Payable	(g-7)	1,200.00	1,200.00	1,200.00	1,200.00	
12	230	Interest Payable	(f-6)	50.00	50.00	50.00	50.00	
13	301	C. R. Byrd, Capital		10,000.00	10,000.00	10,000.00	10,000.00	
14	306	C. R. Byrd, Drawing		500.00	500.00	500.00	500.00	
15	350	Retained Earnings		0.00	0.00	0.00	0.00	
16	400	Service Revenue	(d-4) & (e-5)	10,600.00	10,600.00	10,600.00	10,600.00	
17	631	Advertising Supplies Expens	(a-1)	1,500.00	1,500.00	1,500.00	1,500.00	
18	711	Depreciation Expense	(c-3)	40.00	40.00	40.00	40.00	
19	722	Insurance Expense	(b-2)	50.00	50.00	50.00	50.00	
20	726	Salaries Expense	(g-7)	5,200.00	5,200.00	5,200.00	5,200.00	
21	729	Rent Expense		900.00	900.00	900.00	900.00	
22	905	Interest Expense	(f-6)	50.00	50.00	50.00	50.00	
23								
24		Total:		60,380.00	60,380.00	60,380.00	60,380.00	
25	Net Income			0.00			0.00	
26				60,380.00	60,380.00	60,380.00	60,380.00	
27								

Sheet tab: Working Trial Balance

Status bar: Ready   Average: 2,875.24   Count: 63   Sum: 181,140.00   100%

Figure 4. 9 All inappropriate cells selected and ready for deletion

And with all of the inappropriate values deleted, as shown in Figure 4. 10, the total expenses are shown in Column I as $7,740 while total revenues in Column J show $10,600. This indicates a net income of $2,860. By inserting that value, or writing a formula in Cell I25 to determine it, and then summing Rows 24 and 25 into Row 25 you can confirm that expenses of $7,740 plus net income of $2,860 equal revenues of $10,600. In the balance sheet total assets of $25,450 equal liabilities and owner's equity of $19,590 plus this period's net income of $2,860.

Now that debits equal credits in Row 26 for each financial statement, if the values look appropriate, your working trial balance is complete and you can use the values and accounts to journalize and post (save) them in Peachtree. These particular journal entries were accomplished in Chapter 3.

	L14	▾	× ✓ ƒx						
	A	**B**	**H**	**I**	**J**	**K**	**L**	**M**	
1	Account ID	Account Description	Reference	Income Statement		Balance Sheet			
2	101	Cash				15,200.00			
3	112	Accounts Receivable	(e-5)			200.00			
4	126	Advertising Supplies	(a-1)			1,000.00			
5	130	Prepaid Insurance	(b-2)			550.00			
6	157	Office Equipment				5,000.00			
7	158	Accum Deprec-Office Equip	(c-3)				40.00		
8	200	Notes Payable					5,000.00		
9	201	Accounts Payable					2,500.00		
10	209	Unearned Revenue	(d-4)				800.00		
11	212	Salaries Payable	(g-7)				1,200.00		
12	230	Interest Payable	(f-6)				50.00		
13	301	C. R. Byrd, Capital					10,000.00		
14	306	C. R. Byrd, Drawing				500.00			
15	350	Retained Earnings					0.00		
16	400	Service Revenue	(d-4) & (e-5)		10,600.00				
17	631	Advertising Supplies Expens	(a-1)	1,500.00					
18	711	Depreciation Expense	(c-3)	40.00					
19	722	Insurance Expense	(b-2)	50.00					
20	726	Salaries Expense	(g-7)	5,200.00					
21	729	Rent Expense		900.00					
22	905	Interest Expense	(f-6)	50.00					
23				0.00	0.00	0.00			
24		Total:		7,740.00	10,600.00	22,450.00	19,590.00		
25	Net Income			2,860.00			2,860.00		
26				10,600.00	10,600.00	22,450.00	22,450.00		
27									

Working Trial Balance

Edit

Figure 4. 10   Completed worksheet for Pioneer Advertising Agency

With the journal entries indicated by the worksheet, you can view the income statement and statement of retained earnings for the month ending October 31, 2010, and the balance sheet as of October 31, 2010. The Peachtree presentation values will match the textbook values, with some presentation adjustments – the textbook uses the owner's equity statement and the balance sheet will contain net income values.

MANUALLY CLOSING THE BOOKS

EXTREMELY IMPORTANT NOTE!!!
DO NOT INITIATE OR CLOSE ANY PEACHTREE TEMPLATES WITH THE YEAR-END WIZARD
UNLESS SPECIFICALLY INSTRUCTED TO DO SO BY YOUR INSTRUCTOR!

Closing does not really close accounts or "the books" as it implies or as many individuals think. It determines the balances of nominal or temporary accounts by closing a fiscal year of activities and transfers those balances to real or permanent owner's equity accounts through a specific process. This process provides information for analysis if desired. The closing process can provide specific and total revenues (total sales revenues and total service revenues, then total revenues type issues), specific and total expenses (total salaries expense and total supplies expense, then total expenses), net income and total drawings for the period as well. This "period" statement is the justification for the date reference lines such as "For the Month Ended October 31, 2010" on the income statement, the statement of owner's equity, and the retained earnings statement. The use of this line on the statement of cash flows also indicates that it reports where the cash, not accrual accounting values, came from and went to for the stated period.

Peachtree is an automated closing process which you will see later in the chapter. This does not preclude you from "closing the books" manually as shown in the textbook and this manual process is the first process shown.

To close an accounting period properly you must be able to distinguish between temporary or nominal accounts and permanent or real accounts. And account numbering frequently helps in this effort. Using Pioneer Advertising Agency as an example, on the income statement revenue accounts are numbered in the 4XX range and expense accounts are numbered from 5XX through 9XX with a few excepts. ***Note: ALL*** accounts on the income statement are nominal or temporary accounts and all get closed to the Income Summary account. The owner's drawing account, which is also a nominal or temporary account is closed directly to an owner's equity account. It is not closed to the Income Summary account because drawings are not an income or expense account. Real or permanent accounts, ***ALL*** asset and liability accounts and MOST owner's equity accounts remain open. Drawings and withdrawals accounts for proprietorships and dividends for corporations are owner's equity accounts that get closed.

Since manually closing the books within Peachtree can be easily reversed by deleting the journal entries, the file you have been working with to this point will be utilized – Pioneer Advertising Agency. Figure 4. 11 shows the current general ledger trial balance as of October 31, 2010. Its values agree with those in your textbook.

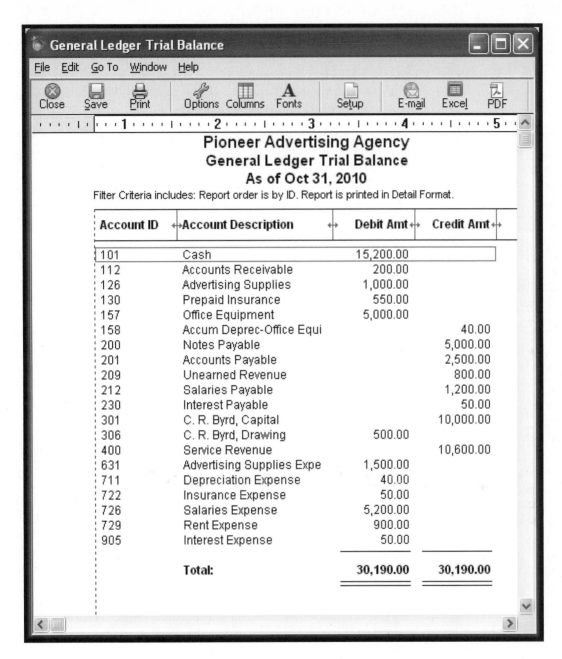

Figure 4. 11   General ledger trial balance report for Pioneer Advertising Agency as of October 31, 2010

The nominal or temporary accounts will be closed in the order of presentation in the financial statements – Income Statement – Revenues then expenses, Statement of Owner's Equity or Retained Earnings Statement – Drawings and Withdrawals for proprietorships and Dividends for corporations.

The following steps will walk you through the manual closing of Pioneer Advertising Agency. Having identified the revenue accounts – those in the 4XX series – 400 – Service Revenues. Its balance, as shown in Figure 4. 11, is a credit value of $10,600. This will be closed to Income Summary account (an income statement account).

Step 1: Open the general journal entry screen. Closing entries are always the last day of the fiscal period. For Pioneer this will be October 31, 2010. The reference is "Closing Entry #1." The debit account is 400 – Service Revenue with a description of "To close revenue accounts." The debit amount is $10,600, as shown in Figure 4. 11. The credit account is 340 – Income Summary. The description should auto fill from the first line. The credit amount is $10,600. Compare your work with that of Figure 4. 12, if you are satisfied, post (save) the journal entry.

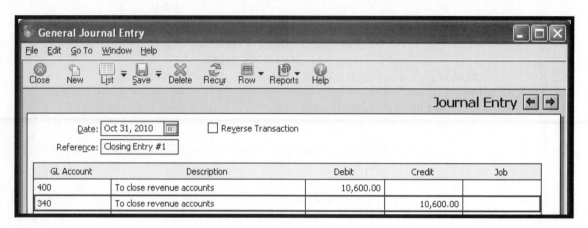

Figure 4. 12 Closing Entry #1 to close the revenue accounts

An interesting look at the income statement as this point will show a loss for the month of October since the revenue account has been set to zero through Closing Entry #1.

Step 2: The next step is to close all expense accounts to the Income Summary account. Peachtree should have advanced the general journal entry screen to October 31, 2010, and a reference of Closing Entry #2, if not, adjust these values. Since expense accounts normally carry debit balances, the Income Summary account will be debited to close them. In the first line of the compound journal entry enter GL (General Ledger) account number 340 – Income Summary. The description is "To close expense accounts." Leave the debit value blank and continue to the multiple credit lines. With the cursor in the GL (General Ledger) account window for the second line try this – since all expense accounts start with a number equal to or greater than 6 – enter 6 – if the first account highlighted in the auto fill options is an expense account, press Enter to accept the account. Now use the down arrow to move to the next line. Enter 6, the first value highlighted for auto fill is the same account as the second line; use the down arrow to highlight the next account. If it is an expense account, press Enter to accept and insert it. Once again, use the down arrow to advance to the next line and press the 6 again and use the down arrows to identify accounts. When all expense accounts have been entered go back and enter the values – as shown on your general ledger trial balance, also shown in Figure 4. 11. Let Peachtree do your mathematics when it can. Figure 4. 13 shows that the journal entry is out of balance by $7,740, the same amount of your loss if you looked at the income statement after closing the revenue account(s). Enter this value into the debit value of the first line and post (save) the journal entry.

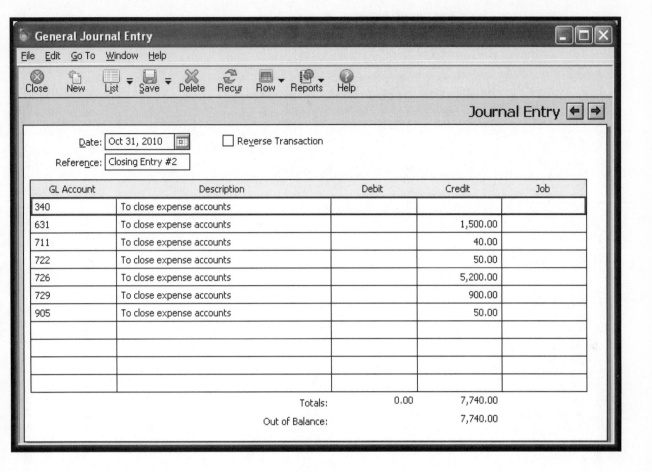

Figure 4. 13   Closing Entry #2 in process showing that expenses total $7,740

Viewing the income statement, Figure 4. 14, shows that all revenue and expense accounts have been closed – reset to zero - for the period. Revenues, expenses, and net income are all $0.00.

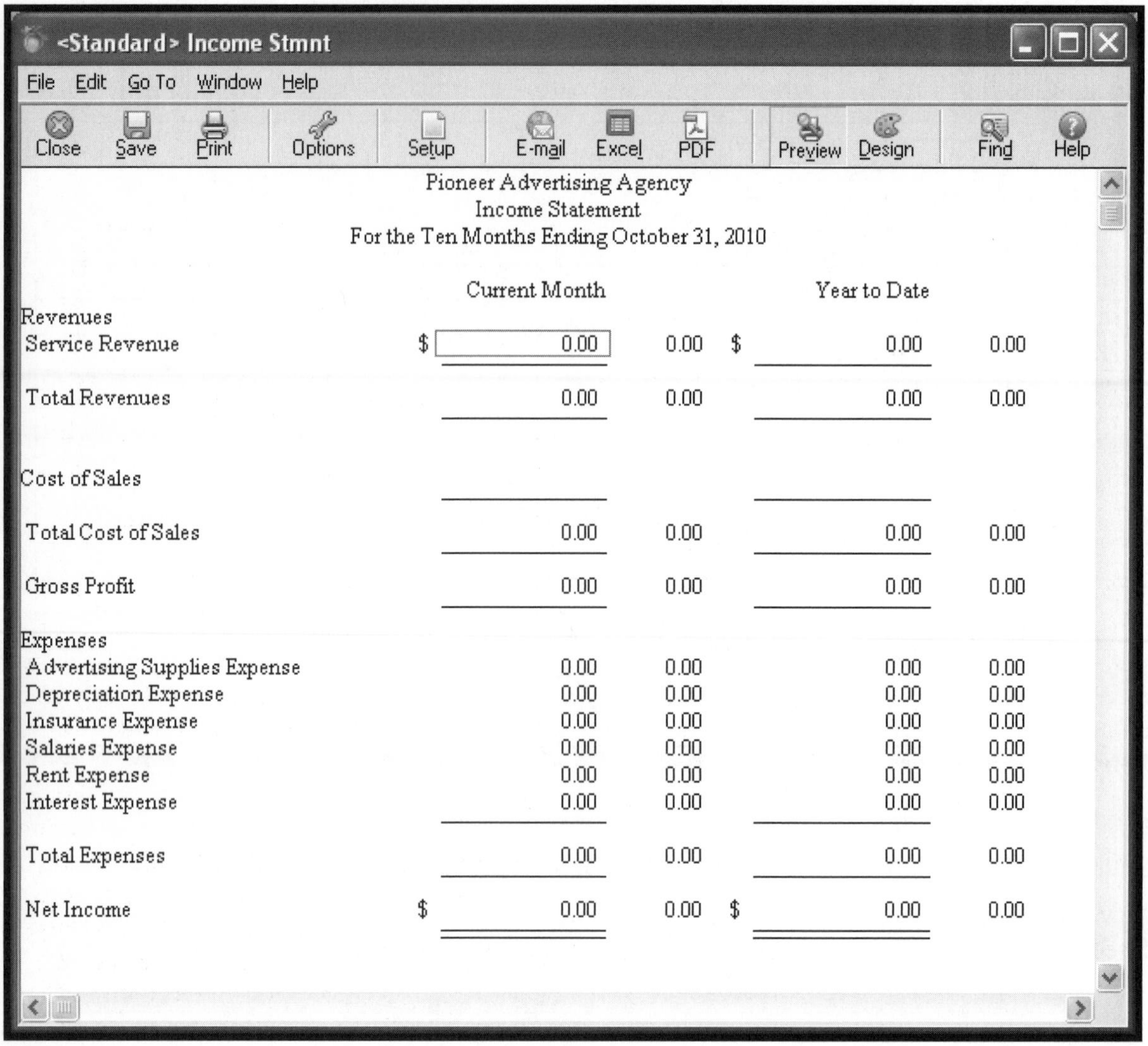

Pioneer Advertising Agency
Income Statement
For the Ten Months Ending October 31, 2010

	Current Month		Year to Date	
Revenues				
Service Revenue	$ 0.00	0.00	$ 0.00	0.00
Total Revenues	0.00	0.00	0.00	0.00
Cost of Sales				
Total Cost of Sales	0.00	0.00	0.00	0.00
Gross Profit	0.00	0.00	0.00	0.00
Expenses				
Advertising Supplies Expense	0.00	0.00	0.00	0.00
Depreciation Expense	0.00	0.00	0.00	0.00
Insurance Expense	0.00	0.00	0.00	0.00
Salaries Expense	0.00	0.00	0.00	0.00
Rent Expense	0.00	0.00	0.00	0.00
Interest Expense	0.00	0.00	0.00	0.00
Total Expenses	0.00	0.00	0.00	0.00
Net Income	$ 0.00	0.00	$ 0.00	0.00

Figure 4. 14 Pioneer's income statement after revenue and expense accounts have been closed

The Income Summary account was created as an Equity - Gets closed account. As such it is shown on the balance sheet in the owner's equity or capital section, Figure 4. 15.

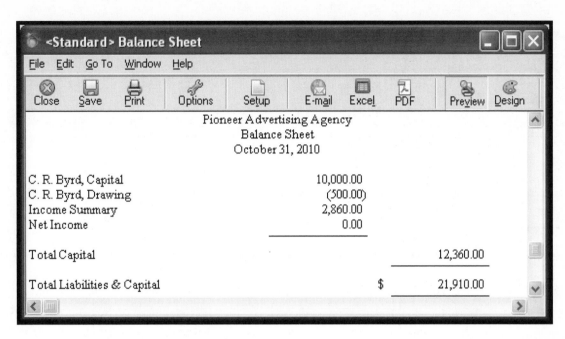

Figure 4. 15 Pioneer's owner's equity or capital section of the balance sheet showing Income Summary of $2,860

As shown in Figure 4. 15, the balance of the Income Summary account is $2,860. The same value as net income on the income statement as the Income Summary account contains the credit balances of Revenues, $10,600 and the debit values of expenses, $7,740. Hence the title of the account – Income Summary.

Step 3; The third journal entry in the closing process is to close the Income Summary account to an owner's equity account. The general journal entry screen should show a date of October 31, 2010, and Closing Entry #3. Make an required adjustments. The debit line will be to GL (General Ledger) account 330 – Income Summary since the account has a credit balance. The description will be "To close net income to capital." The debit amount will be $2,860, the balance of the account and the calculated value of net income. The credit GL (General Ledger) account is 301 – C. R. Byrd, Capital, a real or permanent account. The description should auto fill and the credit value is $2,860. Check your work against Figure 4. 16, when satisfied, post (save) the entry.

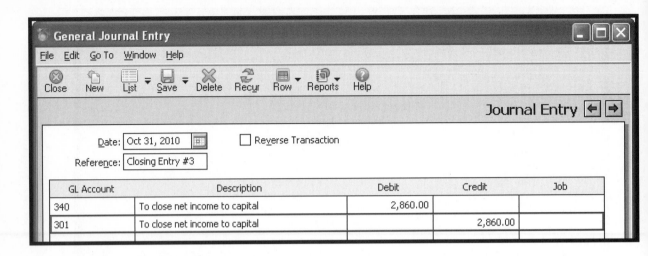

Figure 4. 16 Journal entry to close the Income Summary account to C. R. Byrd, Capital

Step 4: With Closing Entry #3 posted (saved), the next step is to close the C. R. Byrd, Drawing account. Peachtree should have auto filled the date with October 31, 2010, and the reference window to Closing Entry #4. Make any adjustments appropriate. The GL (General Ledger) account number will be 301 – C. R. Byrd, Capital, the description will be "To close drawings to capital" and the debit value will be $500 since the 306 – C. R. Byrd, Drawing account has a debit balance of $500. The credit GL (General Ledger) account is 301 – C. R. Byrd, Drawing, the description should auto fill, and the credit value is $500. Post (save) the journal entry after you compare your work and are satisfied with it as compared with Figure 4. 17.

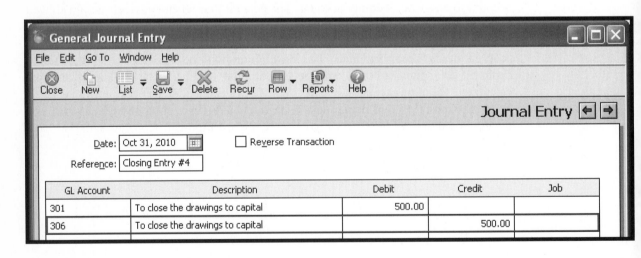

Figure 4. 17 Journal entry to close the drawings account to the capital account of C. R. Byrd

And Figure 4. 18 confirms that the Income Summary account value has been transferred to C. R. Byrd, Capital.

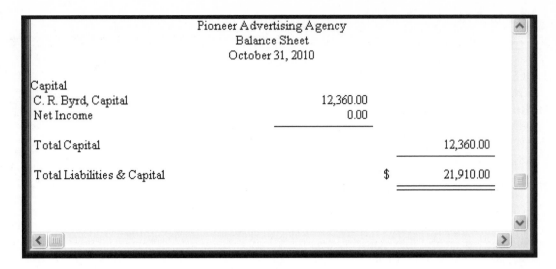

Figure 4. 18 The balance sheet of Pioneer Advertising Agency after all closing entries have been posted (saved)

Figure 4. 19 confirms that no nominal or temporary accounts have a balance.

Pioneer Advertising Agency
General Ledger Trial Balance
As of Oct 31, 2010

Filter Criteria includes: Report order is by ID. Report is printed in Detail Format.

Account ID	Account Description	Debit Amt	Credit Amt
101	Cash	15,200.00	
112	Accounts Receivable	200.00	
126	Advertising Supplies	1,000.00	
130	Prepaid Insurance	550.00	
157	Office Equipment	5,000.00	
158	Accum Deprec-Office Equi		40.00
200	Notes Payable		5,000.00
201	Accounts Payable		2,500.00
209	Unearned Revenue		800.00
212	Salaries Payable		1,200.00
230	Interest Payable		50.00
301	C. R. Byrd, Capital		12,360.00
	Total:	**21,950.00**	**21,950.00**

Figure 4. 19 The general ledger trial balance report of Pioneer Advertising Agency after all closing entries have been posted (saved)

AUTO CLOSING THE BOOKS

EXTREMELY IMPORTANT NOTE!!!
DO NOT INITIATE OR CLOSE ANY
PEACHTREE TEMPLATES WITH THE
YEAR-END WIZARD UNLESS
SPECIFICALLY INSTRUCTED TO DO SO BY
YOUR INSTRUCTOR!

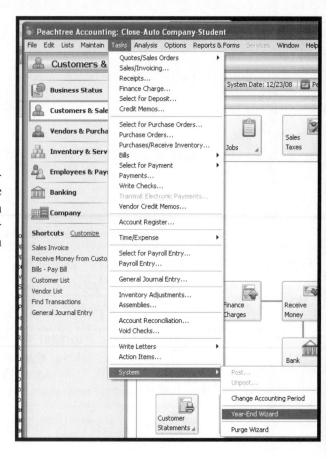

This is a special file for the students - Close-Auto Company-Student – can be closed with the Year-End Wizard which is opened with the path Tasks > Systems > Year-End Wizard, shown in Figure 4. 20.

Figure 4. 20   The path to the Year-End Wizard

Step 1:   To close the company as year-end, select Year-End Wizard. ***WARNING:*** You can accomplish the Year-End Wizard on a fiscal period only once. Do not utilize the Pioneer Advertising Agency file for this demonstration – Use the Close Auto Company Student file as shown, it is a duplicate of the Pioneer file to date.

There are numerous screens that will occur during this process. Many will not be printed here.

Step 2:   Click on "Year-End Wizard" to start the process.

Step 3:   The first screen, titled Year-End Wizard – Welcome, tells you the years open. Click "Next" to continue.

Step 4:   The second screen is titled Year-End Wizard – Close Options. Ensure that Fiscal and Payroll Tax Years is selected. Then click "Next."

Step 5:   **A VERY IMPORTANT STEP!** Peachtree has determined which reports are best printed as permanent records during the closing process. This selection, shown in Figure 4. 21, can consume large amounts of paper but are necessary as you cannot open closed fiscal periods easily. Click "Next" to print and proceed through the closing process.

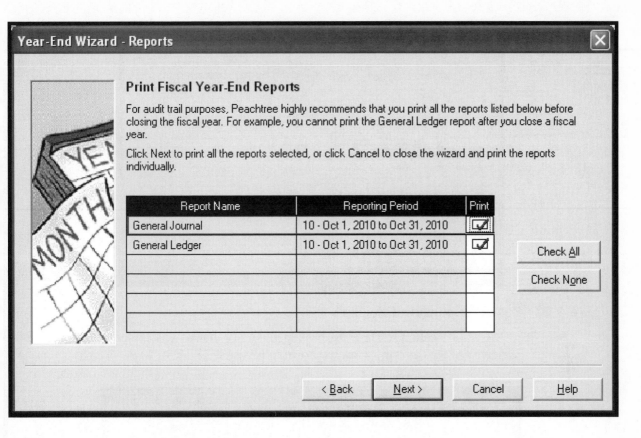

Figure 4. 21   Printing options on the Year-End Wizard process

Step 6:   Year-End Wizard – Internal Accounting Review screen – This screen offers an Internal Accounting Review. This review will check for numerous common errors and violations of GAAP principles. Since the file has been constructed in accordance with the textbook, click on "Next" to bypass this option and continue.

Step 7:   Year-End Wizard – Back Up – In trying to protect your data Peachtree requires you to back up your data before proceeding past this point. Click on "Back Up" and you will be given a new screen – Back Up Company. Ensure that "Include company name in the backup file name" option is selected, as shown in Figure 4. 22.

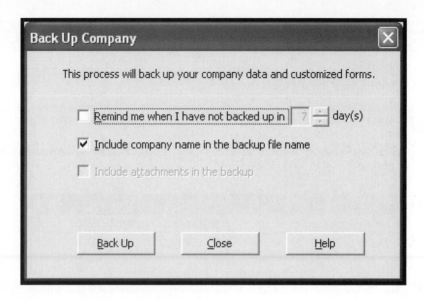

Figure 4. 22   Back Up Company dialog box

Step 8:   Select a location to store the backup file and a name. The preference of many is a date and the company name as shown in Figure 4. 23.

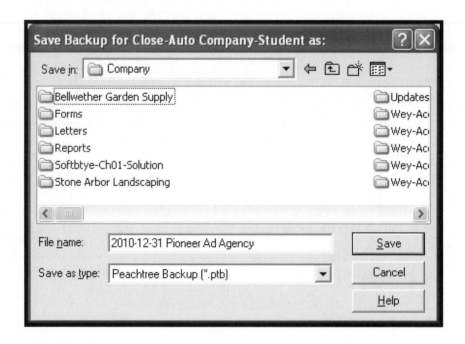

Figure 4. 23   Save Backup For Close Company dialog box

Step 9:   Peachtree then tells you the amount of storage space required, click "OK" to continue. And Peachtree will whiz and whirl when saving the data and present you with the Year-End Wizard Back Up screen again. Click on "Next" to continue.

Step 10:   Year-End Wizard – New Open Fiscal Years – Peachtree tells you the fiscal years that will be open with the next step – 2011 and 2012. Click on "Next" to continue.

Step 11: Year-End Wizard – Confirm Close – This is a second confirmation of the desires – close Fiscal Year 2010 and open Fiscal Years 2011 and 2012. Click on "Next" to continue.

Step 12: Year-End Wizard – Begin Close – The point of no return – and in this special file, Close-Auto Company-Student, it is okay to proceed. Click on "Begin Close," Figure 4. 24.

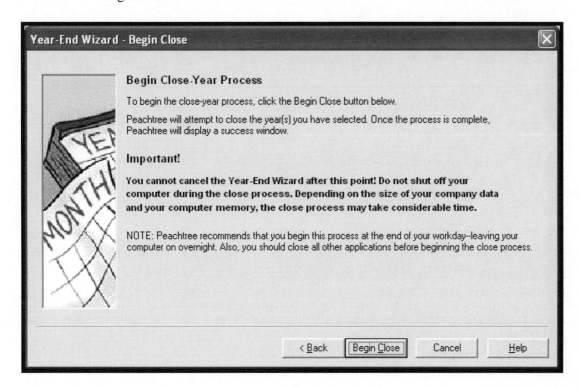

Figure 4. 24 Year-End Wizard – Begin Close dialog box

And Peachtree will whiz and whirl for a bit, depending on the size of the company, and present you with Figure 4. 25 to indicate that the process is complete.

Step 13: And Peachtree once again tells you that Fiscal Year 2010 is closed and Fiscal Years 2011 and 2012 are open. Click on "Finish," Figure 4. 25, to complete the process and return to the company.

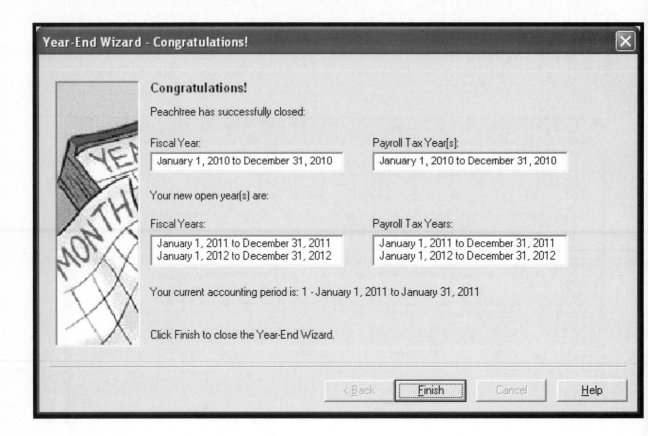

Figure 4. 25   Year-End Wizard – Congratulations dialog box

The company will open into January 2011 as the current accounting period. View the income statement, the statement of retained earnings, and balance sheet. And you will see that all nominal or temporary account have zero balances – they have been closed, and that Retained Earnings, an account normally associated with corporations, contains the value of net income less drawings, withdrawals, (for proprietorships) and dividends (for corporations), $2,360, the same value that C. R. Byrd, Capital increased by in the manual closing process, Figure 4. 26.

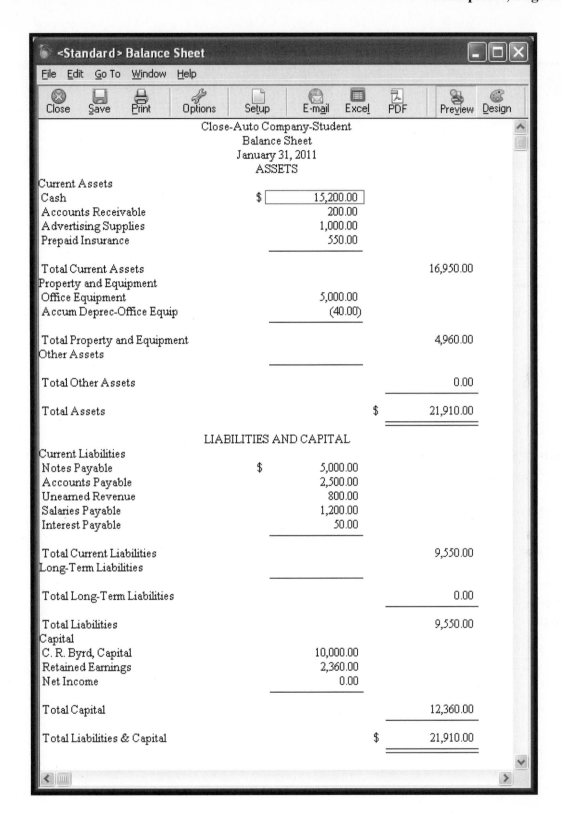

Figure 4. 26 Balance sheet after closing for January 2010

A simple journal entry, shown in Figure 4. 27, would transfer the value of retained earnings, $2,360, to C. R. Byrd, Capital if desired.

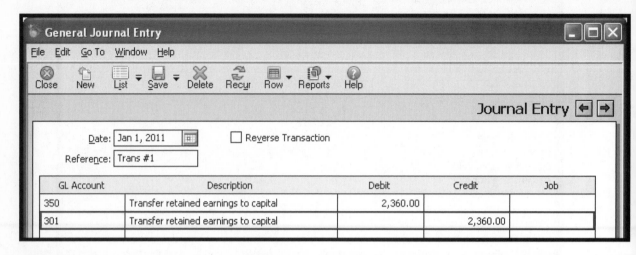

Figure 4. 27 General journal entry to transfer retained earnings to C. R. Byrd, Capital

Comprehensive Do It! Problem, Watson Answering Service, Directory Wey_AP9e_Watson_Answering_Service

Open Watson Answering Service from within your student data set. Preview the general ledger trial balance. You will be presented with the following unadjusted general ledger trial balance, shown below.

Watson Answering Service
General Ledger Trial Balance
As of Aug 31, 2010

Filter Criteria includes: Report order is by ID. Report is printed with Accounts having Zero Amounts and in Detail Format.

Account ID	Account Description	Debit Amt	Credit Amt
101	Cash	5,400.00	
112	Accounts Receivable	2,400.00	
126	Supplies	2,800.00	
130	Prepaid Insurance	1,300.00	
157	Equipment	60,000.00	
157.1	Accum Deprec-Equip		
200	Notes Payable - Short-term		40,000.00
201	Accounts Payable		2,400.00
216	Interest Payable		
231	Notes Payable - Long-term		
301	Ray Watson, Capital		30,000.00
305	Ray Watson, Drawing	1,000.00	
350	Retained Earnings		
400	Service Revenues		4,900.00
530	Depreciation Expense - Eq		
560	Supplies Expense		
610	Advertising Expense	400.00	
718	Interest Expense		
722	Insurance Expense		
726	Salaries Expense	3,200.00	
732	Utilities Expense	800.00	
	Total:	77,300.00	77,300.00

Other data consists of the following:
1. Insurance expires at the rate of $200 per month.
2. There is $1,000 of supplies on hand at August 31.
3. Monthly depreciation is $900 on the equipment.
4. Interest of $500 on the notes payable has accrued during August.

Instructions:
(a) Print the Working Trial Balance.
(b) Compute the values for the adjusting entries and enter them on the working trial balance. Then journalize them using the general journal.
(c) Journalize the recognition of $5,000 of the notes payable as current, $35,000 as long-term notes payable.
(d) Check your work by printing a general ledger trial balance, an income statement, and a balance sheet.
(e) Do not close the temporary accounts using Year-End Wizard unless specifically instructed to do so.

Solution to Demonstration Problem

A portion of the working trial balance:

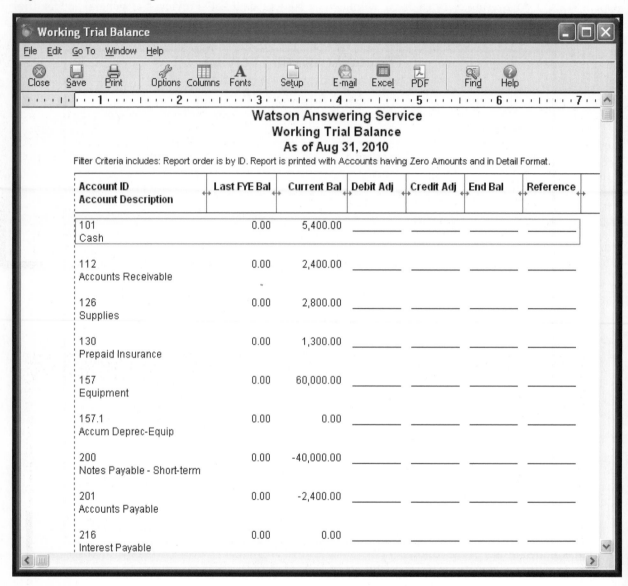

Watson Answering Service
Working Trial Balance
As of Aug 31, 2010

Filter Criteria includes: Report order is by ID. Report is printed with Accounts having Zero Amounts and in Detail Format.

Account ID Account Description	Last FYE Bal	Current Bal	Debit Adj	Credit Adj	End Bal	Reference
101 Cash	0.00	5,400.00				
112 Accounts Receivable	0.00	2,400.00				
126 Supplies	0.00	2,800.00				
130 Prepaid Insurance	0.00	1,300.00				
157 Equipment	0.00	60,000.00				
157.1 Accum Deprec-Equip	0.00	0.00				
200 Notes Payable - Short-term	0.00	-40,000.00				
201 Accounts Payable	0.00	-2,400.00				
216 Interest Payable	0.00	0.00				

General journal entry transferring $5,000 of Notes Payable from the Long Term Liability classification to the Notes Payable account classified as a Current Liability. This transaction makes $5,000 of Notes Payable a current liability, payable within a year.

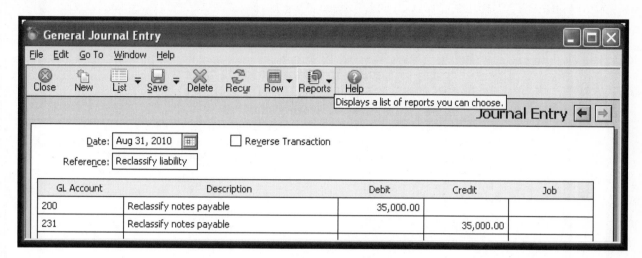

General journal report

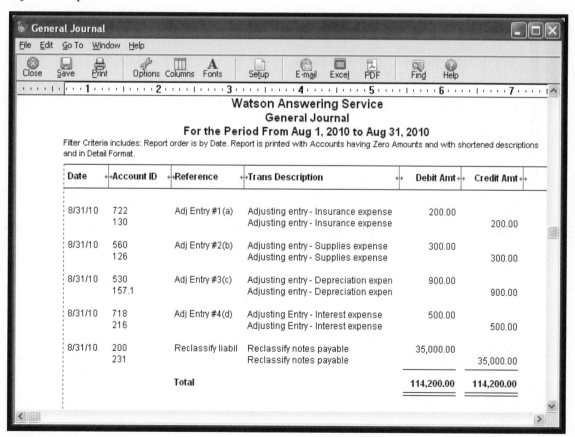

The general ledger trial balance:

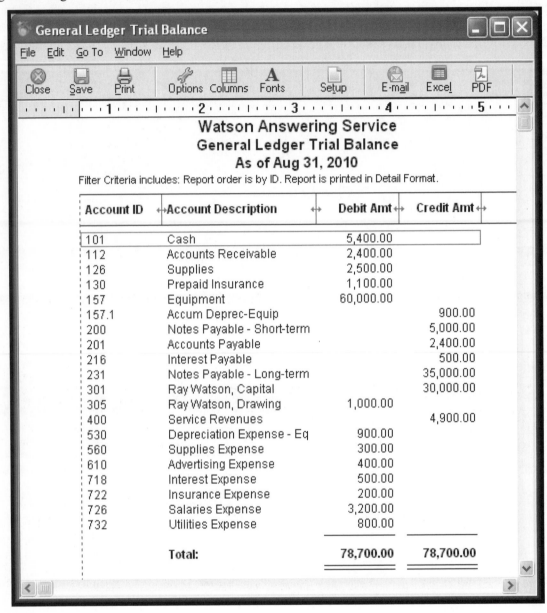

Watson Answering Service
General Ledger Trial Balance
As of Aug 31, 2010

Filter Criteria includes: Report order is by ID. Report is printed in Detail Format.

Account ID	Account Description	Debit Amt	Credit Amt
101	Cash	5,400.00	
112	Accounts Receivable	2,400.00	
126	Supplies	2,500.00	
130	Prepaid Insurance	1,100.00	
157	Equipment	60,000.00	
157.1	Accum Deprec-Equip		900.00
200	Notes Payable - Short-term		5,000.00
201	Accounts Payable		2,400.00
216	Interest Payable		500.00
231	Notes Payable - Long-term		35,000.00
301	Ray Watson, Capital		30,000.00
305	Ray Watson, Drawing	1,000.00	
400	Service Revenues		4,900.00
530	Depreciation Expense - Eq	900.00	
560	Supplies Expense	300.00	
610	Advertising Expense	400.00	
718	Interest Expense	500.00	
722	Insurance Expense	200.00	
726	Salaries Expense	3,200.00	
732	Utilities Expense	800.00	
	Total:	**78,700.00**	**78,700.00**

The income statement of Watson Answering Service

	Current Month			Year to Date	
Revenues					
Service Revenues	$ 4,900.00	100.00	$	4,900.00	100.00
Total Revenues	4,900.00	100.00		4,900.00	100.00
Cost of Sales					
Total Cost of Sales	0.00	0.00		0.00	0.00
Gross Profit	4,900.00	100.00		4,900.00	100.00
Expenses					
Depreciation Expense - Equip	900.00	18.37		900.00	18.37
Supplies Expense	300.00	6.12		300.00	6.12
Advertising Expense	400.00	8.16		400.00	8.16
Interest Expense	500.00	10.20		500.00	10.20
Insurance Expense	200.00	4.08		200.00	4.08
Salaries Expense	3,200.00	65.31		3,200.00	65.31
Utilities Expense	800.00	16.33		800.00	16.33
Total Expenses	6,300.00	128.57		6,300.00	128.57
Net Income	$ (1,400.00)	(28.57)	$	(1,400.00)	(28.57)

Watson Answering Service
Income Statement
For the Eight Months Ending August 31, 2010

The balance sheet of Watson Answering Service

<Standard> Balance Sheet

File   Edit   Go To   Window   Help

Close | Save | Print | Options | Setup | E-mail | Excel | PDF | Preview | Design

Watson Answering Service
Balance Sheet
August 31, 2010
ASSETS

Current Assets		
Cash	$ 5,400.00	
Accounts Receivable	2,400.00	
Supplies	2,500.00	
Prepaid Insurance	1,100.00	
Total Current Assets		11,400.00
Property and Equipment		
Equipment	60,000.00	
Accum Deprec-Equip	(900.00)	
Total Property and Equipment		59,100.00
Other Assets		
Total Other Assets		0.00
Total Assets		$ 70,500.00

LIABILITIES AND CAPITAL

Current Liabilities		
Notes Payable - Short-term	$ 5,000.00	
Accounts Payable	2,400.00	
Interest Payable	500.00	
Total Current Liabilities		7,900.00
Long-Term Liabilities		
Notes Payable - Long-term	35,000.00	
Total Long-Term Liabilities		35,000.00
Total Liabilities		42,900.00
Capital		
Ray Watson, Capital	30,000.00	
Ray Watson, Drawing	(1,000.00)	
Net Income	(1,400.00)	
Total Capital		27,600.00
Total Liabilities & Capital		$ 70,500.00

P4-2A, Porter Company, Directory Wey_AP9e_P4_2A_Porter_Co

The adjusted trial balance columns of the worksheet for Porter Company are as follows:

PORTER COMPANY
Worksheet
For the Year Ended December 31, 2010

Acct No.	Account Titles	Adjusted Trial Balance Dr.	Adjusted Trial Balance Cr.
101	Cash	18,800	
112	Accounts Receivable	16,200	
126	Supplies	2,300	
130	Prepaid Insurance	4,400	
151	Office Equipment	44,000	
152	Accumulated Depreciation – Office Equipment		20,000
200	Notes Payable – Short-term		20,000 10,000
201	Accounts Payable		8,000
210	Notes Payable – Long-term		10,000
212	Salaries Payable		2,600
230	Interest Payable		1,000
301	B. Porter, Capital		36,000
306	B. Porter, Drawing	12,000	
400	Service Revenue		77,800
610	Advertising Expense	12,000	
631	Supplies Expense	3,700	
711	Depreciation Expense	8,000	
722	Insurance Expense	4,000	
726	Salaries Expense	39,000	
905	Interest Expense	1,000	
		165,400	165,400

Instructions:

(a) Write a general journal entry reclassifying the total of notes payable so that only $10,000 of the total of $20,000 is reported as notes payable-short-term with the balance reported as notes payable-long-term.

(b) Follow the path Reports & Forms > General Ledger > General Ledger Trial Balance. While the general ledger trial balance is open, use the "Print" icon to print it as the adjusted trial balance.

(c) Follow the path Reports & Forms > Financial Statements > <Standard> Income Stmnt. While the income statement is open, use the "Print" icon to print it.

(d) Follow the path Reports & Forms > Financial Statements > <Standard> Retained Earnings. While the retained earnings statement is open, use the "Print" icon to print it.

(e) Follow the path Reports & Forms > Financial Statements > <Standard> Balance Sheet. While the balance sheet is open, use the "Print" icon to print it.

(f) Only if specifically instructed, follow the path Tasks > System > Year-End Wizard and follow the instructions to close 2010 and open 2011 and 2012 as current account periods. Select only the reports instructed to select. NOTE: Once the year 2010 is closed, it cannot be reopened easily.

Note: Peachtree reports are accurate for year-end values without closing the fiscal period. The only significant difference is that the balance sheet will have "Net Income" to indicate the income from the current fiscal year. Retained earnings, if shown, is retained income from prior fiscal years.

Note: An Income Summary account, 340, has been established in the chart of accounts permitting manual closing if directed.

P4-5A, Eddy's Carpet Cleaners, Directory
Wey_AP9e_P4_5A_Eddys_Carpet_Cleaners

Laura Eddy opened Eddy's Carpet Cleaners on March 1, 2010. During March 2010, the following transactions were completed:

March	1	Invested $10,000 cash in the business.
	1	Purchased used truck for $6,000, paying $3,000 cash and the balance on account.
	3	Purchased cleaning supplies for $1,200 on account.
	5	Paid $1,200 cash on one-year insurance policy effective March 1.
	14	Billed customers $4,800 for cleaning services.
	18	Paid $1,500 cash on amount owed on truck and $500 on amount owed on cleaning supplies.
	20	Paid $1,800 cash for employee salaries.
	21	Collected $1,400 cash from customers billed on March 14.
	28	Billed customers $2,500 for cleaning services.
	31	Paid gas and oil for month on truck $200.
	31	Withdrew $700 cash for personal use.

The chart of accounts for Eddy's Carpet Cleaners contains the following accounts:

101	Cash	306	L. Eddy, Drawing
112	Accounts Receivable	340	Income Summary
128	Cleaning Supplies	350	Retained Earnings
130	Prepaid Insurance		(Required by Peachtree.)
157	Equipment	400	Service Revenue
158	Accumulated Depreciation—	633	Gas & Oil Expense
	Equipment	634	Cleaning Supplies Expense
201	Accounts Payable	711	Depreciation Expense
212	Salaries Payable	722	Insurance Expense
301	L. Eddy, Capital	726	Salaries Expense

Instructions:
(a)   Using the chart of accounts, given, and the general journal, found through the path Tasks > General Journal Entry, journalize the March transactions.
(b)   Follow the path Reports & Forms > General Ledger > Working Trial Balance to view the working trial balance. Use the "Print" icon to print the working trial balance.
(c)   Enter the following adjustments on the working trial balance and extend the values to the "End Bal" (ending balance) column.
   (1)   Earned but unbilled revenue at March 31 was $700.
   (2)   Depreciation on equipment for the month was $250.
   (3)   One-twelfth of the insurance expired.
   (4)   An inventory count shows $400 of cleaning supplies on hand at March 31.
   (5)   Accrued but unpaid employee salaries were $500.
(d)   Using the chart of accounts, given, and the general journal, found through the path Tasks > General Journal Entry, journalize the adjusting entries.
(e)   Review your work by following the path Reports & Forms > General Ledger > General Journal. While the general journal report is open, use the "Print" icon to print it.

(f) Follow the path Reports & Forms > General Ledger > General Ledger Trial Balance. While the general ledger trial balance is open, use the "Print" icon to print it as the adjusted trial balance.

(g) Follow the path Reports & Forms > Financial Statements > <Standard> Income Stmnt. While the income statement is open, use the "Print" icon to print it.

(h) Follow the path Reports & Forms > Financial Statements > <Standard> Retained Earnings. While the retained earnings statement is open, use the "Print" icon to print it.

(i) Follow the path Reports & Forms > Financial Statements > <Standard> Balance Sheet. While the balance sheet is open, use the "Print" icon to print it.

(j) Only if specifically instructed, follow the path Tasks > System > Year-End Wizard and follow the instructions to close 2010 and open 2011 and 2012 as current account periods. Select only the reports instructed to select. *NOTE:* Once the year 2010 is closed, it cannot be reopened easily.

Note: Peachtree reports are accurate for year-end values without closing the fiscal period. A significant difference is that the balance sheet will have "Net Income" to indicate the income from the current fiscal year. Retained Earnings, if shown, is income earned and retained from prior fiscal years.

Note: An Income Summary account, 340, has been established in the chart of accounts permitting manual closing if directed.

CHAPTER 5

Accounting for Merchandising Operations

OBJECTIVES

- Identify the differences between service and merchandising companies.
- Explain the recording of purchases under a perpetual inventory system.
- Explain the recording of sales revenues under a perpetual inventory system.
- Explain the steps in the accounting cycle for

- a merchandising company.
- Distinguish between a multiple-step and a single-step income statement.
- Explain the computation and the importance of gross profit.
- Determine cost of goods sold under a periodic inventory system.

MERCHANDISING OPERATIONS

Wal-Mart, Kmart, and Target are called merchandising companies because they buy and sell merchandise rather than perform services as their primary source of revenue. Merchandising companies that purchase and sell directly to consumers are called retailers. Merchandising companies that sell to retailers are known as wholesalers. For example, retailer Walgreens might buy goods from wholesaler McKesson; retailer Office Depot might buy office supplies from wholesaler United Stationers. The primary source of revenues for merchandising companies is the sale of merchandise, often referred to simply as sales revenue or sales. A merchandising company has two categories of expenses: cost of goods sold and operating expenses.

Cost of goods sold is the total cost of merchandise sold during the period. This expense is directly related to the revenue recognized from the sale of goods. Sales revenues less cost of goods sold equals gross profit. Gross profit less operating expenses equals net income (or net loss). Cost of goods sold and gross profit are unique to a merchandising company. Neither the account Cost of Goods Sold nor the title gross profit are generally used by a service company.

With Peachtree Complete Accounting you will see accounting for merchandising operations handled differently than in the textbook. To provide the detail for analysis and costing, you should have specific vendors to buy from on account rather than a general accounts payable. You should have specific merchandise items as inventory items to buy and sell rather than a general merchandise inventory. And you should have specific customers to sell to on account rather than a general accounts receivable.

There are numerous issues addressing how Peachtree handles merchandising operations and how these are different in application or reporting as shown in the textbook. Most of these will be addressed in the order presented in the textbook.

PERPETUAL VS. PERIODIC INVENTORY, LIFO, FIFO, AVERAGE COST

When utilizing the power of Peachtree properly (as designed and intented) Peachtree purchases, sales, and inventory actions are detailed and perpetual and you can choose LIFO, FIFO, or average cost. That is, every time you buy something you should be buying a specific item such as Television Set-Model 123-ABC-987 and you should be buying a specific quantity from a specific vendor. When you sell something you should be selling a specific item and quantity which you have in your computerized inventory records, such as one Television Set-Model 123-ABC-987 to specific customer for a specific price. Cost being what you pay and price being what you sell for. This information allows Peachtree to provide the reports that you need to manage your business.

While it is important to know that you owe $750 for the purchase of inventory, it is also important to know that you owe Southeastern Video Suppliers $1,500 for two units of Television Set-Model 123-ABC-987 purchased on May 1, 2010 for $750 each with terms of 2/10, N30. And that you sold one of those units to Cindi Linn on account for $1,100 on May 5, 2010 with the agreement that she will pay within thirty days of the invoice date. The power of Peachtree, when used to its full extent, will tell you income statement information for the month of May 2010 that 1) sales of $1,100 have occurred, 2) that cost of goods sold is $750, 3) that gross profit for this sale is ($1,100 - $750) $350, and 4) that if no other expenses are recognized in association with this sale, that net income related to this sale is $350.

Statement of owner's equity or statement of retained earnings will show that owner's equity has increased by $350 during the month of May 2010.

The balance sheet will show that 1) assets have increased by $750 for the remaining Television Set-Model 123-ABC-987 in inventory, 2) that the asset accounts receivable has increased by $1,100 for the sale on account to Cindi Linn, 3) that liabilities have increased by $1,500 for the purchase of two units of Television Set-Model 123-ABC-987 from Southeastern Video Suppliers, and 4) that owner's equity has increased by $350 due to net income for the month ending May 31, 2010.

And the effort to accomplish these information changes was 1) to record the purchase of the Television Set-Model 123-ABC-987 units to the correct vendor at the correct cost to the correct inventory items on the correct date and 2) to record the sale of the correct inventory unit to the correct customer at the correct price on the correct date. All other computations to prepare the financial and managerial reports – income statement, statement of retained earnings, balance sheet, inventory reports, cost of goods sold reports; aging of payables and receivables was automated by Peachtree.

Both Peachtree Complete Accounting by Sage and QuickBooks by Intuit are, by design, perpetual inventory systems. They track dates, quantities, inventory items, costs, and prices as well as vendors and customers each time a transaction affecting inventory is recorded to give you the information mentioned earlier. QuickBooks, by design, is constrained to average costing while Peachtree offers you the choice of LIFO, FIFO, or Average Cost _**AND**_ these can be controlled as defaults or specific to units. This is, with the power of Peachtree, you can have "Apples" as an inventory item valued with the LIFO concept while you have "Bananas" as an inventory item valued at FIFO, and "Cantaloupes" as an inventory item valued with the average cost concept. All within the same company within the same period, in the same sale, without a problem.

This presents several problems and here are some of them with their solutions. First, you can make purchases using the general journal with a debit to Account 120 – Merchandise Inventory and a credit to Account 201 – Accounts Payable (or Account 101 – Cash) without detail of who you made the purchase from or what you purchased in detail without a problem. This keeps your work in synchronization with the textbook. Second, you can make sales using the general journal with a debit to Account 112 – Accounts Receivable and a credit to Account 401 – Sales without detail of who you sold what items to or what their cost was. Then, later you can enter the cost of goods sold from a manual calculation utilizing the periodic inventory valuation concepts. Any financial or managerial report viewed or printed between the first purchase and the cost of goods sold entry will not reflect the correct financial position of the company and this is accepted in periodic inventory concepts of accounting. This concept allows you to record freight-in charges to Account 120 – Merchandise Inventory without a problem.

Using Peachtree's power of computation – specific vendors, specific customers, specific inventory items, Freight-in will be an expense account since allocating freight-in costs to inventory after it is received exceeds cost/benefit values and can be a complex issue. For a retailer such as Kmart a truck with 40,000 pounds of merchandise which as 62,750 pieces of inventory representing 2,750 different inventory items without specific patterns of weight or cubic footage arrives at the receiving dock with a freight bill of $1,759.73. How much would you allocate to a pen with a cost of $10 and a price of $20 that weighs one quarter pound and occupies one twentieth of a cubic foot of cargo space? How much would you allocate to a ream of paper with a cost of $2.35 that sells for $3.49 that weighs four pounds and occupies one fifth of a cubic foot of cargo space? How much would you allocate to an unassembled desk with a cost of $49.85 and a price of $119.95 that weighs 65 pounds and occupies four cubic feet of cargo space?

So, how do you solve these differences? First, if the setup for the problem tells you periodic inventory the text will tell you to use a general journal entry. If the problem tells you perpetual inventory you will be using specific vendors and customers along with specific inventory items. And your results will match the textbook solutions.

ACCOUNTS PAYABLE DEFAULTS

The use of defaults, when applicable, will greatly ease your workload within Peachtree. Within PW Audio Supply, follow the path Maintain > Default Information > Vendors for the vendor defaults screen, shown in Figure 5. 1.

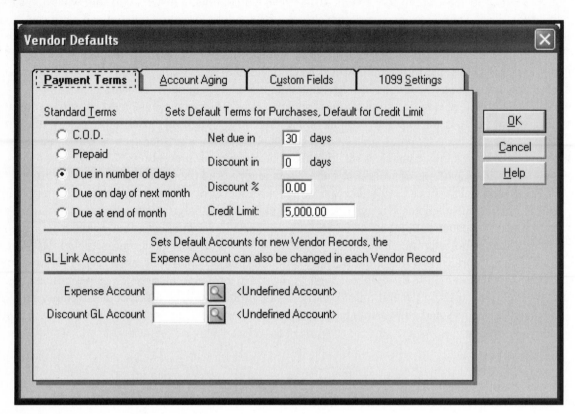

Figure 5. 1   Vendor Defaults screen

> **Step 1:**   Set the Discount in window to "10" for 10 days.
>
> **Step 2:**   Set the Discount % window to "2" for 2%.
>
> **Step 3**:   Set the "Credit Limit" window to "50000" for $50,000.
>
> **Step 4**:   Set the Expense Account to 120 – Merchandise Inventory.
>
> **Step 5:**   Set the Discount GL (General Ledger) account to 120 – Merchandise Inventory.
>
> **Step 6:**   View the Account Aging, Custom Fields, and 1099 Setting, all of which require no changes.
>
> **Step 7:**   Compare your work with Figure 5. 2 and make any necessary changes before clicking on "OK" to save the information.

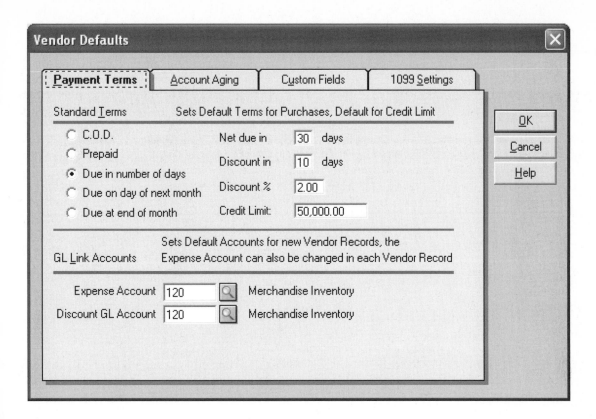

Figure 5. 2 Completed Vendor Defaults screen

ENTERING VENDOR INFORMATION

A vendor is the seller, the merchant, or the manufacturer that has goods, products or merchandise that you plan to buy, increase the price, and resale to your customers. To use the power of Peachtree for detail and analysis, you should set up your vendors before you can make any purchases on account. To do this open up the PW Audio Supply file with Peachtree.

With PW Audio Supply open within Peachtree Complete Accounting:

Step 1: Click on "Maintain" from the main menu bar and then click on "Vendors" from the drop-down menu. You should see the "Maintain Vendors" screen as shown in Figure 5. 3 below.

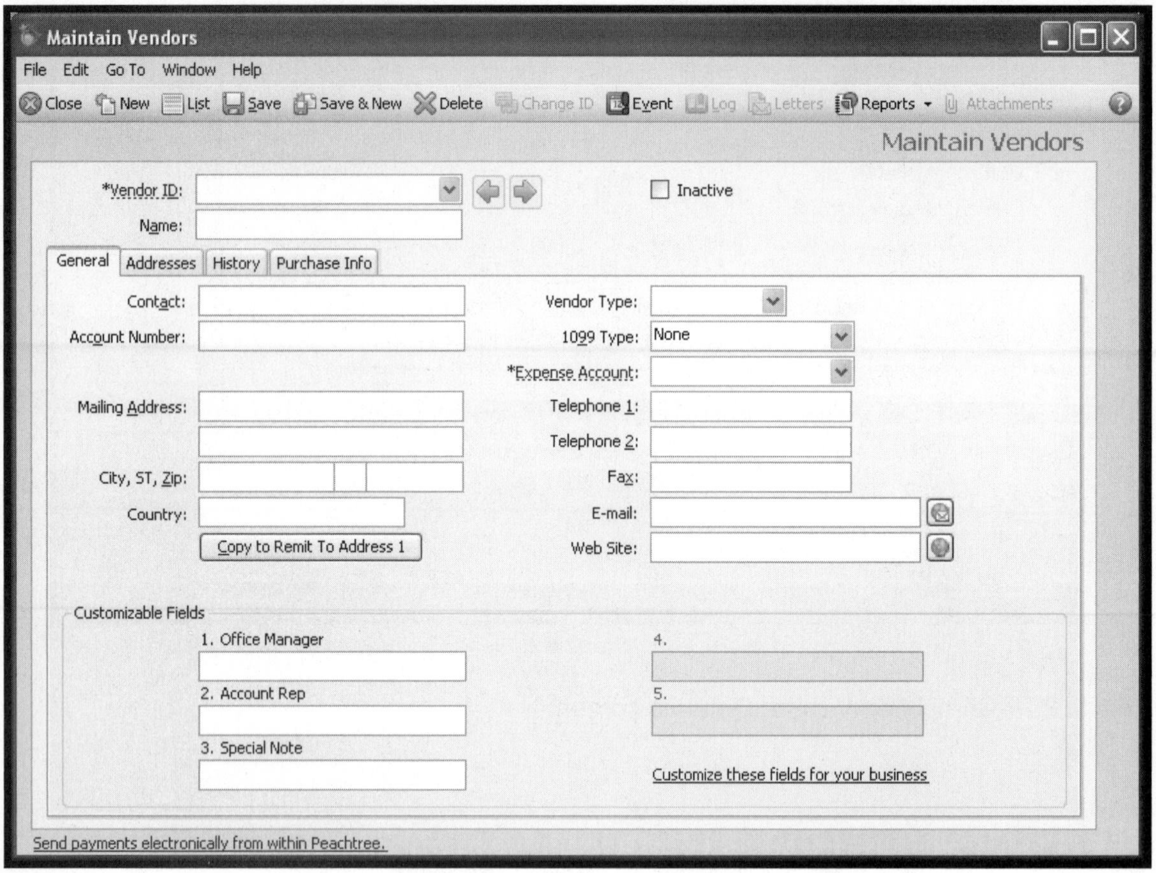

Figure 5. 3   Maintain Vendors screen

There are four tabs on this screen, General, Addresses, History, and Purchase Info. You will fully set up one vendor and other vendors will be abbreviated.

Step 2: Complete the General tab for PW Audio Supply with the following information:

A: The first Vendor ID is V101.

B: The vendor's name is Columbus Import Company.

C: Alyce Merchant is your contact person.

D: Your account number at Columbus Import is 1347.

E: Columbus Import's address is 1492 Queen Isabella Way in Madrid, GA 30341.

F: The Vendor Type is "Whlsler" (Wholesaler). This field is set by the user as desired.

G: Since Columbus Import will not require a 1099 for tax reporting, set 1099 Type to None.

H: Set the Expense Account to 120 – Merchandise Inventory.

I: Set the Telephone 1 field to 555.555.1492. For Peachtree this is a text field – any format you desire – (555) 555-1492, 555-555-1492, is acceptable.

If desired you could put in additional telephone numbers, fax numbers, E-mail addresses, and web sites for the vendor as well as office manager and account representative names.

Step 3: Click on the "Addresses" tab. The default address is that entered on the General tab. If payments are remitted to another address, it could be entered here.

Step 4: Click on the "History" tab. Peachtree will track your actions with the vendor on this tab. No entry is required.

Step 5: Click on the "Purchase Info" tab. You would have to build purchase representatives (your employee) to utilize this field. You can also enter tax ID number information for permanent storage. Airborne is the default method for shipping. This can be changed through the drop-down box for each vendor and the methods and order of presentation is controlled through inventory item defaults. A significant field here is **_Terms and Credit_** – the lower portion of the tab. By default it shows that the net amount is due in 30 days, a discount period of 10 days is set with a 2% discount option and the credit limit is $50,000. If the vendor had dictated other terms clicking on the drop-down arrow to the right of the terms and credit window would allow you to change any of these defaults. Since this vendor has a $25,000 limit on your purchasing account,

Step 6: Click on the drop-down arrow to the right of the terms and credit window.

Step 7: Click on the "Customize terms for this vendor."

Step 8: Change the credit limit field from $50,000 to $25,000.

Step 9:   Your entry should match the one in Figure 5. 4, which contains images of both the general tab and the purchase info tab. Make any corrections before clicking on "Save & New" on the menu bar.

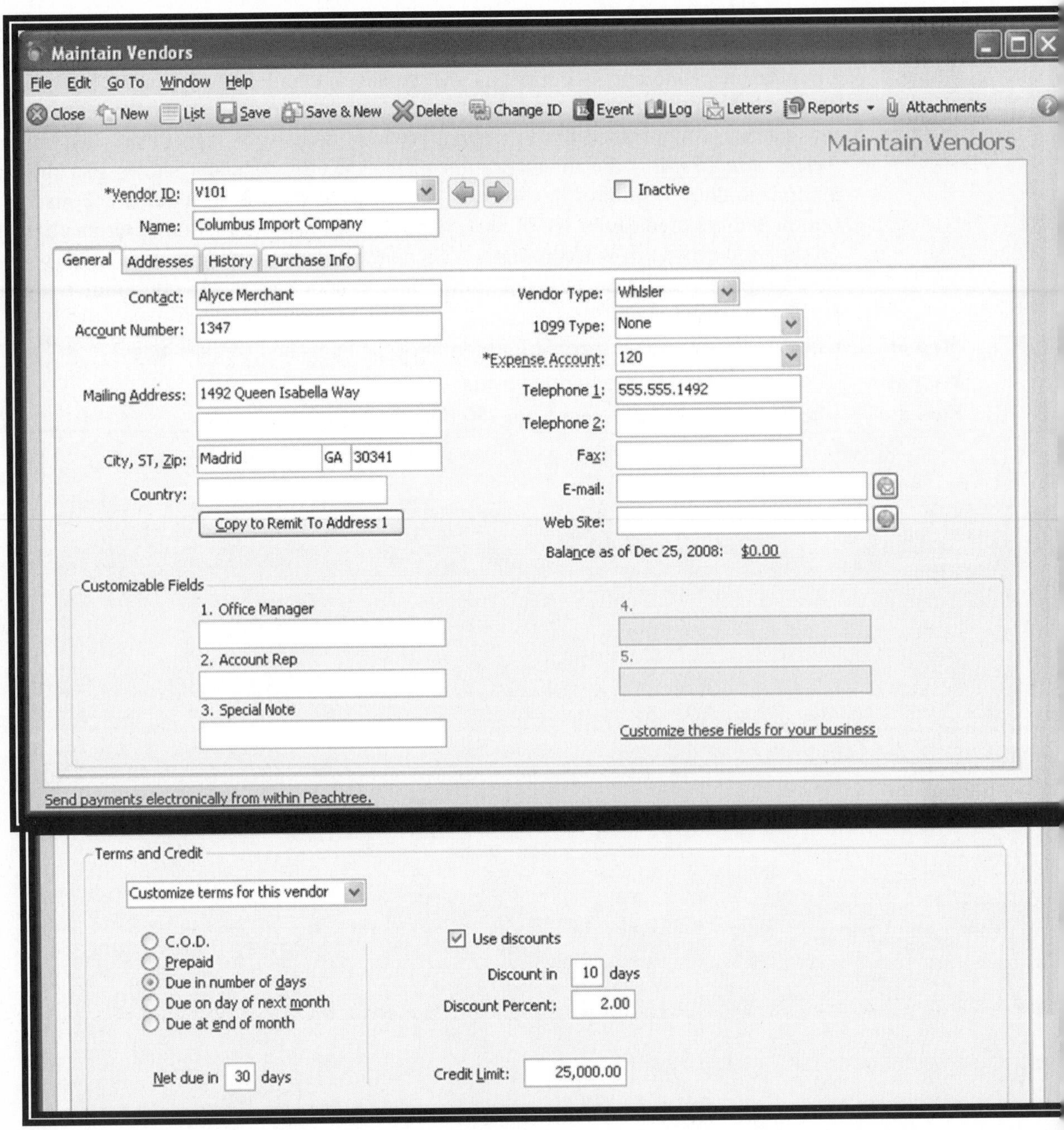

Figure 5. 4   The completed Maintain Vendors screen

Step 10:   Using the information in Table 5.1, enter the three additional vendors. Only the necessary information is given. Accept all the default values for each vendor.

Table 5. 1   Data for Vendors

Vendor ID	V102	V103	V104
Company	Southern Video	Atlanta Television	Ivory Group
Vendor Type	Whlsler	Whlsler	Whlsler
1099?	None	None	None
Expense Acct	120	120	120

Step 11:   Create one vendor for cash purchases. On the General tab place "Cash Vendor" in vendor ID, name, contact, and account number. Ensure that expense account is 120 – Merchandise Inventory. On the purchase info tab customize the terms to C.O.D. as shown in Figure 5. 5.

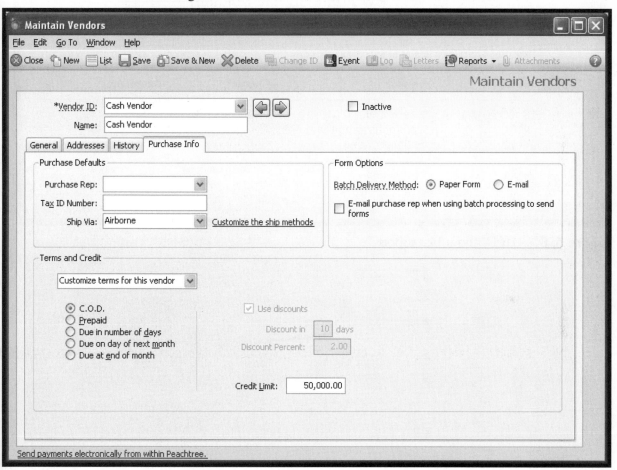

Figure 5. 5   The Purchase Info tab for Cash Vendor

Step 12:   When satisfied with your work, save it.

When finished entering the vendor's data of Table 5. 1 and the cash vendor, follow the path Reports & Forms > Accounts Payable > Vendor List to view the list of vendors in your file, as shown in Figure 5. 6. The vendor list report has additional fields as evident by the slide bar on the bottom of the screen.

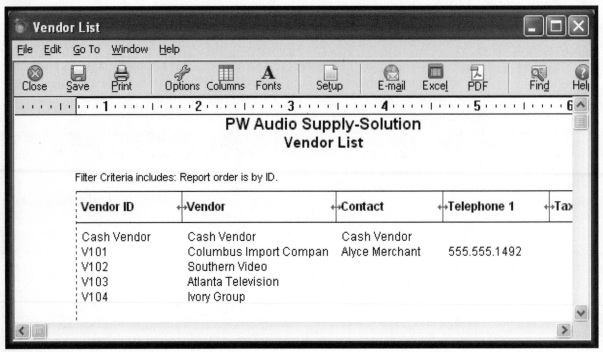

Figure 5. 6   The Vendor List report

INVENTORY DEFAULTS

There are defaults for inventory in a similar manner to those for vendors. Follow the path Maintain > Default Information > Inventory Items for the inventory item defaults screen shown in Figure 5. 7.

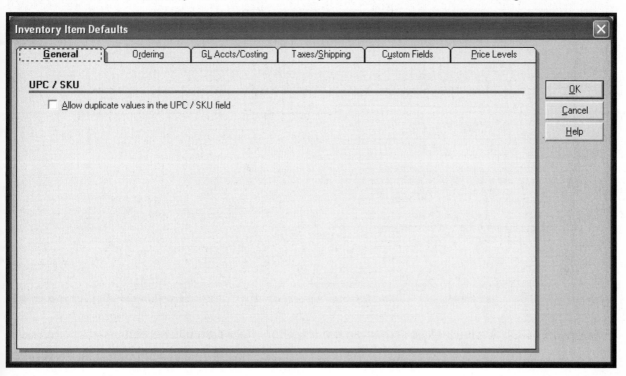

Figure 5. 7   The Inventory Item Defaults screen

There tabs for general, ordering, GL accounts/costing, taxes/shipping, custom fields, and price levels. The general tab has a single choice – Allow duplicate values in the UPC/SKU field. Ensure this is not checked and click into the "Ordering" tab.

The ordering tab has several choices that would be of interest to an operating business such as a warning option if the item is out of stock based on quantity on hand, which is a computer based quantity for both sales invoices and sales orders.

The inventory item defaults GL Accts/Costing tab must be set to save time and effort, Figure 5. 8.

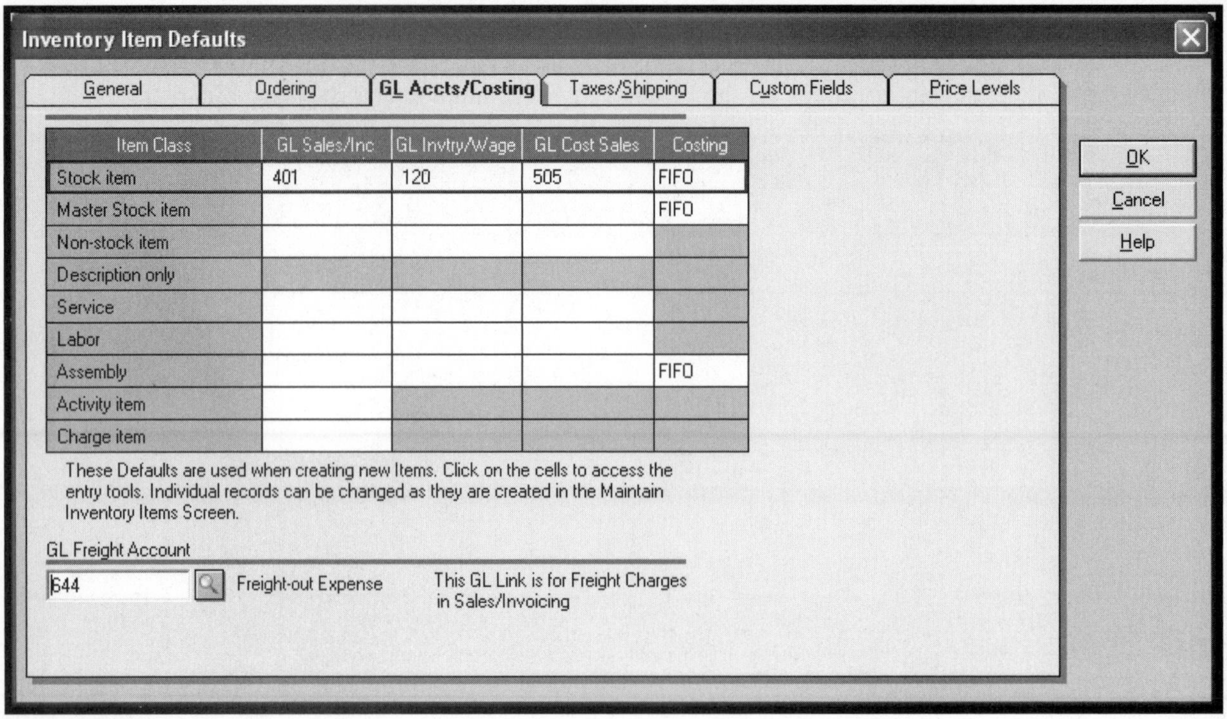

Figure 5. 8   GL Accts/Costing screen on the Inventory Item Defaults screen

By entering the 401 – Sales account in GL Sales/Income window, the 120 – Merchandise Inventory account in the GL Inventory/Wages window, and the 505 – Cost of Goods Sold account in the GL Cost Sales window. The Costing window is where, as a default value, you select your inventory costing concept – LIFO, FIFO, or average costing. This default selection does not curtail changes for specific items – the Apples, Bananas, Cantaloupes example earlier. Since most problems and small businesses use FIFO inventory valuation concepts, select FIFO from the drop-down menu before continuing. The last item is the GL Freight Account. *__As stated in the text to the right of this window, this is for freight charges on sales and sales invoices, not purchases.__* The chart of accounts has Account 644 – Freight-out Expense for this purpose.

The Taxes/Shipping tab controls tax and tax exempt purchases as well as shipping methods. The shipping methods are actually text fields. As an example, to change Cust. Pickup to Self Pickup simply click into the cell for Cust. Pickup and over type the information.

The Custom Fields tab allows you flexibility within Peachtree. If DVD-100 can be substituted with two DVD-50 packages, having a field enabled to document this will preserve that information. Remove the checkmarks from fields not utilized, such as Field 4 and 5 by default.

The Price Levels tab has some powerful capabilities. Frequently manufacturers, wholesalers, and some retailers will have preferred pricing for some customers. Click on the arrow below Edit on the Level 2 line. And Peachtree provides you with a Default Price Level Calculation dialog box, Figure 5. 9. Set the dialog box as shown in Figure 5. 9, Use last cost, increase by percent, 20%, and no rounding. Compare your work with Figure 5. 9, when satisfied click on "OK" to save the price level.

When satisfied with your entries on the inventory item default screen, click on "OK" to save your work.

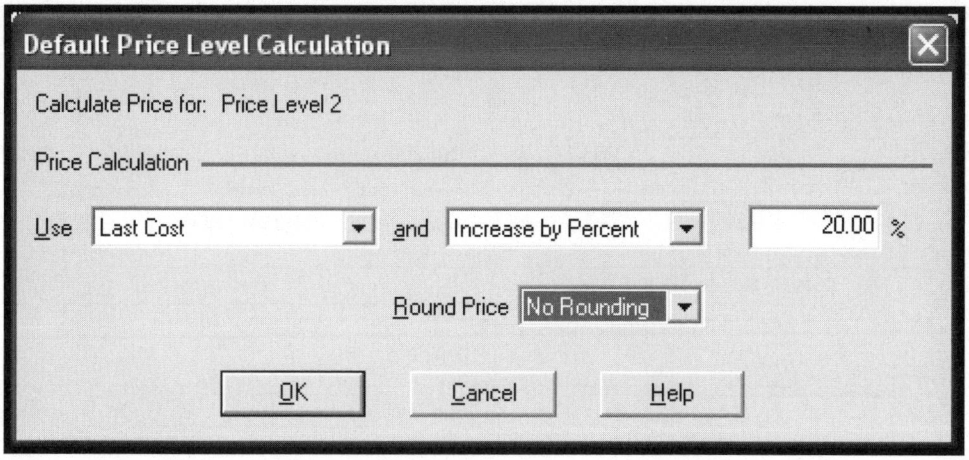

| Default Price Level Calculation | X |

Calculate Price for: Price Level 2

Price Calculation

Use [Last Cost ▼] and [Increase by Percent ▼]   20.00 %

Round Price [No Rounding ▼]

[OK]   [Cancel]   [Help]

Figure 5. 9   Default Price Level Calculation set for Price Level 2

ENTERING INVENTORY INFORMATION

PW Audio Supply sells several different electronic items such as: 19", 25", and 32" color televisions, DVD players, stereo VCRs, standard home stereo component units, surround sound entertainment units, computer monitors, 52" projection televisions, and 74" flat screen wall entertainment centers. They also sell furniture for the three smaller models of color televisions. Each of these inventory items will have a specific inventory identification number and each is sold to PW Audio Supply through the vendors entered earlier. All of these items are considered stock items, meaning that PW Audio Supply carries these items on a continuous basis.

Also notice that you are concerned here only with the sales price of an item and not the actual cost. You will concern yourself with cost when an actual purchase has been made. As you continue, each inventory item mentioned above must be documented in the system.

Step 1:   On the main menu bar, click on "Maintain," and then click "Inventory Items" on the drop-down menu. You will be presented with the screen as shown in Figure 5. 10 on the next page. Notice that several field such as GL Sales Account, GL Inventory Account, GL Cost of Goods Sold Account and Cost Method are already filled in – With data from your inventory item default screen completed earlier.

Figure 5. 10 Maintain Inventory Items screen

Step 2: The first item to be entered is the 19" Color TV. Enter TV19 as the Item ID. Ensure Item Class is Stock. Put 19" Color TV in both the description field immediately below the Item ID field and in the large description field on the General tab.

Step 3: In Peachtree, your items for retail may have ten different pricing levels. In the example you will use only one. The sales price for the 19" Color TV is $225. Enter 225 into the Price Level window. Remember Peachtree wants numbers without dollar signs or commas. Leave Last Unit Cost blank and ensure that Cost Method is FIFO. The default selection can be overridden here for specific items.

Step 4: Leave UPC/SKU, Item Type, and Location blank. Enter "Each" in the units of measurement window.

Step 5: Ensure that the default values of 401 – Sales is entered as the GL Sales Account, 120 – Merchandise Inventory is entered as the GL Inventory Account, and 505 – Cost of Goods Sold is entered as the GL Cost of Sales Account. Item Tax Type can be left at 1.

If this item had a preferred vender it could be entered on this screen.

Step 6: Leave Customs Fields and History tabs as they are.

Step 7: Check your work with Figure 5. 11. When satisfied click on "Save" on the task bar.

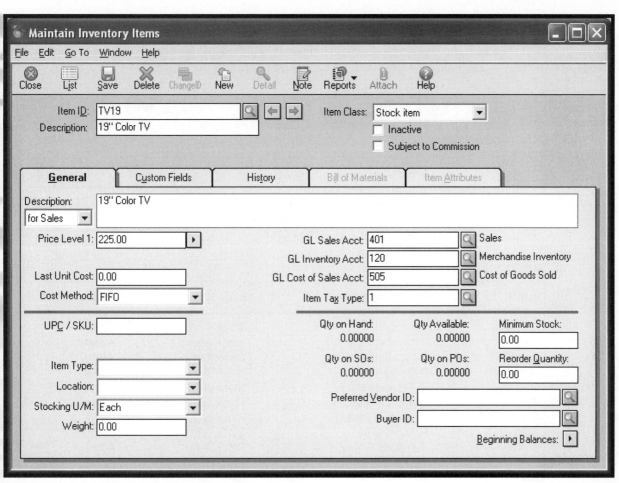

Figure 5. 11 Maintain Inventory Items screen

Step 8: Use Table 5.2 to continue entering inventory items. You have already completed the first entry. Both description fields contain the same data and the Stocking Unit of Measure is Each.

Table 5. 2 Inventory Items

Item ID and Description:	ID Number:	Price Level 1:	Accounts:
19" Color TV	TV19	$225	401, 120, 505
25" Color TV	TV25	$275	401, 120, 505
32" Color TV	TV32	$325	401, 120, 505
DVD Player	DV01	$199	401, 120, 505
Stereo VCR	VC23	$299	401, 120, 505
Home Stereo	ST61	$750	401, 120, 505
Surround Sound	SU85	$950	401, 120, 505
Computer Monitor	MO17	$345	401, 120, 505
Projection System	PROJ	$999	401, 120, 505
Flat Screen System	FLAT	$999	401, 120, 505
19" Cabinet	CAB19	$35	401, 120, 505
25" Cabinet	CAB25	$45	401, 120, 505
32" Cabinet	CAB32	$49	401, 120, 505

Step 8:   View the Item List from your file found in the Inventory Reports option under Reports and Form, Figure 5. 12. You can locate any inventory item by using the left and right green arrows to the right of the Item ID window. When corrections are made make sure you save the work before closing the screen.

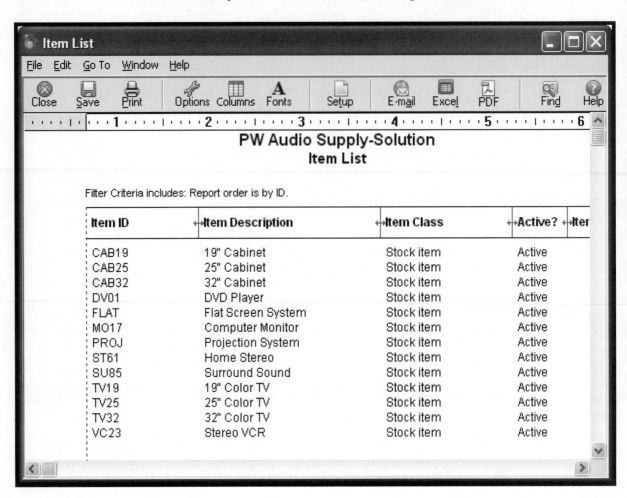

Figure 5. 12   Item List report

ACCOUNTS RECEIVABLE DEFAULTS

The use of defaults, when applicable, will greatly ease your workload within Peachtree. From the Menu Bar, follow the path Maintain > Default Information > Customers for the Customer Defaults screen shown in Figure 5. 13.

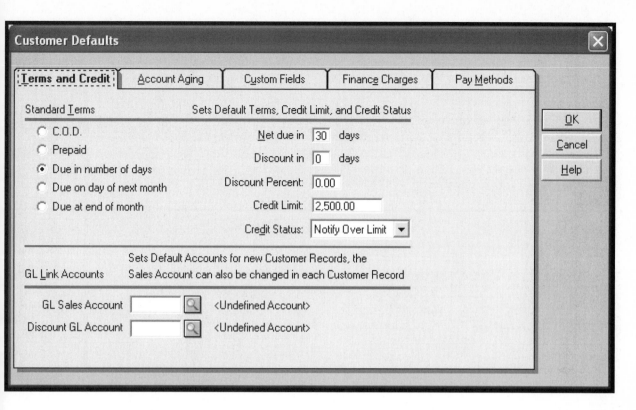

Figure 5. 13 Customer Defaults screen

Most retailers do not offer terms such as 2 percent discount if the invoice is paid within 10 days as a wholesaler might to a retailer. And most of the defaults are set conservatively to protect the seller.

Step 1:   Ensure or set the following values in the upper portion of the Terms and Credit tab. Due in number of days on the left side. On the right side set Net due in 30 days, Discount in 0 days, Discount Percent 0, Credit Limit $2,500, Credit Status: Notify Over Limit.

Step 2:   Set the GL Sales Account to 401 – Sales.

Step 3:   Set the Discount GL (General Ledger) account to 414 – Sales Discounts.

Step 4:   View the Account Aging, Custom Fields, Finance Charges, and Pay Methods tabs but do not make any changes on them.

Step 5:   Compare your work with Figure 5. 14 and make any necessary changes before clicking on "OK" to save the information.

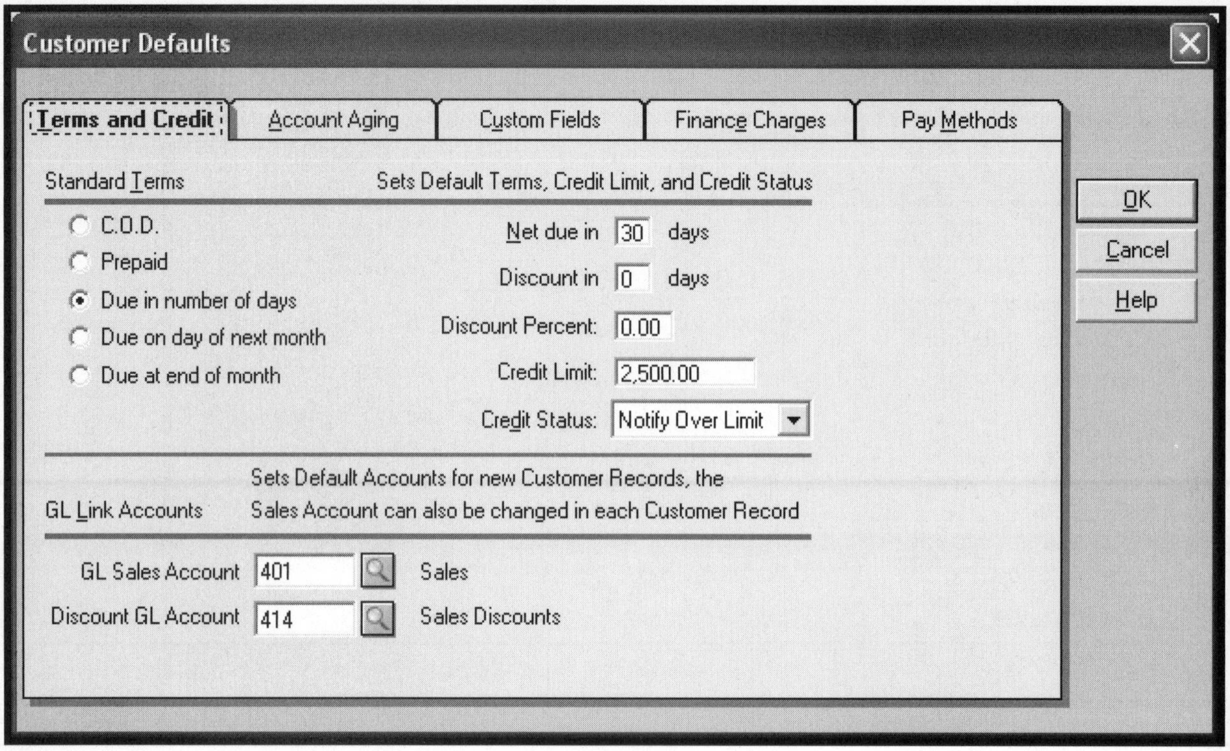

Figure 5. 14   Completed Customer Defaults screen

ENTERING CUSTOMER INFORMATION

A customer or client is someone who makes purchases of products and services from another person. Prospects are those that are considering making purchases but have not yet done so. Peachtree works with both to improve your business.

    With PW Audio Supply open within Peachtree Complete Accounting:

      Step 1:   Click on "Maintain" from the main menu bar and then click on "Customers/Prospects" from the drop-down menu. You should see the "Maintain Customers/Prospects" screen as shown in Figure 5. 15 below.

Figure 5. 15 Maintain Customers/Prospects screen

There are five tabs on this screen, General, Addresses, History, Sales Info, and Payment & Credit. You will fully set up one customer and other customers will be abbreviated.

Step 2:   Complete the General tab with the following information:

A: Enter the customer ID number. Your first customer's ID is C101.

B: Enter the customer's name in the Name box: Adam Zoula. The contact, in the next box, is the same as the customer, Adam Zoula.

C: The GL (General Ledger) account number 1001.

D: Enter Mr. Zoula's address in the proper boxes: 347 Appling Drive, Atlanta, GA 30300.

E: The Country and Sales Tax fields can be left blank.

F: Enter "Retail" in Customer Type. This is a text entry field.

G: Adam's phone number is 555.555.1742.

H: Telephone 2, Fax, E-mail, and Web Site can be left blank.

I: Set the Telephone 1 field to 555.555.1492. For Peachtree this is a text field – any format you desire – (555) 555-1492, 555-555-1492, is acceptable.

Step 3:   View the Addresses tab. Like vendors, a customer can have multiple addresses. The addresses can be used for billing, shipping, and contact information. The address inserted on the General tab is the default address here.

Step 4:   View the History tab. Peachtree will update this tab with purchases information as it occurs.

Step 5:   View the Sales Info tab. By setting Customer Defaults earlier the GL Sales Account should read 401 for the Sales account. If it does not, correct it with the drop-down arrow to the right of the field. The Ship Via options are controlled through Customer Defaults but are selectable here as customer defaults making the sales process simpler if the customer has a consistent delivery method. If the customer makes sales tax exempt purchases the Resale Certificate Number issued by the taxing authority can be recorded here. If the customer has a special pricing level, it can be selected here or applied at the time of the sale. As our economy moves to paper-reduced or paperless events, Peachtree offers Paper Form or E-mail for invoicing. Ensure Paper Form is selected.

Step 8:   View the Payment & Credit tab. The credit card address default is that which was entered on the General tab but can be overridden here. Click on the arrow to the right of the "Terms and Credit" window. Then click on "Customize terms for this customer." Change Adam's credit limit in the lower section of the right side to $3,000. See Figure 5.16.

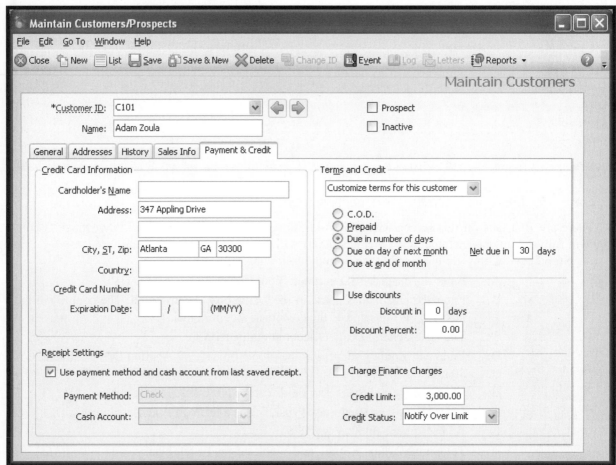

Figure 5. 16   Maintain Customers/Prospects screen in the Payments and Credit tab

Step 9:   Review your work with Figure 5. 16. Make changes as necessary and then click on "Save" on the task bar to save your work.

Step 10: Enter the data in Table 5. 3 into the Maintain Customers/Prospects screen saving each entry with default Payment & Credit terms.

Table 5. 3 Additional customers to be included on Customer list.

Customer ID	*C102*	*C103*	*C104*
Name and Contact	Betty Young	Cathy Xao	Donald Walace
Account Number	1002	1003	1004
Address	987 Amigos Dr.	513 Lake Cir.	1397 Toyta Dr.
	Atlanta, GA 30300	Atlanta, GA 30340	Atlanta, GA 30302

Step 11: The last customer to be set up will be a cash customer. Enter Cash Customer into the Customer ID, Name, Contact, and Account Number fields on the General tab. On the Payments & Credit tab customize the Terms and Credit to C.O.D. and save the record. Compare your work with Figure 5. 17.

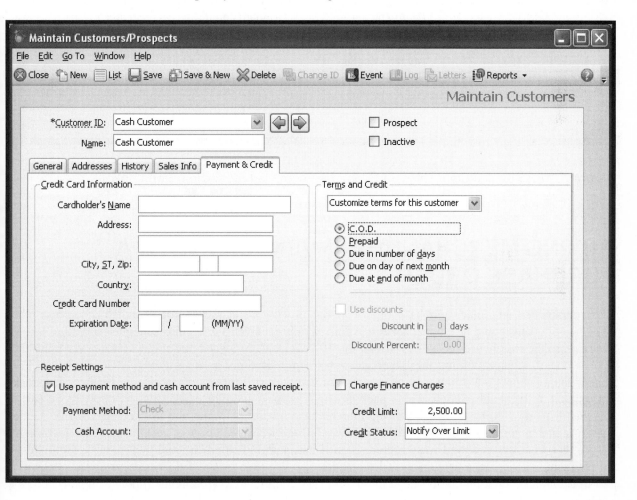

Figure 5. 17 Cash Customer set up

Step 12: View the Customer List under Accounts Receivable reports option. Compare your work with Figure 5. 18. There is more information than shown, simply insure that you have customers C101 through C104 and Cash Customer. Make any necessary corrections.

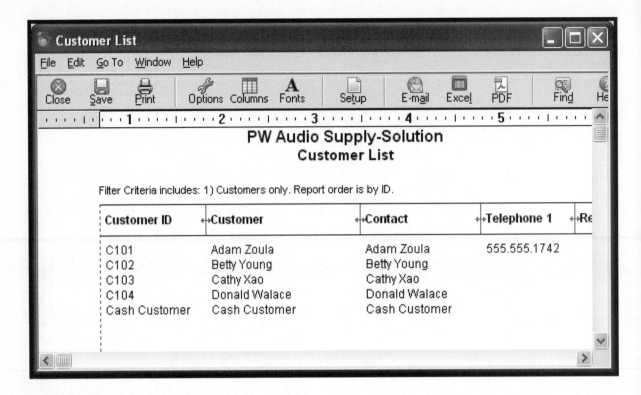

Figure 5. 18   The customer list report from the accounts receivable reports options

BUYING MERCHANDISE INVENTORY WITH A PURCHASE ORDER

Most companies will place purchase orders in the process of acquiring merchandise inventory. The sequence of events could be a buyer for PW Audio Supply received a computer generated notice or verbal notice from the warehouse or sales floor that the 19" cabinets are low or out of stock. After verifying the low or out of stock condition, the buyer generates a purchase order and forwards it to a vendor. The vendor manufactures the cabinet, purchases it from a vendor (manufacturer) or removes it from his stock and ships it to PW Audio Supply with a packing slip and mails an invoice. PW Audio Supply receives the merchandise and records the receipt of the merchandise inventory. When the invoice arrives PW Audio Supply matches the purchase order, the packing slip, the documentation of receipt, and the invoice to ensure that what was received was ordered, even if it is a partial shipment, and then records the liability for payment in accordance with an agreed schedule.

In accordance with that sequence, a purchase order is initiated to Columbus Import Company for 19" cabinets.

Step 1:   Follow the path Tasks > Purchase Orders to open the purchase orders screen shown in Figure 5. 19.

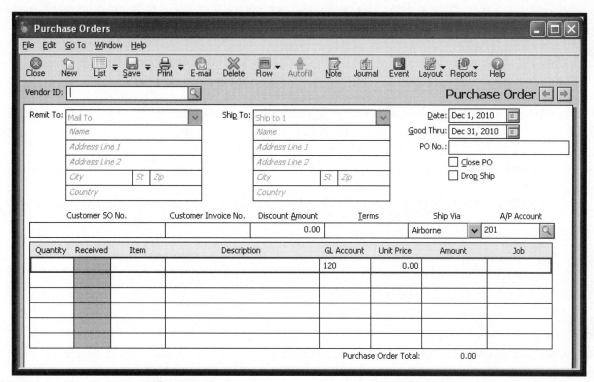

Figure 5. 19   Purchase/Receive Inventory screen for PW Audio Supply

Step 2:   Enter the Vendor ID of V101 or click on the "V101" option from the drop-down menu options associated with the window. Peachtree will insert the information in the Maintain Vendor database into screen. One of the options in Maintain Vendors is to insert multiple addresses for a vendor. On the left side of the main window of this screen there is a "Remit To" box. If this vendor had multiple addresses using the drop-down menu option available for this field would allow you to select any of the addresses in your database.

Step 3:   In the Ship To field in the center of the window you could select any of the multiple addresses you could have setup for PW Audio Supply.

Step 4:   Ensure that the date is December 1, 2010, and change the Good Thru date to December 10, 2010. You can do this by clicking on the Calendar icon to the right of the Good Thru field or clicking into the Good Thru field and pressing the + (plus) or − (minus) keys until the correct date is shown. Then tabbing out of the box, or pressing Enter to accept the value and advance out of the field. Peachtree may advance you out of the field when you select a date from the calendar dialog box.

Step 5:   Utilize 2010-12-01A for the PO No. (Purchase Order Number).

Step 6:   Ensure that the Terms field contains 2% 10, Net 30 Days, the default terms for Columbus.

Step 7:   Utilizing the drop-down options associated with the Ship Via field, select Hand Deliver, Columbus will deliver this purchase on their own truck.

Step 8:   Ensure the A/P Account is 201. If not utilize the drop-down menu option to select this account. Peachtree knows that 201 − Accounts Payable consists of subsidiary accounts and will place this purchase to Columbus Import Company when appropriate.

Step 9: The 19" cabinets must be purchased in a quantity of 12, a vendor constraint, its item identification is CAB19. When you enter the Item field a drop-down menu magnifying glass will appear allowing you to select any of the items you set up in the Inventory database.

Step 10: Ensure that 19" Cabinet appears in the description window and that the GL (General Ledger) account for these items is 120 – Merchandise Inventory.

Step 11: The sales representative quotes $25.47 as the Unit Price and when this value is entered into its window Peachtree extends the value of (12 units at $25.47 each) $305.64 into the Amount window. Peachtree also sums the Purchase Order Total as of this point to $305.64 near the bottom of the screen.

Step 12: Compare your work with Figure 5. 20 before using Save on the menu bar to save it.

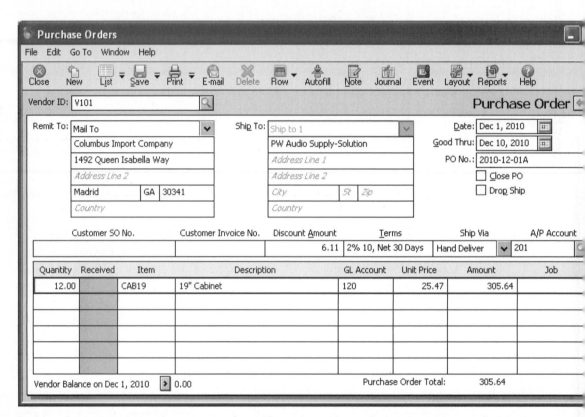

Figure 5. 20 Completed purchase order for 19" cabinets from Columbus Import Company

If you view the income statement and balance sheet at this point you will not see any information related to this purchase order. Unless there are special terms you owe Columbus Import Company nothing until you receive the merchandise. If you view the Purchase Order Report under the Accounts Payable option of Reports & Forms you will see PO No. 2010-12-01A shown for the 19" cabinets.

RECEIVING MERCHANDISE PURCHASED WITH A PURCHASE ORDER

When the twelve 19" cabinets ordered from Columbus Import Company are received on December 7, 2010, the Purchase/Receive Inventory screen found under Tasks of the menu bar is used.

Step 1:   Select or enter V101 for Columbus Import Company into the Vendor ID window.

Step 2:   Select V101 – Columbus Import Company from the drop-down menu options associated with the Vendor ID window. Because this vendor has address information in the database, that information is automatically filled in on the screen.

Note: Peachtree will complete much of the screen for you with the information in the vendor database entered earlier.

Step 3:   Set the date to December 7, 2010.

Step 4:   Set the Invoice No. to 2010-12-06B.

Step 5:   Place a checkmark by clicking into the selection window to the left of Waiting on Bill.

Step 6:   From the drop-down menu options associated with the Apply to Purchase Order No. window, select 2010-12-01A. Peachtree will complete the fields with the appropriate information.

Step 7:   Verify that the purchase order is for twelve CAB19, 19" Cabinets.

Step 8:   Enter "12" in the Received window and Peachtree will extend (12 units × $25.47 per unit) the amount of $305.64 into the Amount window.

Step 9:   Compare your work with Figure 5. 21 and make any necessary correction before using Save on the task bar to save your work.

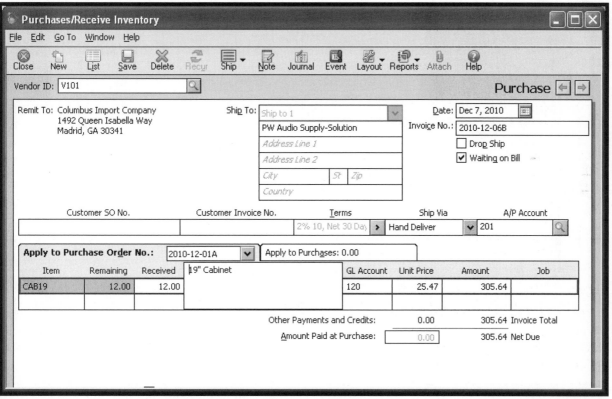

Figure 5. 21   Completed Purchases/Receive Inventory screen for Columbus Import Company

A review of your financial statements now will show that you have inventory and liabilities due to the receipt of this merchandise. However, viewing Accounts Payable Aging will not show this obligation since you are waiting on the invoice.

Note: Packing slips normal only depict items on the purchase order or sales order and the quantities of those items shipped or on back order. The value of those items is not usually depicted.

ENTERING BILLS FROM VENDORS

On December 8, 2010, you receive the invoice for Purchase Order 2010-12-01A in the mail. When you compare it to 1) the Purchase Order, 2) the Packing Slip, and 3) the Receiving Report, all are in agreement that you received what you ordered. To enter the bill into Peachtree:

Step 1:   Follow the path Tasks > Purchase/Receive Inventory from the menu bar to bring up the Purchases/Receive Inventory screen. You can also follow the path Tasks > Bills > Enter Bills.

Step 2:   Select or enter V101 – Columbus Import Company in the Vendor ID window.

Step 3:   Set the date to December 8, 2010.

Step 4:   Enter the Invoice No. of 2010-12-6B.

Step 5:   From the drop-down menu options associated with the Apply to Purchase Order No. window, select Purchase Order 2010-12-01A. And Peachtree will fill in the appropriate windows with the stored data.

Step 6:   The invoice shows that special seasonal pricing has been applied to the purchase. Change the Amount window to $279.75. Peachtree will calculate a Unit Price and display $23.31 in this field.

Step 7:   Compare your work with Figure 5. 22 and make any necessary corrections before using Save on the task bar to save your work.

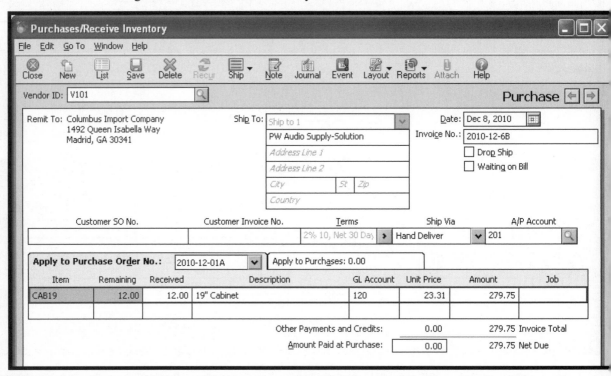

Figure 5. 21   Completed Enter Bill / Purchases/Receive Inventory screen for Invoice 2010-12-6B

Viewing the financials and accounts payable aging now shows this obligation.

PURCHASING AND RECEIVING INVENTORY – ACCOUNTS PAYABLE

Peachtree will also allow you to purchase inventory on account and receive inventory in the same step. And while this action will allow you to "wait for a bill" as shown in the using a purchase order chain of events, this section will assume that you have received an invoice at the time of receipt.

Step 1: Follow the path Tasks > Purchases/Receive Inventory from the menu bar.

Step 2: Select or enter V102 in the Vendor ID window for Southern Video.

Step 3: Set the date to December 2, 2010, and set the Invoice No. to 2010-12-2A.

Step 4: Set the Quantity to 6, the Item to DV01 – DVD Player, ensure the GL (General Ledger) account is 120 – Merchandise Inventory, and set the unit price to $101.45.

Peachtree will extend the value (6 units × $101.45) of $608.70 into the amount column. If given a quantity and a unit price Peachtree will determine the amount. If given a quantity and an amount, Peachtree will determine the Unit Price.

Step 5: Compare your work with Figure 5. 22 before using "Save" on the task bar to save your work.

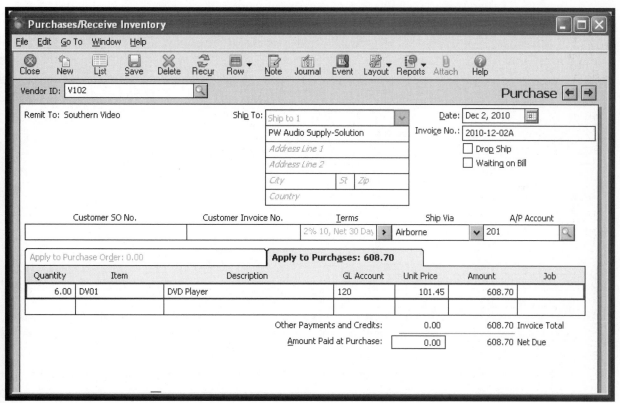

Figure 5. 22 Completed Purchases/Receive Inventory screen for Southern Video

If you view the financial, accounts payable and inventory reports at this point you will see that this action, since you are not waiting on a bill, has affected assets (inventory) and liabilities (accounts payable) and is shown as available inventory since his has been received.

PURCHASING AND RECEIVING INVENTORY – CASH

Peachtree will also allow you to purchase inventory for cash and receive inventory in the same step. To do this:

Step 1:   Follow the path Tasks > Payments from the menu bar.

Step 2:   Enter "Cash Vendor" in the Vendor ID window or select if from the drop-down menu options.

Note: For one-time purchases you can leave the Vendor ID window empty and enter a name into the first line **_UNDER_** the Pay to the Order of window.

Step 3:   Set the check number to 101 and the date to December 3, 2010.

Step 4:   Ensure that the cash account is set to the desired account – 101 – Cash, in this case.

Step 5:   Enter 6 as the quantity and set the Item field to VC23. Peachtree will auto fill description from the inventory database information you entered earlier.

Step 6:   Ensure that the GL (General Ledger) account is set to 120 – Merchandise Inventory.

Step 7:   Set the unit price to $185. Peachtree will extend it into the amount window.

Step 8:   Compare your work with Figure 5. 23 and make any necessary adjustments before using "Save" on the task bar to save your work.

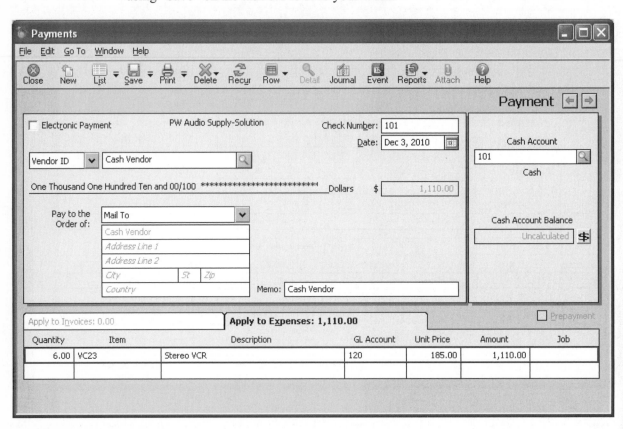

Figure 5. 23   The completed payments screen for the cash vendor

VENDOR CREDIT MEMOS

When a product that has been received is returned to the vendor for some reason vendor credit memos are utilized. Peachtree will automatically deduct the returned value from the accounts payable balance. Suppose that one of the cabinets received from Columbus Import Company is being returned due to damage.

Step 1: Follow the path Tasks > Vendor Credit Memos from the menu bar to open the Vendor Credit Menu screen.

Step 2: Select or enter V101 – Columbus Import Company as the vendor in the Vendor ID window.

Step 3: Set the date to December 9, 2010, and Credit No. to 2010-12-9A.

Step 4: Enter 2010-12-9A in the Return Authorization window.

Step 5: Select Invoice 2010-12-6B from the drop-down options associated with the Apply to Invoice No. window. Peachtree will fill in the appropriate fields from the invoice.

Step 6: Enter the quantity of 1 in the Returned window. Peachtree will extend the value to Amount window.

Step 7: Compare your work with Figure 5. 24 and make any necessary changes before using Save on the menu bar to save your work. Peachtree will update the accounts payable information, inventory quantities, and inventory valuations

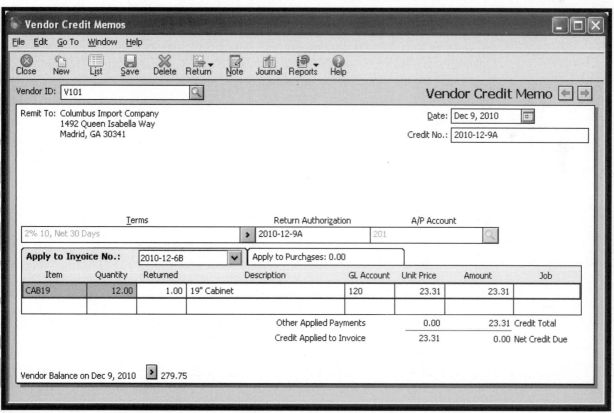

Figure 5. 24 Completed vendor credit memo for Columbus Import Company

If you view the assets – inventory, you will see that Peachtree has adjusted inventory quantities based on this credit memo. It has also adjusted liabilities – accounts payable.

SELLING AND DELIVERING INVENTORY – ACCOUNTS RECEIVABLE

With vendors and inventory set up you can purchase inventory. Now you will sell inventory on account – Accounts Receivable. Much of the options have been set through the default values and as shown earlier, many of these values can be overridden at the time of the event or for a specific customer.

To sell merchandise on account:

Step 1: Follow the path Tasks > Sales/Invoicing from the menu bar to open the Sales/Invoicing screen.

Step 2: Enter C101 or select C101 – Adam Zoula from the drop-down options associated with the Customer ID window.

Note: Peachtree will auto fill much of the customer information into the screen. If the customer has more than one address you can select the appropriate address from the drop-down menu associated with the Ship to window near the center, top of the screen.

Step 3: Set the date to December 10, 2010, and the Invoice No. to 2010-12-10A.

Step 4: Using the drop-down options associated with the Ship Via window select Customer Pickup (Cust. Pickup).

Step 5: On the first Apply to Sales line set the quantity to "1".

Step 6: And Peachtree helps with this one immensely – When you tab or click into the "Item" window, Peachtree displays a magnifying glass to the right side of the window. Click on it to see the items available in inventory, Figure 5. 25. Notice that not only is the Item ID and description, from the Inventory database, shown but Quantities available are shown. Select CAB19 – 19" Cabinet for the first item. And Peachtree puts the default information into the remaining fields of the line.

Step 7: With a quantity of one, select VC23 – Stereo VCR in line two and change its Unit Price to $285.

Step 8: Your Sales/Invoicing screen should have an Invoice Total of $320.00. Check your work and make any necessary adjustments before using "Save" on the task bar to save your work.

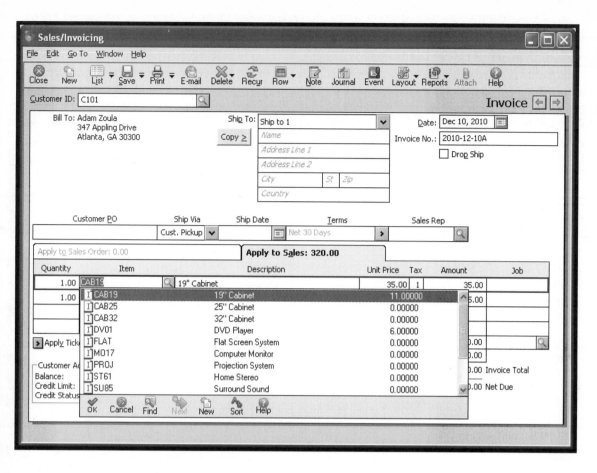

Figure 5. 25   Sales invoicing screen for Adam Zoula's sale

View your financial and accounts receivable reports and you will see that sales and cost of goods sold have been recorded based on this Sales/Invoicing events. Note that accounts receivable and capital (Net income on the balance sheet) have increased and that inventory has decreased.

If you review your inventory reports you will see how this event affected inventory.

SELLING AND DELIVERING INVENTORY – CASH

Now that you can make sales on account, time to handle the customer who walks into the store with cash.

To sell merchandise for cash:

Step 1:   Follow the path Tasks > Receipts from the menu bar to open the receipts screen.

Step 2:   Enter 101212A in the deposit ticket ID window. This is a size constrained field.

Step 3:   Enter or select "Cash Customer" from the drop-down menu options associated with the Customer ID window.

Step 4:   Enter 2010-12-12A in the reference and receipt number windows.

Step 5:   Set the date to December 12, 2010.

Step 6:   From the drop-down menu options associated with Payment Method select Cash.

Step 7:   Ensure that Cash is set as the cash account

Step 8:   In the first line of the Apply to Revenues area, set the quantity to "1", select DV01 – DVD Player as the item and accept the default Unit Price from the Inventory database, $199.

Step 9:   Check your work with Figure 5. 26 and make any corrections necessary before using Save on the task bar to save your work.

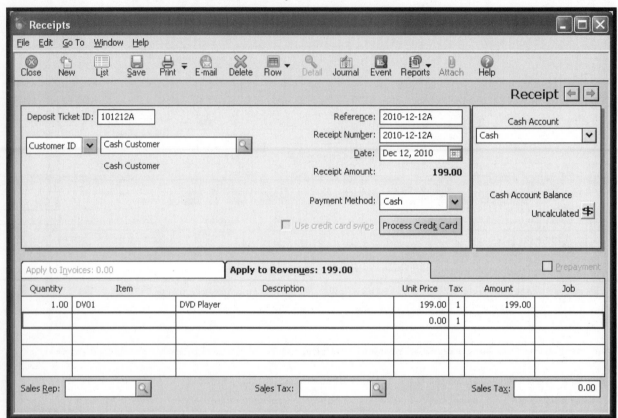

Figure 5. 26   Completed receipts screen for a cash sale

View the financial and managerial reports as this point and you will see the increase in cash and owner's equity – capital as net income and a decrease in inventory on the balance sheet.

You will see an increase in sales, cost of goods sold, and net income on the income statement. Reports such as the Cost of Goods Sold Journal and the Inventory Profitability Report will show the affects of this sale.

REFUNDING A SALE ON ACCOUNTS RECEIVABLE

Refunds on accounts receivable are "reversed" – debited to Inventory and Sales and credited to Accounts Receivable and Cost of Goods sold. Supposed that Adam Zoula would like to return the 19" Cabinet purchased on December 10, 2010, on December 14, 2010.

To accomplish this:

Step 1:   Follow the path Tasks > Credit Memos from the menu bar to open the Credit Memo screen.

Step 2: Select C101 – Adam Zoula in the Customer ID window. Peachtree will auto fill much of the rest of the screen.

Step 3: Set the date to December 14, 2010, and the Credit No. to 2010-12-14A.

Step 4: On the Apply to Invoice No. tab select Invoice No. 2010-12-10A from the options associated with the drop-down options.

Step 5: Enter the quantity of "1" in the Return window of the CAB19, 19" Cabinet line of the presented invoice. Peachtree will extend the value to the Amount field.

Step 6: Compare your work with Figure 5. 27 and make any necessary adjustments before using the Save icon in the task bar to save your work.

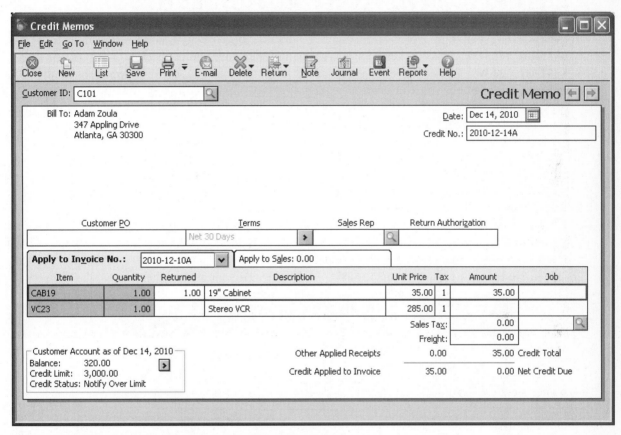

Figure 5. 27 Credit memo screen for Adam Zoula's return

Peachtree will debit the return directly to sales and inventory and credit it to accounts receivable (Adam Zoula) and cost of goods sold. You can review financial and managerial reports to see the impact of this return.

Note: If you are providing the customer a sales allowance – a discounted purchase price rather than bringing the item back, remove the quantity from Returned and the value from Unit Price from the line and enter the Sales Allowance value in the Amount window. Ensure that Peachtree does not "back fill" either the Returned quantity or the Unit Price as these actions may result in units being returned to inventory that are not actually returned.

REFUNDING A SALE ON CASH

When refunds are given to a cash customer the Payments screen, accessed through the path Tasks > Payments can be utilized. This will allow inventory to be returned by Item ID. If an allowance is given the same screen can be utilized without identifying the item. In this case the GL (General Ledger) account needs to be changed to 412 – Sales Returns and Allowances.

ENTERING INVENTORY ADJUSTMENTS

Occasionally, you may need to record adjustments to on-hand quantities of inventory items. The inventory adjustment task makes it easy to make and track these adjustments.

There are two types of inventory adjustments, increases in quantity and decreases in quantity. For an increasing adjustment you will enter a positive quantity and can also enter a unit cost. This will increase your quantity on hand and total inventory value much as a purchase would. If you previously miscounted your inventory and now have more units on hand than recorded you would adjust up.

For a decreasing adjustment you will enter a negative quantity. You cannot enter a unit cost. Peachtree will compute the cost value that these units are being removed in the same manner as a sale, LIFO, FIFO, or Average Cost. A decreasing inventory adjustment will decrease the quantity on hand as well as the total value. For example, if something was stolen or broken, or, if inventory was previously over stated, you would adjust down.

When you make an adjustment, the Cost of Goods Sold, Inventory Total Value, and Inventory G/L accounts are all updated. Assume that the 19" Cabinet, returned by Adam Zoula on December 14, 2010, is determined to be valueless and is not returnable to the vendor. To record this inventory adjustment:

Step 1: Follow the path Tasks > Inventory Adjustments and Peachtree displays the inventory adjustment screen as shown in Figure 5. 28.

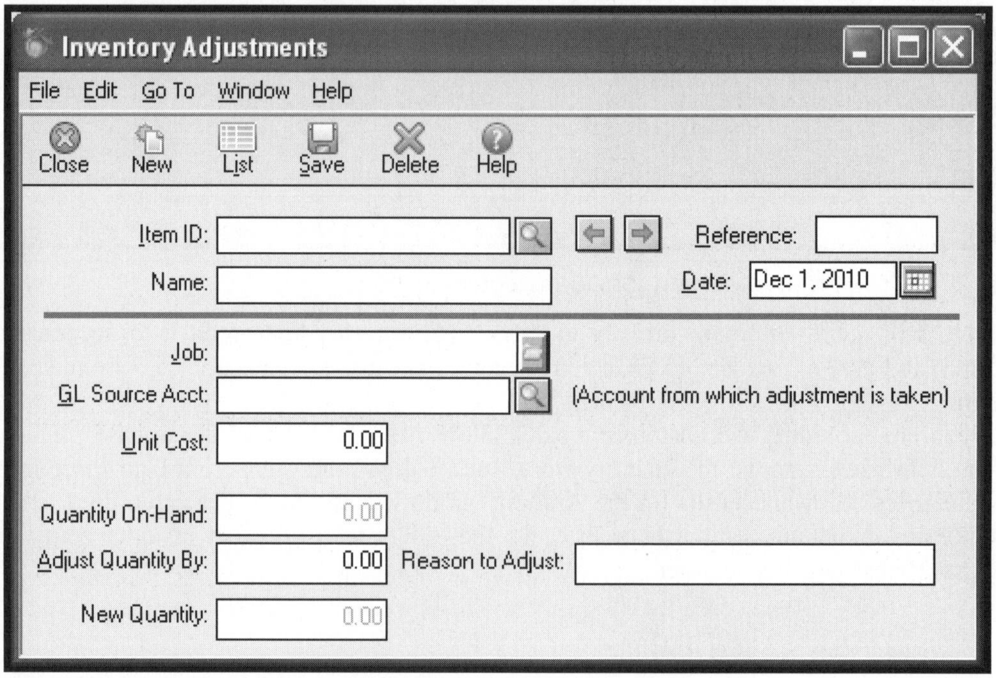

Figure 5. 28   Inventory Adjustments form

Step 2: Enter or select the Item ID, CAB19, 19" Cabinet, in the Item ID window. Peachtree will auto fill the screen for the item. To display a list of existing items, type any character into the field, or click on the magnifying glass to the right of the Item ID window.

Step 3: The reference field is limited to 20 alphanumeric characters. Since this cabinet was returned on a customer credit memo, use that memo, 2010-12-14A, as the reference.

Step 4: Enter the date that the damage or loss was discovered – December 15, 2010, in this example.

Step 5: The GL Source Account should be the Cost of Goods Sold Account. The other account affected by adjustments will be the Merchandise Inventory account.

Step 6: The Unit Cost default is the current cost of the item and no adjustment is necessary.

Step 7: Enter the amount by which to adjust the quantity. The Quantity on Hand is already filled in, and Peachtree calculates the New Quantity after you enter the adjustment.

Step 8: If you know the reason for the adjustment, for example, "Found damage on inspection" or "Theft", you can enter it. Save the adjustment by selecting the appropriate button.

Step 9: Compare your work with Figure 5. 29 and make any appropriate adjustments before using Save on the task bar to save your work.

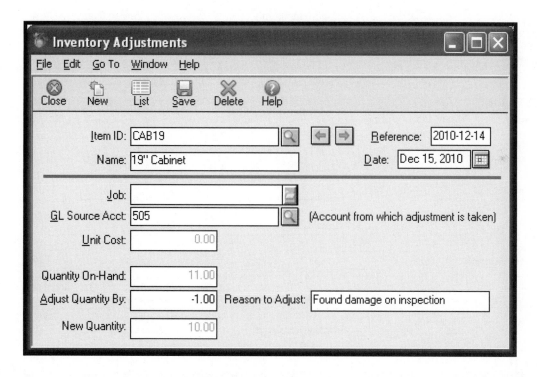

Figure 5. 29 Completed inventory adjustments screen

Viewing the financial and managerial reports will show expenses – 505 – Cost of Goods Sold, has increased and assets – 120 – Inventory and owner's equity – capital, has decreased accordingly.

MULTIPLE-STEP INCOME STATEMENT

The multiple-step income statement is so named because it shows the steps in determining net income (or net loss). Two steps are shown, (1) Cost of sales are subtracted from total revenues and results in gross profit, and (2) operating expenses are deducted from the gross profit and results in net income (or net loss).

The multiple-step income statement for the data entered in this chapter is shown on Figure 5. 30.

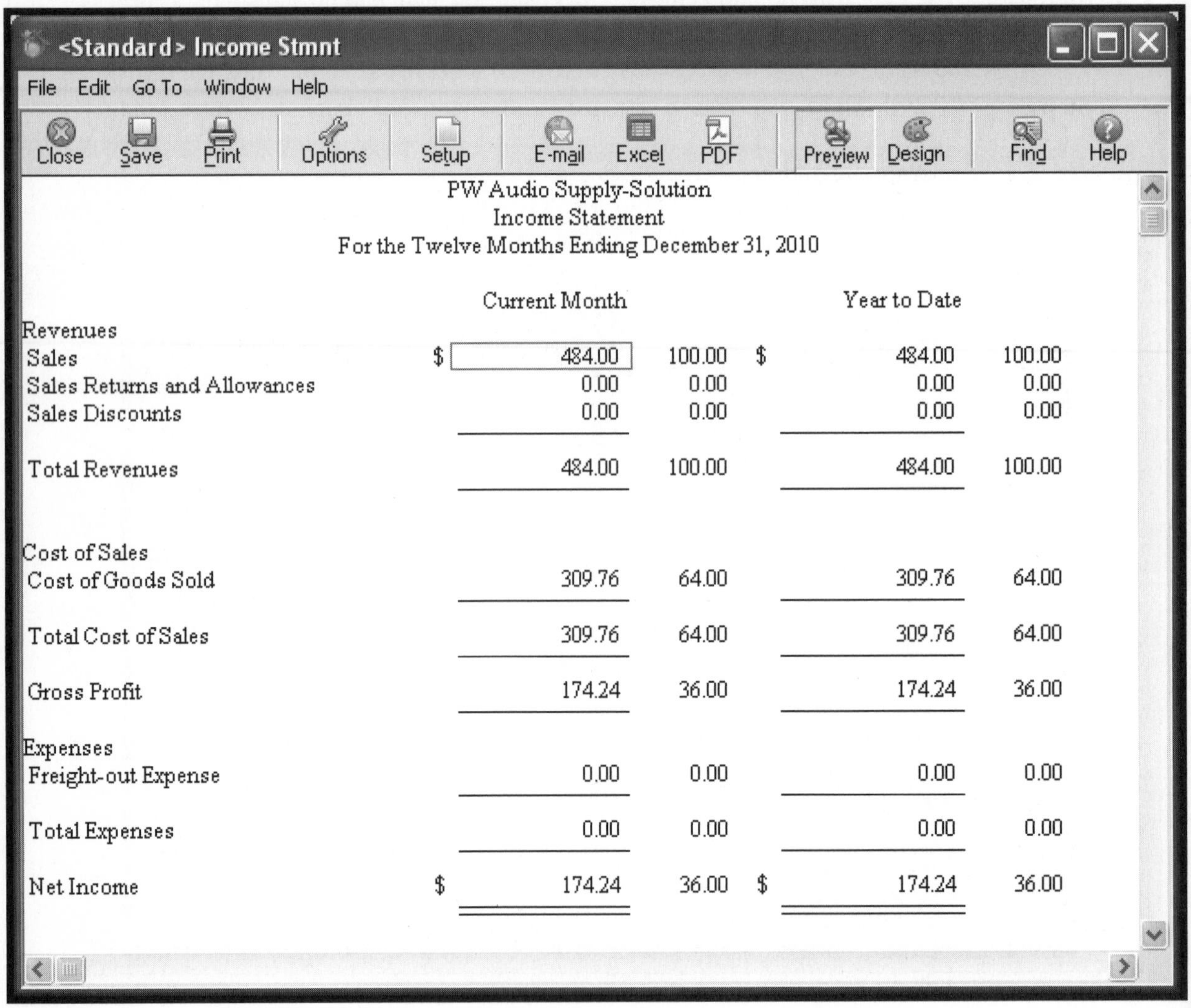

Figure 5. 30 Top portion of income statement showing sales and cost of sales

Comprehensive Do It! Problem, Falcetto Company, Directory
Wey_AP9e_Falcetto_Co_Ch05

The adjusted trial balance columns of Falcetto Company's worksheet for the year ended December 31, 2010, are as follows.

Debit Credit			
Cash	$ 14,500	Accumulated Depreciation	$ 18,000
Accounts Receivable	11,100	Notes Payable	25,000
Merchandise Inventory	29,000	Accounts Payable	10,600
Prepaid Insurance	2,500	Larry Falcetto, Capital	81,000
Store Equipment	95,000	Sales	536,800
Larry Falcetto, Drawing	12,000	Interest Revenue	2,500
Sales Returns and Allowances	6,700		$ 673,900
Sales Discounts	5,000		
Cost of Goods Sold	363,400		
Freight-out	7,600		
Advertising Expense	12,000		
Salaries Expense	56,000		
Utilities Expense	18,000		
Rent Expense	24,000		
Depreciation Expense	9,000		
Insurance Expense	4,500		
Interest Expense	3,600		
	$ 673,900		

Instructions:
Prepare a multiple-step income statement for Falcetto Company. Ensure that the date range is set for the year ended December 31, 2010, through "Options" on the task bar of the income statement report.

Solution to Comprehensive Do It! Problem

<Standard> Income Stmnt   _ □ ×

File   Edit   Go To   Window   Help

Close   Save   Print   Options   Setup   E-mail   Excel   PDF   Preview   Design   Find   Help

Falcetto Company, Chapter 5
Income Statement
For the Twelve Months Ending December 31, 2010

	Current Month			Year to Date	
Revenues					
Sales	$ 536,800.00	101.74	$	536,800.00	101.74
Interest Revenue	2,500.00	0.47		2,500.00	0.47
Sales Returns and Allowances	(6,700.00)	(1.27)		(6,700.00)	(1.27)
Sales Discounts	(5,000.00)	(0.95)		(5,000.00)	(0.95)
Total Revenues	527,600.00	100.00		527,600.00	100.00
Cost of Sales					
Cost of Goods Sold	363,400.00	68.88		363,400.00	68.88
Total Cost of Sales	363,400.00	68.88		363,400.00	68.88
Gross Profit	164,200.00	31.12		164,200.00	31.12
Expenses					
Advertising Expense	12,000.00	2.27		12,000.00	2.27
Depreciation Expense	9,000.00	1.71		9,000.00	1.71
Freight-out Expense	7,600.00	1.44		7,600.00	1.44
Interest Expense	3,600.00	0.68		3,600.00	0.68
Insurance Expense	4,500.00	0.85		4,500.00	0.85
Rent Expense	24,000.00	4.55		24,000.00	4.55
Store Salaries Expense	56,000.00	10.61		56,000.00	10.61
Utilities Expense	18,000.00	3.41		18,000.00	3.41
Total Expenses	134,700.00	25.53		134,700.00	25.53
Net Income	$ 29,500.00	5.59	$	29,500.00	5.59

Note: Peachtree places all revenues accounts at the top of the report and all expense accounts in a single block rather than moving other revenues and gains and other expenses and losses at the bottom of the report.

P5-2A, Olaf Distributing Company, Directory
Wey_AP9e_P5_2A_Olaf_Distributing_Co

Olaf Distributing Company completed the following merchandising transactions in the month of April. At the beginning of April, the ledger of Olaf showed Cash of $9,000 and M. Olaf, Capital of $9,000.

April 2	Purchased 6,900 Toy Trains for $1.00 each on account from Dakota Supply Co., terms 1/10, n/30. Record this action using the Purchases/Receive Inventory screen and Invoice No. 2010-04-02A.
April 4	Sold 4,100 Toy Trains to Train City Models on account for $5,500, FOB destination, terms 1/10, n/30. The cost of the merchandise sold was $4,100. (*Hint:* Leave the Unit Price field blank and insert "5500" in the Amount field and Peachtree will calculate the unit cost of $1.34146 ... automatically and show and insert $1.34 into the Unit Price field.) Record this action using the Sales/Invoicing screen and Invoice No. 2010-04-04A.
April 5	Utilize the write checks screen under Tasks and Check No. 101 to pay Truck'n Transfer Co. $240 for freight on April 4 sale. Ensure Expense Account is set to 644 – Freight-out Expense.
April 6	Received credit from Dakota Supply Co. for merchandise returned $500. Utilize Vendor Credit Memos under Tasks and Credit No. 2010-04-06A. Apply to Invoice No. 2010-04-02A for a quantity of 500 Toy Trains.
April 11	Paid Dakota Supply Co. in full, less discount. Utilize the Payments screen under Tasks, set the check number to 102 and ensure that the appropriate discount is applied with 120 – Merchandise Inventory set as the Discount Account.
April 13	Received collections in full, less discounts, from Train City Models billed on April 4. Utilize the receipts screen under Tasks with 20100413 as deposit ticket ID and 2010-04-13A as reference and receipt number . Ensure receipt is applied to the proper invoice and that the appropriate discount is recognized.
April 14	Purchased 3,800 Toy Trains from a cash vendor (Cash Vendor is set to pay 101 - Cash as the A/P Account) for cash $3,800. Utilize the Purchases/Receive Inventory screen under Tasks with Cash Vendor, Invoice No. 2010-04-14A. Ensure that the A/P Account is set to 101 – Cash.
April 16	Received a cash refund from the Cash Vendor of the Toy Trains for the return of 500 Toy Trains on the cash purchase of April 14, $500. Utilize Vendor Credit Memos and Cash Vendors with Credit No. 2010-04-16A. By applying it to the 2010-04-14A invoice the inventory of Toy Trains will be adjusted appropriately.
April 18	Purchased 4,500 Toy Trains from Skywalker Distributors for $1.00 each, FOB shipping point, terms 2/10, n/30. Set the Invoice No. to 2010-04-18A, ensure that the A/P account is set to 201 – Accounts Payable.
April 20	Paid Truck'n Transfer Co. $100.00 for freight-in on April 18. Use the Write Check screen and check number 103. Ensure that the Expense Account is set to 120 – Merchandise Inventory.
April 23	Utilize the Sales/Invoicing screen to record the sale of 5,120 Toy Trains to Cash Customer for $6,400. Set the Invoice No. to 2010-04-23A and enter the amount of $6,400 in Amount to allow Peachtree to determine the unit price. Because this is a cash customer, click on "Amount Paid at Sale" near the bottom center of the screen. Set the deposit ticket ID to 20100423 and the reference to 2010-04-23A.
April 26	Purchased 2,300 Toy Trains from Cash Vendor for $1.00 each. Utilize the Purchase/Receive Inventory screen and set the Invoice No. to 2010-04-26A. Near the bottom center of the screen enter $2,300 in Amount Paid at Purchase and 2010-04-26A in the reference window.
April 27	Paid Skywalker Distributors in full, less discount. Utilize check number 104 and apply this payment to Invoice 2010-04-18A. Ensure the appropriate discount is applied.

April 29   Made refunds to cash customers for defective merchandise $90. The returned merchandise had a scrap value of $30. Utilize the Journal icon on the task bar to set the debit account to 412 – Sales Returns and Allowances and the credit account to 101 – Cash.

April 30   Sold 2,800 Toy Trains to Train City Models on account for $3,700, terms n/30. Utilize Invoice No. 2010-04-30A and set the Amount to $3,700 and allow Peachtree to calculate the Unit Price. Modify the terms through the drop-down options menu. Cost of goods sold was $2,800.

Olaf Company's chart of accounts includes the following:

101	Cash	401	Sales
112	Accounts Receivable	412	Sales Returns and Allowances
120	Merchandise Inventory	414	Sales Discounts
201	Accounts Payable	505	Cost of Goods Sold
301	M. Olaf, Capital	644	Freight-out
350	Retained Earnings (Required by Peachtree.)		

Instructions:

(a)   Verify the beginning balances and the chart of accounts by viewing the general ledger trial balance.

(b)   Using the chart of accounts, given, record the April transactions as directed. The inventory item, Toy Trains, the customers, and vendors have been set up as shown with costing and perpetual inventory concepts.

(c)   Follow the path Reports & Forms > Financial Statements > <Standard> Income Stmnt. Ensure that the timeframe is set for April 2010. While the income statement is open, use the "Print" icon to print it.

P5-4A, Hafner's Tennis Shop, Directory Wey_AP9e_P5_4A_Hafners_Tennis_Shop

J. Hafner, a former professional tennis star, operates Hafner's Tennis Shop at the Miller Lake Resort. At the beginning of the current season, the ledger of Hafner's Tennis Shop showed Cash $2,500, Merchandise Inventory $1,700, and J. Hafner, Capital $4,200. The following transactions were completed during April.

April 4   Purchased 84 Resort Rally Hats from Wellman Co. for $10.00 each, FOB shipping point, terms 2/10, n/30. Utilize Invoice No. 2010-04-04A

April 6   Paid Truck'n Freight Co. for freight on purchase from Wellman Co. $40. Utilize the Write Check screen and check number 101. Ensure the Expense Account is set to 120 – Merchandise Inventory

April 8   Sold 79 Resort Rally Hats to Club Member for $1,150, terms n/30. The merchandise sold had a cost of $790. Use Invoice No. 2010-04-08A. Enter $1,150 into Amount to allow Peachtree to calculate the Unit Price.

April 10   Received credit of $40 from Wellman Co. for four Resort Rally Hats that were returned. Utilize the Vendor Credit Memos screen and set the Credit No. to 2010-04-10A. Ensure that the memo is applied to 2010-04-04A.

April 11   Purchased 42 Resort Rally Hats from Venus Sports for cash, $10 each. Using the Purchase/Receive Inventory screen, set the Invoice No. to 2010-04-11A and ensure that the A/P Account is set to 101 – Cash.

April 13   Paid Wellman Co. in full. Ensure that the discount amount is appropriate. Use the Payments screen and check number 102.

April 14   Purchased 90 Resort Rally Hats from Serena's Sportswear (Serena's Sportswear is Vendor ID) $10.00 each, FOB shipping point, terms 3/10, n/60. Use Invoice Number 2010-04-14A.

April 15   Received cash refund of $50 for 5 Resort Rally Hats from Venus Sports for damaged merchandise that was returned. Utilize the Vendor Credit Memos screen and a Credit No. of 2010-04-15A. Ensure that the return is applied to Invoice No. 2010-04-11A.

April 17   Paid Truck'n Freight Co. with Check No. 103 for freight on Serena's Sportswear purchase $30.

April 18   Sold 53 Resort Rally Hats to Club Member for $810, terms n/30. The cost of the merchandise sold was $530. Use Invoice No. 2010-04-18A. Enter $810 into Amount to allow Peachtree to calculate the Unit Price.

April 20   Received $500 in cash from Club Member in partial settlement of the account. Record this payment to Invoice 2010-04-08A. Use deposit ticket ID of 100420A and reference and receipt number s of 2010-04-20A.

April 21   Paid Serena's Sportswear in full. Utilize Check No. 104.

April 27   Granted an allowance of $30 to Club Member for tennis clothing that did not fit properly. Utilize the Credit Memos screen setting the Credit No. to 2010-04-27A and applying the value to Invoice No. 2010-04-18A. Remove any entry in Returned (quantity) and Unit Price ensuring $30.00 is entered in Amount.

April 30   Received cash payment from Club Member on account, $660. Utilize deposit ticket ID of 100430A and reference and receipt number 2010-04-30A and apply the payment to Invoice 2010-04-08A for $650 and Invoice 2010-04-18A for $10.

The chart of accounts for the tennis shop includes the following:

101	Cash	350	Retained Earnings (Required by Peachtree.)
112	Accounts Receivable	401	Sales
120	Merchandise Inventory	412	Sales Returns and Allowances
201	Accounts Payable	505	Cost of Goods Sold
301	J. Hafner, Capital	644	Freight-out Expense
306	J. Hafner, Drawing		

Instructions:

(a)   Verify the beginning balances and the chart of accounts by viewing the general ledger trial balance.

(b)   Journalize the April transactions using a perpetual inventory system.

(c)   Print a trial balance on April 30, 2010.

CHAPTER 6

Inventories

OBJECTIVES

- Describe the steps in determining inventory quantities.
- Explain the accounting for inventories and apply the inventory cost flow methods.
- Explain the financial effects of the inventory cost flow assumptions.

- Explain the lower-of-cost-or-market basis of accounting for inventories.
- Indicate the effects of inventory errors on the financial statements.
- Compute and interpret the inventory turnover ratio.

ADVANTAGES OF USING THE PEACHTREE INVENTORY SYSTEM

Peachtree Complete Accounting automatically keeps track of each of the inventory items bought and sold. The quantities are updated after each posted (saved) purchase and sale. The three-step process in tracking inventory in Peachtree involves:

- Entering the item information, which includes the Sales account, the Inventory account, and the Cost of Sales account.
- Using the "Item ID" whenever a purchase or a sale is made.
- Entering adjustments to the inventory, through the Inventory Adjustments Task.

As you saw in the previous chapter, through Maintain Inventory items you can set up your system with the goods and/or services you sell. A Unit Price (or a different pricing scale) can be set up and adjusted. When you enter a purchase or a sale of an item, everything is automatically updated for you. All totals are computed on both the purchasing and sales invoices.

COST METHODS

Using Average Sales Company, Directory Wey_AP9e_Average_Ch06 as an activity file, there are three different cost methods for inventory are available to use as shown in Figure 6. 1. The cost methods, shown on the pull-down menu, are:

- FIFO (First In, First Out)
- LIFO (Last In, First Out)
- Average Cost

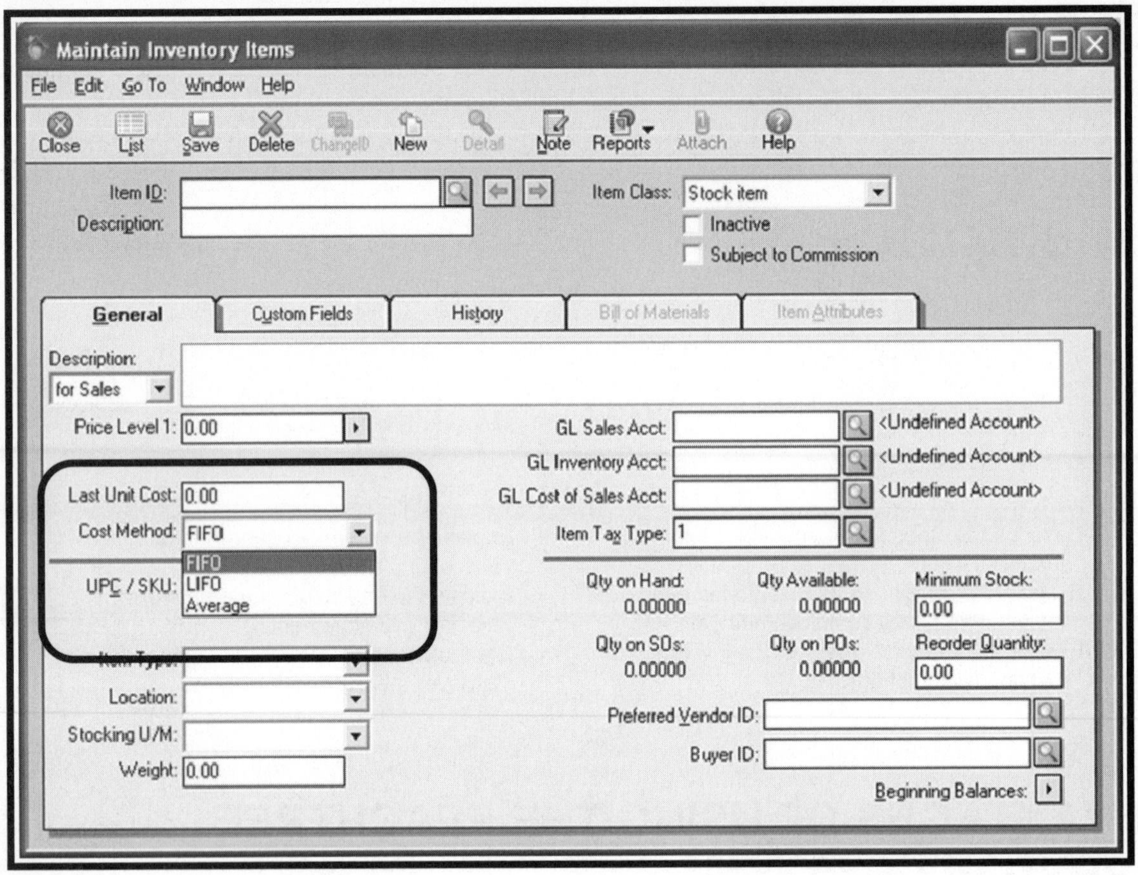

Figure 6. 1   The Maintain Inventory Items screen

AVERAGE COST

The average cost method calculates an average cost upon each acquisition of inventory. Each time you make a purchase, the average cost for that item is recalculated.

Whenever you sell an inventory item that has an average cost type, Peachtree uses the average cost it has been tracking to compute the Cost of Goods Sold. The Cost of Goods Sold is the average cost times the quantity of the item sold. On a daily basis, an entry is made to the Cost of Goods Sold account that encompasses the sales for the day.

Please refer back to your text for additional details and examples.

Example – Average Cost

The company, Average Sales Company, Directory Wey_AP9e_Average_Ch06, on January 1, 2010, buys three AVGUNITS for $1/ea from Vendor 1. On January 15, 2010, three more are purchased for $2.00/each. The average cost thus far would be $1.50 ({[$1 X 3 units] + [$2 X 3 units]} / 6 units). Record these events in Average Sales Company. Use the Purchase/Receive Inventory screen to enter these two transactions.

To view the Item Costing Report:

  Step 1:   From within your student data set, open the "Average Sales Company."

Step 2: From the reports menu, select "Inventory" then double-click on "Item Costing Report."

The Item Costing Report, shown in Figure 6. 2, shows the acquisition of inventory by date, quantity, unit cost, and extended cost as well as aggregate cost of inventory.

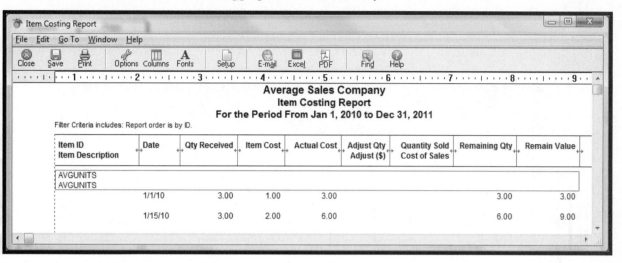

Figure 6. 2 The Item Costing Report with some default columns are hidden.

Example – Adjustments to Inventory

Peachtree makes it easy to conduct a physical inventory count by providing a printable form listing all of the inventory items and providing blanks to the side for an employee to write in the specific count of an inventory item.

To view the Physical Inventory List:

Step 1: From the reports area menu, choose "Inventory."

Step 2: From the reports list click on "Physical Inventory List." The report is shown in Figure 6. 3 below with the inventory count already completed.

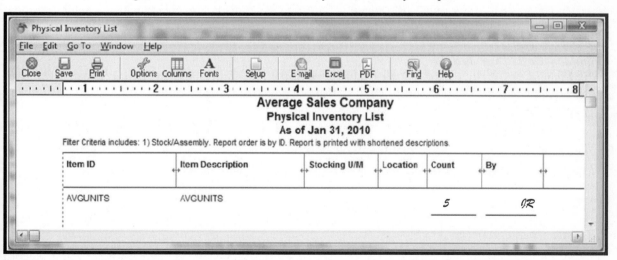

Figure 6. 3 Physical Inventory List report

Based on JR's list taken January 20th, Figure 6. 3, from a "cycle count" it appears that one of the Average Units is missing from the warehouse. To recognize the shortage an inventory adjustment must be made. This can be done through the Inventory Adjustments under the Tasks menu.

Step 1: From the Tasks menu, click on "Inventory Adjustments." The completed entry window is shown in Figure 6. 4.

Step 2: In the blank window, enter the Item ID. Once the Item ID is entered the cost information is automatically generated.

Step 3: The reference number is "2010-01-20." Change the date to January 20, 2010.

Step 4: Enter "-1" (a negative number) in the "Adjust Quantity By" text box.

Step 5: Compare your work with Figure 6. 4 and make any adjustments necessary. Click on "Save" on the task bar to save your work.

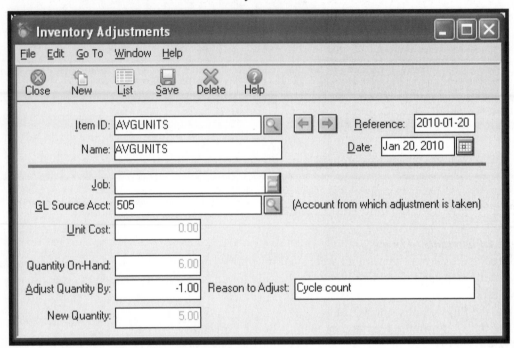

Figure 6. 4 Inventory Adjustments screen

The average cost of our units will remain at $1.50 because this is a mathematical calculation of total acquisition cost divided by total units purchased.

Example – Cost of Goods Sold

On January 25, 2010, Cindi Customer buys three of the remaining AVGUNITS for $6/each. The cost of goods sold would be $4.50 (Average Cost × Quantity Sold or $1.50 × 3 units).

Record Cindi's Purchase:

Step 1: Click on the "Sales" navigation aid. Click on "Sales Invoicing" in the middle section.

Step 2: Complete the invoice (refer back to Chapter 5, if necessary). Cindi purchases three units at $6/each.

Step 3: Check your work with Figure 6. 5 before continuing. The completed invoice is illustrated in Figure 6. 5.

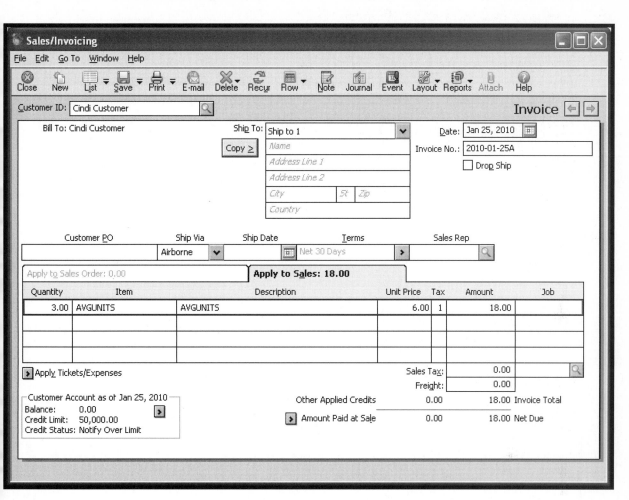

Figure 6. 5 Cindi Customer's invoice

To see how accounts are affected, view the Item Costing Report and compare it to Figure 6. 6, shown here. Notice the report shows how each transaction affects the inventory value.

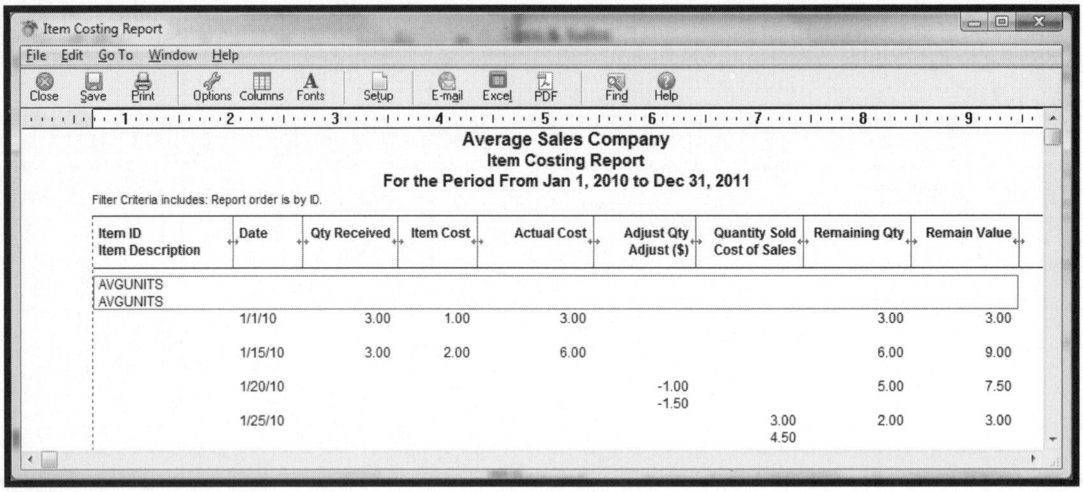

Average Sales Company
Item Costing Report
For the Period From Jan 1, 2010 to Dec 31, 2011

Filter Criteria includes: Report order is by ID.

Item ID Item Description	Date	Qty Received	Item Cost	Actual Cost	Adjust Qty Adjust ($)	Quantity Sold Cost of Sales	Remaining Qty	Remain Value
AVGUNITS AVGUNITS								
	1/1/10	3.00	1.00	3.00			3.00	3.00
	1/15/10	3.00	2.00	6.00			6.00	9.00
	1/20/10				-1.00 -1.50		5.00	7.50
	1/25/10					3.00 4.50	2.00	3.00

Figure 6. 6 Item Costing Report with some default columns are hidden

To see the "Big Picture" and how accounts have been affected, run a general ledger report, shown in Figure 6. 7.

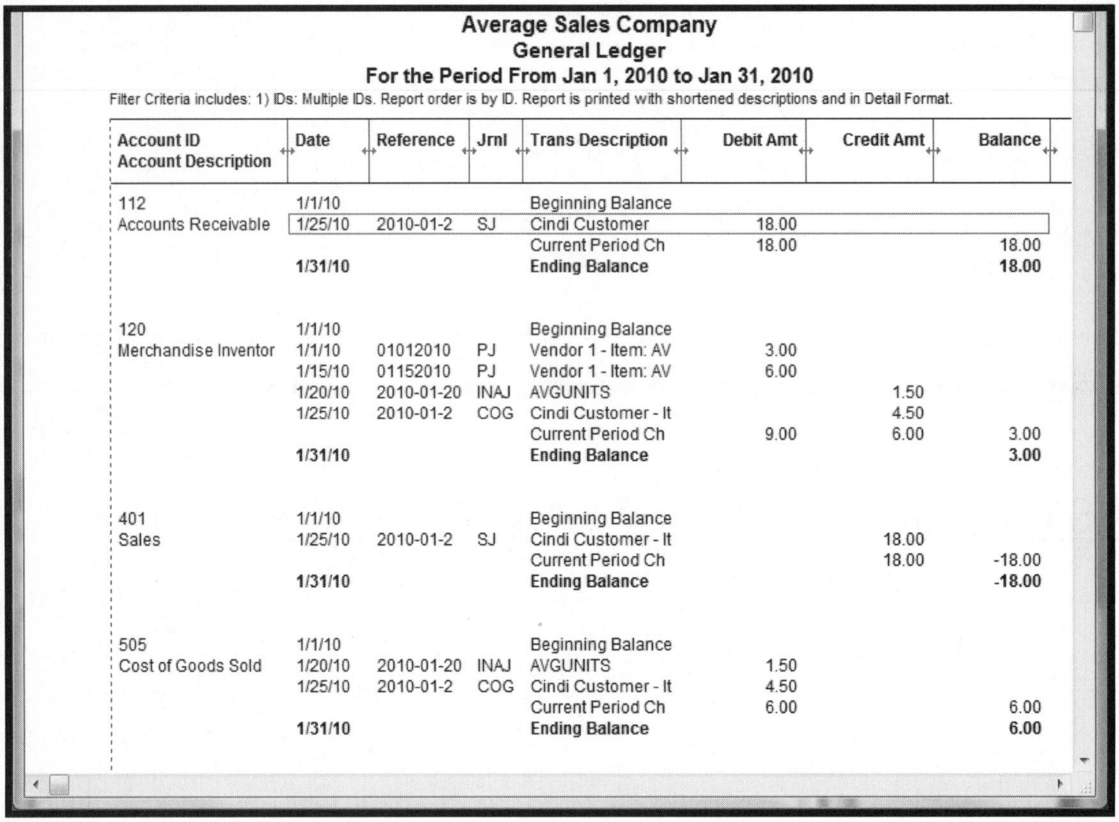

Average Sales Company
General Ledger
For the Period From Jan 1, 2010 to Jan 31, 2010

Filter Criteria includes: 1) IDs: Multiple IDs. Report order is by ID. Report is printed with shortened descriptions and in Detail Format.

Account ID Account Description	Date	Reference	Jrnl	Trans Description	Debit Amt	Credit Amt	Balance
112	1/1/10			Beginning Balance			
Accounts Receivable	1/25/10	2010-01-2	SJ	Cindi Customer	18.00		
				Current Period Ch	18.00		18.00
	1/31/10			**Ending Balance**			**18.00**
120	1/1/10			Beginning Balance			
Merchandise Inventor	1/1/10	01012010	PJ	Vendor 1 - Item: AV	3.00		
	1/15/10	01152010	PJ	Vendor 1 - Item: AV	6.00		
	1/20/10	2010-01-20	INAJ	AVGUNITS		1.50	
	1/25/10	2010-01-2	COG	Cindi Customer - It		4.50	
				Current Period Ch	9.00	6.00	3.00
	1/31/10			**Ending Balance**			**3.00**
401	1/1/10			Beginning Balance			
Sales	1/25/10	2010-01-2	SJ	Cindi Customer - It		18.00	
				Current Period Ch		18.00	-18.00
	1/31/10			**Ending Balance**			**-18.00**
505	1/1/10			Beginning Balance			
Cost of Goods Sold	1/20/10	2010-01-20	INAJ	AVGUNITS	1.50		
	1/25/10	2010-01-2	COG	Cindi Customer - It	4.50		
				Current Period Ch	6.00		6.00
	1/31/10			**Ending Balance**			**6.00**

Figure 6. 7 General ledger report showing select accounts

View the income statement and evaluate the performance of Average Sales Company through Gross Profit. The income statement is shown in Figure 6. 8.

```
┌─────────────────────────────────────────────────────────────────────────┐
│ ⚙ <Standard> Income Stmnt                                    □ ▣ ✕        │
├─────────────────────────────────────────────────────────────────────────┤
│ File  Edit  Go To  Window  Help                                           │
├─────────────────────────────────────────────────────────────────────────┤
│  ⊗     💾    🖨    🔧     📄    ✉     📊   📄   📋  🎨      🔍   ❓          │
│ Close  Save  Print Options Setup E-mail Excel PDF Preview Design Find Help │
├─────────────────────────────────────────────────────────────────────────┤
```

Average Sales Company
Income Statement
For the One Month Ending January 31, 2010

	Current Month			Year to Date	
Revenues					
Sales	$ 18.00	100.00	$	18.00	100.00
Total Revenues	18.00	100.00		18.00	100.00
Cost of Sales					
Cost of Goods Sold	6.00	33.33		6.00	33.33
Total Cost of Sales	6.00	33.33		6.00	33.33
Gross Profit	12.00	66.67		12.00	66.67
Expenses					
Freight-out Expense	0.00	0.00		0.00	0.00
Total Expenses	0.00	0.00		0.00	0.00
Net Income	$ 12.00	66.67	$	12.00	66.67

Figure 6. 8   Average Sales Company's income statement

LAST IN, FIRST OUT (LIFO) INVENTORY

The LIFO method keeps track of the cost you paid for each item. LIFO costs your sales and cost of goods sold as if the item you are selling is the most recently received item.

Select the LIFO method when you charge the most recent inventory costs against revenue. LIFO yields the lowest possible amount of net income in periods of constantly rising costs because the cost of the most recently acquired item more closely approximates the replacement cost of the item. Of course, in periods of declining costs, the effect is reversed.

Please refer back to your text for additional explanation and examples.

Example – LIFO

The company, LIFO Sales Company, on January 1, 2010, buys three LIFOUNITS for $1/ea from Vendor 1. On January 15, 2010, three more are purchased for $2.00/each. Record these events in LIFO Sales Company. Use the Purchase/Receive Inventory screen to enter these transactions.

View an Item Costing Report as explained in Average Sale Company, shown in Figure 6. 9. Note its similarity to the same report under the Average Sales Company.

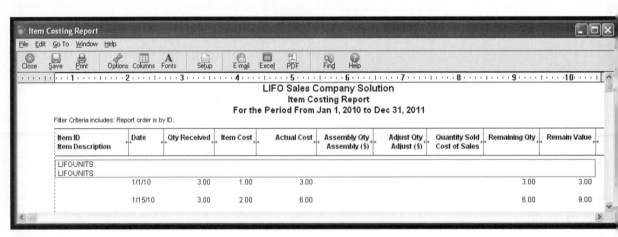

Figure 6. 9   Item Costing Report for LIFO Sales Company

As shown in the Average Sales Company, complete an adjustment for one LIFOUNITS revealed in a cycle count by JR on January 20, 2010 using a reference of 2010-01-20. This is shown in Figure 6. 10.

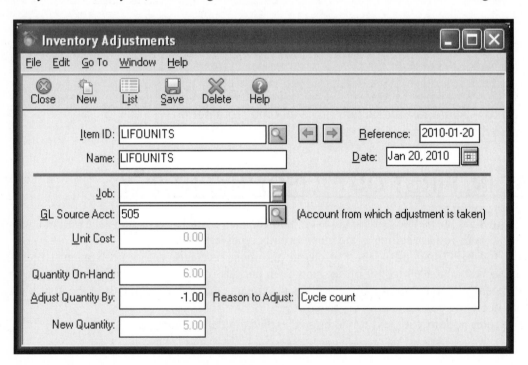

Figure 6. 10   Inventory Adjustments screen for LIFO Sales Company

The affect of this adjustment is shown in Figure 6.11.

Notice that the report tells you that the LIFO cost of the unit adjusted out is $2, shown as -2.00 under the quantity of -1.00.

Item ID **Item Description**	**Date**	**Qty Received**	**Item Cost**	**Actual Cost**	**Assembly Qty** **Assembly ($)**	**Adjust Qty** **Adjust ($)**	**Quantity Sold** **Cost of Sales**	**Remaining Qty**	**Remain Value**
LIFOUNITS LIFOUNITS									
	1/1/10	3.00	1.00	3.00				3.00	3.00
	1/15/10	3.00	2.00	6.00				6.00	9.00
	1/20/10					-1.00 -2.00		5.00	7.00

Figure 6. 11   Item Costing Report for LIFO Sales Company after inventory adjustment

Just as in Average Sales Company Cindi Customer purchases 3 LIFOUNITS on January 25, 2010, for $6 each. Use the screen in Average Sales Company as a model to record the sale. As a result, the remaining value of inventory for LIFO Sales Company is $2 for two $1 units. In Average Sales Company it was $3 for two average costed units at $1.50 each. The LIFO Sales Company Item Costing Report, Figure 6. 12, and the general ledger, Figure 6. 13, follow for comparison to Average Sales Company.

Item ID **Item Description**	**Date**	**Qty Received**	**Item Cost**	**Actual Cost**	**Assembly Qty** **Assembly ($)**	**Adjust Qty** **Adjust ($)**	**Quantity Sold** **Cost of Sales**	**Remaining Qty**	**Remain Value**
LIFOUNITS LIFOUNITS									
	1/1/10	3.00	1.00	3.00				3.00	3.00
	1/15/10	3.00	2.00	6.00				6.00	9.00
	1/20/10					-1.00 -2.00		5.00	7.00
	1/25/10						3.00 5.00	2.00	2.00

Figure 6. 12   Item Costing Report after sale to Cindi Customer

General Ledger

File Edit Go To Window Help

Close Save Print Options Columns Fonts Setup E-mail Excel PDF Find Help

LIFO Sales Company Solution
General Ledger
For the Period From Jan 1, 2010 to Jan 31, 2010

Filter Criteria includes: 1) IDs: Multiple IDs. Report order is by ID. Report is printed with shortened descriptions and in Detail Format.

Account ID / Account Description	Date	Reference	Jrnl	Trans Description	Debit Amt	Credit Amt	Balance
112	1/1/10			Beginning Balance			
Accounts Receivable	1/25/10	2010-01-2	SJ	Cindi Customer	18.00		
				Current Period Ch	18.00		18.00
	1/31/10			Ending Balance			**18.00**
120	1/1/10			Beginning Balance			
Merchandise Inventor	1/1/10	2010-01-0	PJ	Vendor 1 - Item: LI	3.00		
	1/15/10	2010-01-1	PJ	Vendor 1 - Item: LI	6.00		
	1/20/10	2010-01-20	INAJ	LIFOUNITS		2.00	
	1/25/10	2010-01-2	COG	Cindi Customer - It		5.00	
				Current Period Ch	9.00	7.00	2.00
	1/31/10			Ending Balance			**2.00**
201	1/1/10			Beginning Balance			
Accounts Payable	1/1/10	2010-01-0	PJ	Vendor 1		3.00	
	1/15/10	2010-01-1	PJ	Vendor 1		6.00	
				Current Period Ch		9.00	-9.00
	1/31/10			Ending Balance			**-9.00**
401	1/1/10			Beginning Balance			
Sales	1/25/10	2010-01-2	SJ	Cindi Customer - It		18.00	
				Current Period Ch		18.00	-18.00
	1/31/10			Ending Balance			**-18.00**
505	1/1/10			Beginning Balance			
Cost of Goods Sold	1/20/10	2010-01-20	INAJ	LIFOUNITS	2.00		
	1/25/10	2010-01-2	COG	Cindi Customer - It	5.00		
				Current Period Ch	7.00		7.00
	1/31/10			Ending Balance			**7.00**

Figure 6. 13 General ledger for LIFO Sales Company after sale to Cindi Customer showing selected accounts

View the income statement for LIFO Sales Company. It is presented in Figure 6. 14 for comparison.

Figure 6. 14   LIFO Sales Company's income statement

FIRST IN, FIRST OUT (FIFO) INVENTORY

The FIFO method is similar to LIFO and keeps track of the price you paid for each group of units received at the same time at the same unit cost.

Select FIFO when you charge costs against revenue in the order in which costs occur. This method generally yields the highest possible amount of net income during periods of constantly rising prices. Costs increase regardless of whether you have received merchandise prior to the cost increase. In periods of declining cost, the effect is reversed.

Example – FIFO
The company, FIFO Sales Company, on January 1, 2010 buys 3 FIFOUNITS for $1/ea from Vendor 3. Use the Purchases/Receive Inventory screen to enter these transactions. On January 15, 2010, 3 more FIFOUNITS units were purchased at a cost of $2/each. As shown in the Average Sales Company, complete an adjustment for one FIFOUNITS revealed in a cycle count by JR on January 20, 2010 using a reference of 2010-01-20.

Preview the Item Costing Report and compare it to Figure 6. 15.

Item Costing Report

File Edit Go To Window Help

Close Save Print Options Columns Fonts Setup E-mail Excel PDF Find Help

FIFO Sales Company Solution
Item Costing Report
For the Period From Jan 1, 2010 to Dec 31, 2011

Filter Criteria includes: Report order is by ID.

Item ID / Item Description	Date	Qty Received	Item Cost	Actual Cost	Assembly Qty / Assembly ($)	Adjust Qty / Adjust ($)	Quantity Sold / Cost of Sales	Remaining Qty	Remain Value
FIFOUNITS / FIFOUNITS									
	1/1/10	3.00	1.00	3.00				3.00	3.00
	1/15/10	3.00	2.00	6.00				6.00	9.00
	1/20/10					-1.00 -1.00		5.00	8.00

Figure 6. 15 Item Costing Report for FIFO Sales Company

Cindi Customer purchases 3 FIFOUNITS for $6 each on January 25, 2010, just like in Average Sales Company and LIFO Sales Company. Record this event and compare your Item Costing Report and general ledger to Figures 6. 16 and 6. 17.

Item Costing Report

File Edit Go To Window Help

Close Save Print Options Columns Fonts Setup E-mail Excel PDF Find Help

FIFO Sales Company Solution
Item Costing Report
For the Period From Jan 1, 2010 to Dec 31, 2011

Filter Criteria includes: Report order is by ID.

Item ID / Item Description	Date	Qty Received	Item Cost	Actual Cost	Assembly Qty / Assembly ($)	Adjust Qty / Adjust ($)	Quantity Sold / Cost of Sales	Remaining Qty	Remain Value
FIFOUNITS / FIFOUNITS									
	1/1/10	3.00	1.00	3.00				3.00	3.00
	1/15/10	3.00	2.00	6.00				6.00	9.00
	1/20/10					-1.00 -1.00		5.00	8.00
	1/25/10						3.00 4.00	2.00	4.00

Figure 6. 16 Item Costing Report for FIFO Sales Company after Cindi Customer sale

General Ledger — File Edit Go To Window Help

Close | Save | Print | Options | Columns | Fonts | Setup | E-mail | Excel | PDF | Find | Help

FIFO Sales Company
General Ledger
For the Period From Jan 1, 2010 to Jan 31, 2010

Filter Criteria includes: 1) IDs: Multiple IDs. Report order is by ID. Report is printed with shortened descriptions and in Detail Format.

Account ID Account Description	Date	Reference	Jrnl	Trans Description	Debit Amt	Credit Amt	Balance
112	1/1/10			Beginning Balance			
Accounts Receivable	1/25/10	2010-01-2	SJ	Cindi Customer	18.00		
				Current Period Ch	18.00		18.00
	1/31/10			**Ending Balance**			**18.00**
120	1/1/10			Beginning Balance			
Merchandise Inventor	1/1/10	2010-01-0	PJ	Vendor 3 - Item: FI	3.00		
	1/15/10	2010-01-1	PJ	Vendor 3 - Item: FI	6.00		
	1/20/10	2010-01-20	INAJ	FIFOUNITS		1.00	
	1/25/10	2010-01-2	COG	Cindi Customer - It		4.00	
				Current Period Ch	9.00	5.00	4.00
	1/31/10			**Ending Balance**			**4.00**
201	1/1/10			Beginning Balance			
Accounts Payable	1/1/10	2010-01-0	PJ	Vendor 3		3.00	
	1/15/10	2010-01-1	PJ	Vendor 3		6.00	
				Current Period Ch		9.00	-9.00
	1/31/10			**Ending Balance**			**-9.00**
401	1/1/10			Beginning Balance			
Sales	1/25/10	2010-01-2	SJ	Cindi Customer - It		18.00	
				Current Period Ch		18.00	-18.00
	1/31/10			**Ending Balance**			**-18.00**
505	1/1/10			Beginning Balance			
Cost of Goods Sold	1/20/10	2010-01-20	INAJ	FIFOUNITS	1.00		
	1/25/10	2010-01-2	COG	Cindi Customer - It	4.00		
				Current Period Ch	5.00		5.00
	1/31/10			**Ending Balance**			**5.00**

Figure 6. 17   General ledger report for FIFO Sales Company after Cindi Customer sale showing select accounts

View the income statement. Look at the effect on our income and profits. Run a copy of the income statement, which is shown in Figure 6. 18. Notice how the costs have been reflected in Cost of Goods Sold and in Revenue. Compare the FIFO income statement with the one previously generated from LIFO sales.

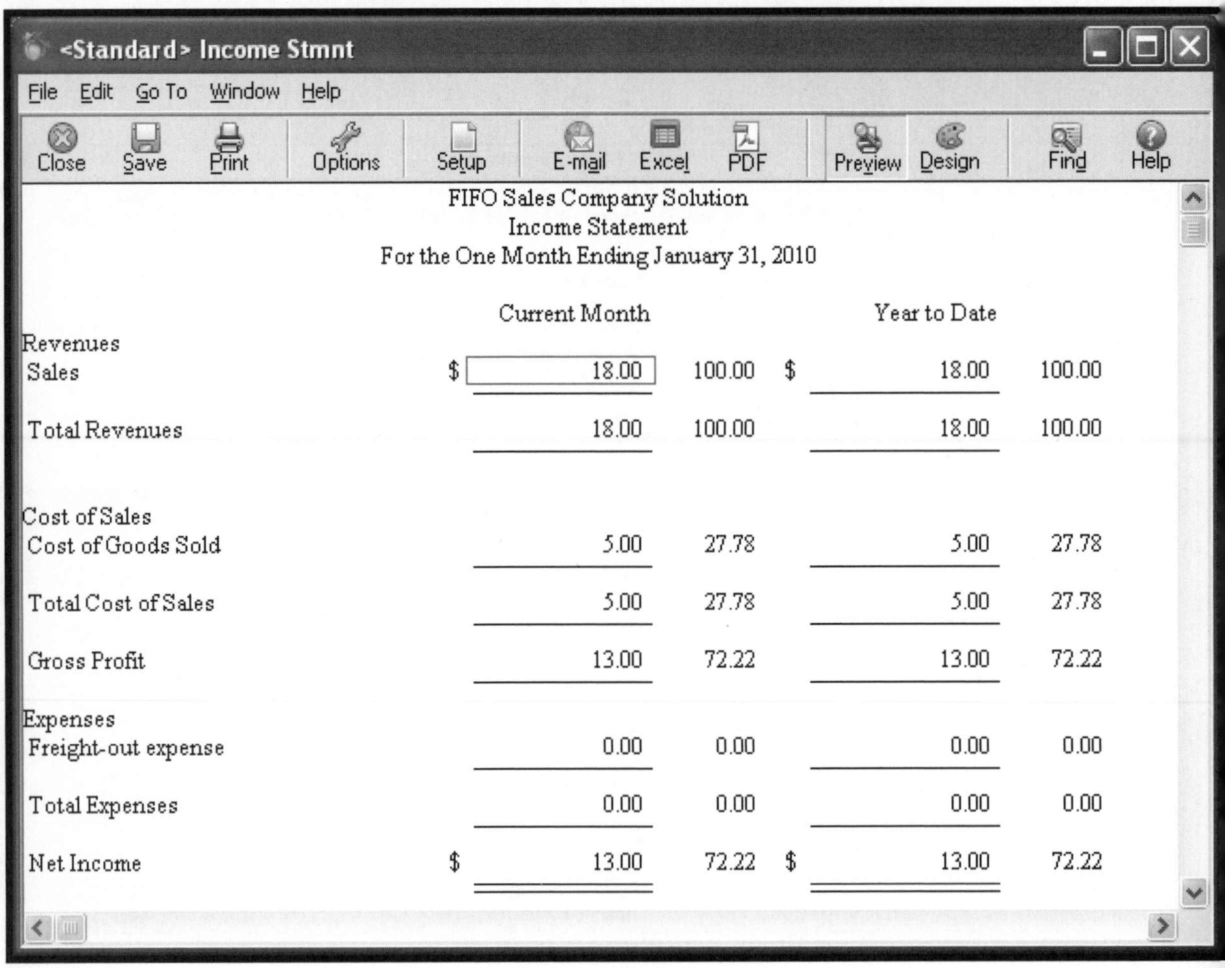

FIFO Sales Company Solution
Income Statement
For the One Month Ending January 31, 2010

	Current Month		Year to Date	
Revenues				
Sales	$ 18.00	100.00	$ 18.00	100.00
Total Revenues	18.00	100.00	18.00	100.00
Cost of Sales				
Cost of Goods Sold	5.00	27.78	5.00	27.78
Total Cost of Sales	5.00	27.78	5.00	27.78
Gross Profit	13.00	72.22	13.00	72.22
Expenses				
Freight-out expense	0.00	0.00	0.00	0.00
Total Expenses	0.00	0.00	0.00	0.00
Net Income	$ 13.00	72.22	$ 13.00	72.22

Figure 6. 18 FIFO income statement after sale to Cindi Customer

INVENTORY REPORTS

Peachtree Complete Accounting provides you with a variety of default reports for organizing and monitoring the inventory process. These reports include listing inventory items, cost, quantity on hand, assembly components, adjustments, and general ledger activity.

To obtain Inventory Reports:

Step 1: Under the "Reports" heading on the menu bar, click on "Inventory."

Step 2: You are presented with the "Inventory" reports selection menu as shown in Figure 6. 19.

Step 3: Select the report required.

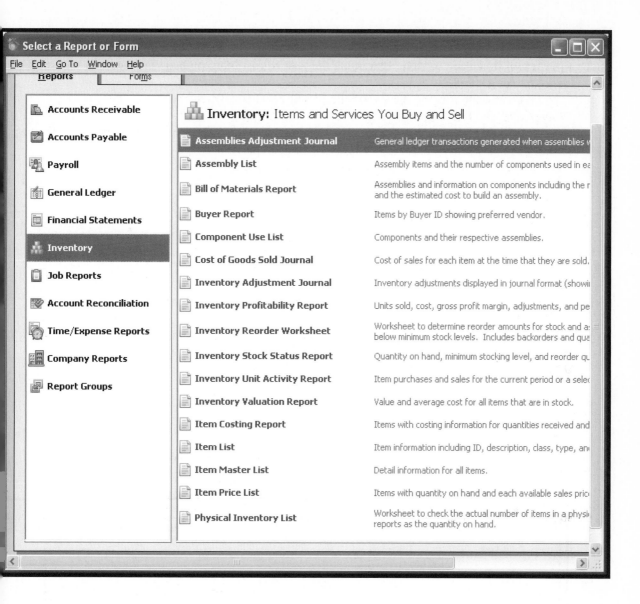

Figure 6. 19 Available Inventory reports

Comprehensive Do It! 2 Problem, Gerald D. Englehart Company, Directory Various

Comprehensive Do It! 2 Gerald D. Englehart Company has the following inventory, purchases, and sales data for the month of March.

Inventory:	March 1	200 units @ $4.00	$ 800
Purchases:			
	March 10	500 units @ $4.50	2,250
	March 20	400 units @ $4.75	1,900
	March 30	300 units @ $5.00	1,500
Sales:			
	March 15	500 units @ $10.00	
	March 25	400 units @ $10.00	

The physical inventory count on March 31 shows 500 units on hand.

Instructions

Under a **perpetual inventory system**, determine the cost of inventory on hand at March 31 and the cost of goods sold for March under:

(a) The FIFO concept utilizing the G-D_E Perpetual-FIFO file, Directory Wey_AP9e_G_D_E_Perpetual_FIFO:

    (1) Journalize the transactions, using Vendor, FIFO Item, Customer, and references/invoices of YYYY-MM-DDA (2010-03-01A for example)

    (2) Verify and print the Cost of Goods Sold Journal.

    (3) Verify and print Inventory Valuation Report.

(b) The LIFO concept utilizing the G-E-D Perpetual-LIFO file, Directory Wey_AP9e_G_D_E_Perpetual_LIFO:

    (1) Journalize the transactions, using Vendor, LIFO Item, Customer, and references/invoices of YYYY-MM-DDA (2010-03-01A for example)

    (2) Verify and print the Cost of Goods Sold Journal.

    (3) Verify and print Inventory Valuation Report.

(c) The average cost concept utilizing the G_D_E Perpetual-Average Cost file, Directory Wey_AP9e_G_D_E_Perpetual_Average:

    (1) Journalize the transactions, using Vendor, Average Cost Item, Customer, and references/invoices of YYYY-MM-DDA (2010-03-01A for example)

    (2) Verify and print the Cost of Goods Sold Journal.

    (3) Verify and print Inventory Valuation Report.

Solution to Comprehensive Do It! Problem - FIFO

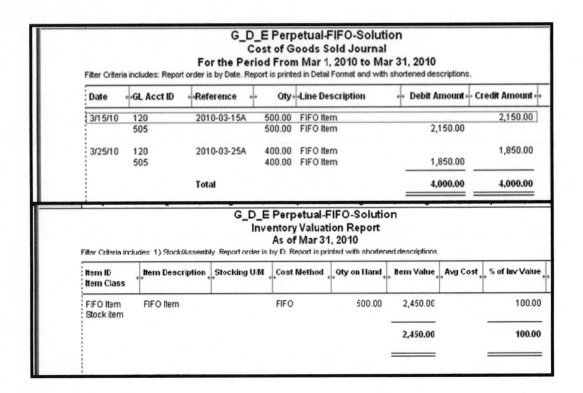

G_D_E Perpetual-FIFO-Solution
Cost of Goods Sold Journal
For the Period From Mar 1, 2010 to Mar 31, 2010

Filter Criteria includes: Report order is by Date. Report is printed in Detail Format and with shortened descriptions.

Date	GL Acct ID	Reference	Qty	Line Description	Debit Amount	Credit Amount
3/15/10	120	2010-03-15A	500.00	FIFO Item		2,150.00
	505		500.00	FIFO Item	2,150.00	
3/25/10	120	2010-03-25A	400.00	FIFO Item		1,850.00
	505		400.00	FIFO Item	1,850.00	
		Total			4,000.00	4,000.00

G_D_E Perpetual-FIFO-Solution
Inventory Valuation Report
As of Mar 31, 2010

Filter Criteria includes: 1) Stock/Assembly. Report order is by ID. Report is printed with shortened descriptions.

Item ID Item Class	Item Description	Stocking U/M	Cost Method	Qty on Hand	Item Value	Avg Cost	% of Inv Value
FIFO Item Stock item	FIFO Item		FIFO	500.00	2,450.00		100.00
					2,450.00		100.00

P6-5A, Pavey Inc., Directory Various

You are provided with the following information for Pavey Inc. for the month ended October 31, 2010. Pavey uses a **_perpetual_** method for inventory as required by Peachtree.

Date	Description	Units	Unit Cost or Selling Price
October 1	Beginning inventory (Entered)	60	$25
October 9	Purchase	120	26
October 11	Sale	100	35
October 17	Purchase	70	27
October 22	Sale	60	40
October 25	Purchase	80	28
October 29	Sale	110	40

Instructions

(a) There are three separate companies set up for this problem Each identified by the type of inventory valuation method it uses. Journal the events affecting inventory in each company. Utilize William Walker as the customer in the Sales/Invoicing screen and Pathway Pavers Inc. as the vendor in the Purchase/Receive Inventory screen. Pavey is purchasing and selling Pavers, which are set up as the only inventory item. All reference and Invoice type numbers are Year-Month-Day-Sequential Alphabet letter for the date. For example 2010-10-01A for October 1, 2010, and 2010-10-09A for October 9, 2010.

(b) Print the Inventory Valuation Report and the Cost of Goods Sold Journal from the Inventory Reports which provides (i) ending inventory, and (ii) cost of goods sold. Print the income statement from Financial Reports which provides (iii) gross profit, and (iv) gross profit rate under each of the following methods.

    (1) LIFO. Use the P6-5A-Pavey Inc.-LIFO, Directory Wey_AP9e_P6_5A_Pavey_Inc_LIFO for this task.

    (2) FIFO. Use the P6-5A-Pavey Inc.-FIFO, Directory Wey_AP9e_P6_5A_Pavey_Inc_FIFO for this task.

    (3) Average-cost. Use the P6-5A-Pavey Inc.-Average Cost, Directory Wey_AP9e_P6_5A_Pavey_Inc_Ave_Cost for this task. (**_Note:_** Peachtree is perpetual method for inventory and as such will not agree with text solution manual which is periodic method.)

(c) Compare results for the three cost flow assumptions.

CHAPTER 7

Accounting Information Systems

OBJECTIVES

- Identify the basic concepts of an accounting information system.
- Describe the nature and purpose of a subsidiary ledger.
- Explain how companies use special journals in journalizing.
- Indicate how companies post a multi-column journal.

BASIC CONCEPTS OF ACCOUNTING INFORMATION SYSTEMS

The accounting information system is the system of collecting and processing transaction data and distributing financial information to interested parties. An Accounting Information System (AIS for short) includes each of the steps in the accounting cycle you have studied in your text. The documents providing evidence of the transactions and events and the records, trial balances, work sheets and financial statements are a result of a solid Accounting Information System. It may be either manual or computerized.

An efficient and effective accounting information system is based on certain principles:

- Cost effectiveness
- Usefulness
- Flexibility

In a manual accounting system, the debits and credits for each transaction were first entered in a book called a journal. The journal record for each transaction is called a journal entry, or simply an entry. Later the journal entries are copied, or posted, to another book called the ledger.

The journal lists the transactions in the order in which they occur, somewhat like a diary; the ledger contains a page for each account and a running balance total. In a manual system, the journal tells the bookkeeper which accounts are to be debited and credited. The bookkeeper carries out these instructions by posting these journal entries to the ledger.

MANUAL VS. COMPUTERIZED SYSTEMS

In a manual accounting system, each of the steps in the accounting cycle is performed by hand. For example, each accounting transaction is entered manually in a journal and each is posted manually to the ledger. To obtain a trial balance or financial statements, manual computations must be made.

In a computerized accounting system, the program is performing these steps in the accounting cycle such as posting and preparing trial balances. Once the journal entry is entered into the application, the software carries out the posting and report generation process. Functions such as billing customers, preparing the payroll, and budgeting are also accomplished inside the computerized system.

Both manual and computerized systems rely on a chart of accounts and account classifications such as assets, liabilities, owner's equity, revenues, and expenses. These accounts are usually identified by a text title and number. Several major advantages are apparent in the computerized system. Unbalanced journal entries generally cannot be posted, posting is automatic, reports are available at the click of a button with little delay, and, with networking, numerous accountants can be working on the books at one time. The disadvantage of computerized accounting systems is the degree of trust without review that is placed on generated information because of the "computer" process.

SUBSIDIARY LEDGERS AND PEACHTREE REPORTS

Imagine a business that has several thousand charge (credit) customers and shows the transactions with these customers using only one general ledger account – Accounts Receivable. It would be impossible to determine the balance owed by a single customer at any specific time. Similarly, the amount you need to pay to a creditor would also be difficult to locate quickly from a single Accounts Payable account in the general ledger. This is why companies use subsidiary ledgers to keep track of individual balances.

A subsidiary ledger, or reports as they are called in Peachtree, is a group of accounts with a common characteristic. For example, all Accounts Receivable (money owed to you by your customers) are contained in one report. The subsidiary ledger frees the general ledger from the details of individual balances. A subsidiary ledger simply is an addition to a second volume or an expansion of the general ledger.

The two most common subsidiary ledgers in Peachtree are as follows:

- The Accounts Receivable Ledger - contains information about the transactions affecting the company's customers. A listing of who owes the company money.
- The Accounts Payable Ledger - contains information about the transactions affecting the company's creditors. A listing of those to whom the company owes money.

THE ACCOUNTS RECEIVABLE LEDGER

The Accounts Receivable Ledger is found under the Reports heading of the menu bar. To run a copy of the Accounts Receivable Ledger for "Bellwether Garden Supply."

Step 1:   Open "Bellwether Garden Supply" from within your student data set.

Step 2: Click on "Reports" on the reports menu and then click on "Accounts Receivable." You will be presented with the complete listing of reports pertaining to "Accounts Receivable" as shown in Figure 7. 1.

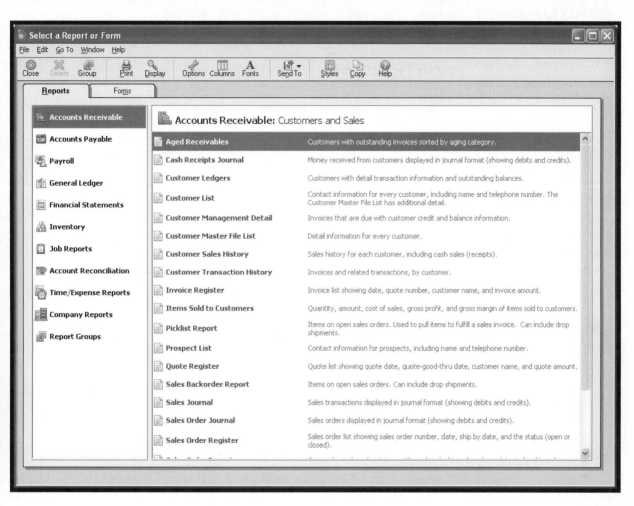

Figure 7. 1 Select a Report or Form screen for Accounts Receivable

Step 3: Click on "Customer Ledgers" under the Report List to obtain a listing of Bellwether's customers and balances, and such. A portion of the report is shown in Figure 7. 2.

Customer Ledgers

Close Save Options Hide Print Setup E-mail Preview Design Find Excel PDF Help

Bellwether Garden Supply
Customer Ledgers
For the Period From Mar 1, 2007 to Mar 31, 2007

Filter Criteria includes: Report order is by ID. Report is printed in Detail Format.

Customer ID Customer	Date	Trans No	Type	Debit Amt	Credit Amt	Balance
ALDRED	3/1/07	Balance Fwd				5,426.94
Aldred Builders, Inc.	3/4/07	10332	SJ	129.97		5,556.91
ARCHER	3/1/07	Balance Fwd				30,734.04
Archer Scapes and Pond	3/4/07	10329	SJ	59.98		30,794.02
	3/15/07	10317	SJ	49.99		30,844.01
	3/15/07		SJ		49.99	30,794.02
	3/15/07	10123	CRJ		23,359.35	7,434.67
ARMSTRONG	3/1/07	Balance Fwd				36,028.36
Armstrong Landscaping	3/2/07	CCM4002	SJ		99.97	35,928.39
	3/5/07	10336	SJ	63.49		35,991.88
	3/8/07	CCM4007	SJ		49.99	35,941.89
	3/15/07	10314	SJ	49.99		35,991.88
	3/15/07	10122	CRJ		10,970.42	25,021.46
	3/15/07	10339	SJ	53.00		25,074.46
CANNON	3/7/07	CC0002	CRJ	158.74	158.74	0.00
Cannon Heathcare Cent	3/12/07	10321	SJ	49.99		49.99
	3/15/07	10329	SJ	635.90		685.89
CHAPPLE	3/7/07	CC0001	CRJ	40.25	40.25	0.00
Chapple Law Offices	3/14/07	10341	SJ	37.10		37.10
	3/15/07	10313	SJ	199.96		237.06
CUMMINGS	3/1/07	Balance Fwd				3,550.68
Cummings Construction	3/1/07	CCM4005	SJ		49.99	3,500.69
	3/13/07	10307	SJ	180.18		3,680.87
	3/15/07	CASH-31503	CRJ	423.89	423.89	3,680.87
DASH	3/1/07	Balance Fwd				1,292.10
Dash Business Systems	3/1/07	10327	SJ	399.90		1,692.00
	3/15/07	10313	CRJ		1,292.10	399.90

Figure 7. 2 Portion of Customer Ledgers for Bellwether Garden Supply

Look at the information provided for Armstrong Landscaping. Each date on which business was conducted with Armstrong is listed, including the beginning balance for the period of $36,028.36, Credit Memos for $99.97 and $49.99 and one cash payment of $10,970.42, and Sales Invoices for $63.49, $49.99 and $53.00 which results in a period end balance of $25,074.46.

THE ACCOUNTS PAYABLE LEDGER

The Accounts Payable Ledger is also found under the Reports heading of the menu bar. To run a copy of the Accounts Payable Ledger for "Bellwether Garden Supply."

Step 1: Open Bellwether Garden Supply in your student data set if it is not already open.

Step 2: Click on "Reports & Forms" on the menu bar and then click on "Accounts Payable." You will be presented with the complete listing of reports pertaining to Accounts Payable as shown in Figure 7. 3.

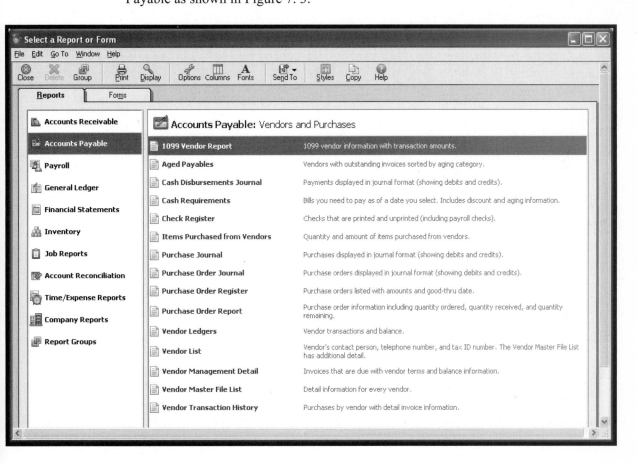

Figure 7. 3 Report listing for Accounts Payable

Step 3: Click on "Vendor Ledgers" under the Report List to obtain a listing of Bellwether's creditors and balances, and such. A portion of the report is shown in Figure 7. 4.

Bellwether Garden Supply
Vendor Ledgers
For the Period From Mar 1, 2007 to Mar 31, 2007

Filter Criteria includes: Report order is by ID.

Vendor ID / Vendor	Date	Trans No	Type	Paid	Debit Amt	Credit Amt	Balance
ABNEY	3/1/07	B1000	PJ			75.00	75.00
Abney and Son Contracto	3/9/07	B1015	PJ	*		195.65	270.65
	3/12/07	VCM30001	PJ	*	195.65		75.00
	3/15/07		CDJ		50.00	50.00	75.00
AKERSON	3/1/07	Balance Fwd					9,398.75
Akerson Distribution	3/7/07	VCM30002	PJ	*	27.20		9,371.55
	3/8/07	4	PJ			5,179.20	14,550.75
	3/13/07		CDJ		1,000.00	1,000.00	14,550.75
	3/14/07	B1016	PJ	*		27.20	14,577.95
CALDWELL	3/1/07	Balance Fwd					21,214.10
Caldwell Tools Company	3/4/07	B1004	PJ			90.00	21,304.10
	3/6/07	B1017	PJ	*		45.90	21,350.00
	3/9/07	VCM30003	PJ	*	45.90		21,304.10
CLINE	3/6/07	B1023	PJ			55.65	55.65
Cline Construction, Inc.	3/15/07	B1006	PJ			400.00	455.65
	3/15/07	10213	CDJ		100.00		355.65
CLOONEY	3/1/07	Balance Fwd					124.68
Clooney Chemical Suppl	3/2/07	B1021	PJ			23.85	148.53
	3/12/07	116655	PJ			297.60	446.13
	3/12/07	10201	CDJ		124.68		321.45
CLOUDET							0.00
Cloudet Property Manage							

Figure 7. 4   Portion listing of Vendor Ledger for Accounts Payable

Look at the information provided for Clooney Chemical Supply. The detail shows a period beginning balance of $124.68, a purchase for $23.85, a purchase for $297.60, and a payment for $124.68 resulting in an ending balance of $321.45.

SPECIAL JOURNALS

In addition to these two subsidiary ledgers there are other special journals such as the sales journal, the cash receipts journal, the purchases journal, and the cash payments journal. While in pencil and paper accounting these would be physical books, in computerized accounting they are screens or forms. Many of Peachtree's reports are titled "journals" and this may present a bit of confusion.

SALES/INVOICE SCREEN

The Sales/Invoicing screen under Tasks from the menu bar is used to record sales of merchandise on account. Sales for cash are entered into the cash receipts screen under Tasks. The Sales/Invoicing screen in Peachtree accepts the information at the time of a sale on an account. The customer can be at the counter, or the merchandise may be shipped to the customer. Within Peachtree the Apply to Sales tab of the Sales/Invoicing screen is primarily driven by inventory items. However, text can be placed in the description windows and values can be entered into the Amount field without an inventory ID. If inventory items are identified with ID, inventory and cost of goods sold are updated when the screen is saved.

From the sales/invoicing screen you can use the arrows near the upper right corner to move through the available screens that have been saved or recorded. Through an option towards the bottom of the screen you can receive cash at the time of the sale. You can use this screen for cash sales if desired but it creates unnecessary additional lines in the general ledger report. Cash sales should be entered in the cash receipts screen. Credit sales of assets other than merchandise would be entered through a general journal entry.

To view the Sales Journal (report):

Step 1: Continue to use the Peachtree demo company, Bellwether Garden Supply.

Step 2: Click on "Reports & Forms" on the menu bar then click on "Accounts Receivable" from the drop-down menu.

Step 3: In the Accounts Receivable reports listing, click on "Sales Journal." A portion of the sales journal is shown in Figure 7. 5.

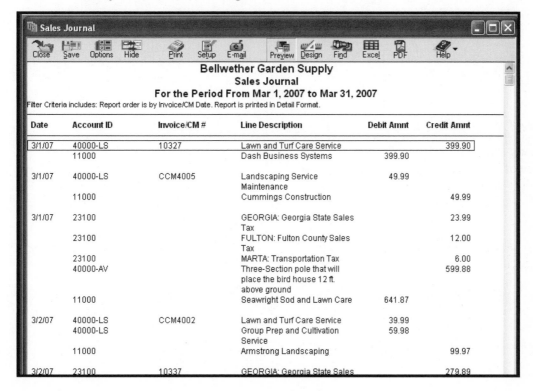

Figure 7. 5   Sales journal for Bellwether Garden Supply

Look at the third entry for March 1, 2007. The 23100 accounts are Sales Taxes Payable accounts related to sales tax liability, the 40000 series accounts are Sales revenue accounts, and the 11000 account is Accounts Receivable showing the total value of the sale - $641.87. This can be verified or clarified by reading Bellwether's chart of accounts within the reports of general ledger. By placing your cursor over an item which results in a magnifying glass as a cursor and double-clicking you will be taken to the original entry for that data.

THE RECEIPTS JOURNAL

The cash receipts within Peachtree are handled through the cash receipts journal which can be accessed through "Tasks." Almost all cash receipts are recorded through the cash receipts journal. If the customer has outstanding invoices for payments Peachtree will present these on the "Apply To Invoices" tab. The "Apply To Revenues" tab can be used for cash sales. This tab can be driven by inventory items. However, it will allow you to text into the description window and values in the Amount window without identifying an inventory item.

When using the "Apply To Invoices" tab, Peachtree will generally calculate a discount if applicable but this value should be checked before accepted.

The cash receipts journal screen creates the cash receipts journal. A portion of this report for Bellwether is shown in Figure 7. 6. To generate a cash receipts journal:

  Step 1: Click on "Reports & Forms" on the menu bar.
  Step 2: Click on "Accounts Receivable" from the drop-down menu.
  Step 3: Click on "Cash Receipts Journal."

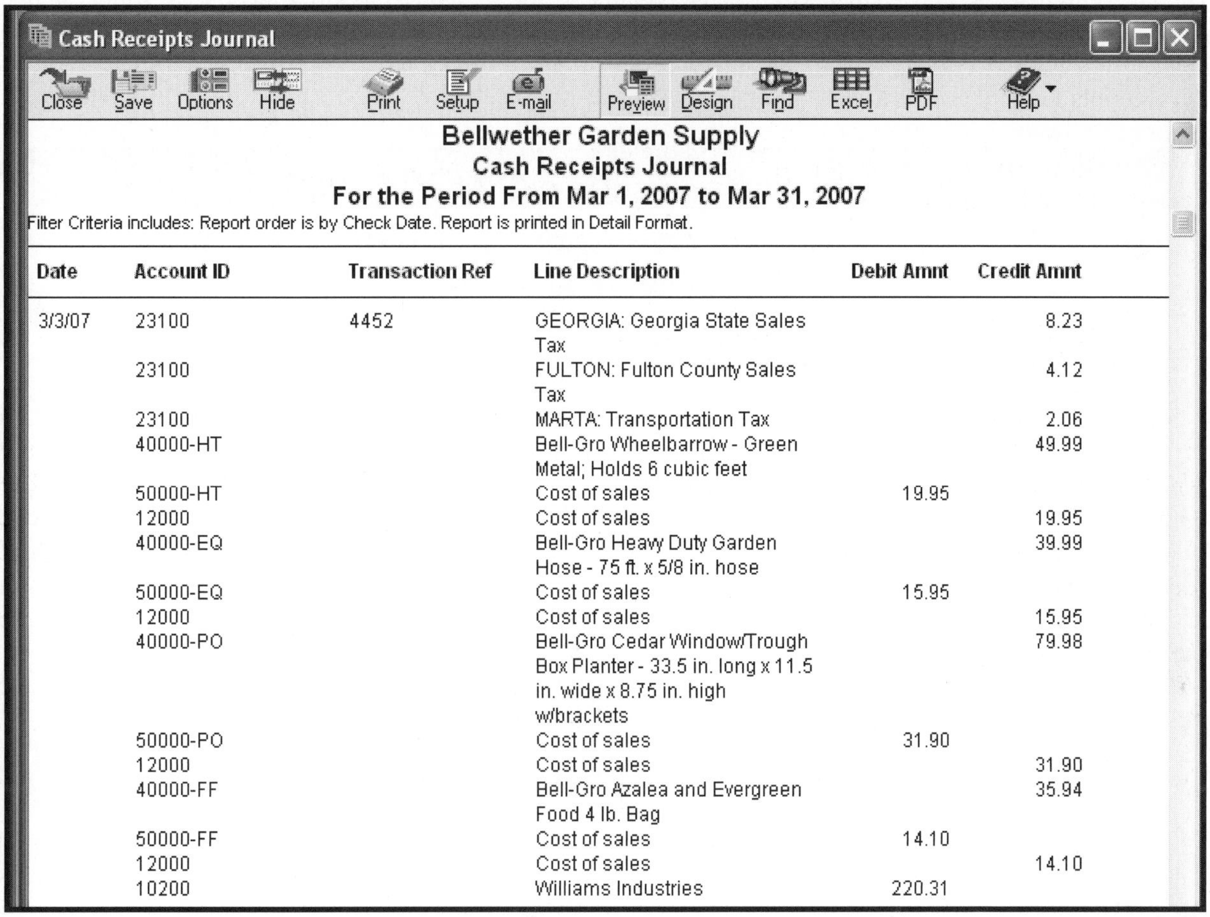

Bellwether Garden Supply
Cash Receipts Journal
For the Period From Mar 1, 2007 to Mar 31, 2007
Filter Criteria includes: Report order is by Check Date. Report is printed in Detail Format.

Date	Account ID	Transaction Ref	Line Description	Debit Amnt	Credit Amnt
3/3/07	23100	4452	GEORGIA: Georgia State Sales Tax		8.23
	23100		FULTON: Fulton County Sales Tax		4.12
	23100		MARTA: Transportation Tax		2.06
	40000-HT		Bell-Gro Wheelbarrow - Green Metal; Holds 6 cubic feet		49.99
	50000-HT		Cost of sales	19.95	
	12000		Cost of sales		19.95
	40000-EQ		Bell-Gro Heavy Duty Garden Hose - 75 ft. x 5/8 in. hose		39.99
	50000-EQ		Cost of sales	15.95	
	12000		Cost of sales		15.95
	40000-PO		Bell-Gro Cedar Window/Trough Box Planter - 33.5 in. long x 11.5 in. wide x 8.75 in. high w/brackets		79.98
	50000-PO		Cost of sales	31.90	
	12000		Cost of sales		31.90
	40000-FF		Bell-Gro Azalea and Evergreen Food 4 lb. Bag		35.94
	50000-FF		Cost of sales	14.10	
	12000		Cost of sales		14.10
	10200		Williams Industries	220.31	

Figure 7. 6 Portion of Cash Receipts Journal report for Bellwether Garden Supply

By reading and being familiar with the chart of accounts you can gain insight as to the actual events of the journal. The first transaction, dated March 3, 2007 with an Account ID of 23100 indicates that sales tax was collected since cash was debited and the Sales Tax Payable account credited for the amount of $8.23.

THE PURCHASES/RECEIVE INVENTORY JOURNAL

Within Peachtree you can issue Purchase Orders and then receive those ordered items through the Purchases/Receive Inventory screen found under Tasks on the menu bar. This is accomplished through the Apply To Purchase Orders tab. For the problems of the textbook, this screen is utilized to purchase and receive inventory at the same time through the Apply To Purchases tab. As with other screens, this screen can be inventory item driven or you can enter text into the description window and value into the Amount window for a one time or seldom acquired item.

While this screen is usually used for purchases and receipts of merchandise on Accounts Payable, there is a options button at the bottom of the screen which allows you to pay some or all of the amount due at the time of recording.

The Purchases/Receive Inventory screen generates the Purchases Journal which is found under Accounts Payable within Reports. A portion of Bellwether's Purchase Journal is shown in Figure 7. 7, below.

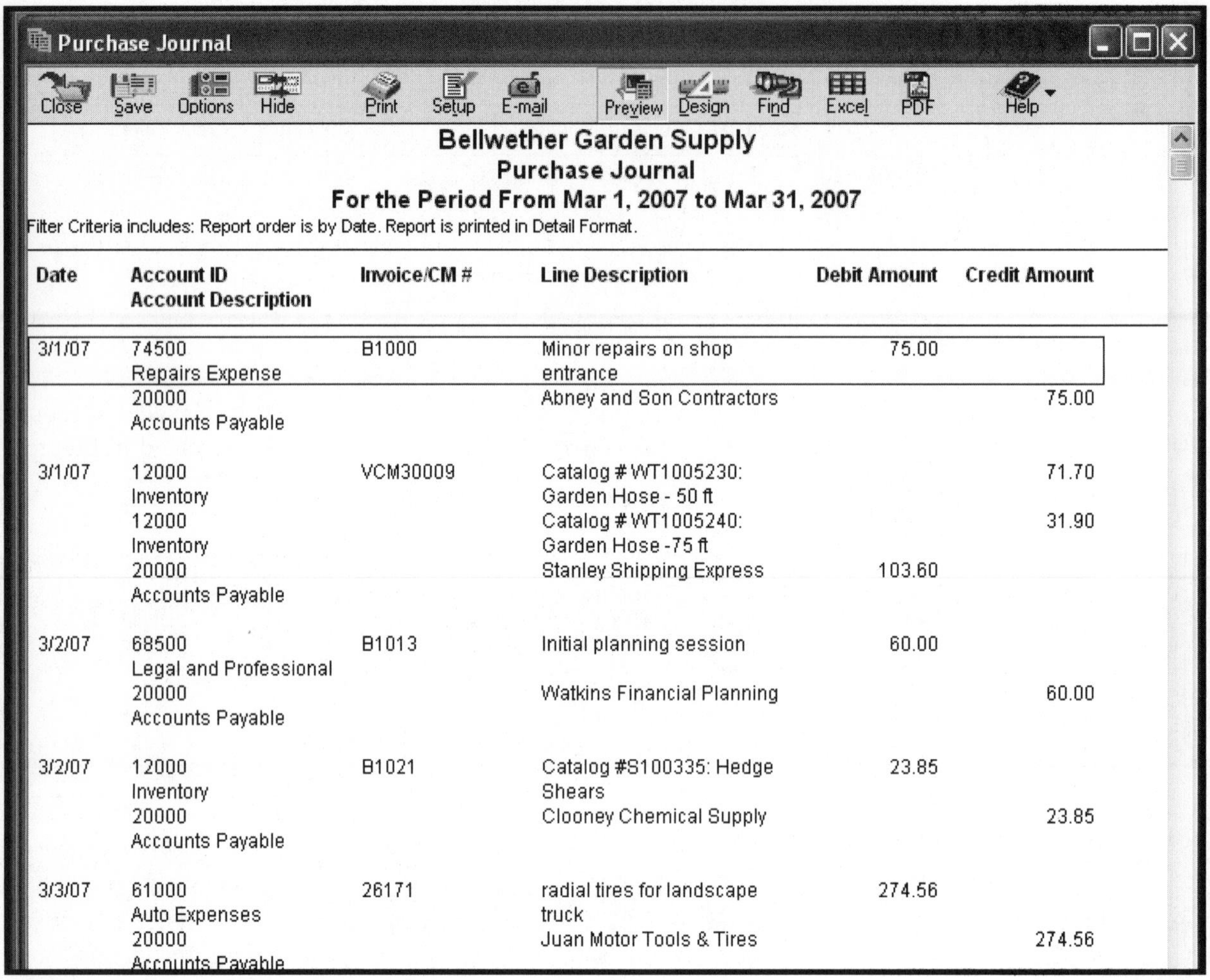

Purchase Journal

Close Save Options Hide Print Setup E-mail Preview Design Find Excel PDF Help

Bellwether Garden Supply
Purchase Journal
For the Period From Mar 1, 2007 to Mar 31, 2007

Filter Criteria includes: Report order is by Date. Report is printed in Detail Format.

Date	Account ID Account Description	Invoice/CM #	Line Description	Debit Amount	Credit Amount
3/1/07	74500 Repairs Expense	B1000	Minor repairs on shop entrance	75.00	
	20000 Accounts Payable		Abney and Son Contractors		75.00
3/1/07	12000 Inventory	VCM30009	Catalog # WT1005230: Garden Hose - 50 ft		71.70
	12000 Inventory		Catalog # WT1005240: Garden Hose -75 ft		31.90
	20000 Accounts Payable		Stanley Shipping Express	103.60	
3/2/07	68500 Legal and Professional	B1013	Initial planning session	60.00	
	20000 Accounts Payable		Watkins Financial Planning		60.00
3/2/07	12000 Inventory	B1021	Catalog #S100335: Hedge Shears	23.85	
	20000 Accounts Payable		Clooney Chemical Supply		23.85
3/3/07	61000 Auto Expenses	26171	radial tires for landscape truck	274.56	
	20000 Accounts Payable		Juan Motor Tools & Tires		274.56

Figure 7. 7 Portion of Purchase Journal report

Notice that there is both a debit and credit column on the report and Account ID explains the depicted information.

THE CASH PAYMENTS JOURNAL

Cash payments are made through the Payments screen under Tasks. This screen resembles a check with additional information and fields. If the payment is being made to a party in the vendor or customer data base, you can select that party through the Vendor ID or Customer ID window. If the check is being written to a party without a data record, you can enter the payee's data directly into the Pay To The Order Of fields. If you select a vendor, Peachtree will offer outstanding invoices on the Apply to Invoices tab. Peachtree will also calculate applicable discounts, these values need to be verified.

If the Apply To Expenses tab is selected, you can designate the account that will be credited in the lower portion of the screen. While the tab is titled Apply To Expenses, all accounts within the chart of accounts are available in the GL (General Ledger) account window. Again, while this appears to be inventory item driven, you can enter text into the description windows and values into the Amount windows without selecting inventory items.

The Payments screen generates the Cash Disbursements Journal (report) found under Accounts Payable within Reports. A portion of Bellwether's Cash Disbursements Journal is presented in Figure 7. 8.

Bellwether Garden Supply
Cash Disbursements Journal
For the Period From Mar 1, 2007 to Mar 31, 2007

Filter Criteria includes: Report order is by Date. Report is printed in Detail Format.

Date	Check #	Account ID	Line Description	Debit Amount	Credit Amount
3/12/07	10201	20000	Invoice: 33112	124.68	
		10200	Clooney Chemical Supply		124.68
3/12/07	10202	20000	Invoice: 44555	360.00	
		10200	Gary, Wilson, Jones, & Smith		360.00
3/12/07	10203	20000	Invoice: LS-6211	550.00	
		10200	Mills Leasing Corp.		550.00
3/12/07	10204	57300-LS	Ground Prep: Chapman Job	215.70	
		57300-LS	Lawn Prep: Hensley Job	119.80	
		10200	Daniel Lawn Pro, Inc.		335.50
3/12/07	10211V	57300-LS	Tree Surgeon Services		450.00
		10200	Paris Brothers Tree Surgeons	450.00	

Figure 7. 8   Portion of the Cash Disbursements Journal report

As with some of the other special journals, this journal has a debit and credit column. A good general knowledge of the chart of accounts helps to read the information.

P7-1A, Grider Company, Directory Wey_AP9e_P7_1A_Grider_Co

Grider Company's chart of accounts includes the following selected accounts already set up within your student data set.

101	Cash		401	Sales
112	Accounts Receivable		414	Sales Discounts
120	Merchandise Inventory		505	Cost of Goods Sold
301	O. Grider, Capital			

On April 1, the accounts receivable ledger of Grider Company showed the following balances:

Ogden	$1,550	Chelsea	$1,200
Eggleston Co.	$2,900	Baez	$1,800

The chart of accounts and the beginning balances have been entered into the Peachtree so they do not need to be inserted or established. Inventory items with sales prices and cost of goods sold has been created for inventory transactions.

The April transactions involving the receipt of cash were as follows:

Apr. 1   The owner, O. Grider, invested additional cash in the business $7,200. Utilize the Journal icon on the Receipts taskbar to identify the 301, O. Grider, Capital account.

4   Received check for payment of invoice 032510A on account from Baez less 2% cash discount. Utilize 040410A as deposit ticket ID, reference and receipt number .

5   Received check for $920 in payment of invoice no. 307 from Eggleston Co. Utilize 040510A as deposit ticket ID, reference and receipt number .

8   Made cash sales of merchandise, item 040810A which as the cost of goods sold set properly, totaling $7,245. The cost of the merchandise sold was $4,347. Utilize Cash Customer in the customer data base. Utilize 040810A as deposit ticket ID, reference and receipt number .

10   Received check for $600 in payment of invoice no. 309 from Ogden. Utilize 041010A as deposit ticket ID, reference and receipt number .

11   Received cash refund from a supplier for damaged merchandise $740. Utilize the Journal icon on the taskbar to set the credit account to 120, Merchandise Inventory. Utilize 041110A as deposit ticket ID, reference and receipt number .

23   Received check for $1,500 in payment of invoice no. 310 from Eggleston Co. Utilize 042310A as deposit ticket ID, reference and receipt number .

29   Received check for payment of account from Chelsea. Utilize 042910A as deposit ticket ID, reference and receipt number .

Instructions:
(a)   Journalize the transactions above using the receipts screen under Tasks on the menu bar.
(b)   All beginning balances and invoice number references have been entered in accounts receivable.
(c)   Print the general ledger trial balance from the general ledger report options and the Customer Ledger from the Accounts Receivable report options.
(d)   Verify the balances of individual accounts receivable.

P7-3A, Lopez Company, Directory Wey_AP9e_P7_3A_Lopez_Co

The chart of accounts for Lopez Company includes the following selected accounts that have already been set up in your student data set:

112	Accounts Receivable	401	Sales
120	Merchandise Inventory	412	Sales Returns and Allowances
126	Supplies	505	Cost of Goods Sold
157	Equipment	610	Advertising Expense

201   Accounts Payable

In July, the following selected transactions were completed. All purchases and sales were on account. The cost of all merchandise sold was 70% of the sales price. There are two inventory items set up for purchases and sales. The "Purchase Item" item should be used for all inventory purchasing events while the "Sales Item" should be used for all inventory sales events. All invoices and references should be in the format of 070110, as dictated by date – this example for July 1, 2010.

July 1   Purchased 11,428.57 pounds of Wangles for $0.70 per pound for a total of $8,000 from Fritz Company using Invoice No. of 070110A.

2   Received freight bill from Wayward Shipping on Fritz purchase $400. Do not set a quantity, enter "Freight bill" in description, and ensure that the GL (General Ledger) account number is 120 – Merchandise Inventory.

3   Made sales to Pinick Company of 1,300 pounds of Wangles for $1.00 per pound using Invoice No. 070310A and to 1,500 pounds of Wangles to Wayne Bros. for $1.00 per pound using Invoice N. 070310B.

5   Purchased 4,571.43 pounds of Wangles from Moon Company for $0.70 per pound using Invoice No. 070510A.

8   Returned 428.57 pounds of Wangles on Invoice No. 070510A using Credit No. 070810A to Moon Company at a value of $0.70 per pound. Use Vendor Credit Memos and select Invoice No. 070510A.

13   Purchased store supplies using Invoice No. 071310A from Cress Supply $720. Do not set a quantity or select an item, ensure that the GL (General Ledger) account number is set to 126 – Supplies.

15   Purchased 5,142.86 pounds of Wangles from Fritz Company at $0.70 per pound and purchased 4,714.29 pounds of Wangles from Anton Company at $0.70 per pound using Invoice No. 071510B.

16   Made sale of 3,450 pounds of Wangles to Sager Company for $1.00 per pound using Invoice No. 071610A and 1,570 pounds of Wangles to Wayne Bros. for $1.00 per pound using Invoice No. 071610B.

18   Received bill for advertising from Lynda Advertisements $600. Use Invoice No. 071810A and ensure that the GL (General Ledger) account number is set to 610.

21   Sales of 310 pounds of Wangles were made to Pinick Company using Invoice No. 072110A at $1.00 per pound and 2,800 pounds of Wangles were sold to Haddad Company for $1.00 per pound using Invoice No. 072110B.

22   Granted allowance to Pinick Company for merchandise damaged in shipment $40 using Credit Memo for customers. Apply this value to Invoice No. 072110A and use the Journal icon on the taskbar to set the account to 412 – Sales Returns and Allowances. Ensure no quantities are recorded as being returned. Hint: Remove value from Unit Price.

24   Purchased 4,285.71 pounds of Wangles from Moon Company for $0.70 per pound using Invoice No. 072410A.

26   Purchased equipment from Cress Supply $900 using Invoice No. 072410A. Ensure the GL (General Ledger) account number is set to 157 – Equipment.

28   Received freight bill from Wayward Shipping on Moon purchase of July 24, $380 using Invoice No. 072810A. Ensure no Item is selected and that the GL (General Ledger) account number is set to 120 – Merchandise Inventory.

30   Sales were made to Sager Company of 5,600 pounds of Wangles for $1.00 using Invoice No. 073010A.

Instructions:
(a)   Journalize the transactions above in the Purchases/Receive Inventory screen and the Sales/Invoicing screen under Task from the menu bar to accomplish these actions unless the event includes other instructions.

(b)   Verify the general and subsidiary ledger accounts. (Assume that all accounts have zero beginning balances.)

(c)   Print the purchases journal and the vendor ledger from the accounts payable reports options, print the sales journal and the customer ledger from the accounts receivable reports option, the general ledger from the general ledger report options, prove the control and subsidiary accounts payable and receivable accounts.

P7-5A, Reyes Co., Directory Wey_AP9e_P7_5A_Reyes_Co

Presented below are the purchases and cash payments journals for Reyes Co. for its first month of operation, July 2010.

		Purchases Journal		
Date		**Account Credited**	**Ref.**	**Merchandise Inventory, Dr.** **Accounts Payable, Cr.**
July	4	G. Clemens		6,800
	5	A. Ernst		8,100
	11	J. Happy		5,920
	13	C. Tabor		15,300
	20	M. Sneezy		7,900
				44,020

		Cash Disbursements Journal				
Date		**Account Debited**	**Other Accounts Dr.**	**Accounts Payable Dr.**	**Merchandise Inventory Cr.**	**Cash Cr.**
July	4	Store Supplies	600			600
	10	A. Ernst		8,100	81	8,019
	11	Prepaid Rent	6,000			6,000
	15	G. Clemens		6,800		6,800
	19	Reyes, Drawing	2,500			2,500
	21	C. Tabor		15,300	153	15,147
			9,100	30,200	234	39,066

In addition, the following transactions have not been journalized for July. The cost of all merchandise sold was 65% of the sales price.

July   1   The founder, D. Reyes, invests $80,000 in cash. Utilize the receipts screen with deposit ticket ID 100701A and reference and receipt number 2010-07-01A. While on the first line of the journal entry, click on "Journal" in the task bar to set the credit account to 301 – D. Reyes, Capital.

July   6   Sell 6,200 units of Sales Item for $1.00 each on account to Ewing Co. $6,200 terms 1/10, n/30. Utilize Invoice No. 2010-07-06A.

July   7   Make cash sales totaling $6,000.   *2010 - 07 - 07A*

July   8   Sell 3,600 units of Sales Item for $1.00 each on account to S. Beauty $3,600, terms 1/10, n/30. Utilize Invoice No. 2010-07-08A.

July   10   Sell 4,900 units of Sales Item for $1.00 each on account to W. Pitts $4,900, terms 1/10, n/30. Utilize Invoice No. 2010-07-10A.

July   13   Receive payment in full from S. Beauty for Invoice 2010-07-08A. Utilize deposit ticket ID 100713A and reference and receipt number 2010-07-13A.

July   16   Utilize the receipts screen to receive payment in full from W. Pitts for Invoice 2010-07-10A. Utilize deposit ticket ID 100716A and reference and receipt number 2010-07-16A.

July   20   Utilize the receipts screen to receive payment in full from Ewing Co for Invoice 2010-07-06A. Use deposit ticket ID 100720A and reference and receipt number 2010-07-20A.

July   21   Sell merchandise on account to H. Prince $5,000, terms 1/10, n/30.

July   29   Returned damaged goods to G. Clemens and received cash refund of $420.

p. 170   Credit!
P. 167

The general ledger includes the following accounts:

101	Cash	306	D. Reyes, Drawing
112	Accounts Receivable	350	Retained Earnings
120	Merchandise Inventory	401	Sales
127	Store Supplies	414	Sales Discounts
131	Prepaid Rent	505	Cost of Goods Sold
201	Accounts Payable	631	Supplies Expense
301	D. Reyes, Capital	729	Rent Expense

Instructions

(a)   Journalize the transactions that have not been journalized in the sales/invoicing screen, the receipts screen, and the general journal entry screen.

(b)   Print the trial balance at July 31, 2010.

(c)   Determine whether the subsidiary ledgers agree with the control accounts in the general ledger.

(d)   The following adjustments at the end of July are necessary.

   (1)   A count of supplies indicates that $140 is still on hand.

   (2)   Recognize rent expense for July, $500.

   Record these entries utilizing the general journal entry screen.

(e)   Print an adjusted trial balance at July 31, 2010.

Financial Reporting Problem, Bluma Co., Directory Wey_AP9e_BYP7_1_Bluma_Co

The following data is given for Bluma Co. for the month of January 2010. Credit sales terms are 2/10, n/30. Each sales and purchase item has been set up in the inventory. Bluma Co. uses a perpetual inventory system and both an accounts receivable and an accounts payable subsidiary ledger. Balances related to both the general ledger and the subsidiary ledger for Bluma are indicated in the working papers. Presented below are a series of transactions for Bluma Co. for the month of January. The cost of all merchandise sold was 60% of the sales price.

Jan.   3   Using the Sales/Invoicing screen, sell 3,100 units of Merchandise on account to B. Richey for $1.00 per unit. Utilize Invoice No. 510.

   3   Using the Sales/Invoicing screen, sell 1,800 units of Merchandise on account to J. Forbes for $1.00 per unit. Utilize Invoice No. 511.

   5   Using the Purchases/Receive Inventory screen to purchase Merchandise from S. Vogel $5,000, terms n/30. Utilize Invoice No. 2010-01-05A. *Note:* Leave the Quantity window blank, insert Merchandise in the Item window, ensure the GL (General Ledger) account window is 120 – Merchandise Inventory, insert $0.60 in the Unit Price window, and

insert $5,000 in the Amount window. Peachtree should insert 8,333.00 in the quantity window when you tab out of the Amount window.

5　Using the Purchases/Receive Inventory screen to purchase Merchandise from D. Lynch $2,200, terms n/30. **_Note:_** Leave the Quantity window blank, insert Merchandise in the Item window, ensure the GL (General Ledger) account window is 120 – Merchandise Inventory, insert $0.60 in the Unit Price window, and insert $2,200 in the Amount window. Peachtree should insert 3,666.67 in the quantity window when you tab out of the Amount window.

7　Use the receipts screen to receive a check from S. LaDew for Invoice 507, $4,000 after discount period has lapsed. Utilize deposit ticket ID 10-01-07 and reference and receipt number 2010-01-07A.

7　Use the receipts screen to receive a check from B. Garcia for Invoice 508, $2,000 after discount period has lapsed. Utilize deposit ticket ID 10-01-07 and reference and receipt number 2010-01-07B.

8　Utilizing the payments screen and check number 101 pay Fast Freight $235 for freight on merchandise purchased. **_Note:_** Do not enter a quantity, item, description, or unit price. Ensure the GL (General Ledger) account is set to "120" – Merchandise Inventory and enter $235 in the Amount window.

9　Utilize the Payments screen to send Check 102 to S. Hoyt for $9,000 less 2% cash discount for Invoice 2009-12-31A.

9　Utilize the Payments screen to send Check 103 to D. Omara for $11,000 less 1% cash discount for Invoice 2009-12-31B.

9　Utilize the credit memo screen to issue credit number 2010-01-09A for 300 units of Merchandise to J. Forbes for merchandise returned. Ensure that the amount is $300.00.

10　Utilize the receipts screen and Cash Customer to record the summary of daily cash sales which is 15,500 units of Merchandise for a total of $15,500. Use deposit ticket ID 10-01-10 and reference and receipt number 2010-01-10A.

11　Sell 1,600 units of Merchandise on account to R. Dvorak $1,600, using Invoice no. 512.

11　Sell 900 units of Merchandise on account to S. LaDew $900, using Invoice no. 513.

12　Pay Land Holding Realty rent of $1,000 for January using the Payments screen and check number 104. Ensure the GL (General Ledger) account is set to 729 – Rent Expense.

13　Receive payment in full from B. Richey less cash discounts. Utilize deposit ticket ID 10-01-13 and reference and receipt number 2010-01-13A.

13　Receive payment in full from J. Forbes less cash discounts. Utilize deposit ticket ID 10-01-13 and reference and receipt number 2010-01-13B.

15　Utilize the write checks screen to issue Check 105 for $800 cash to M. Bluma for personal use. Ensure the Expense Account is set to 306 – M. Bluma, Drawings.

15　View the general ledger report to verify your entries.

16　Purchase 30,000 units of Merchandise from D. Omara for $18,000, terms 1/10, n/30 utilizing Invoice No. 2010-01-16A.

16　Purchase 23,666.67 units of Merchandise from S. Hoyt for $14,200, terms 2/10, n/30 utilizing Invoice No. 2010-01-16B. Note: Do not enter a Quantity, enter Merchandise as the Item and $0.60 as the Unit Price and $14,200 as the Amount. Peachtree should enter the Quantity of 23,666.67 when you tab out of the Amount window.

16　Purchase 2,500 units of Merchandise from S. Vogel for $1,500, terms n/30 utilizing Invoice No. 2010-01-16C.

17　Write Check 106 for $400 to Office Supplies Emporium for office supplies. Ensure the GL (General Ledger) account is set to 125 – Office Supplies.

18　Utilize the Vendor Credit Memos screen to return $200 of Merchandise purchased on Invoice No. 2010-01-16B to S. Hoyt and receive credit. Use Credit No. 2010-01-18A. Leave the Returned (quantity) window blank and enter $200 in the Amount window.

Peachtree should fill the Returned (quantity) window with 333.33 when you tab out of the Amount window.

20	Utilize the receipts screen and Cash Customer to record the summary of daily cash sales which is 20,100 units of Merchandise for a total of $20,100. Use deposit ticket ID 10-01-20 and reference and receipt number 2010-01-20A.
21	Utilize the Payments screen to issue a $15,000 note payable, maturing in 90 days, to R. Moses in payment of balance due of Invoice 2009-12-22A. Enter Notes Payable in the check number window. Once the invoice is selected utilize the Journal icon on the task bar to set the credit account to 200 – Notes Payable. *Note:* This screen allows you to remove the value from Accounts Payable – R. Moses.
21	Receive payment in full for Invoice 513 from S. LaDew less cash discount. Use deposit ticket ID 10-01-21 and reference and receipt number 2010-01-21A.
22	Sell 2,700 units of Merchandise on account to B. Richey, $2,700, invoice no. 514.
22	Sell 1,300 units of Merchandise on account to R. Dvorak, $1,300, invoice no. 515.
22	View the general ledger report to verify your entries.
23	Send check number 117 to D. Omara for full payment, less discount, on Invoice 2010-01-16A.
23	Send check number 118 to S. Hoyt for full payment, less discount, on Invoice 2010-01-16B.
25	Sell 3,500 units of Merchandise on account to B. Garcia for $3,500, utilizing Invoice No. 516.
25	Sell 6,100 units of Merchandise on account to J. Forbes for $6,100, utilizing Invoice No. 517.
27	Purchase Merchandise from D. Omara, $14,500, terms 1/10, n/30. Leave Quantity blank, set Item to Merchandise, ensure Unit Price is $0.60, and set Amount to $14,500. Utilize Invoice No. 2010-01-27A. Peachtree should fill Quantity with 24,166.67 units when you advance out of the window.
27	Purchase 2,000 units of Merchandise from D. Lynch, $1,200, terms n/30. Utilize Invoice No. 2010-01-27B.
27	Purchase 9,000 units of Merchandise from S. Vogel, $5,400, terms n/30. Utilize Invoice No. 2010-01-27C.
27	View the general ledger report to verify your entries.
28	Write Check 119 for $200 to Office Supplies Emporium for office supplies. Ensure the GL (General Ledger) account is set to 125 – Office Supplies.
31	Utilize the receipts screen and Cash Customer to record the summary of daily cash sales which is 21,300 units of Merchandise for a total of $21,300. Use deposit ticket ID 10-01-31 and reference and receipt number 2010-01-31A.
31	Write Check 120 to pay sales salaries of $4,300. Leave Vendor ID blank and insert Cash in the Pay to the Order of window. Ensure the Expense Account is set to 627 – Sales Salaries Expense.
31	Write Check 121 to pay sales salaries of $3,800. Leave Vendor ID blank and insert Cash in the Pay to the Order of window. Ensure the Expense Account is set to 727 – Office Salaries Expense.

Instructions

(a) Record the January transactions as instructed in each event.

(b) Periodically review the general ledger, accounts payable, and accounts receivable reports to verify your entries.

(c) Print the Working Trial Balance report at January 31, 2010. Complete the worksheet using the following additional information.

    (1) Office supplies at January 31 total $900.

    (2)   Insurance coverage expires on October 31, 2010.

    (3)   Annual depreciation on the equipment is $1,500.

    (4)   Interest of $50 has accrued on the note payable.

    (5)   Journal these adjusting entries using references Adj Entry #1 through Adj Entry #4 as appropriate.

(d)   Print the income statement and a statement of retained earnings for the month ended January 31, 2010 and the balance sheet for January 31, 2010.

(e)   Close the Bluma Co., books as of January 31, 2010. The 350 - Income Summary account has been established so Bluma Co. can be closed with manual journal entries utilizing Closing Entry #1 through Closing Entry #5 as a reference. Do not utilize the Year-End Wizard unless specifically instructed to.

(f)   Print the Trial Balance report as of January 31, 2010 and verify its balances.

(g)   Print the Customer Ledgers and the Vendor Ledgers as of January 31, 2010.

CHAPTER 8

Fraud, Internal Control, and Cash

OBJECTIVES

- Define fraud and internal control.
- Identify the principles of internal control activities.
- Explain the applications of internal control principles to cash receipts.
- Explain the applications of internal control to principles to cash disbursements.

- Describe the operation of a petty cash fund.
- Indicate the control features of a bank account.
- Prepare a bank reconciliation.
- Explain the reporting of cash.

INTERNAL CONTROL

Internal control systems have five primary components as listed below.[2]

- **A control environment.** It is the responsibility of top management to make it clear that the organization values integrity and that unethical activity will not be tolerated. This component is often referred to as the "tone at the top."
- **Risk assessment.** Companies must identify and analyze the various factors that create risk for the business and must determine how to manage these risks.
- **Control activities.** To reduce the occurrence of fraud, management must design policies and procedures to address the specific risks faced by the company.
- **Information and communication**. The internal control system must capture and communicate all pertinent information both down and up the organization, as well as communicate information to appropriate external parties.
- **Monitoring.** Internal control systems must be monitored periodically for their adequacy. Significant deficiencies need to be reported to top management and/or the board of directors.

[2]The Committee of Sponsoring Organizations of the Treadway Commission, "Internal Control—Integrated Framework," *www.coso.org/publications/executive_summary_integrated_framework.htm* (accessed March 2008).

PEACHTREE REPORTS THAT AID IN THE CONTROL OF CASH

Segregation of duties involving cash is paramount in assuring an accurate cash flow. For example, one employee may be responsible for cash register receipts. That worker in turn gives the receipts and all paperwork to a second worker who double checks the receipts and records them into Peachtree.

Look at the cash receipts journal (report) for High Cotton Farms.

Step 1:   Open "High Cotton Farms" from within your student data set and familiarize yourself with the chart of accounts.

Step 2:   Review the cash receipts journal report found under "Reports" and "Accounts Receivable", shown in Figure 8. 1.

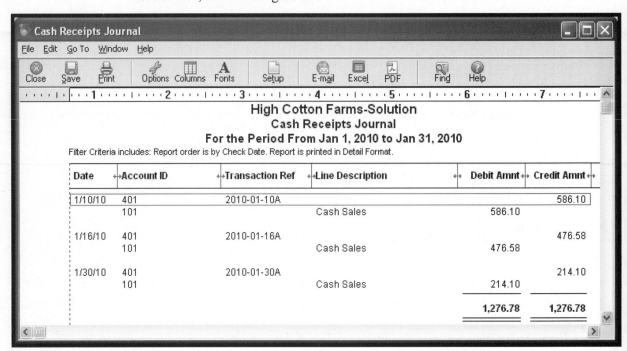

Figure 8. 1   Cash receipts journal report from High Cotton Farms

Notice the date(s) for each transaction along with the account numbers, Sales (#401) and Cash (#101), as shown for each transaction. The transaction reference refers to reference window value and the line description refers the value in the customer ID window of the receipts screen. The amount on the debit side increases the asset account 101 – Cash whereas the amount on the credit side increases the revenue account, 401 – Sales. The cash disbursements journal for High Cotton Farms is shown in Figure 8. 2.

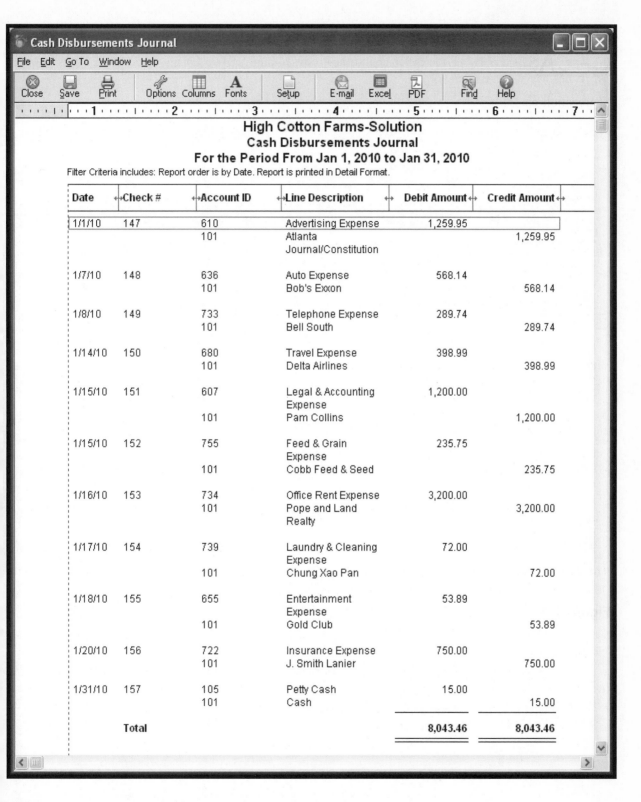

Figure 8. 2   Cash disbursements journal report

Each check is listed as written for the current period. The appropriate expense account number along with the cash account number follows with the line description. Because these are all paid expense items, the debit amount will be for the expense and the credit amount will be for the decrease in the asset Cash. The check register is the next report.

Look at the Check Register Journal for High Cotton Farms.

Step 1:   If not already open, open "High Cotton Farms" from within your student data set.

Step 2:   Run the "Check Register" report found under "Reports" on the menu bar, and click on "Accounts Payable."

Step 3:   Click on "Check Register" to obtain the report shown in Figure 8. 3.

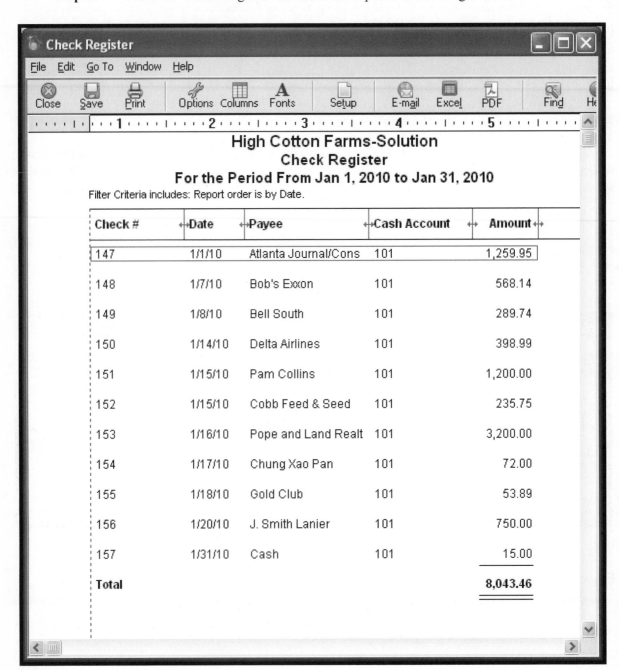

Figure 8. 3   Check register report

Each check that has been written during this accounting period is listed along with to whom it was paid, the cash account charged, and the amount of the check. Remember that a company may have several checking accounts. These may include a general fund checking account, a payroll checking account, and an imprest fund checking account utilized by senior management or officers of the corporation.

ESTABLISHING THE PETTY CASH FUND

Better internal control over cash disbursements is possible when payments are made by check. However, writing a check for small amounts can be impractical and inconvenient. Many businesses handle the situation by setting up a petty cash fund which is a fund used to pay relatively small amounts. It is technically called an imprest system that involves a three-step process:

1. Establishing the fund.
2. Making payments from the fund.
3. Replenishing the fund.

The two essential steps in establishing a petty cash fund are: 1) appointing a petty cash custodian who will be responsible for the fund and 2) determining the size of the fund. Normally, the amount would be set to cover anticipated expenses over the monthly accounting period. To establish the account, you will write a check for $15 directly to the account. Writing a check is easy in Peachtree.

To write a check to the Petty Cash Fund:

Step 1:	On the navigation bar, the left side of the Peachtree desktop, click on "Vendors & Purchases."
Step 2:	In the middle of the "Navigation Aid", Figure 8. 4, click on "Write Checks." Or follow the path Tasks > Write Checks from the menu bar.

Figure 8. 4   Purchases navigation aid

Step 3:	The check writing screen, Figure 8. 5, will appear.
Step 4:	On January 31, 2010, make the check, Number 157, payable to "Cash" or the name of the Petty Cash Custodian; the "Expense Account" will be Account No. 105, the Petty Cash Fund for $15.

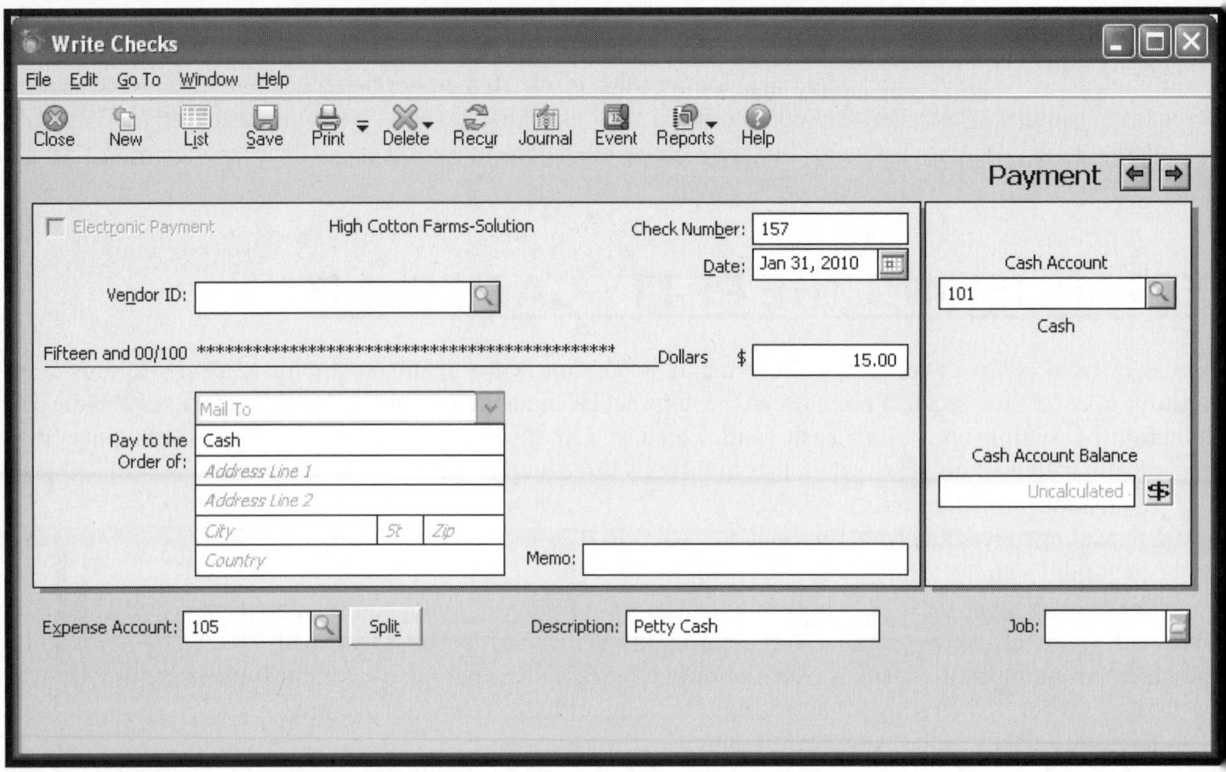

Figure 8. 5   Check writing screen

Often when a check is written it would be charged to or debited to an expense, thus increasing the expense item (a debit) and decreasing cash, an asset (a credit). If you were to increase a cash account, such as Petty Cash, that account would have to be debited also. Do *NOT* save this check. It is already in the system.

MAKING PAYMENTS FROM THE PETTY CASH FUND

The custodian of the petty cash fund has the authority to make payments from the fund. Usually management limits the size of expenditures that may be made. Each payment from the fund should be documented on a prenumbered petty cash receipt or voucher. This would be an internal system that is not available in Peachtree.

REPLENISHING THE PETTY CASH FUND

When the funds in the petty cash fund reach a minimum level, the fund is replenished. The Petty Cash account, number 105, will not be affected by the reimbursement entry. Utilize the Write Check screen to write a check to Petty Cash Fund. However, this time use the "Split" function to document the actual expenditures. On February 1, 2010 it is determined that the petty cash fund must be replenished.

Step 1:   To write the check, Number 158, open the write checks screen under Tasks.

Step 2: On February 1, 2010, it is determined the fund needs replenishing because it is discovered that the fund contains $2. There is a receipt indicating that $5 was spent for postage and that $8 spent for office supplies. Note that "Cash" is entered into the "Pay to the Order of" box.

Step 3: Utilize the "Split" function of write checks to record the Postage Expense of $5 and the Office Supplies Expense of $8. This is shown in Figure 8. 6.

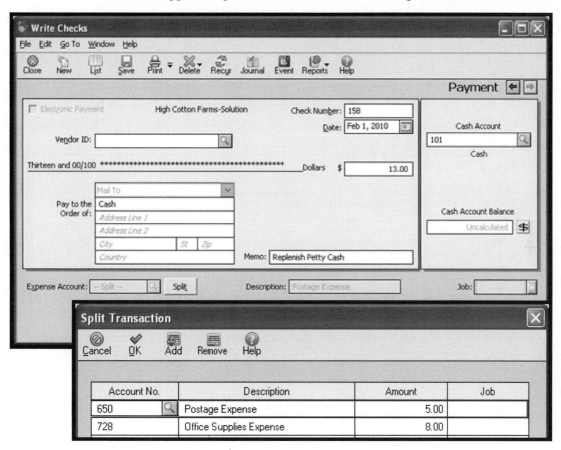

Figure 8. 6 Write checks screen to replenish the petty cash fund

RECONCILING THE BANK ACCOUNT

The bank and the depositor always maintain independent records of the checking account. The two balances are seldom the same at any given time. It is then necessary to understand the differences and determine whether any adjustments are needed. This process is called reconciling the bank account and is an easy automated step in Peachtree.

During the current accounting period, High Cotton had 15 banking transactions; 12 checks numbered 147 – 158 were written and three bank deposits were made. According to High Cotton's books, the Cash account balance is $14.82 as of January 31, 2010. This can be verified in the general ledger as shown in Figure 8. 7.

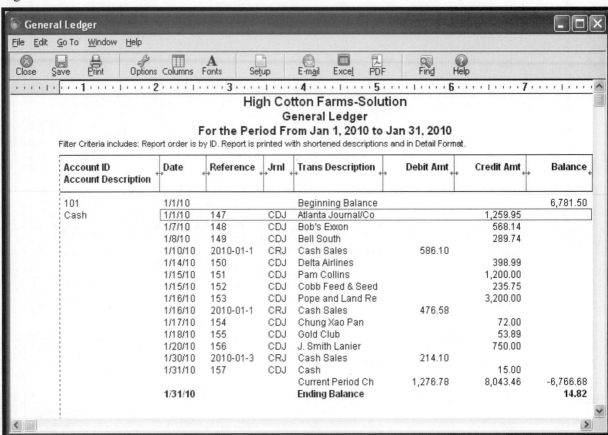

Figure 8. 7   Cash Account from the general ledger

When you received your bank statement, the balance according to the bank is $1,054.61. Checks 151 for $1,200.00 and 155 for $53.89 have not cleared the bank. Neither has the deposit on January 30th for $214.10.

To reconcile your bank account.

Step 1: Click on "Tasks" then toward the bottom of the pull down menu, click on "Account Reconciliation."

Step 2: Enter the account number being reconciled. It will be the Cash account, 101, the Peachtree account number, in the box provided just under the tool bar.

Step 3: At the bottom of the window, by "Statement Ending Balance" enter the balance as shown on the bank statement $1,054.61.

Step 4: Looking at the bank statement you know all but two checks 151 and 155 have cleared the bank. The deposit on January 30 for $214.10 did not clear either. Check the boxes on the account reconciliation screen by clicking in the box for those items that have cleared the bank.

Step 5: Your completed reconciliation should look like that shown in Figure 8. 8. Notice the tally at the bottom of the window. Also, bear in mind that not all information will be shown because scroll boxes (list boxes) are utilized. If you are satisfied with your work click on "OK" on the task bar.

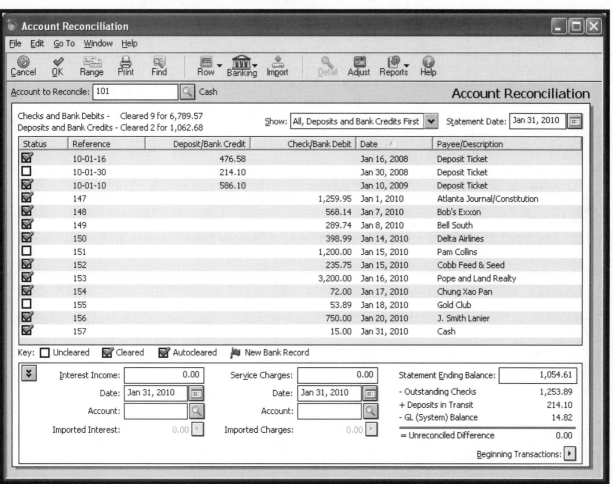

Figure 8. 8 The completed account reconciliation window

In the bottom right corner of the Account Reconciliation screen Peachtree shows you the mathematics of the reconciliation. From the bank's balance it subtracts outstanding checks, adds deposits in transit, and subtracts the GL balance for the account. The difference must equal zero before the account is "reconciled." Ensure that you print the reconciliation report through the "Print" option. These prints are kept in the files for reference and support later.

Comprehensive Do It! Problem, Poorten Company, Directory Wey_AP9e_Poorten_Co

Poorten Company's bank statement for May 2010 shows the following data:

Balance May 1st	$12,650	Balance May 31st	$14,280
Debit Memorandum:		Credit Memorandum	
NSF Check	$175	Collection of note receivable	$505

The cash balance per books at May 31 is $13,319. Your review of the data reveals the following:
1. The NSF check was received from Copple Co., a customer on May 15, 2010 on account, use a general journal entry to reinstate this accounts receivable.
2. The note collected by the bank was a $500, 3-month, 12% note. The bank charged a $10 collection fee. No interest has been accrued. Use the general journal to record this issue.
3. Outstanding Checks at May 31st are numbers 510 and 512 totaling $2,410.
4. There is one Deposit in Transit at May 31st, it is Deposit 05/30/10 for $1,752.
5. A Poorten Company check, number 503, dated May 10, 2010, cleared the bank on May 25, 2010. This check, which was payment on account, was journalized for $325. Use the Payments screen to locate the check, #503, correct the amount recorded to the proper amount, $352, then save the screen.

Instructions:
(a)   Use Peachtree Complete Accounting to prepare a bank reconciliation on May 31, 2010, for the Poorten Company.
(b)   Journalize any entries as directed
(c)   Print the Account Reconciliation screen, the Account Reconciliation report and the Cash Account Register reports found under the Accounts Reconciliation section of Forms & Reports.

Comprehensive Do It! Problem Solution:

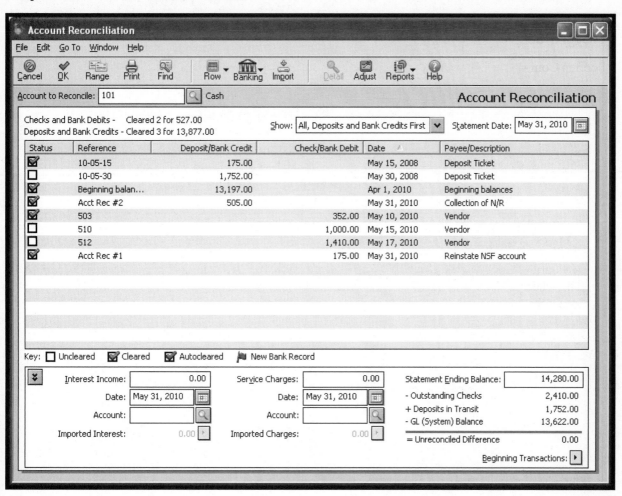

Account Reconciliation

File Edit Go To Window Help

Close Save Print Options Columns Fonts Setup E-mail Excel PDF Find Help

1 . . . . . . 2 . . . . . . 3 . . . . . . 4 . . . . . . 5 6

Poorten Company
Account Reconciliation
As of May 31, 2010
101 - Cash
Bank Statement Date: May 31, 2010

Filter Criteria includes: Report is printed in Detail Format.

Beginning GL Balance				13,197.00
Add: Cash Receipts				1,927.00
Less: Cash Disbursement				(2,762.00)
Add (Less) Other				330.00
Ending GL Balance				13,622.00
Ending Bank Balance				14,280.00
Add back deposits in transi				
	May 30, 2008	10-05-30	1,752.00	
Total deposits in transit				1,752.00
(Less) outstanding checks				
	May 15, 2010	510	(1,000.00)	
	May 17, 2010	512	(1,410.00)	
Total outstanding checks				(2,410.00)
Add (Less) Other				
Total other				
Unreconciled difference				0.00
Ending GL Balance				13,622.00

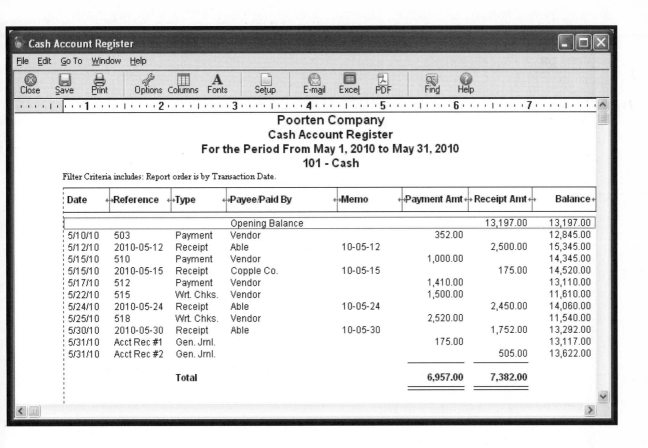

Cash Account Register

File   Edit   Go To   Window   Help

Close | Save | Print | Options | Columns | Fonts | Setup | E-mail | Excel | PDF | Find | Help

Poorten Company
Cash Account Register
For the Period From May 1, 2010 to May 31, 2010
101 - Cash

Filter Criteria includes: Report order is by Transaction Date.

Date	Reference	Type	Payee/Paid By	Memo	Payment Amt	Receipt Amt	Balance
			Opening Balance			13,197.00	13,197.00
5/10/10	503	Payment	Vendor		352.00		12,845.00
5/12/10	2010-05-12	Receipt	Able	10-05-12		2,500.00	15,345.00
5/15/10	510	Payment	Vendor		1,000.00		14,345.00
5/15/10	2010-05-15	Receipt	Copple Co.	10-05-15		175.00	14,520.00
5/17/10	512	Payment	Vendor		1,410.00		13,110.00
5/22/10	515	Wrt. Chks.	Vendor		1,500.00		11,610.00
5/24/10	2010-05-24	Receipt	Able	10-05-24		2,450.00	14,060.00
5/25/10	518	Wrt. Chks.	Vendor		2,520.00		11,540.00
5/30/10	2010-05-30	Receipt	Able	10-05-30		1,752.00	13,292.00
5/31/10	Acct Rec #1	Gen. Jrnl.			175.00		13,117.00
5/31/10	Acct Rec #2	Gen. Jrnl.				505.00	13,622.00
		Total			**6,957.00**	**7,382.00**	

P8-2A, Winningham Company, Directory Wey_AP9e_P8_2A_Winningham_Co

Winningham Company maintains a petty cash fund for small expenditures. The following transactions occurred over a 2-month period.

July   1   Established petty cash fund by writing a check on Cubs Bank for $200.

         15   Replenished the petty cash fund by writing a check for $196.00. On this date, the fund consisted of $4.00 in cash and the following petty cash receipts:

- Freight out, $94.00
- Postage Expense, $42.40
- Entertainment Expense, $46.60
- Miscellaneous Expense, $11.20

         31   Replenished the petty cash fund by writing a check for $192.00. On this date, the fund consisted of $8.00 in cash and the following petty cash receipts:

- Freight out, $82.10
- Charitable Contributions, $45.00
- Postage Expense, $25.50
- Miscellaneous expense, $39.40

August   15   Replenished the petty cash fund by writing a check for $187.00. On this date, the fund consisted of $13.00 in cash and the following petty cash receipts:

- Freight out, $75.60
- Entertainment Expense, $43.00
- Postage Expense, $33.00
- Miscellaneous Expense, $37.00

         16   Increased the amount of the petty cash fund to $300 by writing a check for $100.

         31   Replenished petty cash fund by writing a check for $284.00. On this date, the fund consisted of $16.00 in cash and the following petty cash receipts:

- Postage Expense, $140.00
- Travel Expense, $95.60
- Freight out, $47.10

Instructions:

(a)   Open the Winningham Company from within your student data set and familiarize yourself with the chart of accounts.

(b)   Using the general journal entry screen, journalize the petty cash transactions.

(c)   Print the general journal report and the general ledger for the period July 1, 2010 through August 31, 2010.

(d)   What internal control features exist in this petty cash fund?

P8-5A, Haverman Company, Directory Wey_AP9e_P8_5A_Haverman_Co

Haverman Company maintains a checking account at the Commerce Bank. At July 31, 2010, selected data from the ledger balance and the bank statement are as follows: The bank statement for July 2010 shows the following data. Haverman's checking account is GL (General Ledger) account number 102.

| | Cash in Bank | |
	Per Books	Per Bank
Balance, July 1	$17,600	$16,800
July receipts	81,400	
July credits		82,470
July disbursements	77,150	
July debits		74,756
Balance, July 31	$21,850	$24,514

Analysis of the bank data reveals that the credits consist of $79,000 of July deposits as shown below:
- June 30, 2010, Deposit, $7,000
- July 05, 2010, Deposit, $10,000
- July 10, 2010, Deposit, $10,000
- July 11, 2010, Deposit, $12,000
- July 13, 2010, Deposit, $10,000
- July 19, 2010, Deposit, $10,000
- July 22, 2010, Deposit, $10,000
- July 25, 2010, Deposit, $10,000

A credit memorandum of $3,470 for the collection of a $3,400 note plus interest revenue of $70. (*Hint:* Utilize a general journal entry to record this event.

The July debits per bank consist of checks cleared $74,700 as shown below:
- Check 501, June 25, 2010, $6,200
- Check 502, July 2, 2010, $10,000
- Check 503, July 5, 2010, $10,000
- Check 504, July 10, 2010, $10,000
- Check 505, July 11, 2010, $10,000
- Check 506, July 14, 2010, $10,000
- Check 508, July 23, 2010, $10,000
- Check 509, July 23, 2010, $230
- Check 510, July 24, 2010, $155
- Check 511, July 27, 2010, $8,115

And a debit memorandum of $56 for printing additional company checks. (*Hint:* Utilize the Service Charges window and Account 575 to journalize this value.)

You also discover the following errors involving July checks:

(1)   Check 509 for $230 to a creditor on account that cleared the bank in July was journalized and posted as $320. (*Hint:* Open this check up and correct the amount.)

(2)   A salary check to an employee for $255 was recorded by the bank for $155. (Hint: Assuming you will notify the bank of this error, adjust the Cash in Bank – Per Bank to ($24,514 - $100) to $24,414 for the reconciliation process.)

The June 30 bank reconciliation contained only two reconciling items: deposits in transit $7,000 and outstanding checks of $6,200.

Instructions:

(a)   Open the Haverman Company from within your student data set and familiarize yourself with the chart of accounts.

(b)   Utilize the general journal entry screen to journalize the events known by the bank but not known by you until this statement's receipt.

(c)   Correct the check through the Write Check screen, it is check number 509.

(d)   The error in the salary check must be resolved by requesting a new bank statement with the correction. For the reconciliation, adjust the bank's ending balance to ($24,515 - $100) $24,414.

(e)   Use Peachtree Complete Accounting to prepare a bank reconciliation on July 31 for Haverman Company. Assume that interest has been accrued. Note: the check can be adjusted in its recording process.

(f)   Utilize the account reconciliation capability of Peachtree Complete Accounting under Tasks.

(g)   Print out the account reconciliation report and the general journal report.

CHAPTER 9

Accounting for Receivables

OBJECTIVES
- Identify the different types of receivables.
- Explain how companies recognize accounts receivable.
- Distinguish between the methods and bases companies use to value accounts receivable.
- Describe the entries to record the disposition of accounts receivable.
- Compute the maturity date of and interest on notes receivable.

- Explain how companies recognize notes receivable.
- Describe how companies value notes receivable.
- Describe the entries to record the disposition of notes receivable.
- Explain the statement presentation and analysis of receivables.

TYPES OF RECEIVABLES

The term *receivable* refers to amounts due from individuals and other companies. They are claims that are expected to be collected in cash. Receivables are frequently classified as: Accounts Receivable; Notes Receivable; and Other Receivables.

ACCOUNTS RECEIVABLE

Accounts receivable are the amounts owed by customers on their account. They result from the sale of goods and services. These receivables generally are expected to be collected within 30 to 60 days. They are the most significant type of claim held by a company.

NOTES RECEIVABLE

Notes receivables are claims for which formal instruments of credit are issued as proof of the debt. A note receivable normally requires the debtor to pay interest. Notes and accounts receivable that results from sales transactions are often called trade receivables.

OTHER RECEIVABLES

Other receivables include nontrade receivables such as interest receivable, loans to company officers, advances to employees, and income taxes refundable. These are unusual and are generally classified and reported as separate items on the balance sheet.

Three primary accounting issues are associated with accounts receivable:

- Recognizing the receivable
- Valuing the accounts receivable
- Disposing of accounts receivable.

RECOGNIZING ACCOUNTS RECEIVABLE

Recognizing accounts receivable is relatively straightforward; most of the work was done in Chapter 5. To review, let's work through a sale using a simple company.

Step 1: From within your student data set, open "Jordache Company"

Step 2: Click on "Customer & Sales" at the left of the Peachtree window

Step 3: Click on "Sales/Invoicing" about midway on the navigation aid or follow the path Tasks > Sales/Invoicing from the menu bar.

Step 4: You will be presented with the blank sales invoice.

Step 5: On July 1, 2010, use Polo Co., the Customer ID for the Polo Co. and invoice number 2010-07-01A.

Step 6: Make the "Apply to Sales" entry area to sell Polo 100 pairs of Jeans at $10/each.

Step 7: Make sure the terms read: 2/10, net/30.

Step 8: Check your work with the completed screen as shown in Figure 9. 1.

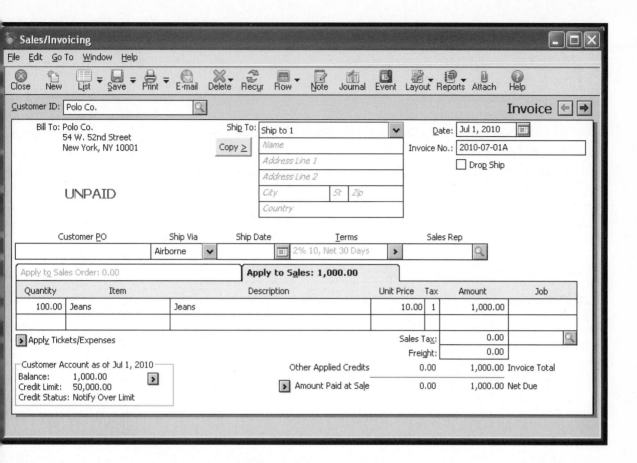

Figure 9. 1 Completed sales invoice for Polo Co.

On July 5, 2010, Polo returns ten pairs of jeans with a sales value of ($10 × 10 pairs) $100. This is a Credit Memo (reducing the asset Accounts Receivable) for the seller.

Step 1:	Follow the path Tasks > Credit Memos from the menu bar.
Step 2:	Select Polo Co. as the Customer ID and Peachtree will present information appropriate to Polo Co. from the database and from history.
Step 3:	Set the date to July 5, 2010, and the Credit No. and Return Authorization to 2010-07-05A.
Step 4:	On the Apply to Invoice No. tab, select Invoice Number 2010-07-01A from the drop-down menu options.
Step 5:	Enter 10 in the Returned window and Peachtree will extend the default Unit Price into the Amount window - $100.00.
Step 6:	Compare your work with Figure 9. 2 before using Save to record your effort. Make any corrections appropriate.

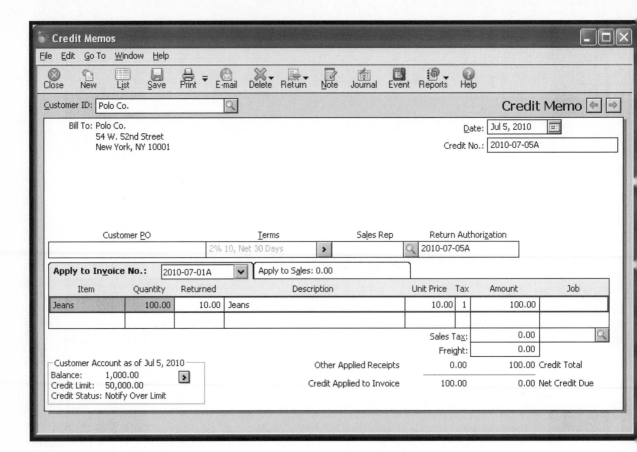

Figure 9. 2   The Credit Memos screen for Polo's returned merchandise

A review of the customer ledgers report at this point will show the $1,000 sale to Polo Co. on July 1, 2010, and the credit memo of $100 on July 5, 2010 which results in a balance of $900 for Polo Co.

On July 11, 2010, payment from Polo is received for the balance due which should include a discount of ([$1,000.00 - $100.00] × 2%) $18 because Polo returned $100 of the original $1,000 purchase and they paid within the 10-day time limit.

Step 1:   Follow the path Tasks > Receipts from the menu bar to open the receipts screen.

Step 2:   Set the deposit ticket ID to 10-07-11, set the reference and receipt number to 2010-07-11A, set the Date to July 11, 2010.

Step 3:   In the Customer ID window select Polo Co. from the drop-down menu options. Peachtree will fill in portions of the screen with information from the database and from the history of Polo Co.

Step 4:   Ensure that Invoice 2010-07-01A is selected. Peachtree has "applied" the credit memo to the invoice so the amount due is $900. Verify or adjust the discount to ([$1,000.00 - $100.00] × 2%) $18 and Peachtree should calculate the payment due of $882. If Peachtree does not, enter the correct value in the Amount Paid window.

Step 5:   Compare your work with Figure 9. 3 before using the "Save" icon on the task bar to record your work. Make any adjustments necessary.

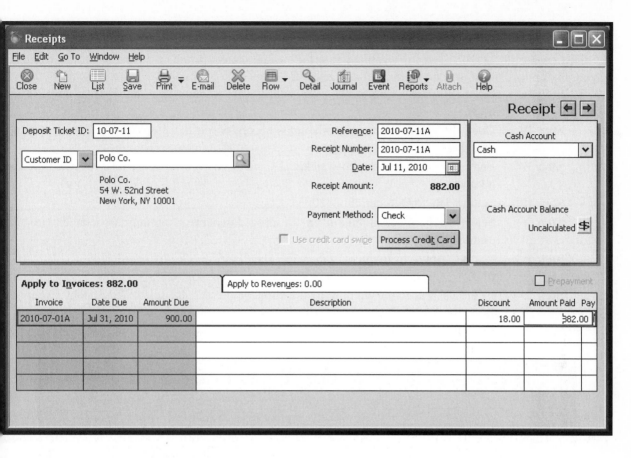

Figure 9. 3   The completed receipts screen for Polo Co.'s payment on July 11, 2010

A review of the Customer Ledgers report will now show the purchase, the credit memo value, the discount amount, and the payment.

WRITE OFF OF A CUSTOMER BAD DEBT

In some cases customers will not pay money owed, and the accounts receivable must be written off to bad debt expense. There are two methods for writing off bad debts.

Direct Method: Each invoice that is a bad debt is recorded as a debit to Bad Debt Expense and a credit to the specific by customer Accounts Receivable account as the bad debt is recognized. Unless bad debts losses are insignificant, the direct method is not acceptable for financial reporting purposes.

Allowance Method: A percentage of your accounts receivables is written off periodically or at the end of each fiscal year. The amount that is written off depends on the percentage of bad debt you believe your company incurs throughout the year. Normally, you would make a general journal entry affecting an accounts receivable (used as a contra-asset) account titled "Allowance for Doubtful Accounts" and Bad Debt Expense (an expense account). Then, each invoice is written off to Allowance for Doubtful Accounts as the bad debt is recognized.

To directly write off an invoice(s) whether partially paid or not paid at all in Accounts Receivable as a bad debt, follow the procedure below.

On July 5, 2010, Zaxby's Restaurant, Customer ID Zaxby's Restaurant, purchased 50 table clothes for $15 each. Record this event through the Sales/Invoice screen, use Invoice No. 2010-07-05B.

On October 20, 2010, it was determined that the restaurant went out of business and will not be paying their bill. Thus, it is to be written off as a bad debt

Step 1: Open "Jordache Company" from within your student data set, if it is not already open.

Step 2: Open the receipts screen available as an option on the drop-down menu associated with Tasks.

Step 3: Enter 10-10-20 as the deposit ticket ID, and 2010-10-20A as the reference and receipt number.

Step 4: Set the date to October 20, 2010.

Step 5: Select Zaxby's Restaurant from the drop-down menu options associated with the customer ID window.

Step 6: On the "Apply to Invoices" tab, select the "Pay" check box next to Invoice 2010-07-05B.

Step 7: In the cash account window to the right of the screen, select "Bad Debt Expense" from the drop-down menu options.

Step 8: Compare your with Figure 9. 4 and make any adjustments necessary before using the Save icon on the task bar to record your entry.

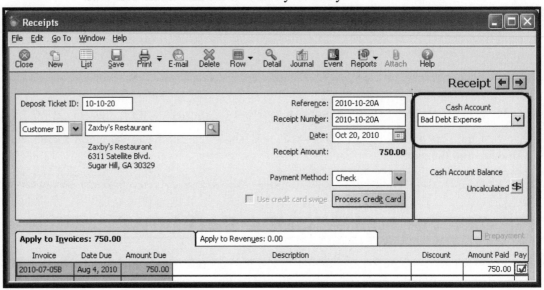

Figure 9. 4   Receipts screen used to write off bad debt as a direct write off

View the customer ledgers report, ensure you set the date through Options, to July 1, 2010 through October 31, 2010, and you will see the sale to Zaxby's on July 5, 2010, and the write-off of this sale on October 20, 2010 resulting in a zero balance. A general journal entry will not accomplish this write-off since it must be recorded into the specific accounts receivable account of Zaxby's. The receipts screen allows this access and interaction.

ALLOWANCE FOR UNCOLLECTIBLE ACCOUNTS

Under the direct write-off method, bad debts expense is seldom recorded in a period in which the revenue was recorded. No attempt is made to match bad debts expense to sales revenues in the income statement. On the other hand, the allowance method of accounting for bad debts involves estimating uncollectible accounts at the end of each period. This method provides better matching of associated expenses with revenues on the income statement and ensures that receivables are stated at their cash (net) realizable value, which is the net amount expected to be received in cash. It excludes amounts that the company estimates it will not collect. Receivables are therefore reduced by estimated uncollectible receivables on the balance sheet through use of this method.

The allowance method is required for financial reporting purposes when bad debts are material in amount. The allowance for doubtful accounts is entered through a general journal entry similar to the entry in Figure 9. 5.

To illustrate the allowance method, assume Jordache Company has credit sales of $1,200,000. Of that amount, $200,000 remains uncollected at the end of year, December 31st. The credit manager estimates 6% or $12,000 of these sales will be uncollectible. The general journal entry made on December 31, 2010, is shown in Figure 9. 5, below.

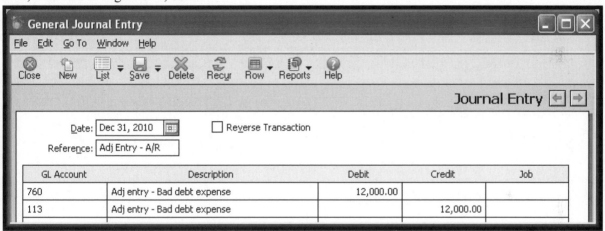

Figure 9. 5   Completed general journal entry for uncollectible accounts

Now, when the Zaxby's Restaurant account is identified as uncollectible, the cash account is set to Allowance for Doubtful Accounts, as shown in Figure 9. 6. Then it is saved.

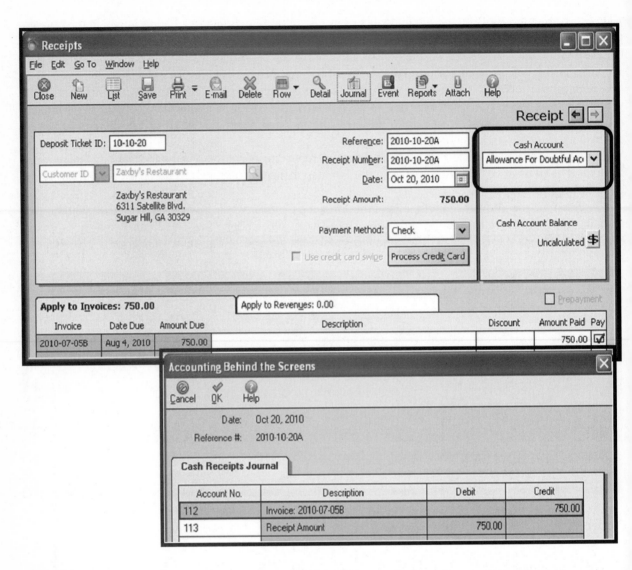

Figure 9. 6 Receipts screen used to write off bad debt with the allowance method

Note: If the desired account is not shown in the drop-down selection menu for the Cash Account, click on "Journal" on the task bar near the top of the receipts screen and select the proper account.

Once again, as noted in the direct write-off method, the receipts screen is utilized to access the specific Accounts Receivable account – Zaxby's. A general journal entry will not allow this access.

AGED RECEIVABLES REPORT

An aging schedule for accounts receivable is a listing of customer balances that are classified by the length of time they have been unpaid.

To obtain a sample aging report:

Step 1: Open Bellwether Garden Supply, Peachtree's tutorial company.

Step 2: Click on "Reports," then click on "Accounts Receivable."

Step 3: Click on "Aged Receivables" on the reports list.

A portion of the aged receivables report is shown in Figure 9. 7. Compare that with additional information provided in your text. Data may not be the same on your system. However, the basic format of the information should be similar. Scroll through the report and you will see that Bellwether has aged accounts – Cummings Construction has invoices in the 31-60 day range while Everly Property Management has invoices in the 61-90 day range.

Bellwether Garden Supply
Aged Receivables
As of Mar 31, 2007

Filter Criteria includes: Report order is by ID. Report is printed in Detail Format.

Customer ID Customer Contact Telephone 1	Invoice/CM #	0 - 30	31 - 60	61 - 90	Over 90 days	Amount Due
ALDRED Aldred Builders, Inc. Tony Aldred 770-555-0654	10129 10332	5,426.94 129.97				5,426.94 129.97
ALDRED **Aldred Builders, Inc.**		**5,556.91**				**5,556.91**
ARCHER Archer Scapes and Ponds Nancy Archer 770-555-4660	10209 10329 10317	7,374.69 59.98 49.99 -49.99				7,374.69 59.98 49.99 -49.99
ARCHER **Archer Scapes and Pond**		**7,434.67**				**7,434.67**

Figure 9. 7 Portion of Aged Receivables Report from Bellwether Garden Supply

RECOVERY OF AN UNCOLLECTIBLE ACCOUNT

Assume that on November 30, 2010, Zaxby's submits a check in the amount of $500 as final payment of the accounts receivable which has already been written off. To "recover" this amount utilize the Sales/Invoicing screen and enter the appropriate data for Zaxby. After entering the relevant data – Customer ID, Date, Invoice No, enter $500 in the Amount window. Then click on "Journal" on the task bar to allow selection of non-default accounts. Debit 112 – Accounts Receivable, and credit 113 – Allowance for Doubtful Accounts, as shown in Figure 9. 8.

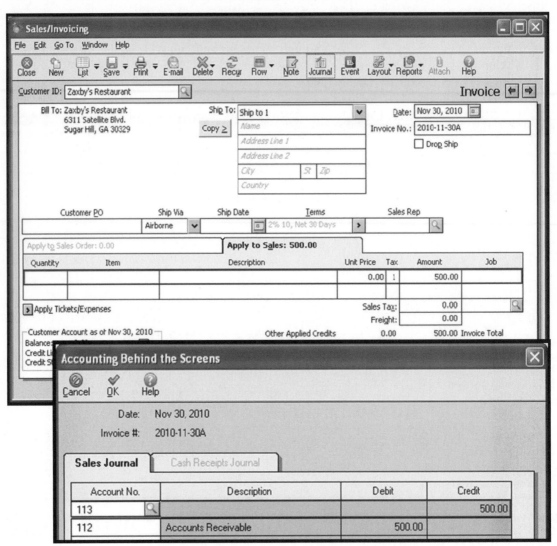

Figure 9. 8   Reinstating a portion of the Zaxby's write-off for collection

When "Save" on the task bar is utilized to record this reinstatement, the collection through the receipts screen can be accomplished. One of the tools that Peachtree offers is the "Events" icon on the task bar. When the "Events" icon is clicked you can record a note associated with this journal entry.

CREDIT CARD SALES

Credit card sales are usually considered cash sales by the retailer. Upon receipt of credit card sales slips from the retailer, the bank immediately adds that amount to the seller's bank account. Credit card slips are recorded on the deposit much like the way in which checks are recorded. A fee ranging from 2 to 6 percent of the credit card sales is charged to the seller.

Before you can begin recording credit card transactions in Peachtree Complete Accounting, you must consider the following questions.

When are credit card payments deposited into the company's bank account? Are payments received when the bank receives the credit card transactions (within 24 hours)? Or, is payment received three or more days after submitting the transaction record?

When does the bank debit from your bank account the credit card processing fee? Is the processing fee deducted from each customer's credit card use? Or, does the credit card company charge one processing fee for the entire month?

SET UP PEACHTREE TO ACCEPT CREDIT CARD RECEIPTS

Before you can record a credit card receipt from a customer, you must first set up an expense account in the chart of accounts in which to charge the credit card processing fees. Again, make sure Jordache Company is open in your student data set. To verify that account 765 is Credit Card Processing Expense:

Step 1: Click on "Maintain" from the main menu bar. Select "Chart of Accounts." Peachtree displays the Maintain Chart of Accounts window.

Step 2: Use the drop down arrow to verify the existence of the 765 – Credit Card Processing Expense account.

If you receive the entire credit card payment in one lump sum, then no other special accounts are required. However, if there is a delay between the time your customer makes the charge and when the credit card company reimburses you, you may want to set up unique accounts receivable accounts to track money owed by the credit card company. Still using Jordache Company verify that account 122 is AMEX Receivable.

You also must set up the credit card company that deposits money in your bank account as a vendor, not a customer. This way you can record and track processing-fee expenses.

SET UP A CREDIT CARD VENDOR FOR CUSTOMER RECEIPTS

You must set up a vendor from whom you will receive monthly credit card reimbursements. (This is the process, which has been completed for you.)

Step 1: From the Maintain menu, within the Jordache Company, select Vendors. Peachtree displays the Maintain Vendors window.

Step 2: Enter a vendor ID that represents the credit card (e.g., AMEX).

Step 3: Enter a vendor name that represents the bank or finance company of your credit card (e.g., American Express or Wachovia Bank Visa).

Step 4:   Select account 765, the Credit Card Processing Expense account as the Expense Account default.

Step 5:   Enter any additional information, as needed on the General tab. Then, select the Purchase Info tab. If the terms for this vendor were not the same as the default terms, this is where you could set them accordingly.

Step 6:   When finished entering vendor information, select Save, and close the window.

ENTER CUSTOMER CREDIT CARD RECEIPTS

When recording credit card receipts, always enter customer payments using "Receipts" from the Tasks menu. Apply the customer credit card receipts to open invoices or to revenue (prepayment). You cannot manage credit card receipts effectively when using the Amount Paid field in "Invoicing." You will also be unable to edit the invoice, if needed, later.

To keep the customer's ledger accurate and up-to-date, record the amount paid in Receipts as the "full" amount of the credit card charge, regardless of how the bank handles processing fees.

NOTES RECEIVABLE

Credit may also be granted in exchange for a promissory note, which is a written promise to pay a specified amount of money on demand or at a specific time. Promissory notes may be used when individuals or companies lend or borrow money; when the amount of the transaction and the credit period exceed normal limits or in settlement of accounts receivable.

On January 17, 2010, Mills Company purchased 1,000 towels on account. On February 28, 2010, it was agreed that the Accounts Receivable value of $7,500 would be placed on an interest bearing Notes Receivable by Jordache. This invoice is in your student data set.

The receipts screen can be utilized to convert this Accounts Receivable to a Notes Receivable. This will allow you to apply the value to the invoice.

Open the Receipt screen shown in Figure 9. 9. Use the "Receipt" process from the Navigation Bar to make the entry changing the Cash Account to the Notes Receivable Account as shown. Change the Cash Account to 115 – Notes Receivable. If 115 – Notes Receivable is not available in the Cash Account window, enter the value, $7,500, in the Amount Paid window then click on the "Journal" icon on the task bar to set the accounts. This screen will allow you to apply the value of the note to outstanding invoices as shown in the lower section of the screen.

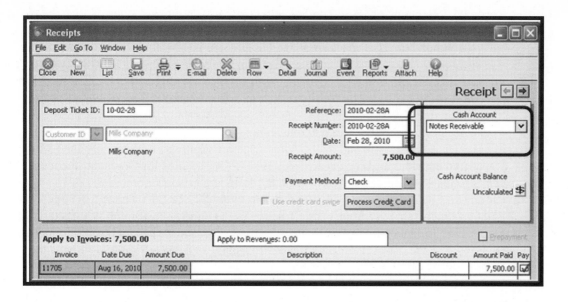

Figure 9. 9   Transferring an amount from accounts receivable to notes receivable

When this note is collected the receipts screen is again utilized. During collection you may have to use the Journal icon on the task bar to set the accounts appropriately.

Comprehensive Do It! Problem, Falcetto Company-Chapter 9, Directory Wey_AP9e_Falcetto_Co_Ch09

The following selected transactions relate to Falcetto Company.

Mar.   1   Sold 4,000 Pots for Potter for $5.00 each to Potter Company, terms 2/10, n/30. Utilize Invoice No. 2010-03-01A.

   11   Received payment in full from Potter Company for balance due. Utilize deposit ticket ID 10-03-11 and reference and receipt number 2010-03-11A. Ensure that the appropriate discount is applied to Invoice 2010-03-01A.

   12   Accepted Juno Company's $20,000, 6-month, 12% note for balance due. Using the receipts screen, utilize deposit ticket ID 10-03-12 and reference and receipt number 2010-03-12A. Ensure that Notes Receivable – Current is set in the Cash Account window.

   13   Made Falcetto Company Credit Card sales for $13,200. Within the Sales/Invoicing screen, utilize Falcetto Company Credit Cards with Invoice No. 2010-03-13A and 1,320 units of Credit Card Sales at $10.00 each.

   15   Made Visa credit card sales totaling $6,700. A 3% service fee is charged by Visa. Utilize the receipts screen, deposit ticket ID 10-03-15 and reference and receipt number 2010-03-15A as well as 670 units of Credit Card Sales items at $10.00 each.

Apr. 11   Sold accounts receivable of $8,000 to Harcot Factor. Harcot Factor assesses a service charge of 2% of the amount of receivables sold. Utilize the receipts screen with deposit ticket ID 10-04-11 and reference and receipt number 2010-04-11A. Set the Customer ID window to Accts Receivable as these accounts are being "resolved" – removed from the records in the sale of receivables. Utilize Invoice 2010-02-13A and ensure that the discount amount is $160.00. Use the Journal icon on the task bar to ensure that 770 – Service Charge Expense is appropriately debited before clicking "OK" and then "Save."

13 Received collections of $8,200 on Falcetto Company credit card sales. Utilize the receipts screen and Falcetto Credit Card Customer with deposit ticket ID 10-04-13 and reference and receipt number 2010-04-13A as well as Invoice 2010-03-13A.

13 Added finance charges of 1.5% to the remaining balance of Falcetto Company credit card sales. Utilize the Sales/Invoicing screen with Invoice No. 2010-04-13A. Use the Journal icon on the task bar to set the debit account to 112 – Accounts Receivable and 410 – Interest Revenue.

May 10 Wrote off as uncollectible $16,000 of accounts receivable. Falcetto uses the percentage-of-sales basis to estimate bad debts. After selecting Apply to Revenues on the receipts screen and ensure that the Cash Account is set to Allowance for Doubtful Accounts. This can be selected with the Journal icon on the task bar.

June 30 Credit sales recorded during the first 6 months total $2,000,000. The bad debt percentage is 1% of credit sales. At June 30, the balance in the allowance account is $3,500. Utilize the general journal entry screen to record only the allowance for doubtful accounts value.

July 16 One of the accounts receivable written off in May was from J. Simon, who pays the amount due, $4,000, in full. Utilize Receipts – twice, deposit ticket ID 10-07-16, reference and Receipts Numbers 2010-07-16A to reinstate the account and 2010-07-16B to collect it.

Instructions
(a) Prepare the journal entries for the transactions.
(b) Print the general ledger for the range January 1, 2010 through December 31, 2010.

P9-6A, Mendosa Company, Directory Wey_AP9e_P9_6A_Mendosa_Co

Mendosa Company closes its books monthly. On September 30, 2010, selected ledger account balances are:

Notes Receivable	$33,000
Interest Receivable	170

Notes receivable include the following:

Date	Maker	Face	Term	Interest
August 16	Chang Inc.	$8,000	60 days	8%
August 25	Hughey Co.	$9,000	60 days	10%
September 30	Skinner Corp.	$16,000	6 months	9%

Interest is computed using a 360-day year. During October, the following transactions were completed. Peachtree Complete Accounting does not have a method of computing Notes Receivable. You should use the general journal for your entries.

Oct. 7 Made sales of $6,900 on Mendosa credit cards.

12 Made sales of $900 on MasterCard credit cards. The credit card service charge is 3%.

15 Added $460 to Mendosa customer balance for finance charges on unpaid balances.

15 Received payment in full from Chang Inc. on the amount due.

24 Received notice that the Hughey note has been dishonored. (Assume that Hughey is expected to pay in the future.)

Instructions:

(a) Journalize the October transactions.

(b) Print the balance sheet for Mendosa Company prior to making any adjusting entries.

(c) Journalize the adjusting entries for accrued interest receivable as of October 31st.

(d) Print the General Journal report.

(e) Print the balance sheet as of October 31st. Compare the changes in accounts receivable and notes receivable between the unadjusted and adjusted balances.

CHAPTER 10

Plant Assets, Natural Resources, and Intangible Assets

OBJECTIVES

- Describe how the cost principle applies to plant assets.
- Explain the concept of depreciation.
- Compute periodic deprecation using different methods.
- Describe the procedure for revising periodic depreciation.
- Distinguish between revenue and capital expenditures, and explain the entries for

- each
- Explain how to account for the disposal of a plant asset.
- Compute periodic depletion of natural resources.
- Explain the basic issues related to accounting for intangible assets.
- Indicate how plant assets, natural resources, and intangible assets are reported.

SETTING UP A PLANT ASSET ACCOUNT

Plant assets are tangible resources that are used in the operations of a business and are not intended for sale to customers. In accounting, they are also called "Property, Plant, and Equipment"; "Plant and Equipment"; or "Fixed Assets." These assets are generally long-lived and are expected to provide services to the business for a number of years. With the exception of land, plant assets decline in service potential over their useful lives.

Plant assets often are split into four classes:

Land – the building site

Land Improvements – driveways, parking lots, fences, underground sprinkler systems, etc.

Buildings – stores, offices, factories, and warehouses

Equipment – check-out counters, cash registers, office furniture, factory machinery, and delivery equipment

In Peachtree, all property, plant, and equipment; plant and equipment; or fixed assets will be classified as "Fixed Assets" when the account is created as shown in Figure 10. 1. On the balance sheet, they are classified as Property and Equipment.

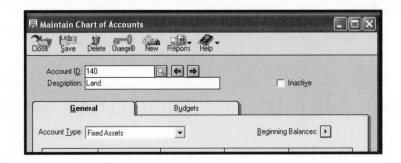

Figure 10. 1 Example of a fixed asset in maintain chart of accounts

Accumulated depreciation is a contra asset account to depreciable (fixed) assets. For example, depreciation will be charged against buildings, machinery, and equipment. The depreciable basis is the difference between an asset's cost and its estimated salvage value. Recording depreciation is a way to indicate that assets have declined in service potential during the period. Accumulated depreciation represents total depreciation taken to date on the assets.

An example from "Maintain Chart of Accounts" is shown in Figure 10. 2.

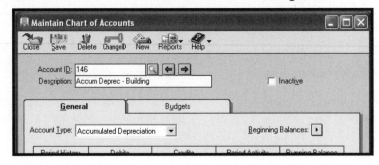

Figure 10. 2 Example of accumulated depreciation in maintain chart of accounts

Peachtree does not provide any special way of entering transactions for the purchase of Fixed Assets or entering transactions for Accumulated Depreciation besides a general journal entry, which was covered previously. Depreciable calculations must be done in a fixed asset manager or Excel and entered as a general journal entry.

CREATING THE FIXED ASSET ACCOUNT(S)

Three accounts will be created in this exercise. The first account to be created is for the purchase of a warehouse, account 148, and accumulated depreciation for the warehouse, account 149.

Step 1: Open "Blair Electronics" from within your student data set that you have been working with.

Step 2: The account number for "Warehouse" is 148, the account type will be Fixed Assets.

Step 3: The account number for "Accum Deprec – Warehouse" is 149, the account type will be Accumulated Depreciation.

Step 4: Access chart of accounts through Maintain from the menu bar.

Step 5: Enter "148" in Account ID, the number of the account.

Step 6: Enter "Warehouse" in description.

Step 7: Use the drop down arrow in Account type to find and select "Fixed Assets."

Step 8: Click on "Save."

The date entry is shown in Figure 10. 3, shown here.

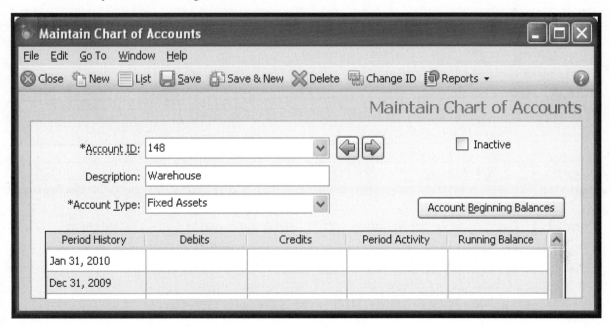

Figure 10. 3 Chart of accounts construction

The construction of Account 149, Accumulated Depreciation – Warehouse parallels this construction. The differences are 1) the account title must be abbreviated to fit the window so "Accum Deprec – Warehouse" which is adequate to identify the account is used. From the Account Type drop down selection, find and select "Accumulated Depreciation." Now build "Deprec Expense – Warehouse", number 619, type – expense if it is not already in your chart of accounts. (**Note:** These accounts have already been constructed for you – this is provided to ensure you know the account building process.)

MAKING THE ENTRY

Step 1: Make sure the Blair Electronics data file you have been working with is open. You will be making a compound general journal entry on June 18, 2010 to purchase land for $150,000 and a warehouse on that land for $250,000.

Step 3: Using the general journal entry screen, debit Land for $150,000 and Warehouse for $150,000, credit cash for $100,000, the down payment, and credit Notes Payable – Long-term for the balance of $300,000 for this acquisition. The journal entry is shown in Figure 10. 4, below. Then save the journal entry.

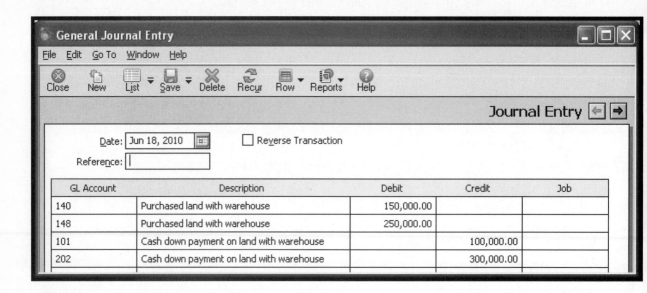

Figure 10. 4 Compound general journal entry to show purchase of land & warehouse

Using the straight line method of depreciation, it has been determined that the useful life of the warehouse will be 20 years and that the salvage value will be $15,000. Based on those figures, the monthly depreciation for the building will be $979.17

Cost of the Building – Salvage Value = Depreciable Value $250,000 – 15,000 = $235,000

Depreciable Value / 20 years = Yearly Depreciation $235,000 / 20 = $11,750

Yearly Depreciation / 12 months = Monthly Depreciation $11,750 / 12 = $979.17

RECURRING TRANSACTIONS FOR MONTHLY DEPRECIATION FOR THE WAREHOUSE

You learned how to make basic entries and adjusting entries earlier. However, since this will be a recurring transaction, one that happens the same way, every time, Peachtree can automate that step for you.

Step 1:   Make the general journal entry at the end of the month as you normally would to expense depreciation.

Step 2:   Debit the 619 – Deprec Expense –Warehouse account for $979.17.

Step 3:   Credit the 149 – Accumulated Depreciation – Building Account No. 149 for $979.17. Do not save the journal entry yet. The entry is shown in Figure 10. 5

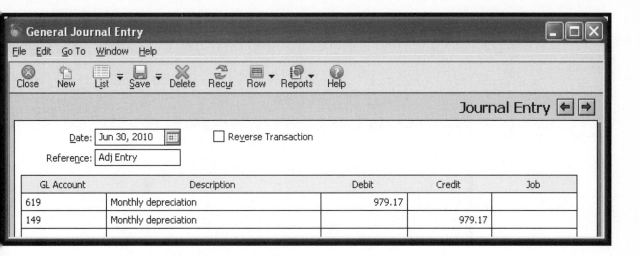

Figure 10. 5   Adjusting entry for depreciation

> **Step 4:**   Instead of saving the transaction as you did previously, click on "Recur" on the task
> bar as shown in Figure 10. 6 below.

Figure 10. 6   Menu bar for general journal entry

> **Step 5:**   You will be presented with the pull down menu as shown in Figure 10. 7. Click
> "Monthly" and enter "19" (June 2010 through December 2011) as the number of
> accounting periods this transaction will occur. Peachtree will only recognize
> accounting periods – months through the end of the available periods.

> **Step 7:**   Click "OK" and on the last day (the dialog box states the 30th) of every month for the
> next 19 months, Peachtree will automatically make this entry for you.

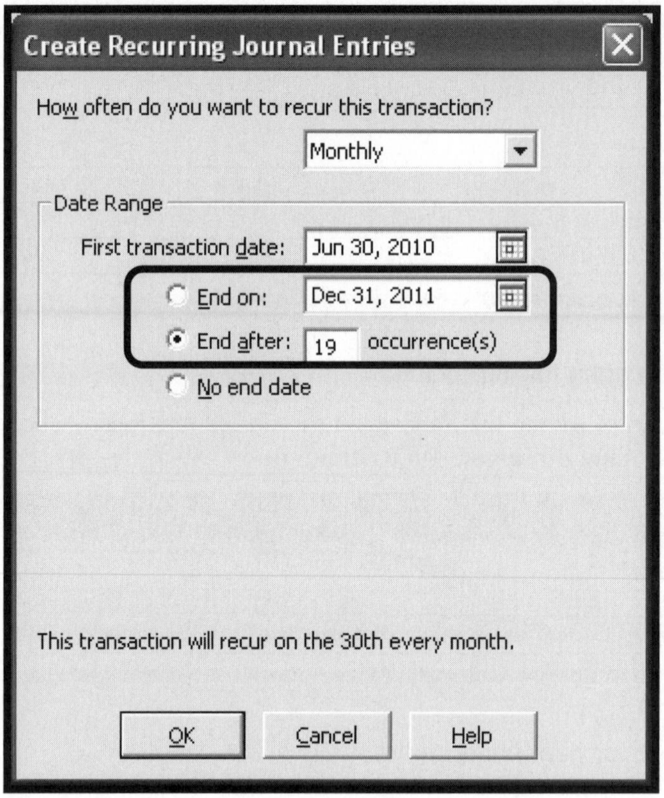

Figure 10. 7   Create Recurring Journal Entries screen

View the balance sheet for the period January 1, 2010 through December 31, 2011, for Blair Electronics. Look specifically at the assets section of the report, Figure 10. 8. Notice the addition of the new accounts. Also, notice the accumulated depreciation account for the warehouse.

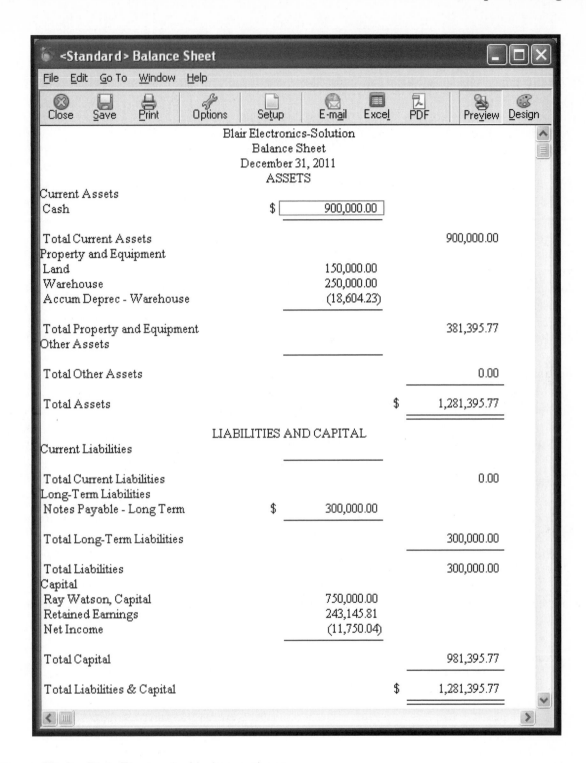

Figure 10. 8 Blair Electronics' balance sheet

REVISING PERIODIC DEPRECIATION

Occasionally things change in business. Blair Electronics used the following calculation to determine monthly depreciation:

Cost of the Building – Salvage Value = Depreciable Value	$250,000 – 15,000 = $235,000
Depreciable Value / 20 years = Yearly Depreciation	$235,000 / 20 = $11,750
Yearly Depreciation / 12 months = Monthly Depreciation	$11,750 / 12 = $979.17

And, based on that information, a recurring journal entry for depreciation was recorded which is posted for nineteen periods – June 2010 through December 2011. An energy and effort saving feature of Peachtree.

Assume that Blair has determined that there is only fourteen years left in the life of this warehouse as of January 1, 2011 and salvage value remains at $15,000.

To date the book value is ($250,000 – [$979.17 × 7])	$243,145.81
Adjusted depreciable value as of January 1, 2011 ($243,145.81 - $15,000)	$228,145.81.
Depreciable Value / 14 years = Yearly Depreciation	$228,145.81 / 14 = $16,296.13
Yearly Depreciation / 12 months = Adjusted Monthly Depreciation	$16,296.13 / 12 = $1,358.01

Since the revision is effective January 1, 2011, and Peachtree has 19 journal entries already recorded the steps to handle this are an adjustment to Peachtree's data.

Step 1: Open the General Journal report for viewing and set the options to display the range of January 2011.

Step 2: Double-click on the line depicting the adjusting entry for depreciation in 149 – Accumulated Depreciation – Warehouse dated January 31, 2011.

Step 3: With the adjusting entry for depreciation of the warehouse dated January 31, 2011 change the value from $979.17 to $1,358.01 in both the debit and credit lines.

Step 4: Click on the Save icon on the task bar and Peachtree presents the Change Recurring Journal Entries dialog box, shown in Figure 10. 9.

Step 5: The default selection for the Change Recurring Journal Entries dialog box is "This transaction only." Since this is change to all of the following recurring journal entries, ensure that "This transaction and all remaining" is selected. The Number remaining value of 11 does not include the January 31, 2011 journal entry so all twelve recurring journal entries for the year 2011 will be changed after you click on "OK."

Step 6: View the general ledger for the range of January 1, 2010 through December 31, 2011 to verify the values of $979.17 are recorded in 2010 and $1,358.01 is recorded in the 2011 entries for accounts 149 and 619.

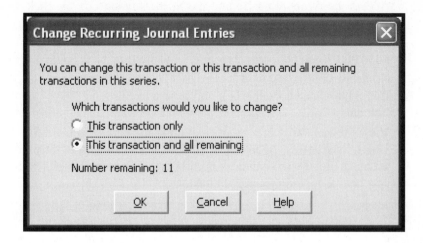

Figure 10. 9   Change Recurring Journal Entries dialog box

RETIREMENT OF FIXED ASSETS

When disposing of fixed assets the first step is always ensuring that depreciation is up to date for the calculation of gains and losses on disposal. Blair is going to sell the warehouse and the land it is on for $400,000 in cash on December 31, 2011. All gains and losses will be recorded to the warehouse in this example. To verify the book value of this sale the following are applicable:

Price of the land – Depreciation not applicable	$150,000.00
Purchase price of the warehouse	$250,000.00
Less: Depreciation for the year 2010 ($979.17 × 7 months)	$6,854.19
Less: Depreciation for the year 2011 ($1,358.01 × 12 months)	16,296.12
Book value of the warehouse	$226,849.69
Sale price on December 31, 2011	$400,000.00
Less: Value of the land	150,000.00
Less: Book value of the warehouse, December 31, 2011	226,849.69
Gain on disposal	23,150.31

This disposal must remove all values associated with the ownership of the land and the warehouse. Since it is a cash transaction:

Step 1: Using the general ledger report or the general ledger trial balance report for the date December 31, 2011, verify that Accumulated Depreciation – Warehouse is $23,150.31. Peachtree has made the necessary adjusting entries.

Step 2: Using the receipts screen, set the deposit ticket ID to 11-12-31 and the reference and receipt number to 2011-12-31A.

Step 3: Set the date to December 31, 2011.

Step 4: Put "Land Investors, Inc." in the Name window of the Customer ID area. This will preclude the necessity to set up this one time event as a customer.

Step 5: Enter the text and values shown in Figure 10. 10. Note that the second value of $23,150.31 is a negative value.

Step 6: Access the Accounting Behind the Scenes dialog box by clicking on Journal on the task bar.

Step 7: Set the accounts as shown in the bottom portion of Figure 10. 10. The last value, $400,000 is calculated by Peachtree. Ensure that the account is Cash – 101.

Step 8: Compare your work with Figure 10. 10 before clicking on OK on the Accounting Behind the Scenes dialog box and before clicking on "Save" on the receipts screen's task bar.

Step 9: View the general ledger report including the date December 31, 2011, and verify the 140 – Land, 148 – Warehouse, and 149 – Accumulated Depreciation – Warehouse accounts are all zero balance and that the balance of the 440 – Gain/Loss on Disposal account has a credit (negative) balance of $23,150.31.

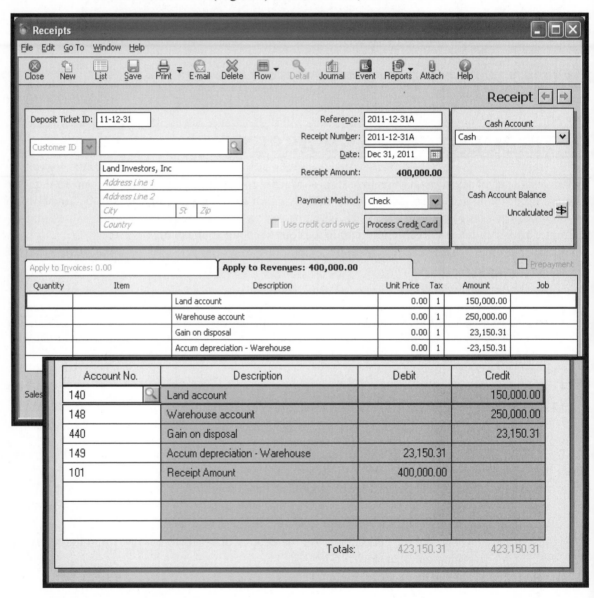

Figure 10. 9 Receipts screen and Behind the Scenes dialog box for the disposal of the land and warehouse

Comprehensive Do It! 2 Problem, Skyline Limousine Co.-Chapter 10, Directory Wey_AP9e_Skyline_Limousine_Co_Ch10

On January 1, 2010, Skyline Limousine Co. purchased a limo at an acquisition cost of $28,000. The vehicle has been depreciated by the straight-line method using a 4-year service life and a $4,000 salvage value. The company's fiscal year ends on December 31. **Note:** To keep this problem within two reporting periods adjustments need to be made as directed.

Instructions
(a)   (1)   Record the purchase of the limousine for $28,000 on January 1, 2010, with cash.

        (2)   Record the appropriate value of straight-line depreciation for the limousine assuming a salvage value of $4,000 for the timeframe of January 1, 2010, through January 14, 2014. Date this general journal entry January 31, 2010.

        (3)   Record the disposal of the limousine as of January 14, 2014, is if it is scrapped with no salvage value using a general journal entry dated January 31, 2010.

(b)   (1)   Record the purchase of the limousine for $28,000 on February 1, 2010, with cash.

        (2)   Record the appropriate value of straight-line depreciation for the limousine assuming a salvage value of $4,000 for the timeframe of February 1, 2010, through August 13, 2013. Date this general journal entry February 28, 2010.

        (3)   Record the disposal of the limousine as of August 13, 2013, for $5,000 cash using a general journal entry dated February 28, 2010.

(c)   Print the general ledger, a special report for this problem located in Reports > General Ledger.

(d)   Print the general journal report for the range January 1, 2010 through February 28, 2010.

(d)   Print the income statement for the range January 1, 2010 through January 31, 2010, to show the e affects of Instruction (a).

(e)   Print the income statement for the range February 1, 2010 through February 28, 2010, to show the affects of Instruction (b).

e

Comprehensive Do It! Problem Solution: (Partial)

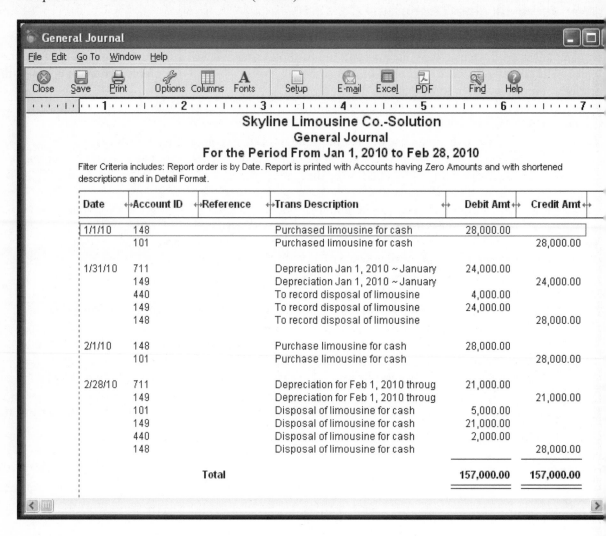

General Journal

File Edit Go To Window Help

Close Save Print Options Columns Fonts Setup E-mail Excel PDF Find Help

Skyline Limousine Co.-Solution
General Journal
For the Period From Jan 1, 2010 to Feb 28, 2010

Filter Criteria includes: Report order is by Date. Report is printed with Accounts having Zero Amounts and with shortened descriptions and in Detail Format.

Date	Account ID	Reference	Trans Description	Debit Amt	Credit Amt
1/1/10	148		Purchased limousine for cash	28,000.00	
	101		Purchased limousine for cash		28,000.00
1/31/10	711		Depreciation Jan 1, 2010 ~ January	24,000.00	
	149		Depreciation Jan 1, 2010 ~ January		24,000.00
	440		To record disposal of limousine	4,000.00	
	149		To record disposal of limousine	24,000.00	
	148		To record disposal of limousine		28,000.00
2/1/10	148		Purchase limousine for cash	28,000.00	
	101		Purchase limousine for cash		28,000.00
2/28/10	711		Depreciation for Feb 1, 2010 throug	21,000.00	
	149		Depreciation for Feb 1, 2010 throug		21,000.00
	101		Disposal of limousine for cash	5,000.00	
	149		Disposal of limousine for cash	21,000.00	
	440		Disposal of limousine for cash	2,000.00	
	148		Disposal of limousine for cash		28,000.00
		Total		157,000.00	157,000.00

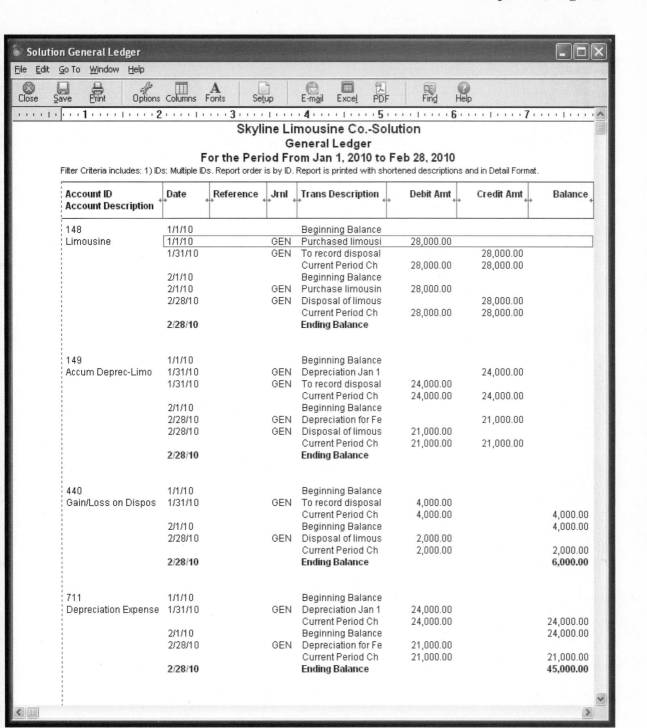

Solution General Ledger

File Edit Go To Window Help

Close Save Print Options Columns Fonts Setup E-mail Excel PDF Find Help

Skyline Limousine Co.-Solution
General Ledger
For the Period From Jan 1, 2010 to Feb 28, 2010

Filter Criteria includes: 1) IDs: Multiple IDs. Report order is by ID. Report is printed with shortened descriptions and in Detail Format.

Account ID Account Description	Date	Reference	Jrnl	Trans Description	Debit Amt	Credit Amt	Balance
148	1/1/10			Beginning Balance			
Limousine	1/1/10		GEN	Purchased limousi	28,000.00		
	1/31/10		GEN	To record disposal		28,000.00	
				Current Period Ch	28,000.00	28,000.00	
	2/1/10			Beginning Balance			
	2/1/10		GEN	Purchase limousin	28,000.00		
	2/28/10		GEN	Disposal of limous		28,000.00	
				Current Period Ch	28,000.00	28,000.00	
	2/28/10			**Ending Balance**			
149	1/1/10			Beginning Balance			
Accum Deprec-Limo	1/31/10		GEN	Depreciation Jan 1		24,000.00	
	1/31/10		GEN	To record disposal	24,000.00		
				Current Period Ch	24,000.00	24,000.00	
	2/1/10			Beginning Balance			
	2/28/10		GEN	Depreciation for Fe		21,000.00	
	2/28/10		GEN	Disposal of limous	21,000.00		
				Current Period Ch	21,000.00	21,000.00	
	2/28/10			**Ending Balance**			
440	1/1/10			Beginning Balance			
Gain/Loss on Dispos	1/31/10		GEN	To record disposal	4,000.00		
				Current Period Ch	4,000.00		4,000.00
	2/1/10			Beginning Balance			4,000.00
	2/28/10		GEN	Disposal of limous	2,000.00		
				Current Period Ch	2,000.00		2,000.00
	2/28/10			**Ending Balance**			**6,000.00**
711	1/1/10			Beginning Balance			
Depreciation Expense	1/31/10		GEN	Depreciation Jan 1	24,000.00		
				Current Period Ch	24,000.00		24,000.00
	2/1/10			Beginning Balance			24,000.00
	2/28/10		GEN	Depreciation for Fe	21,000.00		
				Current Period Ch	21,000.00		21,000.00
	2/28/10			**Ending Balance**			**45,000.00**

CHAPTER 11

Current Liabilities and Payroll Accounting

OBJECTIVES

- Explain a current liability, and identify the major types of current liabilities.
- Describe the accounting for notes payable.
- Explain the accounting for other current liabilities.
- Explain the financial statement presentation and analysis of current liabilities.
- Describe the accounting and disclosure

requirements for contingent liabilities.
- Compute and record the payroll for a pay period.
- Describe and record employer payrolls taxes.
- Discuss the objectives of internal control for payroll.

CURRENT LIABILITIES

Proper financial reporting often requires classified balance sheets and Peachtree provides them as the default presentation. Using Peachtree's example company, Bellwether Garden Supply, Figure 11. 1 is the liabilities section of Bellwether's balance sheet as of March 31, 2007. (You need not open Bellwether at this time.) Notice that liabilities is divided into two sections. Current liabilities such as accounts payable, accrued expenses, and sales tax payable are shown in the first section and a subtotal of $174,580.91 in this example, is presented for them. Long-term liabilities follows current liabilities, notes payable-noncurrent in this case, and a subtotal of $4,000, in this example, is presented. Then current and long-term liabilities is totaled to $178,580.91.

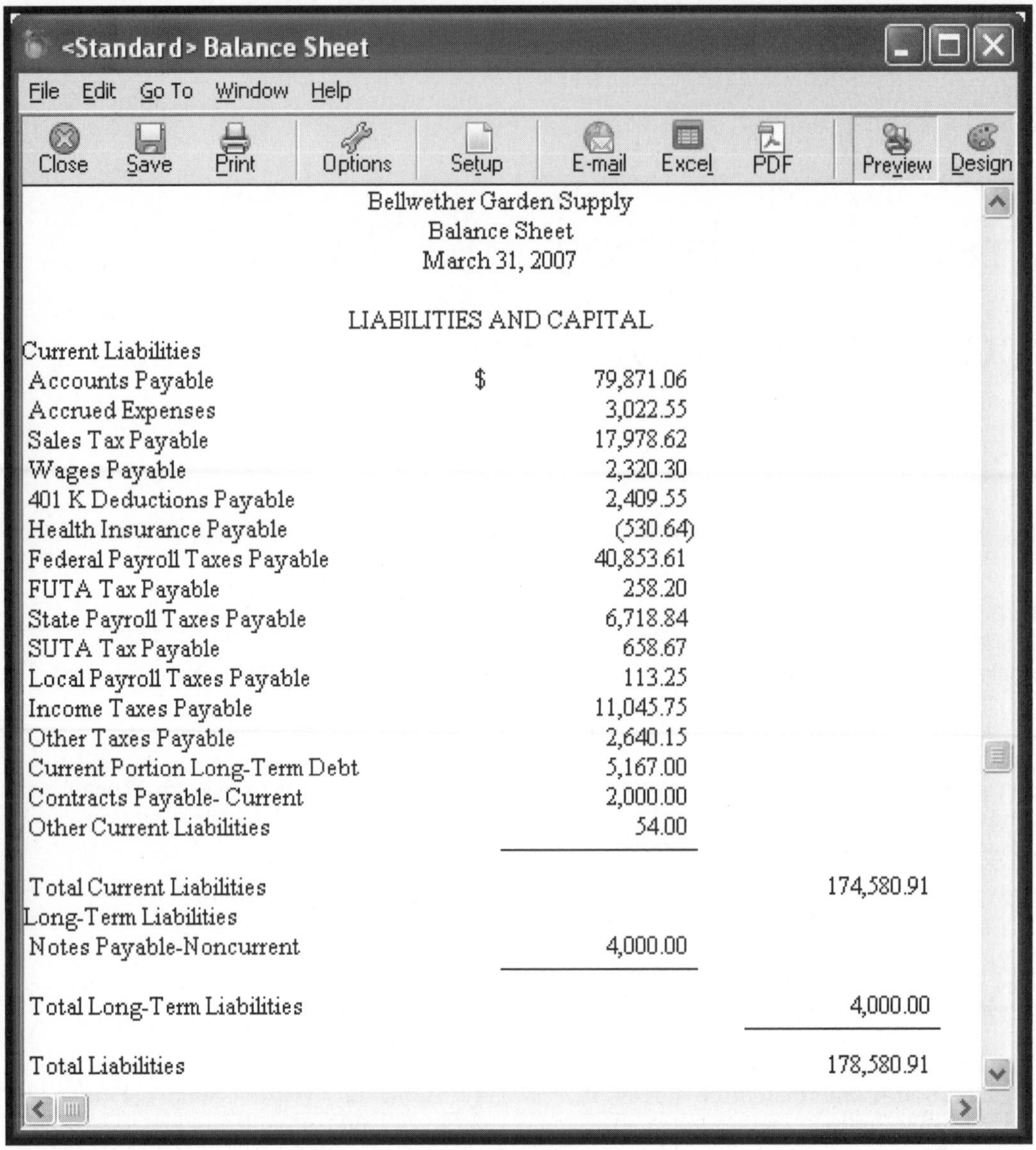

Bellwether Garden Supply
Balance Sheet
March 31, 2007

LIABILITIES AND CAPITAL

Current Liabilities			
Accounts Payable	$	79,871.06	
Accrued Expenses		3,022.55	
Sales Tax Payable		17,978.62	
Wages Payable		2,320.30	
401 K Deductions Payable		2,409.55	
Health Insurance Payable		(530.64)	
Federal Payroll Taxes Payable		40,853.61	
FUTA Tax Payable		258.20	
State Payroll Taxes Payable		6,718.84	
SUTA Tax Payable		658.67	
Local Payroll Taxes Payable		113.25	
Income Taxes Payable		11,045.75	
Other Taxes Payable		2,640.15	
Current Portion Long-Term Debt		5,167.00	
Contracts Payable- Current		2,000.00	
Other Current Liabilities		54.00	
Total Current Liabilities			174,580.91
Long-Term Liabilities			
Notes Payable-Noncurrent		4,000.00	
Total Long-Term Liabilities			4,000.00
Total Liabilities			178,580.91

Figure 11. 1 Bellwether Garden Supply partial balance sheet as of March 31, 2007

How does Peachtree know what to put where in the report? Account type or classification. Peachtree has numerous Account Types or classifications and they are, with financial statement placement:

Income Statement:

- Income – Income Statement
- Cost of Sales (Cost of Goods Sold)
- Expenses

Retained Earnings Statement:

- Equity – Doesn't close (Capital, Owner's equity)
- Equity – Gets closed
- Equity – Retained Earnings

Balance Sheet
    Assets:
        Current Assets:
            Cash
            Accounts Receivable
            Inventory
            Other Current Assets
        Property and Equipment:
            Fixed Assets – Balance Sheet
            Accumulated Depreciation
        Other Assets"
            Other Assets – Balance Sheet – Other Assets
    Liabilities:
        Current Liabilities:
            Accounts Payable
            Other Current Liabilities
        Long-Term Liabilities:
            Long Term Liabilities
    Capital:
        Equity – Doesn't close (Capital, Owner's equity)
        Equity – Retained Earnings
        Net Income – Peachtree processes revenues and expenses as soon as they are recorded through the income statement to the statement of retained earnings and then to the balance sheet. The sum of revenues less expenses is held in the Capital section of the balance sheet under the title of Net Income until the Year-End Wizard closes the nominal accounts and moves these values to Retained Earnings.
        Withdrawals and Dividends – Peachtree presents withdrawals and dividends on the statement of retained earnings and in the Capital section of the balance sheet, similar to Net Income, until the Year-End Wizard closes the nominal accounts and moves these values to Retained Earnings.

    This Account Type or classification is established during the construction of the account through the drop-down menu options as shown in Figure 11. 2.

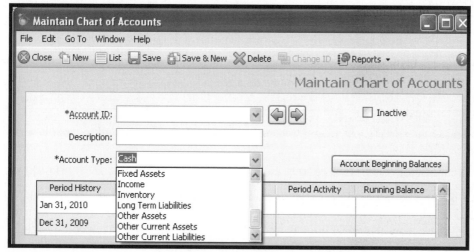

Figure 11. 2 Partial listing of account type or classification options

With the exception of Equity – Retained Earnings, an account required by Peachtree for its processing of revenues, expenses, and withdrawals or dividends, the account type or classification given to an account can be changed as needed. This global change is not recommended as ALL transactions to this account title will be changed causing possible alternations not expected in the general ledger and financial reports. The recommended methodology is to create a new account and transfer the value with a journal entry.

JOURNAL ENTRIES FOR CURRENT LIABILITIES

Open the Payroll Tax Example Company from within the student data set. All of the accounts have been established. Using the textbook presentation, First National Bank agrees to lend $100,000 on March 1, 2010, if Payroll Tax Example Company (PTEC) signs a $100,000, 12%, four-month note. With an interest-bearing promissory note, the amount of assets received upon issuance of the note generally equals the note's face value. PTEC therefore will receive $100,000 cash and will make the following journal entry utilizing the Receipt screen within Peachtree. Use deposit ticket ID of 10-03-01 and reference and receipt number 2010-03-01A. Change Customer ID to Vendor ID to select First National Bank. Using the Journal icon on the task bar ensure that the credit account is 200 – Notes Payable–Current after the value is entered in the Amount window. The description text is "To record issuance of 12%, 4-month note to First National Bank." Compare your work with Figure 11. 3, make any adjustments necessary before using the Save icon on the task bar to record your work.

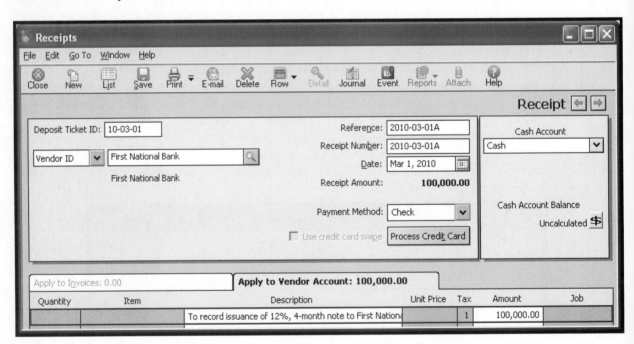

Figure 11. 3 Receipts screen to record the cash receipt associated with the note payable

The note payable is due July 1, 2010, with interest incurred to that date. The interest expense is computed by Face Value of Note × Annual Interest Rate × Time in Terms of One Year or $100,000 × 12% × (4 months/12 months), or $4,000. To record the interest expense incurred through June 30, 2010, of $4,000, a general journal entry, Figure 11. 4, is written. Record and save this entry as shown.

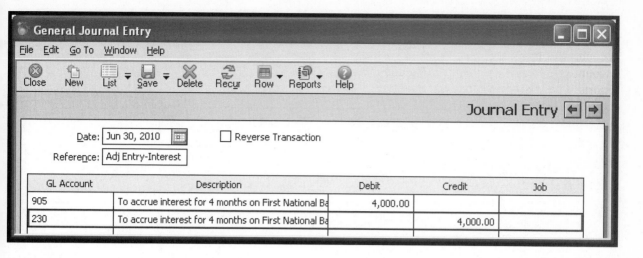

Figure 11. 4 Receipts screen to record the cash receipt associated with the note payable

When PTEC pays the note at maturity, July 1, 2010, you need to write a check. Using the Write Check screen, write check number 101, Date July 1, 2010, select First National Bank from the Vendor ID drop-down options. Enter the amount $104,000 in the $ (Dollars) window. Entering the note payable account number, if known, in the Memo window helps First National Bank associate the check with the note. Click on "Split" to the right of the expense account window which will allow you to record the debits of the check to more than one account. The accounts are 200 – Notes Payable-Current for $100,000, the face value of the note, and 230 – Interest Payable, the interest incurred during the note's life. Compare your Write Check Screen with Figure 11. 5 and make any necessary adjustments before using Save on the task bar to record the check.

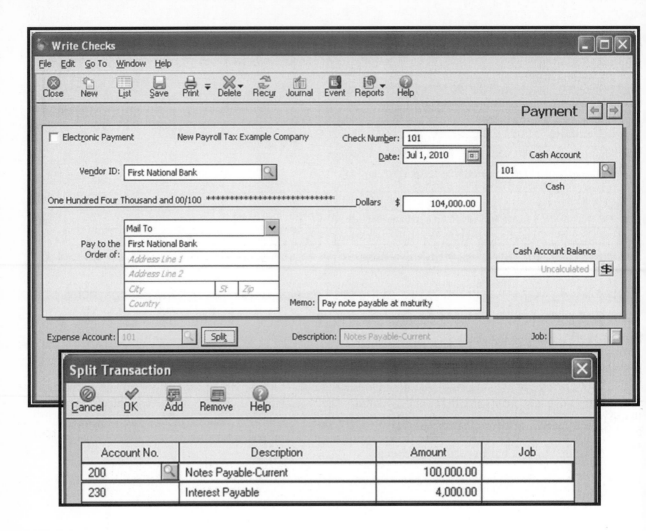

Figure 11. 5 Write check screen to resolve the note payable at maturity

The events shown here are "associated" through the screens and actions of their timeline. With Peachtree, the receipts screen is utilized to accept the money brought into PTEC with the Note Payable. Then a general journal entry is utilized to record the recognition of interest expense incurred. And, finally, the write checks screen with its Split function, is utilized to pay off the note and interest upon maturity. You can view reports such as the general ledger, the income statement, and the balance sheet to see how this series of events has affected PTEC. Since this series of events has taken place between March 1, 2010, and July 1, 2010, you will need to use the Options icon on the task bar to change the displayed periods.

SETTING UP SALES TAXES

Sales taxes are set up through the path Maintain > Sales Taxes and select "Set Up A New Sales Tax" as shown in Figure 11. 6.

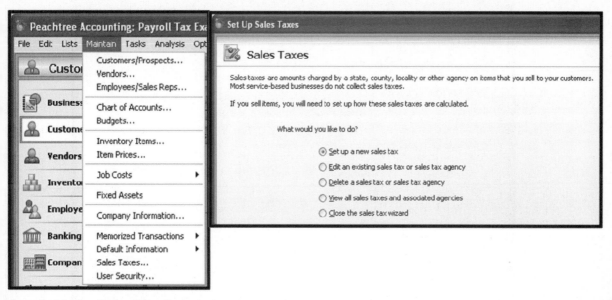

Figure 11. 6   Sales Tax Setup screen

While Peachtree can have multiple tax rates and multiple taxing agencies, this process will set up a single tax rate for a single taxing agency. The next step is to set the tax rate. The tax rate, 6%, is entered in the What is the Total Rate That You Will Charge? window of the Set Up Sales Taxes screens as shown in Figure 11. 6. Ensure that the How Many Individual Rates Make Up This Total Rate? window is set to 1 as shown in Figure 11. 7. Then click on Next near the bottom right corner of the screen to advance the Wizard.

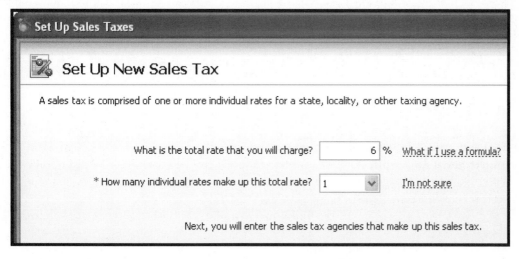

Figure 11. 7   Set Up Sales Taxes, Rates and number of rates

The next screen asks the Sales Tax Agency ID. This is a very limited text window. Entry GA to identify the State of Georgia as the taxing agency. In the Sales Tax Agency Name window enter GA Dept of Revenue, as shown in Figure 11. 8. The Georgia Department of Revenue has been set up in Vendors as GA Dept of Revenues for selection as to which vendor you submit sales taxes collected to. Ensure that only a single tax rate is utilized and that the tax rate is still set at 6%. Utilize Account 245 – Sales Taxes Payable in the Select An Account To Track Sales Taxes. Compare your work with Figure 11. 8 and make any adjustments necessary before clicking on "Next" to advance the Wizard.

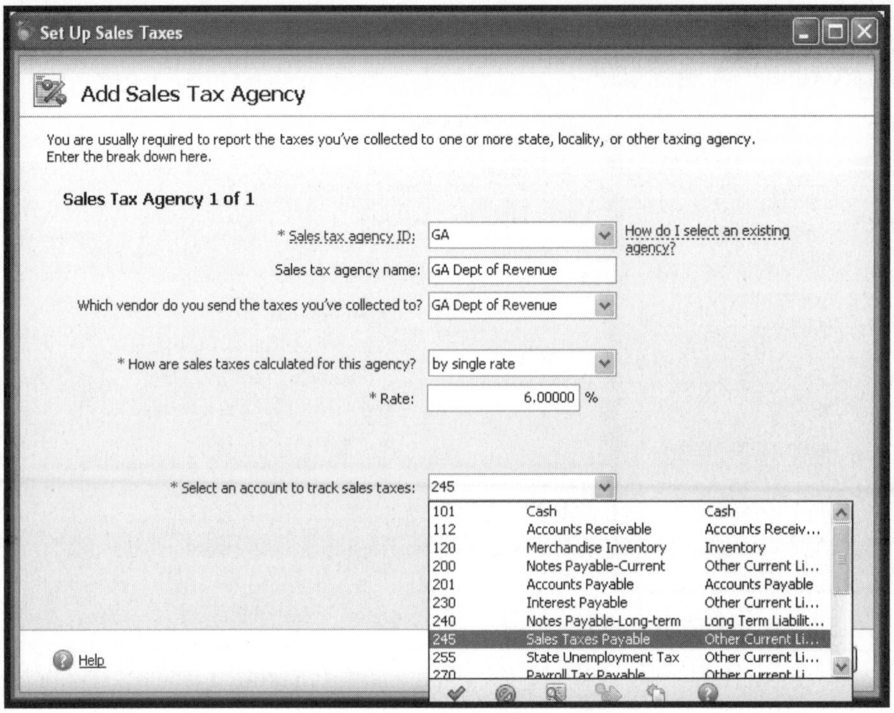

Figure 11. 8 Set Up Sales Taxes, Add Sales Tax Agency

In the Sales Tax Entered window set the Sales Tax ID to GA for Georgia. Enter GA State Sales Tax in the Sales Tax Name window and ensure that you do not charge sales tax on freight. Compare your work with Figure 11. 9 and make any adjustments before completing the process by clicking on "Finish."

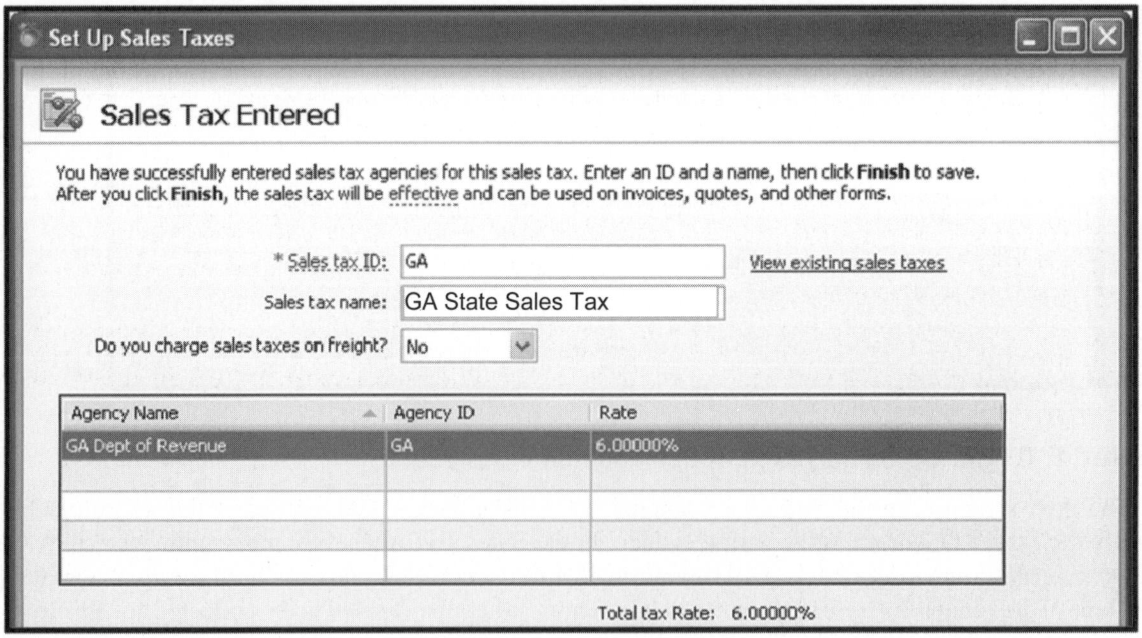

Figure 11. 9 Set up sales taxes, sales taxes entered screen

If Peachtree takes you back to the starting dialog box, Figure 11. 6, close the dialog box to complete the process.

COLLECTING SALES TAXES

Once the taxing agency has been set up so Peachtree will calculate and record the collection of sales taxes, you can apply sales taxing to sales. Follow the path Tasks > Sales/Invoicing and select Cash as the customer for a sale on January 10, 2010, with an Invoice No. of 2010-01-10A. The sale is five hundred Juno Jumpers for $20.00 each. This sale will extend to sale value of $10,000.00. From the magnifying glass option select GA – GA State Sales Tax – 6%, the only option, from the list. Peachtree will calculate the sales tax of $600.00 and identify it as GA. ***DO NOT*** save your work yet but compare it with Figure 11. 10.

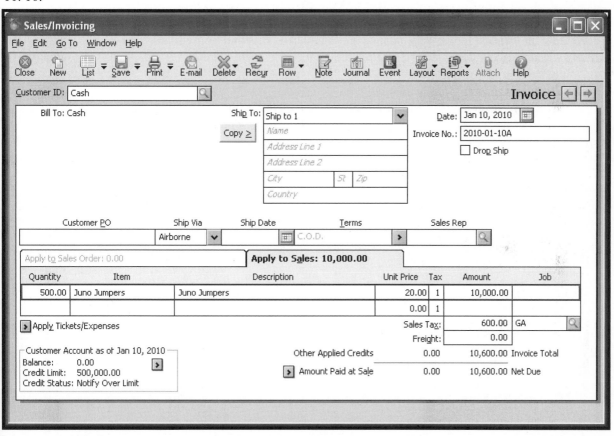

Figure 11. 10 Sales/Invoicing with sales taxes applied

Suppose that a portion of the sale is exempt from sales for some reason. In the second line of the Sales/Invoicing screen set the quantity to 10 and select Pots for Potter as the item. Ensure that $5.00 appears as the unit price. After you click into the tax window for the second line select 2 from the drop-down menu or simply type it in. Then tab or advance out of the window to extend the values. Since "2" is titled Exempt in the taxation options, no sales taxes are applied to the second item. Confirm that the sales tax value has remained at $600.00 – 6% of the $10,000.00 of Juno Jumpers.

Compare your work with Figure 11. 11 and make any corrections necessary before saving it.

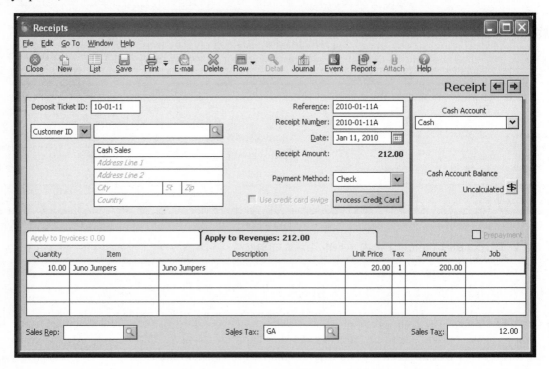

Figure 11. 11 Sales/Invoicing with sales taxes applied to only one of two items

Review the general ledger and balance sheet under reports and you will see that your company now has 245 – Sales Taxes Payable for $600 related to the sale on Invoice No. 2010-01-10A on January 10, 2010. When sales taxes must be remitted to the taxing agency you can utilize "Pay Bills" or "Write Checks" to submit the appropriate amount.

When a cash sale is made utilizing the receipts screen and sales taxes are collected the presentation is slightly different. Using Figure 11. 12 of the receipts screen as a guide, enter the deposit ticket ID of 10-01-11. Manually enter "Cash Sales" in the "Name" window rather than select Cash (customer) from the Customer ID options. Utilize reference and receipt number 2010-01-11A with a date of January 11, 2010. The sale is ten Juno Jumpers for $20.00 each and ensure that the tax code is set to 1. From the drop-down menu options associated with the sales tax window at the bottom select GA – GA State Sales Tax – 6%, the only option, from the list. And Peachtree will calculate the sales tax of $12.00

Figure 11. 12 Receipts screen for a cash sale with sales taxes collected

The value shown in receipt amount, below the reference, receipt number, and date area, of $212.00 indicates the amount collected. Compare your work with Figure 11. 12 and make any necessary corrections before saving your work.

If you review reports such as the general ledger or the balance sheet you will see that the value owed as sales taxes payable has been updated for this sale.

UNEARNED REVENUES

As shown in the Weygandt Accounting Principles text, assume that PTEC has sold ten thousand season tickets for $50.00 each on August 6, 2010, and one-fifth of the ticket value is earned for each of the five home games during the season. Two accounts have been set up for these events – 212 – Unearned Football Ticket Rev(enue) and 403 – Football Ticket Revenue. A customer – Football Fans – has been set up for this event and the account credited will be 212 – Unearned Football Ticket Rev(enue).

Utilize the receipts screen under Tasks to record the sale. The deposit ticket ID is 10-08-06, the reference and receipt number is 2010-08-06A with a date of August 6, 2010. The customer ID is Football Fans. Click on the prepayment box approximately two-thirds of the way down the right side of the dialog box. This changes several areas of the Apply to Revenues section of the screen. Enter the text "Football Tickets – 10,000 at $50.00 each, five game pack" in the description to describe the events of the receipt and enter the value (10,000 × $50.00) $500,000 in the amount window. While your cursor is still on the first journal line, click on the Journal icon on the task bar and set the credit account to 212 – Unearned Football Ticket Rev(enue). Compare your work with Figure 11. 13 and make any adjustments necessary before saving the transaction.

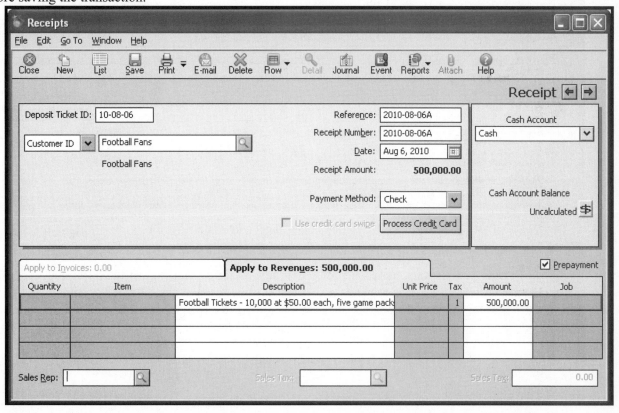

Figure 11. 13 Receipts screen for a prepayment of ten thousand football tickets for $50.00 each

If you view your income statement at this time you will not see any revenue for the prepayment as it is not a sale. While the balance sheet will show an increase in cash, this increase is balanced by an increase in unearned football ticket revenue.

When the first football game is played on September 9, 2010, one-fifth of the ticket revenue, $100,000, is earned. Utilize the sales/invoice screen under Tasks. Set the customer ID to "Football Fans," the date to September 7, 2010, and the Invoice No. to 2010-09-07A. Enter (10,000 / 5) 2,000 as the quantity, and "Football Ticket" as the Item. Verify that the unit price is $50 with a 2 in the tax window and the amount is $100,000. Click on "Journal" while your cursor is still on the first line of the journal entry and set the debit account to 212 – Unearned Football Ticket Rev(enue). This will reduce the liability being recorded for the prepayment recorded on August 6, 2010. Compare your work with Figure 11. 14 and make any corrections necessary before saving it.

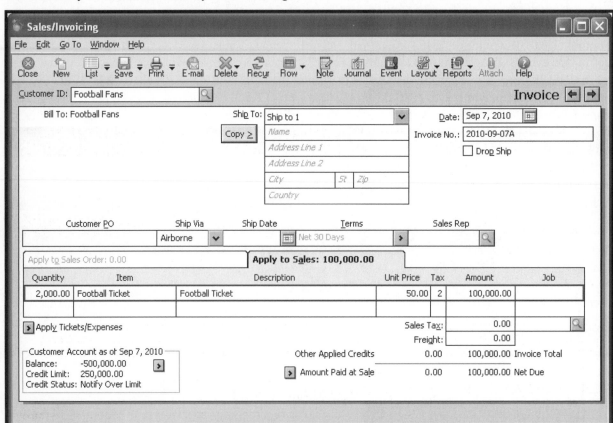

Figure 11. 14 Sales/Invoicing screen to document the earning of prepaid funds

If you review your income statement for PTEC at this time you will see the $100,000 in football ticket revenue without an associated increase in the cost of goods sold since Peachtree has no data on the cost of these tickets. Viewing the balance sheet will show the decrease in unearned football ticket revenue and the increase in net income for the conversion of the prepayment to revenue.

RECORDING A CONTINGENT LIABILITY

Contingent liabilities are required to correctly report the events and liabilities of the company. To record the contingent liability associated with warranties two accounts have been created – 225 – Estimated Warranty Liability and 625 – Warranty Expense.

Utilizing the values within the Weygandt Accounting Principles textbook, assume that in 2010 PTEC sells 10,000 washers and dryers at an average price of $600 each. (The entries associated with these sales have been recorded.) The selling price includes a one-year warranty on parts. PTEC expects that 500 units (5%) will be defective and that warranty repair costs will average $80 per unit. In 2010, the company honors warranty contracts on 300 units, at a total cost of $24,000. At December 31, it is necessary to accrue the estimated warranty costs on the 2010 sales. PTEC computes the estimated warranty liability as $40,000.

On December 31, 2010, PTEC makes an adjusting entry utilizing the general journal entry screen with a reference of Adj Entry-Warranty. The debit account is 625 – Warranty Expense and the credit account is 225 – Estimated Warranty Liability. The description is "To accrue estimated warranty costs." The debit and credit value, as computed, is $40,000. Check your adjusting entry with Figure 11. 15 and make any appropriate corrections before continuing.

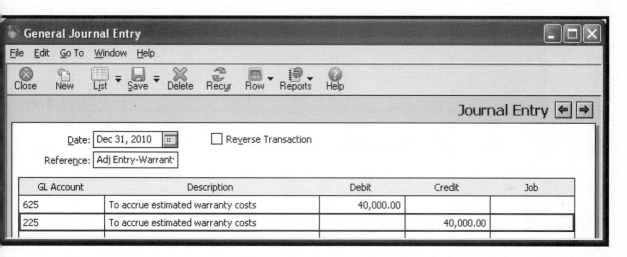

Figure 11. 15 Adjusting entry for warranty liability

An important aspect of this journal entry is that it records only an estimated, contingent liability. When warranty work is accomplished utilizing repair parts, items bought as inventory items within Peachtree, these items must be "consumed" or removed from inventory as the work is accomplished otherwise inventory and the contingent liability will be overstated and costs are understated. Assuming that twelve thousand Wringers and twelve thousand Wetters, both established inventory items with a cost of $1.00 each, are the only parts utilized to repair the returned units, utilize the Inventory Adjustments screen found under Tasks to record the warranty repairs. This allows you to record the use of inventory items correctly.

The first Item ID used is Wetters. Set the reference to Warranty and the Date to December 31, 2010. Set the GL Source Acct to 225 – Estimated Warranty Liability and adjust quantity by a ***NEGATIVE*** twelve thousand. Enter Warranty Repairs in the Reason to Adjust window. Compare your work with Figure 11. 16 and make any corrections necessary before saving the adjustment.

Utilize the same process and information to record the use of twelve thousand Wringers. Then check your general ledger to ensure that the only two accounts affected are 1) 225 – Estimated Warranty Liability debited for two entries of $12,000 and, 2) 120 – Merchandise Inventory credited for two entries of $12,000 each on December 31, 2010, each on December 31, 2010. The use of other screens to accomplish this task may result in a cost of goods sold issue – **_NOT_** a correct process, or may leave the quantity of inventory items misstated. As stated in the textbook, warranty repairs affect **_ONLY_** inventory values and warranty liability obligations, and as such, in Peachtree, they affect inventory quantities, and warranty liabilities.

Figure 11. 16 Inventory Adjustments screen utilized to record warranty work

PAYROLL OVERVIEW

The payroll process can be automated when using Peachtree Complete Accounting following the setup process for the business and for each of your employees. Once you have set up the defaults and records you select the employee, enter the hours worked for employees earning wages or the salary period for salaried employees. Then Peachtree computes the payroll which includes creating payroll reports and paycheck. Payroll checks can be printed in batches or on an individual basis.

One of the most complex issues associated with payroll is the tax obligation. There are taxes that only the employee bears, there are taxes only the employer bears because he has employees, and there are taxes that both the employee and employer bear. Some of these taxes are unlimited and increase as a percentage rate as the annual increases while some others are a fixed percentage until a cap value is attained after which no future deductions are made in the tax year. These complex tax obligations may best be handled by Peachtree's subscription payroll service and subscription maintained tax tables. These tax tables are referred to as "Global Tax Tables" as once installed within Peachtree, they are available for all companies the accountant is providing services to. These additional cost services are not available to Peachtree Complete Accounting Educational version user. However, the tax tables, which expired at an earlier date due to changes, are installed and available for educational purposes. If the accountant desires, he/she can manually install and maintain the tax tables for his/her company. Both the manual installation and manual maintenance of the tax tables are beyond the scope of this textbook.

To maintain consistency amongst the many classrooms most accounting textbooks provide you tax information as basic percentages or as specific values. This chapter will show you both aspects of payroll – automated by Peachtree followed by manually for textbook accounting.

NAVIGATION AIDS PAYROLL

Open Payroll Tax Example Company (PTEC) from within the student data set if it is not already open to follow this example. The Payroll Navigation Aid is brought up by clicking on "Payroll Setup Wizard" in the Maintain submenu under Default Information of Peachtree, as shown in Figure 11. 17.

Figure 11. 17 The path to the Payroll Setup Wizard

The first screen to address in the Payroll Setup Wizard is setting the state – Georgia (GA), unemployment percentage rate – 6.2%, and accounts. Figure 11. 18 shows you the settings, which have been accomplished for you. A nice feature on this screen is that when an account is selected, the account title is shown. Once the data is entered and verified, you would click Next to advance the Wizard.

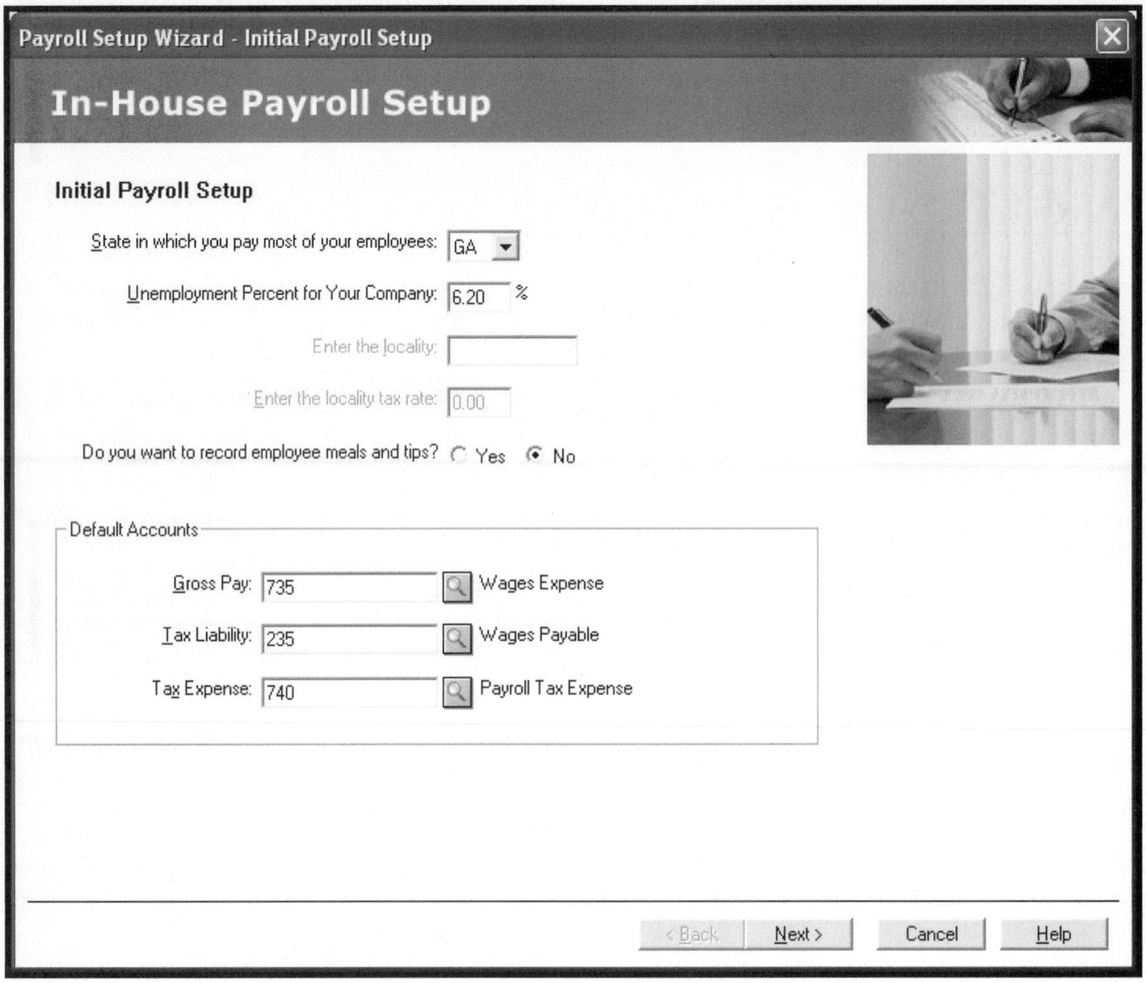

Figure 11. 18 The initial payroll setup screen of the payroll setup wizard

While Peachtree has the capability of handling 401(k) deductions, click Next to advance the Wizard after you ensure that you have selected "Not Offered."

While Peachtree has the capability of tracking Vacation and Sick Time, click Next to advance the Wizard after you ensure that you have selected Not Tracked in both sections of the dialog box.

Click Finish to complete the setup. The next event is to setup employees.

EMPLOYEES DEFAULTS

By setting up employee defaults, much of the data entry can be standardized as defaults. Follow the path Maintain > Default Information > Employees from the main menu and drop-down menu options. Peachtree will present the Employee Default screen shown in Figure 11. 19.

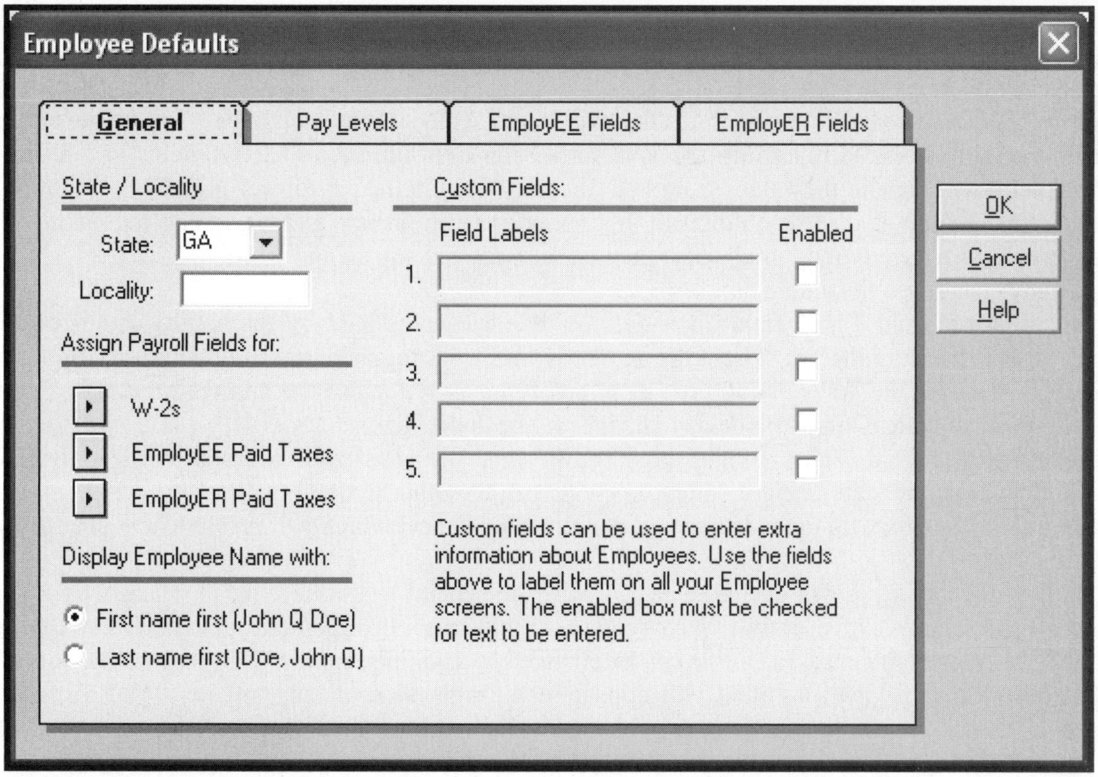

Figure 11. 19 The Employee Defaults screen opened to the General tab

The default State/Locality is set in the upper left side of the tab. This can be changed for each employee during setup for a specific employee. There are three pop-up menus associated with "Assign Payroll Fields for." All three are shown in Figure 11. 20.

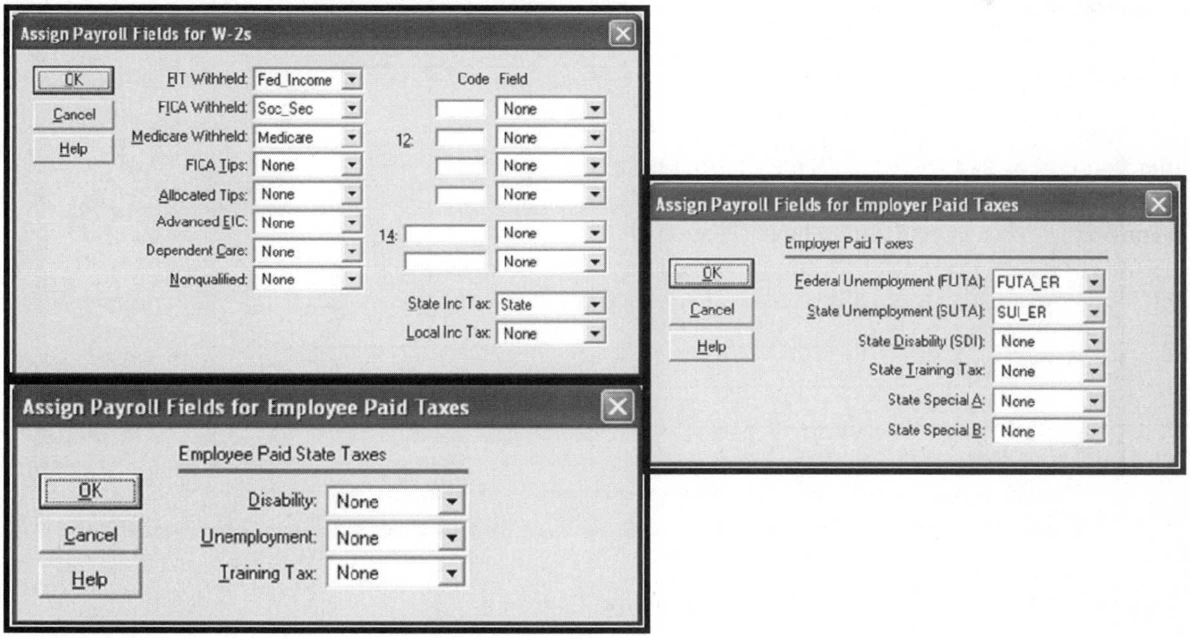

Figure 11. 20 The three pop-up dialog boxes associated with "Assign Payroll Fields for"

As a general rule Peachtree is very well structured in this aspect, and no adjustments should be made without a complete understanding of how these defaults will affect the payroll process. These screens are addressed so you know they are there.

The W-2s dialog box defines the fields that will be presented on the employee's W-2. These are titles from the payroll process to blocks on the W-2 form. The first line says FIT Withheld (Federal Income Tax Withheld) will contain the values from Fed_Income (Tax) in the payroll records. The rest follow this pattern. A change on this screen could result in a major error on income and taxes reported on the W-2 of the employee. As a "safety measure," close the box with the red square and white X or Cancel which will preclude any changes to the dialog box.

The Employee Paid Taxes dialog box defines the state taxes paid by the employee for disability, unemployment, and training tax. These are federally and state regulated taxes which a tax professional can address. As with the W-2s dialog box, as a "safety measure," close the box with the red square and white X or Cancel which will preclude any changes to the dialog box.

The Employer Paid Taxes dialog box shows that the employer bears a burden for federal unemployment tax and state unemployment tax. As with the other dialog boxes in this area, as a "safety measure," close the box with the red square and white X or Cancel which will preclude any changes to the dialog box.

The Pay Levels tab, shown in Figure 11. 21, sets the general ledger account to which wages (hourly pay levels) and salaries expenses will be charged to. In this case, all wages and salaries will be charged to account 735 – Wages Expense. Each line can be changed by clicking into the G/L Account block and then clicking on the magnifying glass that will appear in the right side of the window. Then accounts can changed in the same manner as accounts are selected when making journal entries.

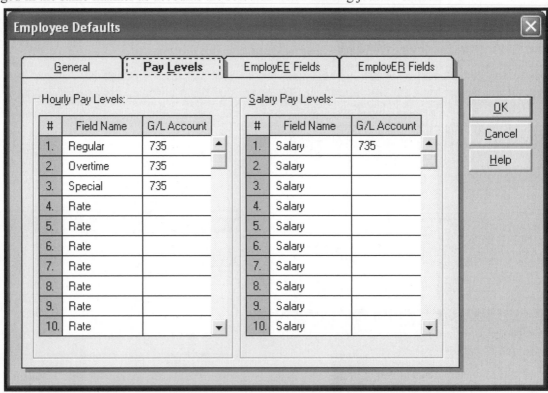

Figure 11. 21 The Pay Levels tab of Employee Defaults

The Employee Fields tab shows which taxes the employee (EE) pays through payroll. This dialog box, Figure 11. 22, shows that the employee pays Federal Income Tax, Social Security, Medicare, and State Income Tax. It also sets 237 – Payroll Taxes Payable, as the default account for all withheld taxes during the payroll process. These accounts can be changed in the same manner as explained earlier – click into the G/L Account window, click on the magnifying glass that appears and select the desired account.

Figure 11. 22 Employee Fields of the Employee Defaults

The Employer Fields tab, Figure 11. 23, shows that the employer is bearing the burden for Social Security, Medicare, Federal Unemployment Insurance, and State Unemployment Insurance. The values for these taxes is being recorded to the general ledger account 237 – Payroll Taxes Payable and to 740 – Payroll Tax Expense. As with other tabs and windows, these accounts can be changed by clicking into the window, then clicking on the magnifying glass that appears and selecting the desired account.

Figure 11. 23 Employer Fields of the Employee Defaults

Once all of the values have been entered, clicking on OK will save the data entered into all four tabs and the dialog box will close.

SETTING UP AN EMPLOYEE

From the Maintain option on the main menu bar, select Employees/Sales Reps and Peachtree presents the Maintain Employees/Sales Reps screen, shown in Figure 11. 24.

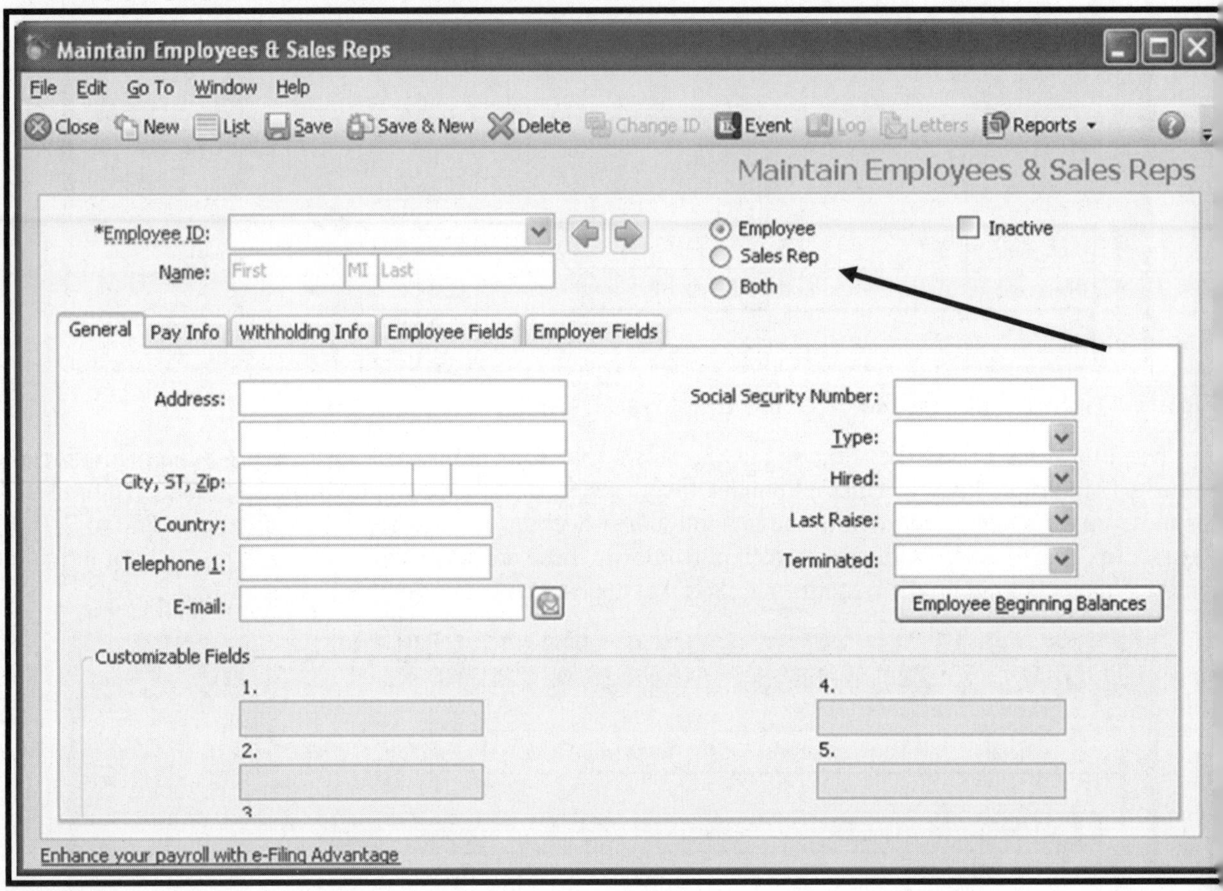

Figure 11. 24 Maintain Employees/Sales Reps screen open to the General tab

The first selection is whether the individual is an employee, sales rep, or both. You can also make employees inactive by checking the box to the right of this area with a mouse click. The employee ID is a text field which accepts most alphanumerical values. PTEC has chosen numbers as employee IDs. Enter the data from Table 11. 1 into Peachtree. Employee 21, Mike Crofton is shown as the example.

ID	**21**	**5**	**20**
Name:	Mike Crofton	John Caine	Karen Cattz
Address	340 14th St., NE	15 W. Peachtree St.	21 5th St., NW
City/ST/Zip	Atlanta, GA 30344	Atlanta, GA 30321	Marietta, GA 30321
SSN	256-90-5881	255-10-4467	010-14-7375
Phone	770.555.1943	770.555.7950.	404.555.9959
Date Hired	4/12/00	7/1/97	7/4/98
Last Raise	4/12/08	5/14/09	7/4/09
Filing Status	Married/Joint – 2 allowances	Married/Joint – 1 allowance	Single – 3 allowances
Pay Method	Salary	Hourly	Hourly
Frequency	Weekly	Weekly	Weekly
Hour/pay period	40	40	40
Regular Pay Rate	$575.00	$35.00	$25.00
Overtime Pay	None	$52.50	$37.50

Table 11. 1   Employee listing for Payroll Tax Example Company payroll

Figure 11. 25 shows the General tab filled in with Mike's data. Check your work with Figure 11. 25 and make the appropriate adjustments before clicking on the Pay Info tab.

Figure 11. 25 Mike Crofton's General tab for the Maintain Employees/Sales Reps dialog box

The Pay Info tab, shown in Figure 11. 26, provides for the selection of hourly or salary payroll tasks. Mike is salaried with a salary of $575 per week. So, set the Pay Method to Salary, as shown, through the drop-down menu associated with the Pay Method window. Mike is paid weekly, as all PTEC are, so set Weekly in the Pay Frequency window through the associated drop-down menu options. Enter Mike's weekly salary, $575.00, in the Salary Pay Rate window associated with the Regular line. Peachtree will calculate that Mike's annual salary is $29,900, shown in the bottom right corner of the screen. Compare your work with Figure 11. 26 before clicking into the Withholding Info tab.

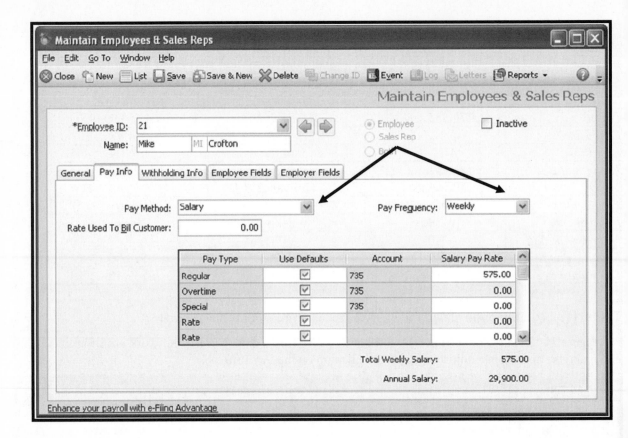

Figure 11. 26 Mike Crofton's pay information tab for the maintain employees/sales reps dialog box

On Mike's Withholding Info tab, Figure 11. 27, Mike's marital status and allowances declared on his Federal W-4 are entered. Many state and local governments have specific forms for their withholdings but allow the use of the Federal W-4 to reduce paperwork. Mike, as stated in Table 11. 1, is married and filing jointly for federal, state, and any local income taxes. While set in the screen print, Local can be ignored in this case. An important option here is the Additional Withholdings windows. If Mike has more than one job or his spouse is employed, Mike may want additional withholding to preclude an excessive burden when the annual tax return is filed and the associated fines and interest for under withholdings. The Federal, State, and Local Filing Status is set through a drop-down menu options list with each window. Allowances is a numerical entry. **_Note:_** The term "Allowances" is a statement or value declared on the W-4 while the term "Exemptions" is a term associated with the tax return. Compare your work with that of Figure 11. 27 and make any necessary adjustments before advancing to the Employee Fields tab.

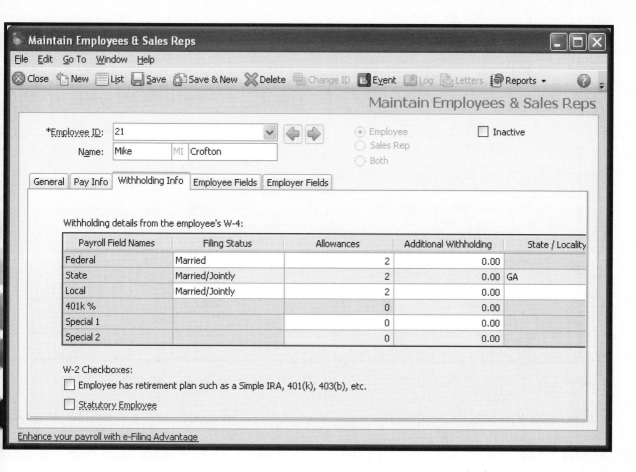

Figure 11. 27 Mike Crofton's withholding info tab

The Employee Fields tab, shown in Figure 11. 28, controls which taxes the employee bears through employment. The tax can be deselected, if appropriate, on this tab. This default values of this tab are set through the Employees Defaults dialog box's Employee Fields tab, addressed earlier. There are no changes on this tab for Mike.

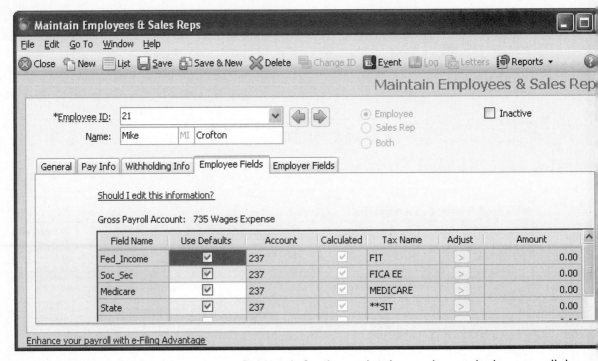

Figure 11. 28 Mike Crofton's employee fields tab for the maintain employees/sales reps dialog box

The Employer Fields tab shown in Figure 11. 29, shows the tax burden caused by PTEC having employees. This tab has its default values set through the Employees Default screen and, like the Employee Fields tab, can be changed as necessary. Click on Save & New and enter the other employees for PTEC shown in Table 11 .1.

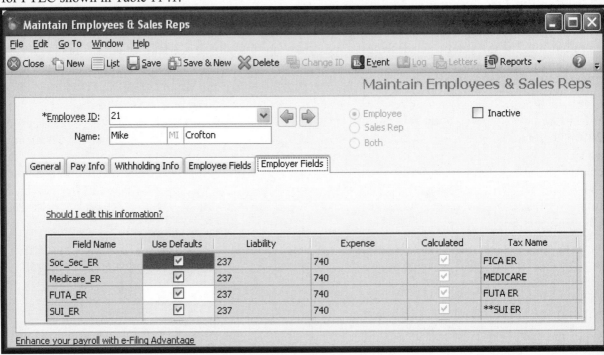

Figure 11. 29 Mike Crofton's employer fields tab

As all of the tabs properly filled in with the information from Table 11. 1 for each employee click on "Save" on the task bar to record the information. When something changes for an employee you can locate that employee's record by dropping down the complete list of available records by clicking on the down arrow to the right of Employee ID window and then double-clicking on appropriate record. The list of employees is shown in Figure 11. 30. You can also use the left and right arrows to the right of the Employee ID window to work your way through the list.

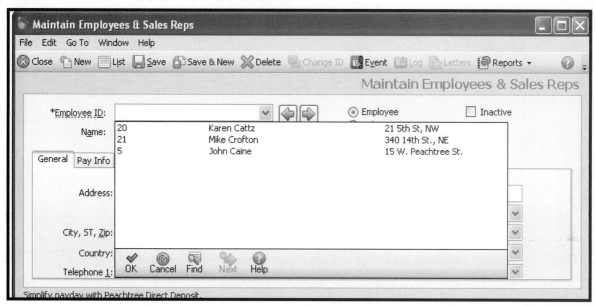

Figure 11. 30 The employee listing available through the maintain employees/sales reps dialog box

PAYING EMPLOYEES

Using the installed tax tables for deductions, follow the path Tasks > Select for Payroll Entry to access the Select Employees – Filter Selection dialog box, shown in Figure 11 .31. Set the pay end date to January 8, 2010. This can be done with the direct entry of 01/08/10 in the window or by utilizing the calendar accessible through the calendar icon to the right of the window. When the date is set, remove all the checkmarks from the Include Pay Frequencies area EXCEPT Weekly. Ensure both hourly and salary are selected in the "Include Pay Methods" area. And ensure that ALL employees are selected in the Include Employees area. Compare your work with Figure 11. 31 and make any adjustments before clicking on OK.

Figure 11. 31 The Select
Employees – Filter
Selection dialog box

The next screen is the select employees to pay screen, shown in Figure 11. 32. Within this screen set the check date to January 15, 2010. Ensure that all three employees are selected for pay with the red checkmarks on the right column. Assume that Karen only worked 32 hours during this pay period. Change the default value of 40 in the Hours column for Karen to 32. When you tab into another window notice that Peachtree updates the check amount window. If PTEC utilized a separate checking account for payroll, recommended, it would be selected in the upper right corner area. Compare your work with Figure 11. 32 and make any adjustments necessary before selecting "Print" on the task bar.

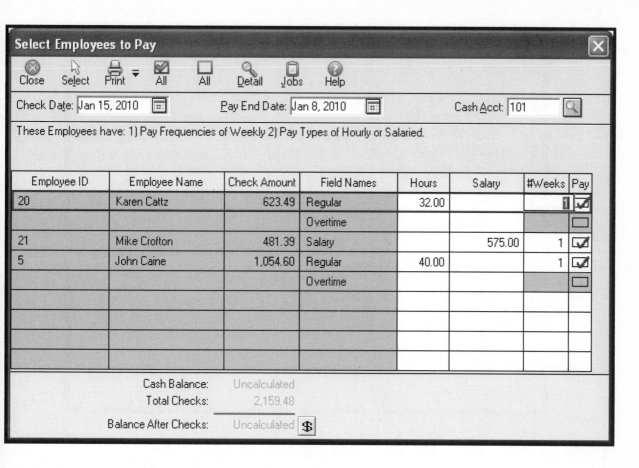

Figure 11. 32 The Select Employees to Pay dialog box

When you click on "Print" on the task bar, Peachtree presents you with a print forms dialog box, shown in Figure 11. 33. Set the first check number field value to "111" and accept the rest of the default values – which assume you have a standardized check form in your printer. And then click "Print." And your checks are printed.

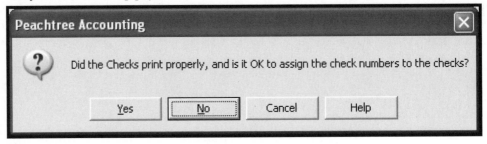

Figure 11. 33 The Select Employees – Filter Selection dialog box

To ensure that your employees are paid, Peachtree asks, with Figure 11 .34, if your checks printed properly. If you click No, Peachtree will NOT post the checks to the check register or the general ledger and it will take you back to set up payroll.

Figure 11. 34 Did the checks printer properly" dialog box

VOIDING CHECKS

Occasionally a check will need to be voided for one or more reasons. Follow the path Tasks > Void Checks from the main menu bar. And Peachtree provides the dialog box shown in Figure 11. 35. You must set the Account ID to the proper account, PTEC only has one checking or cash account, 101. Then you need to set the date the check is to be voided on. In this example that is January 15, 2010. And then select the check to be voided. In Figure 11. 35 Check 101 to First National Bank is selected. If Void is clicked now that check will be voided. Since we do not need to void any of the checks, close the dialog box.

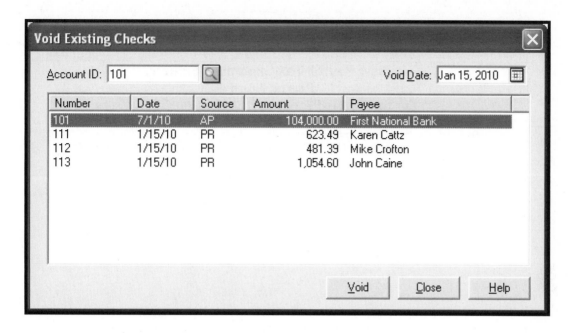

Figure 11. 35 Void existing checks dialog box

PAYROLL REPORTS

Payroll reports are accessible through Payroll on the dropdown menu from Reports & Forms option on the main menu bar. A portion of the Payroll Journal is shown in Figure 11. 36. This common report shows the date, employee name, gross amount, amount of the various taxes and the net amount of the check as well as the check number.

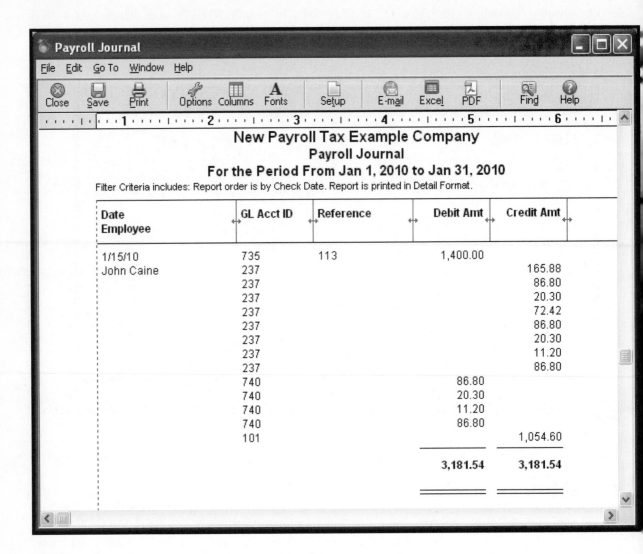

Figure 11. 36 Payroll Journal report

PAYROLL ENTRIES USING THE GENERAL JOURNAL

A general journal entry will frequently address the requirements of textbook accounting. In Figure 11. 37, a basic general journal entry for payroll is presented. As stated in the textbook the company computes the payroll entry for January 14, 2010, as:

Jan. 14, 10	Office Salaries Expense	5,200.00	
	Wages Expense	12,010.00	
	FICA Taxes Payable		1,376.80
	Federal Income Taxes Payable		3,490.00
	State Income Taxes Payable		344.20
	United Way Payable		421.50
	Union Dues Payable		115.00
	Salaries and Wages Payable		11,462.50
	To record payroll for the week ending January 14, 2010		

Utilizing the accounts of PTEC, follow the path Tasks > General Journal Entry to open the general journal entry screen. Using the provided information, write the journal entry. Figure 11. 37 is a screen print of the general journal entry.

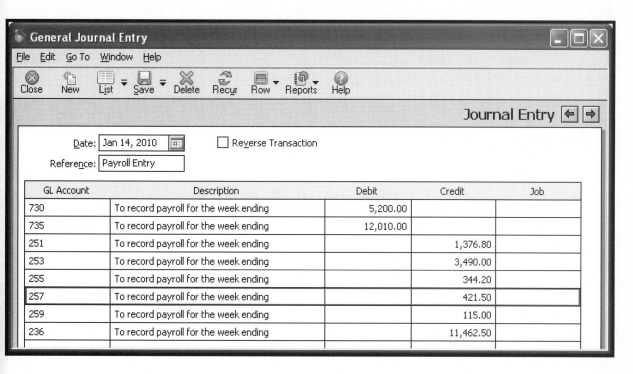

Figure 11. 37 General journal entry for to record payroll obligations

The general journal process, effective for the classroom, does not prepare checks to be printed or to record in individual employee's earnings and taxation issues. Once the payroll liability is recorded, a general journal entry is written to pay the salaries and wages. This general journal entry is shown in Figure 11. 38. Make any necessary corrections necessary before saving your journal entry.

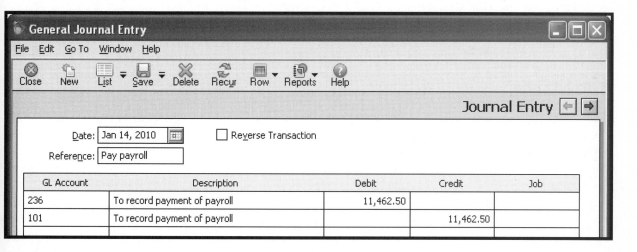

Figure 11. 38 General journal entry for payroll

The employer's tax obligation is as follows for this general journal entry process:

Jan. 14, 10	Payroll Tax Expense	2,443.82	
	FICA Taxes Payable		1,376.80
	Federal Unemployment Taxes Payable		137.68
	State Unemployment Taxes Payable		929.34
	To record employer's payroll taxes on January 14 payroll		

Utilize the general journal entry screen to write the journal entry shown in Figure 11. 39. Make any adjustments necessary before saving the entry.

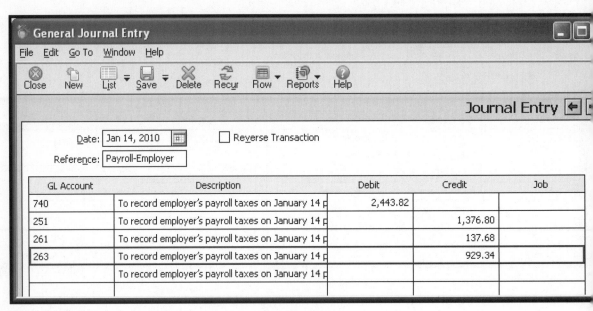

Figure 11. 39 General journal entry for payroll tax expense

Comprehensive Do It! Problem, Indiana Jones Company, Directory
Wey_AP9e_Indiana_Jones_Co

Indiana Jones Company had the following selected transactions in 2010. Assume the Peachtree Complete Accounting Payroll system was not used and all entries are general journal entries. Open the Indiana Jones Company in your student data set. Since the tax tables of Peachtree do not accurately portray these values for payroll, use the general journal to record these events.

Feb 1   Signs a $50,000, 6-month, 9%- interest bearing note payable to Citibank and receives $50,000 in cash.

    10   Cash register sales total $43,200, which includes an 8% sales tax.

    28   The payroll for the month consists of Sales Salaries $32,000 and Office Salaries $18,000. All wages are subject to 8% FICA taxes. A total of $8,900 federal income taxes are withheld. The salaries are paid on March 1.

Feb 28   The following adjustment data are developed:

    (1) Interest expense of $375 has been incurred on the note.

    (2) Employer payroll taxes include 8% FICA taxes, a 5.4% state unemployment tax and a 0.8% federal unemployment tax.

    (3) Some sales were made under warranty. Of the units sold under warranty, 350 are expected to become defective. Repair costs are estimated to be $40 per unit.

Instructions:

(a)   Familiarize yourself with the problem's chart of accounts within the Peachtree Complete Accounting in your student data set.

(b)   Journalize the February transactions.

(c)   Journalize the adjusting entries at February 28th.

(d)   Print the general journal for February 2010.

Solution to Comprehensive Do It! Problem

General journal report for February 2010:

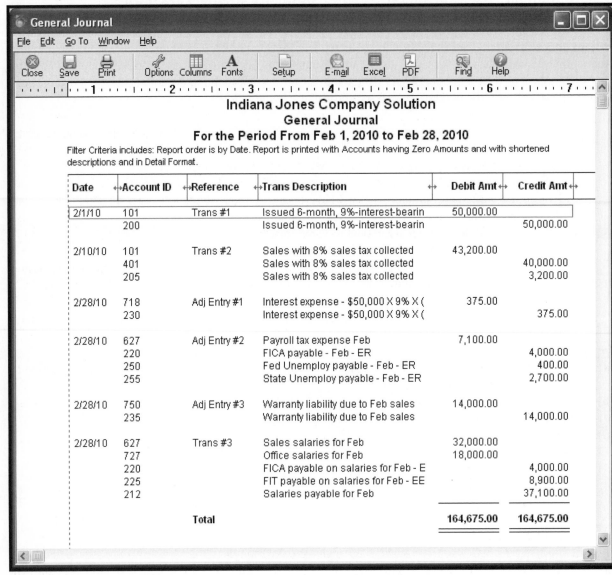

General Journal

File   Edit   Go To   Window   Help

Close   Save   Print   Options   Columns   Fonts   Setup   E-mail   Excel   PDF   Find   Help

Indiana Jones Company Solution
General Journal
For the Period From Feb 1, 2010 to Feb 28, 2010

Filter Criteria includes: Report order is by Date. Report is printed with Accounts having Zero Amounts and with shortened descriptions and in Detail Format.

Date	Account ID	Reference	Trans Description	Debit Amt	Credit Amt
2/1/10	101	Trans #1	Issued 6-month, 9%-interest-bearin	50,000.00	
	200		Issued 6-month, 9%-interest-bearin		50,000.00
2/10/10	101	Trans #2	Sales with 8% sales tax collected	43,200.00	
	401		Sales with 8% sales tax collected		40,000.00
	205		Sales with 8% sales tax collected		3,200.00
2/28/10	718	Adj Entry #1	Interest expense - $50,000 X 9% X (	375.00	
	230		Interest expense - $50,000 X 9% X (		375.00
2/28/10	627	Adj Entry #2	Payroll tax expense Feb	7,100.00	
	220		FICA payable - Feb - ER		4,000.00
	250		Fed Unemploy payable - Feb - ER		400.00
	255		State Unemploy payable - Feb - ER		2,700.00
2/28/10	750	Adj Entry #3	Warranty liability due to Feb sales	14,000.00	
	235		Warranty liability due to Feb sales		14,000.00
2/28/10	627	Trans #3	Sales salaries for Feb	32,000.00	
	727		Office salaries for Feb	18,000.00	
	220		FICA payable on salaries for Feb - E		4,000.00
	225		FIT payable on salaries for Feb - EE		8,900.00
	212		Salaries payable for Feb		37,100.00
		Total		164,675.00	164,675.00

P11-1A, Mane Company, Directory Wey_AP9e_P11_1A_Mane_Co

On January 1, 2010, the ledger of Mane Company, found in your student data set, contains the following liability accounts:

Accounts Payable	$52,000
Sales Taxes Payable	7,700
Unearned Service Revenue	16,000

There is a "Credit Customer" established and sales tax of 8% for all of these transactions. During January, the following selected transactions occurred:

Jan   5   Use the deposit ticket ID of 10-01-05 and reference and receipt number 2010-01-05A within the receipts screen to sell 700 units of "Jan 5 Sales Item" at $30 each, for cash totaling $22,680, which includes 8% sales taxes. Ensure that the screen is taxed.

12   Provided services for customers who had made advance payments of $10,000. The receipts were recorded on Jan 01, 2010, with reference 2010-01-01PP. Use the receipts screen and Apply to Invoices with reference 2010-01-12A to apply the value to the prepayment of Invoice 2010-01-01PP. Utilize the Journal icon to ensure that the debit account is properly set o Unearned Service Revenues and that the credit account is set to Service Revenue.

14   Use the write checks screen to submit collected sales taxes to Vendor ID Sales Tax for the sales taxes collected in December 2009 ($7,700), use check #101 and ensure that Expense Account is set to 215 – Sales Taxes Payable.

20   Use the Sales/Invoicing to sell 800 units of "Jan 20 Sales Item" at $50 each to Credit Customer, plus 8% sales tax. Ensure that the screen is taxed. This new product is subject to a 1-year warranty.

21   With deposit ticket ID of 10-01-21 and reference and receipt number of 2010-01-21A, use the receipts screen to record borrowing $18,000 from UCLA Bank on a 3-month, 9%, $18,000 note. Change the Customer ID window to Vendor ID for UCLA Bank. Use the Journal icon to set the debit account to 101 – Cash and the credit account to 200 – Notes Payable.

25   Use the receipts screen and Cash Customer with deposit ticket ID 10-01-25 and reference and receipt number 2010-01-25A to sell 575 units of Jan 25 Sales Item at $20 each for cash totaling $12,420, which includes 8% sales taxes. Ensure that the screen is taxed.

Instructions:
(a)   Open the company from within your student data set and familiarize yourself with the chart of accounts.

(b)   Record the January transactions as indicated.

(c)   Use the general journal entry screen to journalize the adjusting entries at January 31st for:
   (1) The outstanding notes payable, and
   (2) Estimated warranty liability, assuming warranty costs are expected to equal 7% of sales of the "Jan 20 Sales Item" on January 20, 2010.

(d)   Print the general journal report, the general ledger for the month of January 2010, and the balance sheet at January 31, 2010.

P11-4A, Armitage Company, Directory Wey_AP9e_P11_4A_Armitage_Co

The following payroll liability accounts are included in the ledger of Armitage Company on January 1, 2010.

FICA Tax Payable	$ 760.00
Federal Income Tax Payable	1,204.60
State Income Tax Payable	108.95
Federal Unemployment Tax Payable	288.95
State Unemployment Tax Payable	1,954.40
Union Dues Payable	870.00
Wages Payable	360.00

In January, the following transactions occurred:

Jan 10 Sent check for $870 to union treasurer for union dues.

12 Deposited check for $1,964.60 in Federal Reserve bank for FICA tax payable and federal income tax payable obligations.

15 Purchased U.S. Savings Bonds for employees by writing check for $360.

17 Paid State Income Taxes Payable withheld from employees.

20 Paid federal and state unemployment taxes.

31 Completed monthly payroll register, which shows Office Salaries Expense $26,600, Store Wages Expense $28,400, FICA Tax (Payable) withheld $4,400, Federal Income Tax Payable $2,158, State Income Tax Payable $454, Union Dues Payable $400, United Fund Contributions Payable $1,888 and net Wages Payable $45,700.

31 Prepared payroll checks for the net pay and distributed checks to employees.

At January 31st, the company also makes the following accrued adjustments pertaining to employee compensation.

1. Employer payroll taxes: FICA taxes 8%, federal unemployment taxes 0.8%, and state unemployment taxes 5.4%

2. Vacation pay: 6% of gross earnings.

Instructions:

(a) Familiarize yourself with the chart of accounts for Armitage Company from within your student data set.

(b) Use the general journal screen to journalize the January transactions.

(c) Use the general journal screen to journalize the adjustments pertaining to employee compensation at January 31.

(d) Print the general journal report.

CHAPTER 12

Accounting for Partnerships

OBJECTIVES

- Identify the characteristics of the partnership form of business organization.
- Explain the accounting entries for the formation of a partnership.
- Identify the bases for dividing net income or net loss.
- Describe the form and content of partnership financial statements.
- Explain the effects of the entries to record the liquidation of a partnership.

PARTNERSHIP FORM OF ORGANIZATION

There are basic rules for partnerships set forth by The Uniform Partnership Act. These rules outline the formation and operation of partnerships and are recognized in most states. This act defines a partnership as an association of two or more persons to carry on as co-owners of a business for profit. Partnerships are common in retail establishments and in small manufacturing companies. Accountants, lawyers, and doctors find it desirable to form partnerships with other professionals in their field. Partnerships are easy to form in Peachtree Complete Accounting.

SETTING UP A PARTNERSHIP IN PEACHTREE

The partnership of A. Rolfe and T. Shea has been set up as U.S. Software in your student data set. During the creation of this company "Partnership," as shown in Figure 12. 1, was chosen as the business type. The create a new company screen is available under "File" from the menu bar.

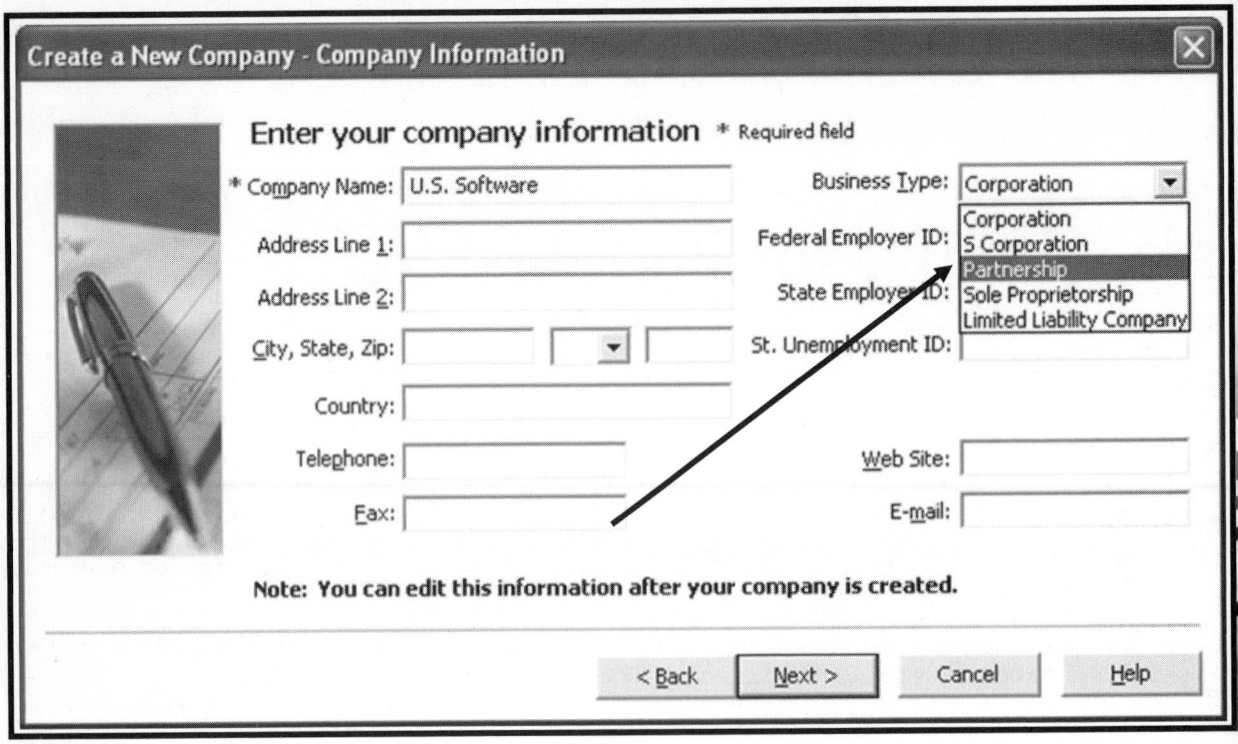

Figure 12. 1   Business type section of create a new company information

On January 2, 2010, each of the partners contributes cash and other assets to the company as shown in Table 12. 1. Use two general journal entries, one for A. Rolfe and one for T. Shea, to record the initial contributions to U.S. Software by the partners using the values in Table 12. 1, as listed below.

| | Book Value | | Market Value | |
	A. Rolfe	T. Shea	A. Rolfe	T. Shea
Cash	$ 8,000	$ 9,000	$ 8,000	$ 9,000
Office equipment	5,000		4,000	
Accumulated depreciation	(2,000)			
Accounts receivable		4,000		4,000
Allowance for doubtful accounts		(700)		(1,000)
	$11,000	$12,300	$12,000	$12,000

Table 12. 1   Detail of partners' contributions to form U.S. Software

Check your general journal entry screens for A. Rolfe and T. Shea with Figure 12. 2, shown below. Make adjustments necessary before saving the journal entries.

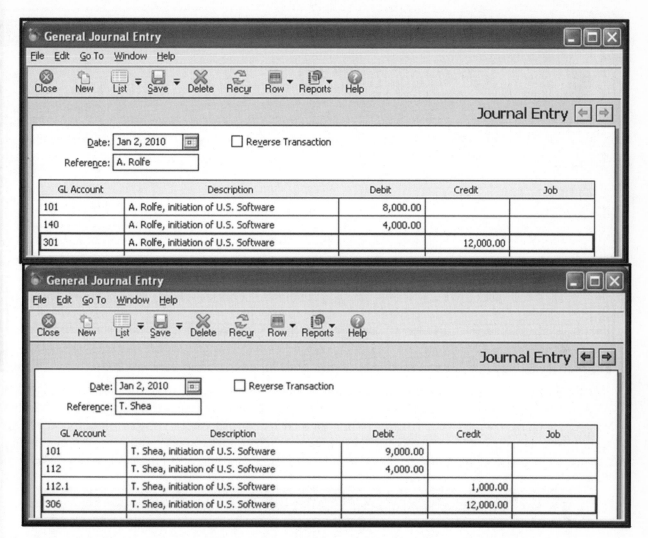

Figure 12. 2   General journal entries for the initial contributions into U.S. Software

During the month of January 2010, the U.S. Software earns $32,000 in service revenues from Cash Customers. Use the receipts screen to record the receipt of cash paid by the Cash Customers. Use deposit ticket ID of 10-01-31 and reference and receipt number 2010-01-31A. Ensure that the Date is set to January 31, 2010. "Cash Customer" is set up in the customer database with a default account of 407 – Service Revenues. Compare your work with Figure 12. 3 and make any necessary adjustments before saving your work.

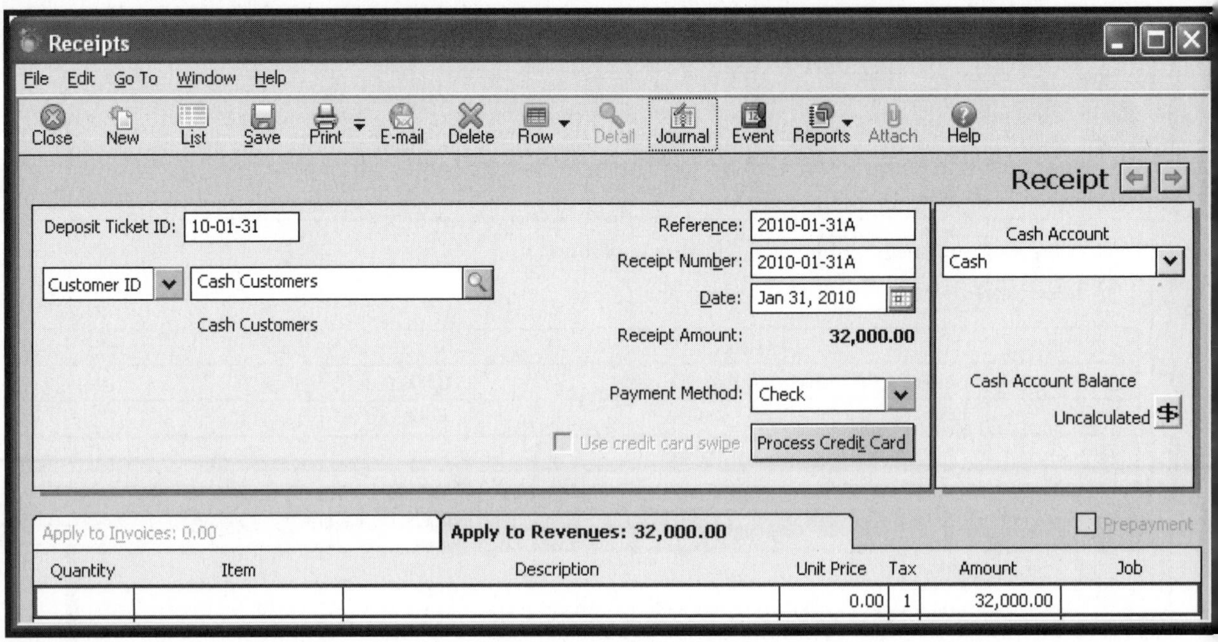

Figure 12. 3   Receipts screen for services rendered for cash during January 2010

During January 2010, A. Rolfe made drawings of $8,000 and T. Shea made drawings of $6,000. Both A. Rolfe and T. Shea have been set up as Vendors to ease the process of writing checks. Utilizing the write checks screen, write Check 101 to A. Rolfe for $8,000 and write Check 102 to T. Shea for $6,000 to record these drawing events. Date both checks January 31, 2010. Ensure that the Expense Account is set to the appropriate drawing account. For A. Rolfe, compare your work with Figure 12. 4 and make any necessary adjustments before saving the check.

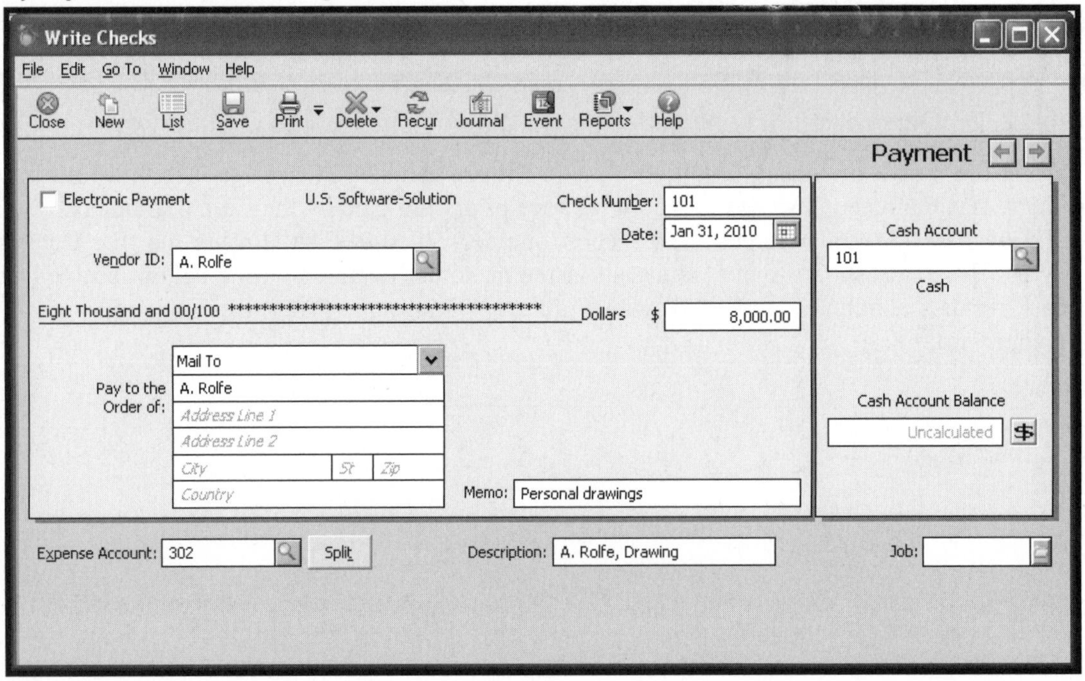

Figure 12. 4   Check 101 for A. Rolfe's drawings

View the balance sheet for U.S. Software as of January 31, 2010, shown in Figure 12. 5. Peachtree has recorded the income from the income statement into the Capital section, $32,000, and it has recorded the contributions and drawings for the period.

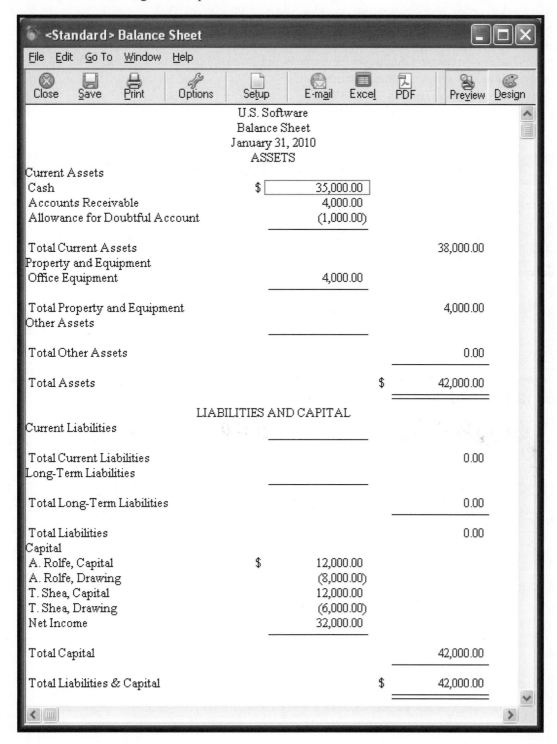

Figure 12. 5   The balance sheet for U.S. Software before closing accounts

While the revenue (income for Peachtree), expense, and drawing (Equity that gets closed for Peachtree) accounts are automatically closed by the Year-End Wizard, to maintain the parallel with the textbook, general journal entries will be written to close these accounts at the end of January 2010.

The proper order is to close revenue (income for Peachtree) then expense accounts to income summary followed by closing the income summary account to the capital accounts. Then the drawing (Equity that gets closed for Peachtree) accounts are closed to the capital accounts.

Note: The 360 – Income Summary account is not an account normally needed by Peachtree. It is provided to allow this series of journal entries.

The first entry, dated January 31, 2010, is to close the revenue (income for Peachtree). The revenue account has a credit balance of $32,000. Compare your work with Figure 12. 6 and make any necessary adjustments before saving it.

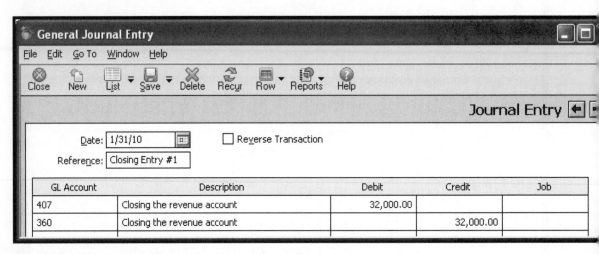

Figure 12. 6   The general journal entry to close the revenue account

The second entry is to close, with a 50~50 distribution, of the income summary account to A. Rolfe and T. Shea's capital accounts. Compare your work with Figure 12. 7 and make any adjustments necessary before saving the journal entry.

General Journal Entry

File   Edit   Go To   Window   Help

Close   New   List   Save   Delete   Recur   Row   Reports   Help

Journal Entry

Date: 1/31/10   ☐ Reverse Transaction
Reference: Closing Entry #2

GL Account	Description	Debit	Credit	Job
360	To close the Income Summary account to capital	32,000.00		
301	To close the Income Summary account to capital		16,000.00	
306	To close the Income Summary account to capital		16,000.00	

Figure 12. 7   The general journal entry to close the income summary account

The third and fourth journal entries in this closing process are to close A. Rolfe and T. Shea's drawing accounts to their capital accounts. Compare your closing entries with those in Figure 12. 8 and make any necessary adjustments before saving them.

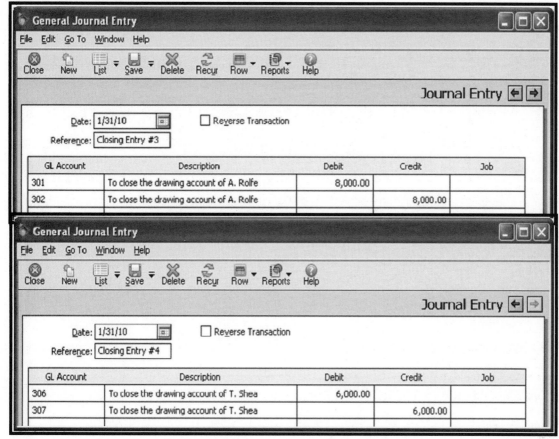

Figure 12. 8   The general journal entry to close the drawing accounts

Now view the balance sheet, Figure 12. 9, and notice the changes. The drawing and net income values have been incorporated into the capital accounts for each partner. If the Peachtree Year-End Wizard had been utilized to close the accounts net income would have been recorded to Retained Earnings where a general journal entry would have to be written to manually allocate it to the partners.

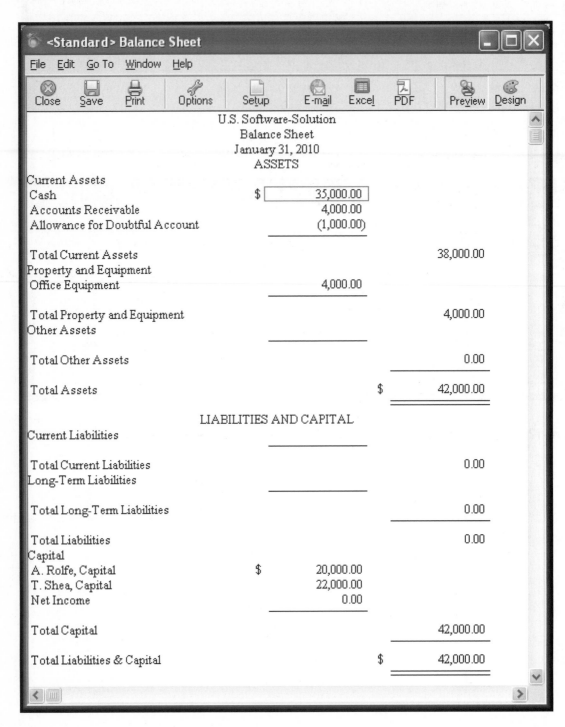

Figure 12. 9   The balance sheet after the manual closing entries

FMV

P12-1A, Pasa Company, Directory Wey_AP9e_P12_1A_Pasa_Co

The post-closing trial balances of two proprietorships on January 1, 2010, are presented below.

	Patrick Company		Samuelson Company	
	Debit	**Credit**	**Debit**	**Credit**
Cash	$14,000		$12,000	
Accounts receivable	17,500		26,000	
Allowance for doubtful accounts		$3,000		$4,400
Merchandise inventory	26,500		18,400	
Equipment	45,000	21	29,000	
Accumulated depreciation-				
Equipment		24,000		11,000
Notes payable		18,000		15,000
Accounts Payable		22,000		31,000
Patrick, Capital		36,000		
Samuelson, Capital				24,000
	$103,000	$103,000	$85,400	$85,400

Patrick and Samuelson decide to form a partnership, Pasa Company, with the following agreed upon valuations for noncash assets.

	Patrick Company	Samuelson Company
Accounts receivable	$17,500	$26,000
Allowance for doubtful accounts	4,500 ✔	4,000
Merchandise inventory	28,000	20,000
Equipment	23,000	16,000

All cash will be transferred to the partnership, and the partnership will assume all the liabilities of the two proprietorships. Further, it is agreed that Patrick will invest an additional $5,000 in cash, and Samuelson will invest an additional $19,000 in cash.

Instructions:
(a) Open the file and familiarize yourself with the chart of accounts.
(b) Prepare separate journal entries to record the transfer of each proprietorship's assets and liabilities to the partnership.
(c) Journalize the additional cash investment by each partnership.
(d) Print the general journal report.
(e) Print the balance sheet for the partnership on January 1, 2010.

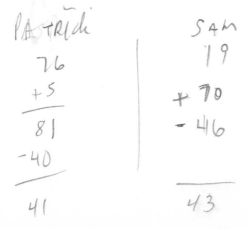

P12-3A, New Yorker Company, Directories Wey_AP9e_P12_3A_New_Yorker Co_(a)(b) and (c)

The partners in New Yorker Company decide to liquidate the business when the balance sheet shows the following.

NEW YORKER COMPANY
Balance Sheet
May 31, 2010

Assets		Liabilities	
Cash	$27,500	Notes payable	$13,500
Accounts receivable	25,000	Accounts payable	27,000
Allowance for doubtful accounts	(1,000)	Wages payable	4,000
Merchandise inventory	34,500	M. Mantle, Capital	33,000
Equipment	21,000	W. Mays, Capital	21,000
Accumulated depreciation-			
Equipment	(5,500)	D. Snider, Capital	3,000
Total	$101,500	Total	$101,500

The partners share income and loss 5:3:2. During the process of liquidation, the following transactions were accomplished in the following sequence.
1. A total of $55,000 was received from converting noncash assets into cash.
2. Gain or loss on realization was allocated to partners.
3. Liabilities were paid in full.
4. D. Snider paid his capital deficiency.
5. Cash was paid to the partners with credit balances.

Instructions:
(a) Open the P12-3A_New Yorker Co (a) & (b) file and familiarize yourself with the chart of accounts.
(b) Prepare the entries to record the transactions.
(c) Print the general journal report.
(d) Open the P12-3A_New Yorker Co (c) file and familiarize yourself with the chart of accounts. Assume that Snider is unable to pay the capital deficiency.
   (1) Prepare the entries to record the transactions 1, 2, and 3.
   (2) Prepare the entry to allocate Snider's debit balance to Mantle and Mays.
   (3) Print the general journal report.
   (4) Print the balance sheet for the partnership on May 31, 2010.

CHAPTER 13

Corporations: Organization and Capital Stock Transactions

OBJECTIVES

- Identify the major characteristics of a corporation.
- Differentiate between paid-in capital and retained earnings.
- Record the issuance of common stock.

- Explain the accounting for treasury stock.
- Differentiate preferred stock from common stock.
- Prepare a stockholders' equity section.

THE CORPORATE FORM OF ORGANIZATION

A corporation is defined as "an artificial being, invisible, intangible and existing only in contemplation of law." The definition as stated in 1819 by then Chief Justice John Marshall laid the foundation for the prevailing legal interpretation that a corporation is an entity separate and distinct from its owners.

The initial step in forming a corporation is to file an application with the appropriate state office in which incorporation is desired. The application will contain:

- The corporate name
- The purpose of the proposed corporation
- The amounts, kinds, and number of shares of capital stock to be authorized
- The names of the incorporators
- The shares of stock to which each has subscribed

When chartered, the corporation may begin selling ownership rights in the form of shares of stock. When a corporation has only one class of stock that stock is identified as common stock. Each share of common stock gives the stockholder certain ownership rights. The authorization of capital stock does not result in a formal accounting entry and has no immediate effect on either corporate assets or stockholders' equity.

In a corporation, as compared to a sole proprietorship, owners' equity is now identified as "Stockholders' Equity," "Shareholders' Equity," or "Corporate Capital." Two sections of capital are now presented on the balance sheet, Paid in Capital (contributed) and Retained Earnings (earned capital from income). The distinction between paid-in capital and retained earnings is important from both a legal and accounting point of view. Legally, dividends can be declared out of retained earnings. Many states forbid paying dividends out of paid-in capital. From an analysis standpoint, continued existence and growth of a corporation is based on earnings. Paid-in capital is the total amount of cash and other assets paid in to the corporation by stockholders in exchange for capital stock.

RETAINED EARNINGS

Throughout the text and student data sets Peachtree has required a retained earnings account. This is where the results of the equation revenues less expenses less dividends ends up in the closing process. The definition of retained earnings is net income that is retained in a corporation. Peachtree records net income in the retained earnings account as earnings occur automatically through the Year-End Wizard.

THE NEW CORPORATION

Setting up the new corporation.

Step 1: Open the "Hydro-Slide" company found within your student data set and familiarize yourself with the chart of accounts.

Step 2: Verify that Hydro-Slide is a corporation through Maintain – Company Information.

Step 3: On January 1, 2010, Hydro-Slide issues 1,000 shares of $1 par value common stock at par for cash. Remember that you can enter infrequent investors, customers, and vendors names directly in the "Name" window below Customer ID without building a file for that individual. Use the receipts screen to record the issuance of the stock. Use the "Journal" button on the task bar to set the account to 310 – Common Stock. Ensure that appropriate text is used as a description. The receipts screen is shown in Figure 13. 1.

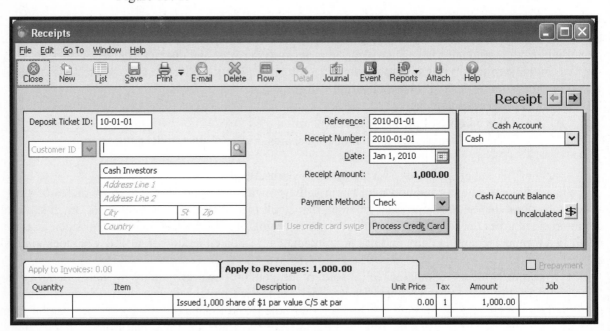

Figure 13. 1 Receipts entry for initial stock issuance

Using the receipts screen and the "Journal" icon on its task bar, record the issuance of an additional 1,000 shares of the $1 par value common stock for cash at $5 per share on January 5, 2010 by Hydro-Slide. Compare your work with Figure 13. 2 and make any necessary adjustments before saving.

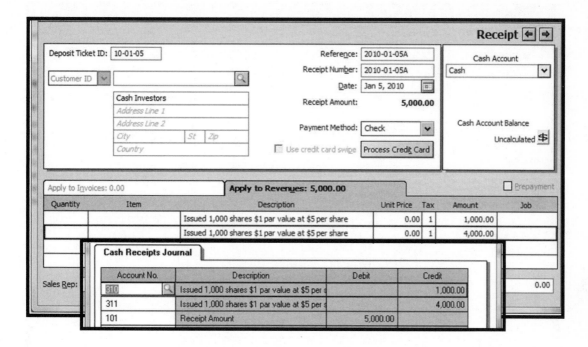

Figure 13. 2   Receipts entry for the additional stock issuance

After the issuance of the common stock on January 1st and 5th, the (modified for display) balance sheet of Hydro-Slide would show the proper differentiation of values in the capital section. This is shown in Figure 13. 3.

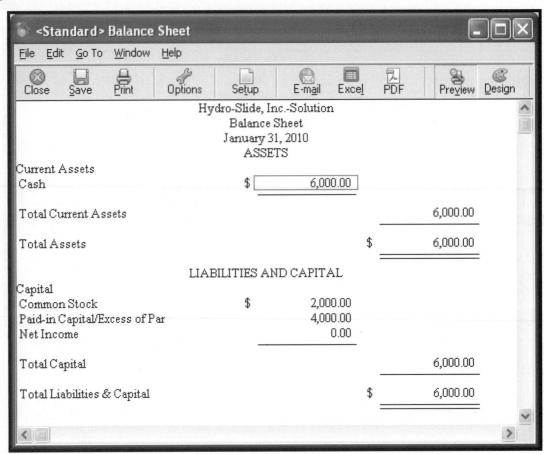

Figure 13. 3 The (modified for presentation) balance sheet of Hydro-Slide after the issuance of the stock

Note: At this point Hydro-Slide in Peachtree has not recorded any revenue or expenses while your textbook version has $27,000 in retained earnings.

ISSUING COMMON STOCK FOR SERVICES OR NONCASH ASSETS

Continuing with Hydro-Slide as the company rather than Jordan Company referenced in the Weygandt Accounting Principles textbook, assume that Hydro-Slide is billed $5,000 for legal services during incorporation. The legal firm agrees to accept 4,000 shares of $1.00 par value common stock in payment of their bill. At the time of the exchange, there is no established market price for the Hydro-Slide stock. In this case, the market value of the consideration received, $5,000, is more clearly evident. Using a general journal entry, record the transaction as of January 10, 2010. Check your work with Figure 13. 4 and make any necessary corrections before saving it.

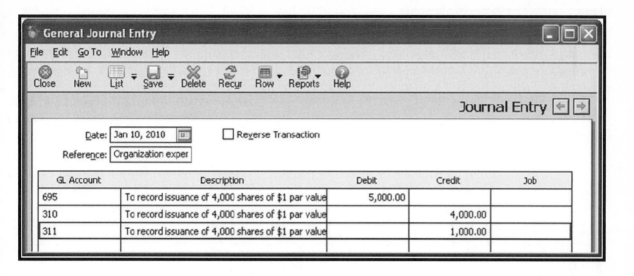

Figure 13. 4   The general journal entry resolving organization expenses with the issuance of stock

Continuing with Hydro-Slide as the company, assume that Hydro-Slide issues 50,000 shares of $1.00 par value common stock (adjusted from your textbook) to acquire land recently advertised for sale at $90,000. The most clearly evident value in this noncash transaction is the market price of the consideration given, $80,000. Using a general journal entry, record the transaction as of January 11, 2010. Check your work with Figure 13. 5 and make any necessary corrections before saving it.

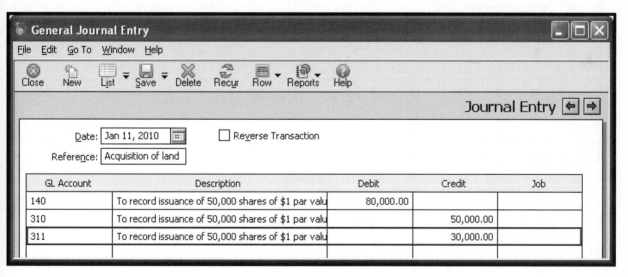

Figure 13. 5   The general journal entry for the acquisition of land through the issuance of stock

TREASURY STOCK

Treasury stock is a "contra equity" account that represents a corporation's own stock that has been issued, fully paid for by a stockholder, and reacquired by the corporation. Treasury stock, a different classification than an investment in another company through a stock purchase, is never an asset of the corporation. Treasury Stock – Common Stock is an equity account that does not close.

Step 1: To keep the activity in one month, on January 15, 2010, Hydro-Slide purchases back from shareholders 4,000 shares of its common stock as Treasury Stock for $8 per share. Utilize the 315 – Treasury Stock – Common Stock to record this event.

Step 2: Utilize the write checks screen and check number 101 to purchase the treasury stock. Enter "Shareholders" in the Pay to the Order of:" window. Ensure that the Expense Account is set to 315 – Treasury Stock – Common Stock. Compare your work with Figure 13. 6 and make any adjustments necessary before saving your work.

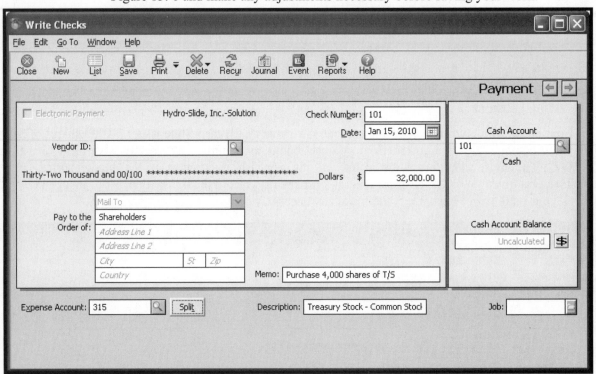

Figure 13. 6   Write checks entry to record purchase of treasury stock

When you view the balance sheet for Hydro-Slide you will see a DEBIT/negative value of $32,000 in the capital section representing the acquisition of the treasury stock. The shareholders' equity section of Hydro-Slide's balance sheet should appear the same as Figure 13. 7.

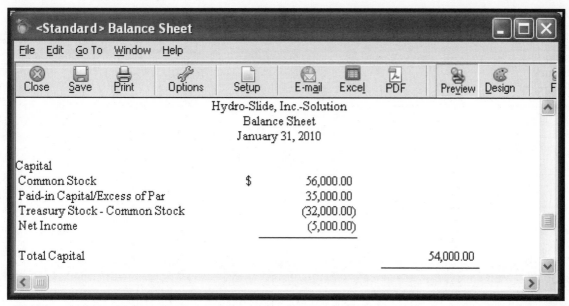

Figure 13. 7   The shareholders' equity section of Hydro-Slide's balance sheet after the treasury stock acquisition

On January 20, 2010, to remain with Hydro-Slide and in one fiscal period, Hydro-Slide sells one thousand of the shares of treasury stock it purchased on January 15, 2010, for $10.00 per share. The first issue to resolve the is purchase price of these shares - $8.00 per share. Therefore the amount CREDITED to the 315 – Treasury Stock-Common Stock account will be (1,000 shares × $8.00 per share) $8,000. The amount DEBITED to 101 – Cash will be (1,000 shares × $10.00 per share) $10,000. The difference, computed as $10,000 - $8,000 or as 1,000 shares × ($10.00 - $8.00), $2,000, will be CREDITED to 316 – Paid-in Capital-Treasury Stock. Utilize the receipts screen and the "Journal" option on its task bar to record this event. Check your work with Figure 13. 8 and make any necessary corrections before saving it.

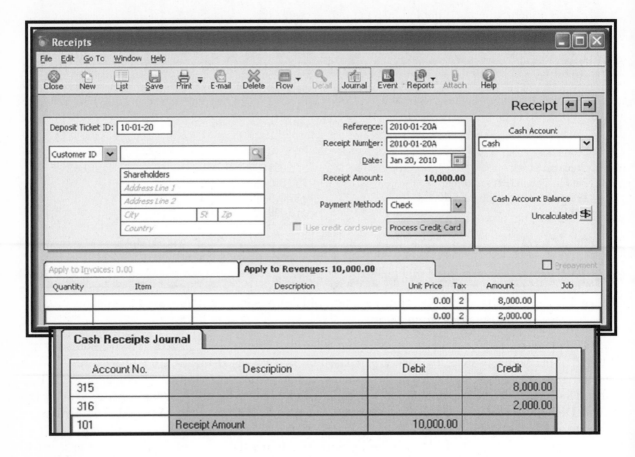

Figure 13. 8 Hydro-Slide's receipts screen to reissue the treasury stock

When you view the balance sheet for Hydro-Slide at this point you will see a new category for values – those associated with account 316 – Paid-in Capital-Treasury Stock. Figure 13. 9.

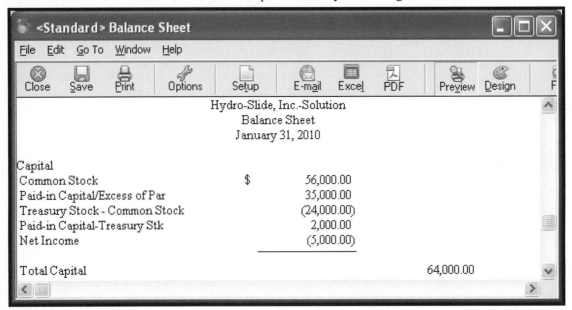

Figure 13. 9 Hydro-Slide's balance sheet after the reissuance of the treasury stock

Notice that the net income value, generated by Peachtree, has not changed. The issuance of stock and treasury stock **_IS NOT_** a revenue event and will not appear on the income statement.

Assuming that on January 25, 2010, again, to remain within one accounting period and with Hydro-Slide, Hydro-Slide sells or reissues eight hundred shares of its treasury stock for $7.00 per share. The first issue to resolve the is purchase price of these shares - $8.00 per share. Therefore the amount CREDITED to the 315 – Treasury Stock-Common Stock account will be (8000 shares × $8.00 per share) $6,400. The amount DEBITED to 101 – Cash will be (8000 shares × $7.00 per share) $5,600. The difference, computed as $6,400 - $5,600 or as 800 shares × ($8.00 - $7.00), $800, will be DEBITED to 316 – Paid-in Capital-Treasury Stock. Utilize the receipts screen and the Journal option on its task bar to record this event. Because 101 – Cash is the automatic debit account and all other accounts are CREDITED, you must enter a "nonstandard" value in the receipts screen. Enter the $6,400 to be credited to 315 – Treasury Stock-Common Stock on the first line of the journal entry section. Then enter a NEGATIVE $800 in the second line of the journal entry section. A NEGATIVE value in the DEBIT column is actually a CREDIT. Then utilize the Journal icon on the task bar to set the accounts to 315 – Treasury Stock-Common Stock for the $6,400 and 316 – Paid-in Capital-Treasury Stock. Check your work with Figure 13. 10 and make any necessary corrections before saving it.

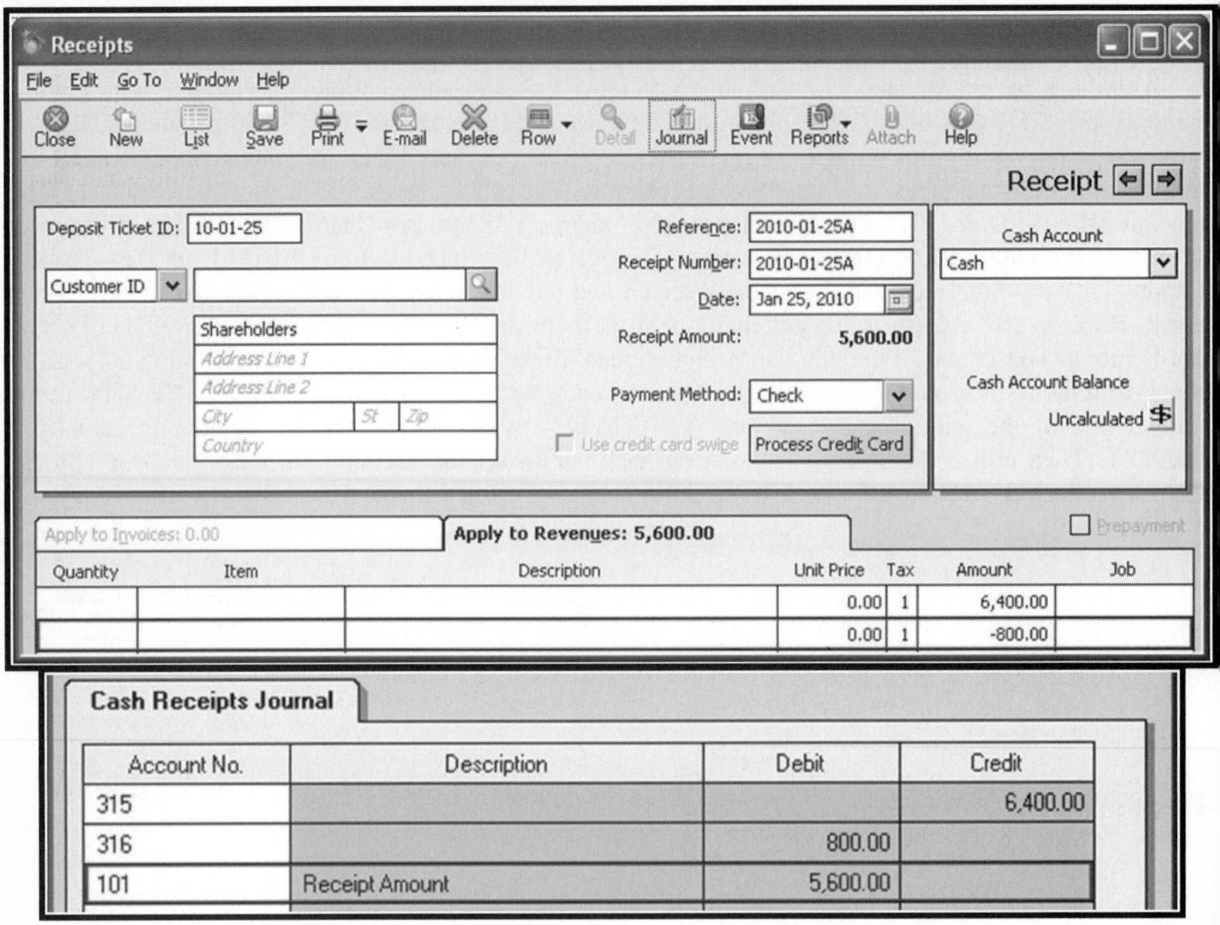

Figure 13. 10 Hydro-Slide's receipts screen for the second reissuance of the treasury stock

View the balance sheet for Hydro-Slide and notice the changes as well as the items that did not change. Common stock, paid-in capital in excess of par value, and net income have not changed while treasury stock-common stock and paid-in capital-treasury stock has. Compare your Hydro-Slide balance sheet with Figure 13. 11.

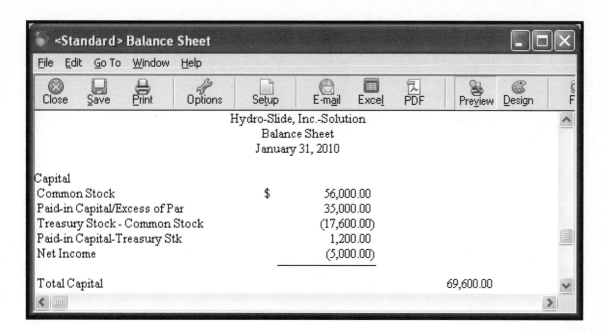

Figure 13. 11 Hydro-Slide's balance sheet after the second reissuance of the treasury stock

PREFERRED STOCK

Preferred stock accounts have been established as 300 – Preferred Stock and 301 – Paid-in Capital in Excess of Par Value Preferred Stock. Remember that Peachtree is text limited in the description field of chart of accounts so this ends up "Paid-in Capital/Excess-Par-P/S."

Staying with Hydro-Slide in January 2010, Hydro-Slide issues 10,000 shares of $10 par value preferred stock for $12 cash per share on January 11, 2010. Utilize the receipts screen and the "Journal" icon on the task bar to record this event. Compare your work with Figure 13. 12 and make any necessary adjustments before saving it.

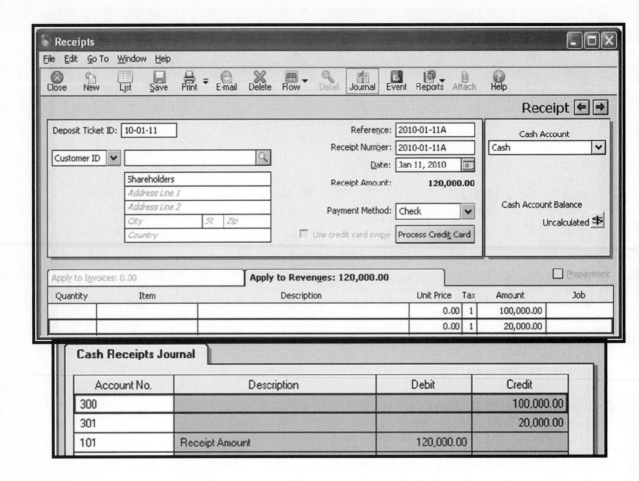

Figure 13. 12 Hydro-Slide's Receipt screen for the issuance of preferred stock

And Figure 13. 13 shows the additional categories of values in Hydro-Slide's capital section of the balance sheet.

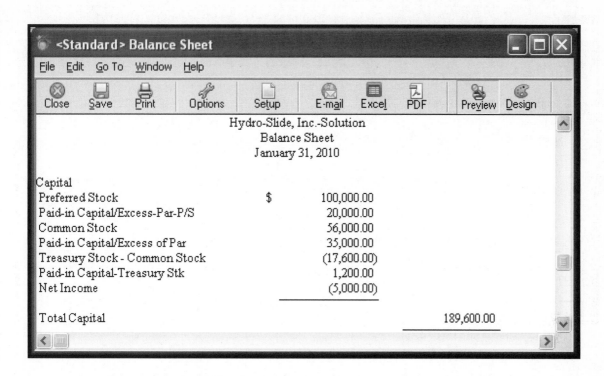

Figure 13. 13 Hydro-Slide's balance sheet after the issuance of preferred stock

303 – Dividends – Preferred Stock and 313 – Dividends – Common Stock have both been established as Equity-Gets Closed accounts for your use as needed.

Comprehensive Do It! Problem, Rolman Corporation, Directory Wey_AP9e_Rolman_Corp,

The Rolman Corporation is authorized to issue 1,000,000 shares of $5 par value common stock. In its first year, 2010, the company has the following stock transactions:

Jan 10   Issued 400,000 shares of stock at $8 per share. Reference JE #1.

July 1   Issued 100,000 shares of stock for land. The land had an asking price of $900,000. The stock is currently selling on a national exchange at $8.25 per share. Reference JE #2.

Sept 1   Purchased 10,000 shares of common stock for the treasury (Treasury Stock) at $9 per share. Reference JE #3.

Dec 1   Sold 4,000 shares of the treasury stock at $10 per share. Reference JE #4.

Instructions:

(a)   Open the Rolman Corporation file within your student data set and familiarize yourself with the chart of accounts.

(b)   Use the general journal entry screen to journalize the transactions on the dates indicated.

(c)   Print the general journal report for the year ended December 31, 2010, and the balance sheet as of December 31, 2010.

(d)   The journal entry to recognize the $200,000 in retained earnings has been made for you.

Solution to the Comprehensive Do It! Problem

The general journal report for Rolman Corporation for the year ended December 31, 2010.

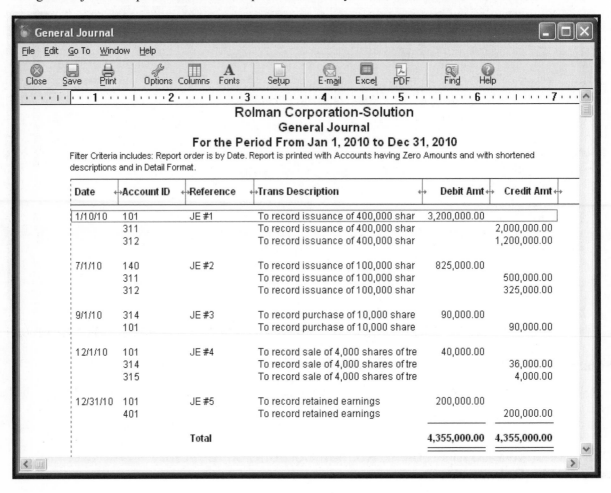

	General Journal

Rolman Corporation-Solution
General Journal
For the Period From Jan 1, 2010 to Dec 31, 2010

Filter Criteria includes: Report order is by Date. Report is printed with Accounts having Zero Amounts and with shortened descriptions and in Detail Format.

Date	Account ID	Reference	Trans Description	Debit Amt	Credit Amt
1/10/10	101	JE #1	To record issuance of 400,000 shar	3,200,000.00	
	311		To record issuance of 400,000 shar		2,000,000.00
	312		To record issuance of 400,000 shar		1,200,000.00
7/1/10	140	JE #2	To record issuance of 100,000 shar	825,000.00	
	311		To record issuance of 100,000 shar		500,000.00
	312		To record issuance of 100,000 shar		325,000.00
9/1/10	314	JE #3	To record purchase of 10,000 share	90,000.00	
	101		To record purchase of 10,000 share		90,000.00
12/1/10	101	JE #4	To record sale of 4,000 shares of tre	40,000.00	
	314		To record sale of 4,000 shares of tre		36,000.00
	315		To record sale of 4,000 shares of tre		4,000.00
12/31/10	101	JE #5	To record retained earnings	200,000.00	
	401		To record retained earnings		200,000.00
		Total		**4,355,000.00**	**4,355,000.00**

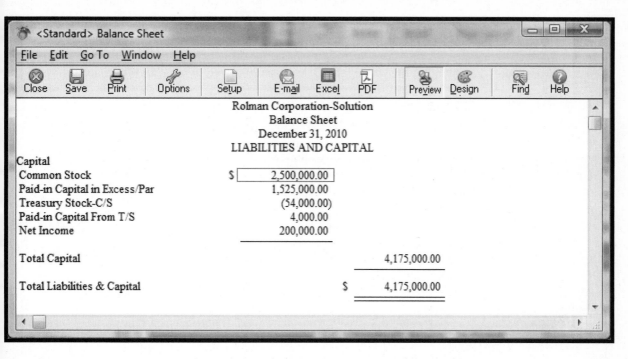

The capital section of Rolman Corporation's balance sheet as of January 31, 2010.

P13-1A, Franco Corporation, Directory Wey_AP9e_P13_1A_Franco_Corp

Franco Corporation was organized on January 1, 2010. It is authorized to issue 10,000 shares of 8%, $100 par value preferred stock, and 500,000 shares of no-par common stock with a stated value of $2 per share. The following stock transactions were completed during the first year.

Jan	10	Issued 80,000 shares of common stock for cash at $4 per share
Mar	1	Issued 5,000 shares of preferred stock for cash at $105 per share
Apr	1	Issued 24,000 shares of common stock for land. The asking price of the land was $90,000. The fair market value of the land was $85,000
May	1	Issued 80,000 shares of common stock for cash at $4.50 per share.
Aug	1	Issued 10,000 shares of common stock to attorneys in payment of their bill of $30,000 for services rendered in helping the company organize.
Sept	1	Issued 10,000 shares of common stock for cash at $5 per share
Nov	1	Issued 1,000 shares of preferred stock for cash at $109 per share

Instructions:
(a) Open the Franco Corporation file from within your student data set and familiarize yourself with the chart of accounts.

(b) Use the general journal entry screen to journalize the transactions.

(c) Print the general journal report for the year ended December 31, 2010, and the balance sheet as of December 31, 2010.

P13-4A, Vargas Corporation, Directory Wey_AP9e_P13_4A_Vargas_Corp

Vargas Corporation is authorized to issue 20,000 shares of $50 par value, 10% convertible preferred stock and 125,000 shares of $3 par value common stock. On January 1, 2010, the ledger contained the following stockholders' equity balances:

Cash	$1,785,000
Preferred Stock (10,000 shares)	500,000
Paid In Capital in Excess of Par Value – Preferred	75,000
Common Stock (70,000 shares)	210,000
Paid In Capital in Excess of Par Value – Common	700,000
Retained Earnings	300,000

During 2010, the following transactions occurred:

Feb	1	Issued 2,000 shares of preferred stock for land having a fair market value of $125,000.
Mar	1	Issued 1,000 shares of preferred stock for cash at $65 per share.
July	7	Issued 16,000 shares of common stock for cash at $7 per share.
Sept	1	Issued 400 shares of preferred stock for a patent. The asking price of the patent was $30,000. Market values were preferred stock $70 per share and patent indeterminable.
Dec	1	Issued 8,000 shares of common stock for $7.50 per share.
Dec	31	Net income for the year was $260,000. No dividends were declared. (Use a general journal entry debiting cash and crediting sales.)

Instructions:
(a) Open Vargas Corporation found within the student data sets and familiarize yourself with the chart of accounts.
(b) Verify the beginning balances.
(c) Use the general journal entry screen to journalize the transactions.
(d) Print the general journal report and general ledger for the year ended December 31, 2010, and the balance sheet as of December 31, 2010.
(e) Do not close Vargas using the Year-End Wizard to move sales from income to retained earnings unless specifically instructed to by your instructor.

CHAPTER 14

Corporations: Dividends, Retained Earnings, and Income Reporting

OBJECTIVES

- Prepare the entries for cash dividends and stock dividends.
- Identify the items reported in a retained earnings statement.
- Prepare and analyze a comprehensive

stockholders' equity section.
- Describe the form and content of corporation income statements.
- Compute earnings per share.

DIVIDENDS

While there are several types of dividends available to a corporation, this text will focus on Cash Dividends. A Cash Dividend is a cash distribution of retained earnings to shareholders on a per share basis. All shareholders within the same class – common stock or preferred stock – will get the same amount per share. But all shareholders may not hold the same number of shares so some shareholders will receive more while others receive less. Some shareholders may also hold two or more classes of stock. Dividends are usually expressed in percentage of par – 2% of par which would be $2 per share if par or stated value is $100 per share or as a value such as $2 per share – par value is not a factor in the amount per share paid. If there is preferred stock or cumulative preferred stock, dividends payable to these classes must be paid before common stock receives dividends.

For a corporation to pay a cash dividend it must have:

- Retained Earnings
- Adequate Cash
- A Board of Directors' authorization

VIOLATIONS OF CONCEPTS – MUST READ!

This chapter of the Peachtree text will be using one company, Makers Inc., to show the events of the chapter. As such, each event is independent of any other events unless stated. One event may be based on a company with only common stock while the next may be based on a company with a complex stock structure. The dates are adjusted as necessary to ease of viewing reports. Makers Inc. had been established with cash, preferred stock, common stock, and retained earnings for these events. There are some violations you must be aware of. If the example in the textbook states that the par value of the common stock is $1.00 and 100,000 shares of common stock are outstanding, the balance of the common stock account MUST be $100,000. The value Makers Inc. may be something else. And when a company has a complex stock structure the preferred stock shareholders must receive their proper entitle before common stock shareholders receive their entitle. With Makers Inc. in this chapter, common stock may be addressed while preferred stock is ignored. These types of stipulations are violated in this chapter with Markers Inc. in an attempt to minimize opening and closing companies for this chapter's accomplishments. And, following the textbook, you should use the retained earnings account for recording dividend declarations. *REMEMBER* each event is considered in isolation unless otherwise stated.

PEACHTREE ENTRIES FOR CASH DIVIDENDS

Three dates are important in connection with dividends: 1) the declaration date, 2) the record date, and 3) the payment date. There is normally about a month between the dates. Accounting entries are required for the declaration date and the payment date.

On the declaration date, the board of directors formally announces or declares (authorizes) the cash dividend. The announcement is made to the shareholders. And, at that point, the obligation is binding and cannot be rescinded. The corporation has now entered into a liability for the declared dividends.

With Makers Inc. from within your student data set open, assume that on January 1, 2010, the directors of Makers Inc. declare a 50¢ per share cash dividend on 100,000 shares of $10 par value common stock. The dividend is (100,000 shares × $0.50 per share) $50,000.

Using the general journal entry screen, journalize the recognition of this newly created liability. The debit account will be 350 – Retained Earnings, as stated in the text. The credit account will be 228 – Dividends Payable – C/S. The amount will be (100,000 shares × $0.50 per share) $50,000. Compare your work with Figure 14. 1 and make any necessary adjustments before saving your journal entry.

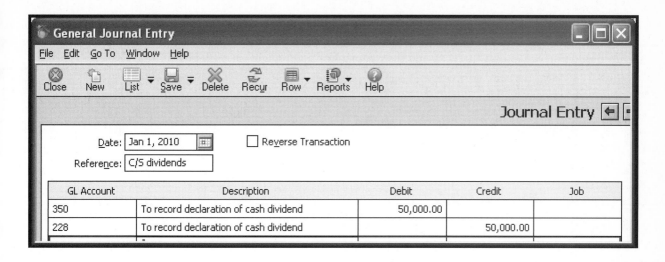

Figure 14. 1   General journal entry to declare common stock dividends

The next step is the record date, which identifies the stockholders who will receive the dividend. The stockholder must be owner of record on the record date to receive the dividend. No accounting entry is required for the date of record. For this example assume that the record date is January 10, 2010.

On the payment date, assume it to be January 20, 2010, dividend checks are mailed to the stockholders and the payment of the dividend is recorded. Use the write checks screen and check Number 101 to write the check to the common stock shareholders. Compare your work with Figure 14. 2 and make any necessary adjustments before saving.

Figure 14. 2   Write check screen to pay common stock dividends

When you view the 101 – Cash, 228 – Dividends Payable – Common Stock, and 350 – Retained Earnings accounts in the general ledger for the month of January 2010, you will see the recording of the obligation on January 1, 2010, and the payment of that obligation on January 20, 2010.

Makers Inc.-Solution
General Ledger
For the Period From Jan 1, 2010 to Jan 31, 2010

Filter Criteria includes: 1) IDs: Multiple IDs. Report order is by ID. Report is printed with shortened descriptions and in Detail Format.

Account ID Account Description	Date	Reference	Jrnl	Trans Description	Debit Amt	Credit Amt	Balance
101	1/1/10			Beginning Balance			
Cash	1/1/10	Beginning	GEN	Beginning balance	13,500,000.00		
	1/20/10	101	CDJ	Common Stock Sh		50,000.00	
				Current Period Ch	13,500,000.00	50,000.00	13,450,000
	1/31/10			Ending Balance			13,450,000.
228	1/1/10			Beginning Balance			
Dividends Payable -	1/1/10	C/S dividen	GEN	To record declarati		50,000.00	
	1/20/10	101	CDJ	Common Stock Sh	50,000.00		
				Current Period Ch	50,000.00	50,000.00	
	1/31/10			Ending Balance			
350	1/1/10			Beginning Balance			
Retained Earnings	1/1/10	Beginning	GEN	Beginning balance		2,500,000.00	
	1/1/10	C/S dividen	GEN	To record declarati	50,000.00		
				Current Period Ch	50,000.00	2,500,000.00	-2,450,000
	1/31/10			Ending Balance			-2,450,000.

Figure 14. 3   The filtered (limited account presentation) general ledger of Makers Inc.

Recall that these are independent transactions. Assume that Makers Inc. has a complex stock structure with 1,000 shares of 8%, $100 par value cumulative preferred stock and has 50,000 shares of $10 par value common stock outstanding. The dividend per share for preferred stock is ($100 par value × 8%) $8.00. The required annual dividend for preferred stock is therefore (1,000 shares × $8.00 per share) $8,000. On February 1, 2010, the directors declare a $6,000 cash dividend with a record date of February 5, 2010, and a distribution date of February 10, 2010. In this case, the entire declared dividend amount goes to preferred stockholders because of the preferred stock dividend preference of $8,000 is more than the value being declared, $6,000.

As with the common stock dividends in the previous example, utilize the general journal entry screen to record this obligation on February 1, 2010, and the write checks screen with check number 102 dated February 10, 2010, to pay the obligation. Compare your work with Figure 14. 4 and make any necessary adjustments before saving your work.

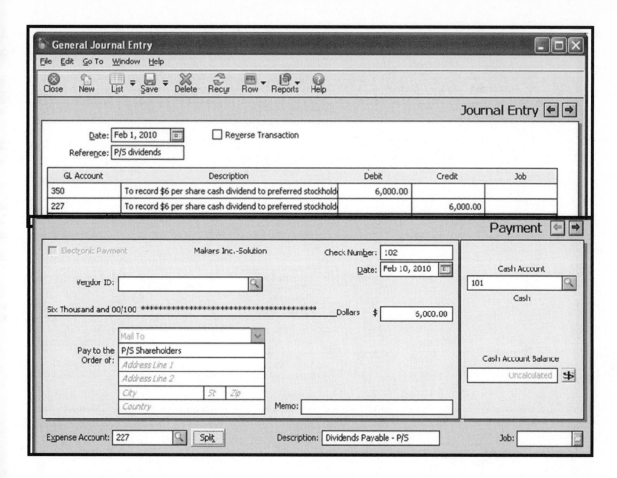

Figure 14. 4 Makers Inc. general journal entry and check number 102 for preferred stock dividends

View the general ledger for Makers Inc. and use the "Options" icon on the task bar to set the date to February 1, 2010 to February 28, 2010 with account IDs of 101 – Cash, 227 – Dividends Payable – P/S, and 350 – Retained Earnings, as shown in Figure 14. 5. And the obligation incurred by the declaration of dividends on February 1, 2010, and the payment of those dividends on February 10, 2010, is shown. Compare your general ledger report with Figure 14. 5.

General Ledger

File Edit Go To Window Help

| Close | Save | Print | Options | Columns | Fonts | Setup | E-mail | Excel | PDF | Find | Help |

Makers Inc.-Solution
General Ledger
For the Period From Feb 1, 2010 to Feb 28, 2010

Filter Criteria includes: 1) IDs: Multiple IDs. Report order is by ID. Report is printed with shortened descriptions and in Detail Format.

Account ID Account Description	Date	Reference	Jrnl	Trans Description	Debit Amt	Credit Amt	Balance
101	2/1/10			Beginning Balance			13,450,000.0
Cash	2/10/10	102	CDJ	P/S Shareholders		6,000.00	
				Current Period Ch		6,000.00	-6,000.00
	2/28/10			**Ending Balance**			**13,444,000.0**
227	2/1/10			Beginning Balance			
Dividends Payable - P	2/1/10	P/S dividen	GEN	To record $6 per s		6,000.00	
	2/10/10	102	CDJ	P/S Shareholders -	6,000.00		
				Current Period Ch	6,000.00	6,000.00	
	2/28/10			**Ending Balance**			
350	2/1/10			Beginning Balance			-2,450,000.0
Retained Earnings	2/1/10	P/S dividen	GEN	To record $6 per s	6,000.00		
				Current Period Ch	6,000.00		6,000.00
	2/28/10			**Ending Balance**			**-2,444,000.0**

Figure 14. 5   Makers Inc. filtered general ledger regarding preferred stock dividends in February 2010

As a continuation of the preferred stock dividends, on February 1, 2011, the board of Makers Inc. declares $50,000 in dividend payments. The first issue that must be resolved is the dividends in arrears, $2,000, on preferred stock from 2010. The second issue is the entitlement of $8,000 to preferred stock shareholders for 2011 resulting in preferred stock shareholders being entitled to the first $10,000 declared. The balance, ($50,000 - $10,000) $40,000 is the amount due to common stock shareholders. As with the earlier entries, utilize the general journal entry screen to record the obligation incurred by the declaration of dividends and the write checks screen with check number 103 dated February 10, 2011 to pay the dividends. In writing the check use the Split option near the lower portion of the screen to set the accounts properly. Compare your work with Figure 14. 6 and make any necessary corrections before saving your work.

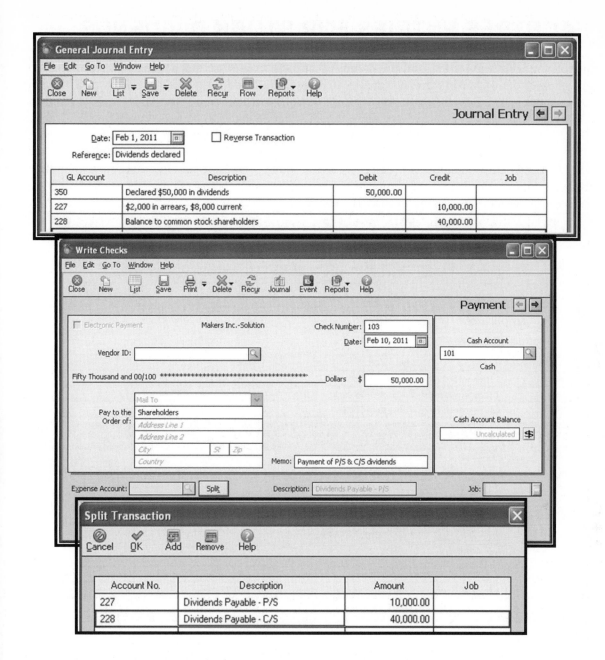

Figure 14. 6   Makers Inc. general journal entry and check for the declaration of dividends in February 2011

View the general ledger, using the "Options" icon, to set the date range to February 1, 2011 to February 28, 2011 to see the affect on the numerous accounts associated with these events.

PEACHTREE ENTRIES FOR STOCK DIVIDENDS

Still working with Makers Inc. and the premise that these events are independent, on April 1, 2010, the board of directors of Makers Inc. declares a 10% stock dividend on its 50,000 shares of $10 par value common stock with a record date of April 10, 2010, and a distribution date of April 20, 2010. The current fair market value of its stock is $15 per share. The number of shares to be issued is (10% × 50,000 shares) 5,000 shares. Therefore the total amount to be debited to retained earnings is (5,000 × $15) $75,000. Utilize the general journal entry screen to record the obligation and distribution. Account 375 – Common Stock Dividends Distributable has been set up as an Equity – Doesn't get closed account. Compare your work with Figure 14. 7 and make any necessary adjustments before saving them. Since no cash is transferred in these events, the use of the write checks screen is inappropriate.

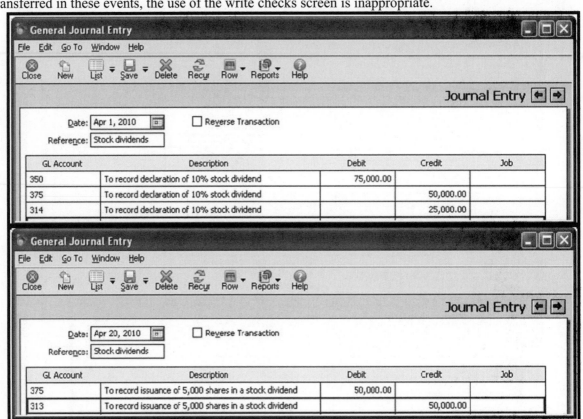

Figure 14. 7   Makers Inc. general journal entries for stock dividends in April 2010

There is a progression of value changes within the capital section of Makers Inc.'s balance sheet. This is shown in Figure 14. 8. The top panel is the capital section before the declaration on April 1, 2010. The middle panel is after the declaration on April 1, 2010. Notice that the distributable amount is now shown and retained earnings is reduced, as dictated by the journal entry of April 1, 2010. The third panel shows the affects of the April 20, 2010, journal entry. The distributable value is now incorporated into the common stock account and now these newly issued stocks can vote.

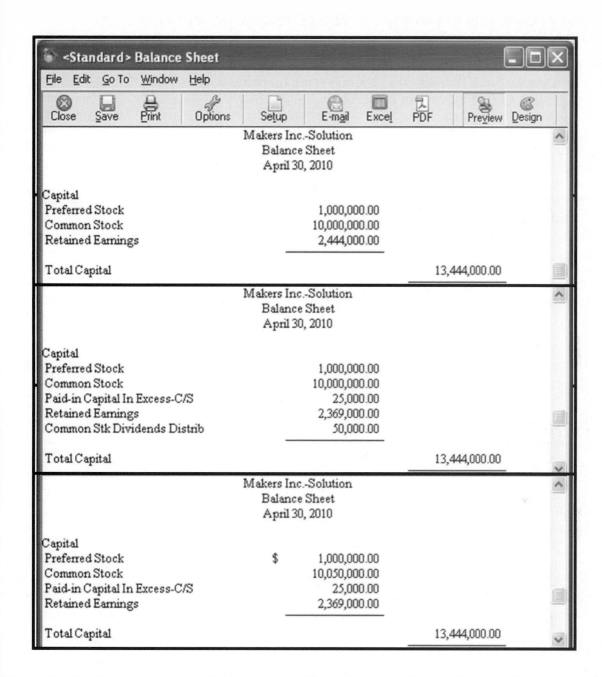

Figure 14. 8 The progression of the journal entries' effects on Makers Inc.'s capital section of the balance sheet

Comprehensive Do It! Problem, Hayslett Corporation, Directory Wey_AP9e_Hayslett_Corp

On January 1, 2010, Hayslett Corporation had the following stockholders' equity accounts.

Common Stock ($10 par value, 260,000 shares issued and outstanding)	$2,600,000
Paid-in Capital in Excess of Par Value	1,500,000
Retained Earnings	3,200,000

Beginning balances and the chart of accounts have been entered. During the year, the following transactions occurred.

April	1	Utilize the general journal entry screen to record the declaration of a $1.50 cash dividend per share to stockholders of record on April 15, payable May 1.
May	1	Utilize the write checks screen to write check number 101 to pay the dividend declared in April.
June	1	Announced a 2-for-1 stock split. Prior to the split, the market price per share was $24.
Aug.	1	Utilize the general journal entry screen to record the declaration of a 10% stock dividend to stockholders of record on August 15, distributable August 31. On August 1, the market price of the stock was $10 per share.
	31	Utilize the general journal entry screen to record the issued the shares for the stock dividend.
Dec.	1	Utilize the general journal entry screen to record the declaration of a $1.50 per share dividend to stockholders of record on December 15, payable January 5, 2009.
	31	Utilize the general journal entry screen to record the net income for the year was $600,000. (Record this as a debit to Cash and a credit to Retained Earnings since no sales events are given in the text.)

Instructions

(a)   Journalize the transactions and the closing entry for net income.

(b)   Print the balance sheet as of December 31, 2010.

Hayslett Corporation's general journal report

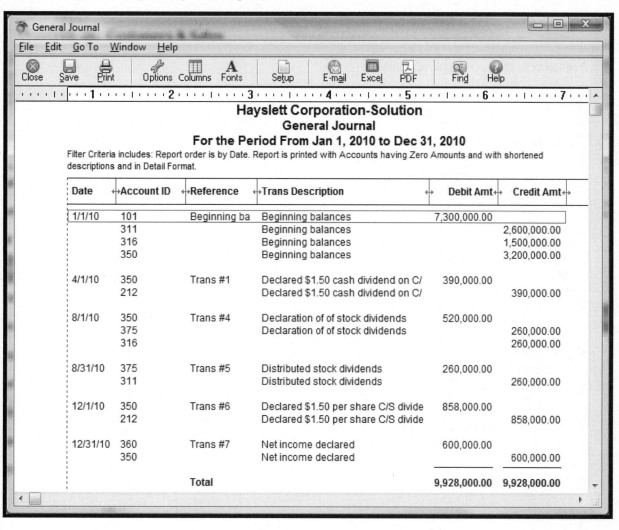

General Journal

File Edit Go To Window Help

Close Save Print Options Columns Fonts Setup E-mail Excel PDF Find Help

Hayslett Corporation-Solution
General Journal
For the Period From Jan 1, 2010 to Dec 31, 2010

Filter Criteria includes: Report order is by Date. Report is printed with Accounts having Zero Amounts and with shortened descriptions and in Detail Format.

Date	Account ID	Reference	Trans Description	Debit Amt	Credit Amt
1/1/10	101	Beginning ba	Beginning balances	7,300,000.00	
	311		Beginning balances		2,600,000.00
	316		Beginning balances		1,500,000.00
	350		Beginning balances		3,200,000.00
4/1/10	350	Trans #1	Declared $1.50 cash dividend on C/	390,000.00	
	212		Declared $1.50 cash dividend on C/		390,000.00
8/1/10	350	Trans #4	Declaration of of stock dividends	520,000.00	
	375		Declaration of of stock dividends		260,000.00
	316				260,000.00
8/31/10	375	Trans #5	Distributed stock dividends	260,000.00	
	311		Distributed stock dividends		260,000.00
12/1/10	350	Trans #6	Declared $1.50 per share C/S divide	858,000.00	
	212		Declared $1.50 per share C/S divide		858,000.00
12/31/10	360	Trans #7	Net income declared	600,000.00	
	350		Net income declared		600,000.00
			Total	**9,928,000.00**	**9,928,000.00**

Hayslett Corporation's balance sheet as of December 31, 2010

Hayslett Corporation-Solution
Balance Sheet
December 31, 2010

ASSETS

Current Assets		
Cash	$ 7,510,000.00	
Total Current Assets		7,510,000.00
Property and Equipment		
Total Property and Equipment		0.00
Other Assets		
Total Other Assets		0.00
Total Assets		$ 7,510,000.00

LIABILITIES AND CAPITAL

Current Liabilities		
Dividends Payable	$ 858,000.00	
Total Current Liabilities		858,000.00
Long-Term Liabilities		
Total Long-Term Liabilities		0.00
Total Liabilities		858,000.00
Capital		
Common Stock	2,860,000.00	
Paid-in Capital in Excess-C/S	1,760,000.00	
Retained Earnings	2,032,000.00	
Net Income	0.00	
Total Capital		6,652,000.00
Total Liabilities & Capital		$ 7,510,000.00

P14-1A, Carolinas Corporation, Directory Wey_AP9e_P14_1A_Carolinas_Corp

On January 1, 2010, Carolinas Corporation had the following stockholders' equity accounts:

Common Stock ($20 par value, 60,000 shares issued and outstanding)	$1,200,000
Paid In Capital in Excess of Par Value	200,000
Retained Earnings	600,000

During the year, the following transactions occurred:

Feb	1	Declared a $1 cash dividend per share to stockholders of record on February 15, payable March 1.
Mar	1	Paid the dividend declared in February.
Apr	1	Announced a 2-for-1 stock split. Prior to the split, the market price per share was $36.
July	1	Declared a 10% stock dividend to stockholders of record on July 15, distributable July 31. On July 1, the market price of the stock was $13 per share.
July	31	Issued the shares for the stock dividend.
Dec	1	Declared a $0.50 per share dividend to stockholders of record on December 15, payable January 5, 2010.
Dec	31	Determined that net income for the year was $350,000. (Record this as a debit to Cash and a credit to Retained Earnings since no sales events are given in the text.)

Instructions:
(a) Open the Carolinas Corporation file from within your student data set and familiarize yourself with the chart of accounts.
(b) Use the general journal entry screen to journalize the transactions.
(c) Print the general journal report and the retained earnings statement for the year 2010. Print the balance sheet as of December 31, 2010.

P14-2A, Hashmi Company, Directory Wey_AP9e_P14_2A_Hashmi_Co

The stockholders' equity accounts of Hashmi Company at January 1, 2010 are as follows:

Preferred Stock, 6%, $50 par	$600,000
Common Stock, $5 par	800,000
Paid-In Capital in Excess of Par Value - Preferred Stock	200,000
Paid-In Capital in Excess of Par Value - Common Stock	300,000
Retained Earnings	800,000

There are no dividends in arrears on preferred stock. During 2010, the company had the following transactions and events.

July	1	Declared a $0.50 cash dividend on common stock.
Aug	1	Discovered $25,000 understatement of 2009 depreciation. Ignore income taxes.
Sept	1	Paid the cash dividend declared on July 1
Dec	1	Declared 10% stock dividend on common stock when the market value of the stock was $18 per share.
Dec	15	Declared a 6% cash dividend on preferred stock payable January 15, 2011.
	31	Determined that net income for the year was $355,000. (Record this as a debit to Accounts Receivable and a credit to Sales since no sales events are given in the text.)
	31	Recognized a $200,000 restriction of retained earnings for plant expansion. Since Peachtree will only allow one Retained Earnings account, this is a text note, no action required.

Instructions:
(a) Open Hashmi Company found within your student data set and familiarize yourself with the chart of accounts and verify the beginning balances of the stockholders' equity accounts.
(b) Use the general journal entry screen to journalize the transactions and events.
(c) Print the general journal report and the retained earnings statement for the year ended December 31, 2010. Print the balance sheet as of December 31, 2010.

CHAPTER 15

Long-Term Liabilities

OBJECTIVES

- Explain why bonds are issued.
- Prepare the entries for the issuance of bonds and interest expense.
- Describe the entries when bonds are redeemed or converted.
- Describe the accounting for long-term notes payable.
- Contrast the accounting for operating and capital leases.
- Identify the methods for the presentation and analysis of long-term liabilities.

BOND BASICS

To obtain large amounts of long-term capital, corporate management usually must decide whether to issue stock (equity financing) or issue bonds (debt financing). Bonds are a form of interest bearing notes payable. They are usually sold in denominations of $1,000. For the issuing company, bond interest paid is a deduction for taxes, interest expense, while dividends paid on the company's stock is not. A disadvantage of bonds is that interest payments are required in accordance with the terms of the bond issue – annually, semiannually, or quarterly. If any of these recurring payments are not made the bond is in default. Recurring or periodic stock dividends are not a formal requirement and need not be declared. The default of bond interest payments will most likely incur legal action, a loss of faith and reputation of the issuing company, and decline in the issuer's credit rating and therefore an increase in their risk, resulting in higher interest requirements in the future.

Terms related to bonds are:

Face value – the amount of principal that the issuer must pay upon redemption. This is frequently $1,000 but can be any value determined by the issuer.

Contractual interest rate, also known as stated or nominal interest rate – the annual rate of interest printed or stated on the bond itself. This value is part of the factor used in determining the present value of the issue and the actual interest payment being made.

Effective interest rate, also known as market interest – the actual interest rate on the open market for similar financial instruments in risk and time. This value is part of the factor that will determine the present value of the issue and the period interest expense.

Life – the life of a bond issue is usually stated in whole years – 5 years, 10 years, etc. This is stated on the bond itself and in the issue documents. Bond lives general do not exceed 40 years.

Periods of the bond – this is the number of times the bond will pay interest during its life. If the bond is a 10-year bond paying interest semiannually the periods of the bond is (10 years × 2 interest payments per year) 20 periods.

> ***Period interest rate*** – the face interest is stated as an annual percentage rate although the interest may be paid more frequently. If interest payments are made more often than annually, the face annual interest rate must be divided by the number of interest payments being made annually. For example, if the face interest rate is 10% and the bonds pay semiannual interest the period interest rate is (10% / 2 interest payments per year) 5%. Period interest rate must be calculated for contractual and effective interest.
>
> ***Double check*** – there is a simple check process for period interest – years of the issue × face rate must equal periods of the bond × period interest rate. In the example if the bond is a 10-year, 10% bond paying semiannual interest, 10 years × 10% must equal 20 periods × 5%. This should be done with contractual and effective interest values.

In authorizing a bond issue, the corporation's board of directors stipulates the number of bonds to be issued, the denomination of the bonds, the total face value, and the contractual interest rate. The contractual interest rate is the rate used to determine the amount of cash interest the borrower (the company) pays to the investor. This is often referred to as the stated rate. Although the contractual rate is stated as an annual rate, it can be paid as stated in the issue – annually, semiannually, quarterly or monthly. Semiannually is the most common.

BONDS AT FACE VALUE

Bonds may be issued at face value, below face value (a discount) or above face value (a premium). This is determined by the relationship of contractual interest rate to effective or market interest rate. If the contractual interest rate is 10% and the market interest rate for this risk level and duration of bonds is 11%, these bonds will sell at a discount. This discount adjusts the total value of the issue and the interest payments to effective or market interest. If the contractual interest rate is 10% and the market interest rate for this risk level and duration of bonds is 9%, these bonds will sell at a premium. This premium adjusts the total value of the issue and the interest payments to effective or market interest. Discounts and premiums are not bad or good, they are mathematical adjustments to the issue to effective or current market interest rates. If the bond contractual interest rate is the same as effective interest, the bond will sell at face value. Computing the present value of a bond issue is addressed completely in text.

There are three versions of Candlestick Corporation within your student data set. "Candlestick Corp – Discount" for bond issuances at a discount, "Candlestick Corp – Face" for bond issuances at face value, and "Candlestick Corp – Premium" for bond issuances at a premium. This will allow you to accomplish all three events in the same chart of accounts and retain your work without interference.

The board of directors decided to issue bonds on January 1, 2010. The issue will be for 100 bonds with a face value of $1,000 each, the contractual or face interest rate is 10%, the life of the bonds are 5 years and the bonds pay semiannual interest payments on July 1 for the period January 1 through June 30, and on January 1 for July 1 through December 31.

> **Step 1:**   Open the Candlestick Corp – Face from within your student data set and familiarize yourself with the chart of accounts.

Step 2:   Utilize the receipts screen to journalize the issuance of the bonds on January 1, 2010. Use deposit ticket ID 10-01-01 and reference and receipt number 2010-01-01F. Use Bondholders in the Name window of the Pay to the Order of area on all entries. Utilize the Journal icon on the task bar to set the credited account to 211 – Bonds Payable. Compare your work with Figure 15. 1 and make any necessary adjustments before saving it.

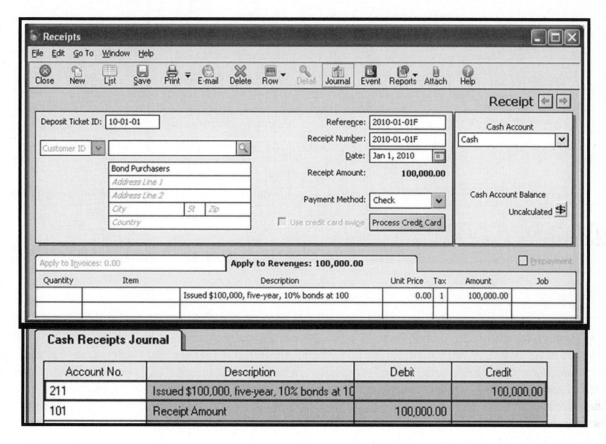

Figure 15. 1   Receipts screen for the issuance of bonds at face value

On July 1st Candlestick must make the first interest payment of the bond's term.   Utilize the write check screen to write check number 101 and set the date to July 1, 2010. The amount is (Principal × Rate × Time or $100,000 × 10% × (6/12)) $5,000. Enter Bondholders in the name window of the "Pay to the Order of" area and set the Expense Account to 718 – Interest Expense. Compare your work with Figure 15. 2 and make any adjustments necessary before saving it.

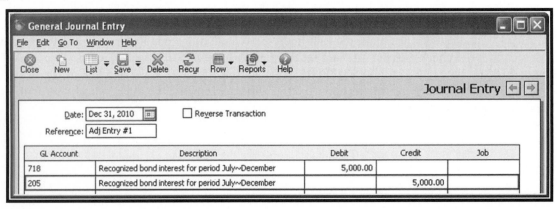

Figure 15. 2   Write check screen to the payment of interest on July 1, 2010

The next event associated with the bond is the interest accrued from July 1, 2010, through December 31, 2010, to correctly record and report interest expense and interest payable for the fiscal year of 2010. This is done with a general journal entry. Utilizing the general journal entry screen, set the date to December 31, 2010, use a reference of Adj Entry #1, a debit account of 718 – Interest Expense and a credit account of 205 – Interest Payable. The description can be Recognized bond interest for period July~December. The debit and credit amount is (Principal × Rate × Time or $100,000 × 10% × (6/12)) $5,000. Compare your work with Figure 15. 3 and make any necessary adjustments before saving your work.

Figure 15. 3   General journal entry to record the interest expense and interest payable as of December 31, 2010

On January 1, 2011, the interest obligation incurred on December 31, 2010, is paid with check number 102. Utilize the write check screen and compare your work with Figure 15. 4 and make any necessary adjustments before saving your work.

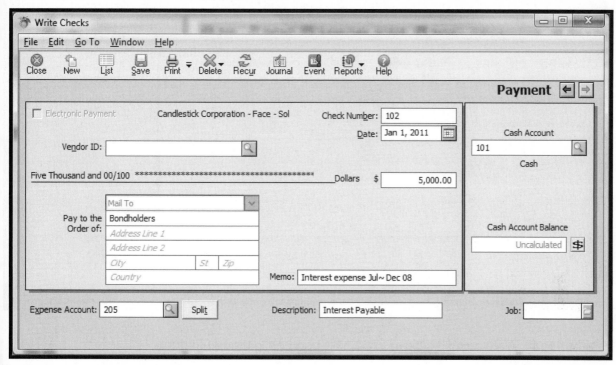

Figure 15. 4 Write checks screen to pay interest incurred on December 31, 2010, and paid on January 1, 2011

When this bond matures, a check will be written for the last interest payment and another check will be written for the payment of the bond. The check for interest will be similar to checks 101 and 102. You would write check number 103 dated January 1, 2015, as shown in Figure 15. 5 to accomplish this.

Note: This check is out of Peachtree's accessible accounting periods. Do not attempt to record or save it as it will require Peachtree to initiate the Year-End Wizard and close the preceding fiscal years.

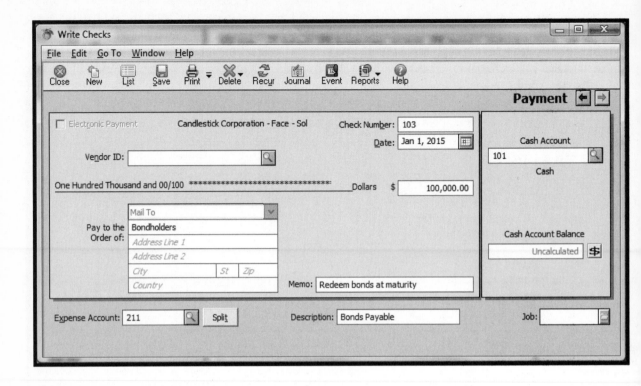

Figure 15. 5   Write checks screen to pay the bond obligation at maturity

BONDS AT A DISCOUNT

Restating what was said early, bonds are not issued at a discount because the issuer is bad or untrustworthy. They are issued at a discount because the interest rate, which is usually set months before the bond was actually issued, is **_LOWER_** than the market interest rate for the risk and the life of the bond. For this example you will be using Candlestick Corporation – Discount from within your student data set. In this example Candlestick's board of directors has dictated that a bond issue of $100,000 with a life of five years paying an interest rate of 10% with interest payable on July 1 and January 1 be accomplished. On the date of issue, January 1, 2010, the market interest for comparable bonds is 12%, higher than Candlestick's 10% so the bonds issue for a cash value of $92,639. This difference of $7,361 is referred to as the discount on bonds payable and is NOT an expense but a contra account to bonds payable in the liabilities section of the balance sheet.

Utilize the receipts screen of Candlestick Corp. - Discount to record the issuance of the bonds. Set the deposit ticket ID to 10-01-01 and the reference and receipt number to 2010-01-01D and the date to January 1, 2010. You can enter text into the description windows of the journal area, as shown, and these will transfer to the Journal screen accessed through the "Journal" icon on the task bar. Because there is a discount associated with this transaction, enter $100,000 in the first line's amount window. Then enter a **_NEGATIVE_** $7,361 in the second line's Amount window, as shown. Then click on the "Journal" icon on the task bar and set the accounts to 211 – Bonds Payable and 212 – Discount on Bonds Payable, as shown in Figure 15. 6. Compare your work with Figure 15. 6 and make any necessary adjustments before saving your work.

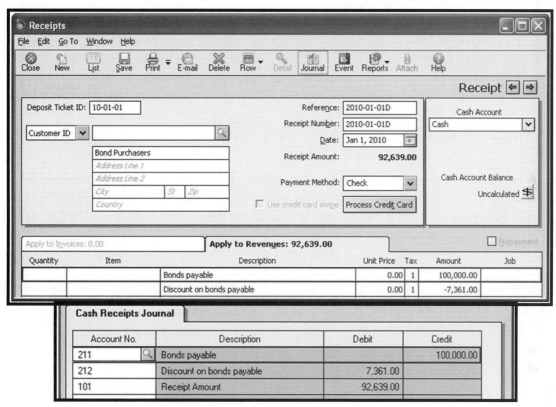

Figure 15. 6   Receipts screen for the issuance of the bonds at a discount

How this discount on bonds payable is presented, as compared to the bonds issued at face value, is shown in the partial balance sheet of Figure 15. 7. The upper panel is taken from Candlestick Corporation's bond issue at face value, the lower panel is taken from Candlestick's bond issuance at a discount.

Candlestick Corporation - Face - Sol
Balance Sheet
January 31, 2010

LIABILITIES AND CAPITAL

Long-Term Liabilities
Bonds Payable $ 100,000.00

Total Long-Term Liabilities   100,000.00

Candlestick Corporation - Discnt - Sol
Balance Sheet
January 31, 2010

LIABILITIES AND CAPITAL

Long-Term Liabilities
Bonds Payable $ 100,000.00
Discount on Bonds Payable   (7,361.00)

Total Long-Term Liabilities   92,639.00

Figure 15. 7 Candlestick's balance sheet showing bonds payable at face and at a discount at issue date

Using Illustration 15B-2 from the textbook, shown here as Figure 15. 8, the discount on bonds payable will be amortized utilizing the effective interest method. As such, the first interest payment will amortize $558 and the carrying value of the bond will increase from $92,639 to ($92,639 + $558) $93,197.

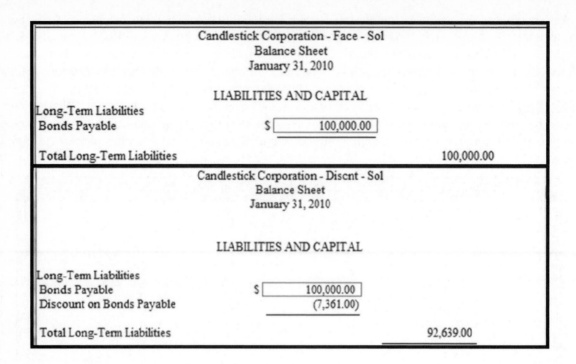

CANDLESTICK, INC.
Bond Discount Amortization
Effective-Interest Method—Semiannual Interest Paym
10% Bonds Issued at 12%

B	C		D
(A) Interest to Be Paid (5% × $100,000)	(B) Interest Expense to Be Recorded (6% × Preceding Bond Carrying Value)		(C) Discount Amortization (B) − (A)
$ 5,000	$ 5,558	(6% × $92,639)	$ 558
5,000	5,592	(6% × $93,197)	592
5,000	5,627	(6% × $93,789)	627
5,000	5,665	(6% × $94,416)	665
5,000	5,705	(6% × $95,081)	705
5,000	5,747	(6% × $95,786)	747
5,000	5,792	(6% × $96,533)	792
5,000	5,840	(6% × $97,325)	840
5,000	5,890	(6% × $98,165)	890
5,000	5,945*	(6% × $99,055)	945
$50,000	$57,361		$7,361

Figure 15. 8 Effective interest method table for Candlestick's discount on bonds payable

Since Candlestick pays the interest incurred from January 1 through June 30 on July 1, utilize the write checks screen to write check number 111 dated July 1, 2010, with a credit to 101 – Cash for $5,000, this is entered in the window to the right of the dollars line on the check face. The 718 – Interest Expense account is ***DEBITED*** for the sum of $5,000, the amount paid to the bond holders, and the amount amortized, $558, from the effective interest table, $5,558. A ***NEGATIVE*** (CREDIT) value of $558 is placed into the 212 – Discount on Bonds Payable account of the second journal line. Since the discount on bonds payable was entered as a DEBIT value offsetting the cash received, $92,639, for the obligation incurred by bonds payable - $100,000, this discount is amortized by CREDIT values over the term of the bond. Compare your work with Figure 15. 9 and make any necessary adjustments before saving it.

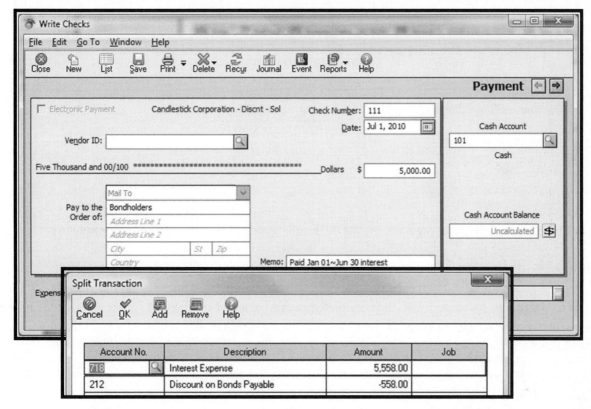

Figure 15. 9   Write checks screen for the first interest payment on bonds payable

View your balance sheet for July 31, 2010, shown in Figure 15. 10, and notice that the bonds payable value has ***NOT*** changed. But, the discount on bonds payable has ***DECREASED*** by the $558 and the carrying value has ***INCREASED*** by $558 to $93,197. Compare this report with Figure 15. 7.

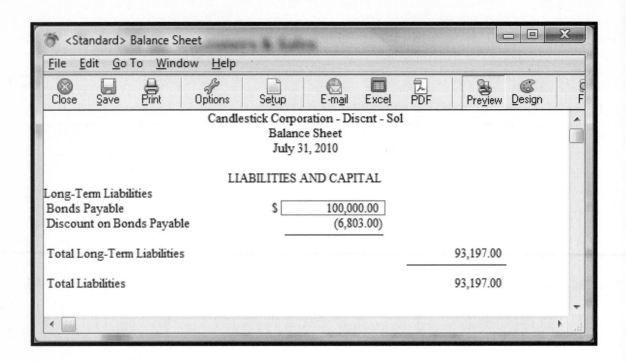

Figure 15. 10 Candlestick's balance sheet showing long-term liabilities after the interest
payment of July 1, 2010

The next event associated with the bond is the interest accrued from July 1, 2010, through December 31, 2010, to correctly record and report interest expense, interest payable, and bond carrying value for the fiscal year of 2010. This is done with a general journal entry. Utilizing the general journal entry screen, set the date to December 31, 2010, use a reference of Adj Entry #1, a debit account of 718 – Interest Expense for the sum of the interest to be paid, $5,000, and the amortization of the discount on bonds payable for the SECOND period from Figure 15. 8, $592, totaling $5,592. Credit account of 205 – Interest Payable for the amount the bond holders will receive, $5,000. The descriptions can be seen in Figure 15. 11. Compare your work with Figure 15. 11 and make any necessary adjustments before saving your work.

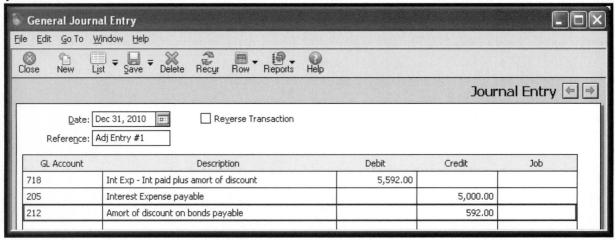

Figure 15. 11 General journal entry to record the interest expense, amortization of discount on bonds payable, and interest payable as of December 31, 2010

On January 1, 2011, the interest obligation incurred on December 31, 2010, is paid with check number 112. Utilize the write check screen and compare your work with Figure 15. 12 and make any necessary adjustments before saving your work.

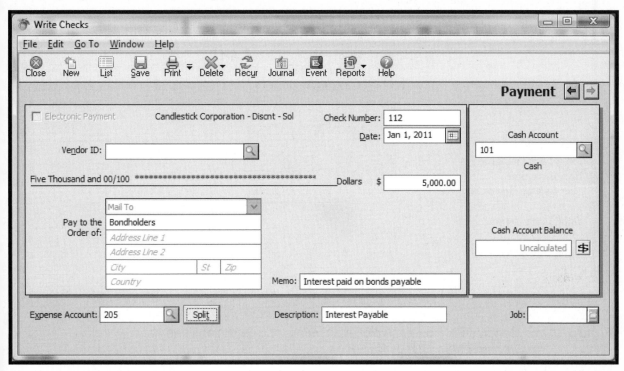

Figure 15. 12 Write checks screen to pay interest incurred on December 31, 2010 and paid on January 1, 2011

And, as shown in Figure 15. 13, the discount on bonds payable and the bond carrying value has changed again due to the December 31, 2010, adjusting entry. This change follows that of the effective interest table of Figure 15. 7.

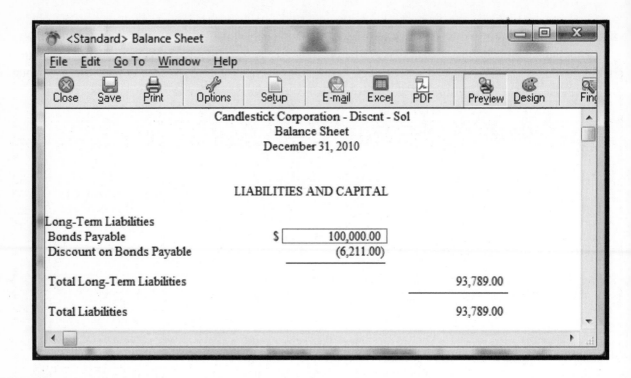

Figure 15. 13 Candlestick's balance sheet showing long-term liabilities as of December 31, 2010

When this bond matures, a check will be written for the last interest payment and another check will be written for the payment of the bond. The check for interest and the amortization of discount on bonds payable will be similar to Checks 111 and 112. You would write check number 113 dated January 1, 2015, similar to Figure 15. 5 to accomplish this.

Note: This check is out of Peachtree's accessible accounting periods. Do not attempt to record or save it as it will require Peachtree to initiate the Year-End Wizard and close the preceding fiscal years.

BONDS AT A PREMIUM

Restating what was stated early, bonds are not issued at a premium because the issuer is an above average company or extremely trustworthy. They are issued at a premium because the interest rate, which is usually set months before the bond was actually issued, is ***HIGHER*** than the market interest rate for the risk and the life of the bond. For this example you will be using Candlestick Corporation – Premium from within your student data set. In this example Candlestick's board of directors has dictated that a bond issue of $100,000 with a life of five years paying an interest rate of 10% with interest payable on July 1 and January 1 be accomplished. On the date of issue, January 1, 2010, the market interest for comparable bonds is 8%, LOWER than Candlestick's 10% so the bonds issue for a cash value of $108,111. This difference of $8,111 is referred to as the Premium on Bonds Payable and is NOT a revenue but an adjunct account (same type – debit or credit - balance as its associated account) to Bonds Payable in the liabilities section of the balance sheet.

Utilize the receipts screen of Candlestick Corp. - Premium to record the issuance of the bonds. Set the deposit ticket ID to 10-01-01 and the reference and receipt number to 2010-01-01P and the date to January 1, 2010. You can enter text into the description windows of the journal area, as shown, and these will transfer to the journal screen accessed through the "Journal" icon on the task bar. Because there is a premium associated with this transaction, enter $100,000 in the first line's amount window. Then enter $8,111 in the second line's amount window, as shown. Then click on the "Journal" icon on the task bar and set the accounts to 211 – Bonds Payable and 213 – Premium on Bonds Payable, as shown in Figure 15. 14. Compare your work with Figure 15. 14 and make any necessary adjustments before saving your work.

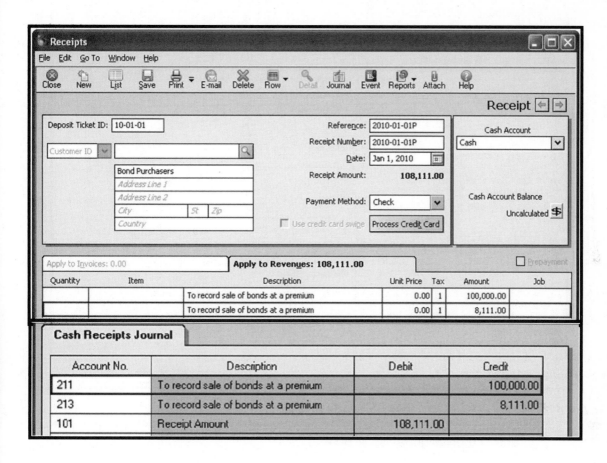

Figure 15. 14 Receipts screen for the issuance of the bonds at a premium

How this premium on bonds payable is presented, as compared to the bonds issued at face value, and at a discount, is shown in the partial balance sheet of Figure 15. 15. The upper panel is taken from Candlestick Corporation's issue at face value, the middle panel is taken from Candlestick's issuance at a discount, and the lower panel is Candlestick's issuance at a premium.

Candlestick Corporation - Face - Sol		
Balance Sheet		
January 31, 2010		
LIABILITIES AND CAPITAL		
Long-Term Liabilities		
Bonds Payable	$ 100,000.00	
Total Long-Term Liabilities		100,000.00

Candlestick Corporation - Discnt - Sol		
Balance Sheet		
January 31, 2010		
LIABILITIES AND CAPITAL		
Long-Term Liabilities		
Bonds Payable	$ 100,000.00	
Discount on Bonds Payable	(7,361.00)	
Total Long-Term Liabilities		92,639.00

Candlestick Corporation - Premium - Sol		
Balance Sheet		
January 31, 2010		
Long-Term Liabilities		
Bonds Payable	$ 100,000.00	
Premium on Bonds Payable	8,111.00	
Total Long-Term Liabilities		108,111.00

Figure 15. 15 Candlestick's presentation of bonds payable at face, at a discount at issue date, and at a premium at issue date

Using Illustration 15B-4 from the textbook, shown here as Figure 15. 16, the premium on bonds payable will be amortized utilizing the effective interest method. As such, the first interest payment will amortize $676 and the carrying value of the bond will decrease from $108,111 to ($108,111 - $676) $107,435.

B	C	D
	CANDLESTICK, INC. **Bond Premium Amortization** **Effective-Interest Method—Semiannual Interest Paym**	
(A) **Interest to Be Paid** **(5% × $100,000)**	**(B)** **Interest Expense** **to Be Recorded** **(4% × Preceding Bond** **Carrying Value)**	**(C)** **Premium** **Amortization** **(A) − (B)**
$ 5,000	$ 4,324 (4% × $108,111)	$ 676
5,000	4,297 (4% × $107,435)	703
5,000	4,269 (4% × $106,732)	731
5,000	4,240 (4% × $106,001)	760
5,000	4,210 (4% × $105,241)	790
5,000	4,178 (4% × $104,451)	822
5,000	4,145 (4% × $103,629)	855
5,000	4,111 (4% × $102,774)	889
5,000	4,075 (4% × $101,885)	925
5,000	4,040* (4% × $100,960)	960
$50,000	$41,889	$8,111

Figure 15. 16 Effective interest method table for Candlestick's discount on bonds payable

Since Candlestick pays the interest incurred from January 1 through June 30 on July 1, utilize the write checks screen to write check number 131 dated July 1, 2010, with a credit to 101 – Cash for $5,000, this is entered in the window to the right of the dollars line on the check face. The 718 – Interest Expense account is DEBITED for the sum of $5,000, the amount paid to the bond holders, less the amount amortized, $676, from the effective interest table, $4,324. Account 213 – Premium on Bonds Payable is debited for $676 in the second journal line. Since the Premium on Bonds Payable was entered as a CREDIT value offsetting the cash received, $108,111, for the obligation incurred by Bonds Payable - $100,000, this premium is amortized by DEBIT values over the term of the bond. Compare your work with Figure 15. 17 and make any necessary adjustments before saving it.

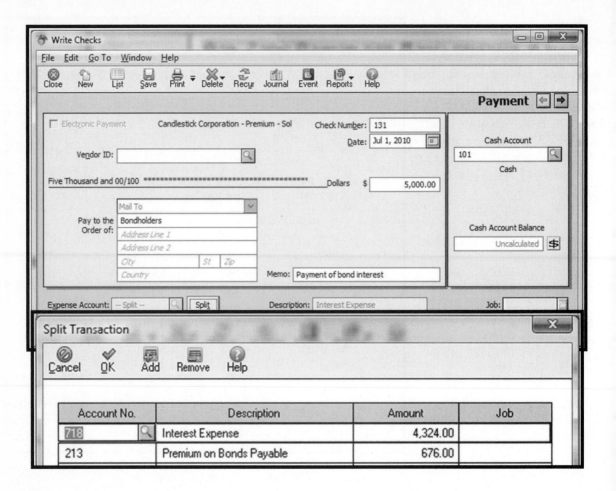

Figure 15. 17 Write checks screen for the first interest payment on bonds payable

View your balance sheet for July 31, 2010, shown in Figure 15. 18, and notice that the bonds payable value has **_NOT_** changed. But, the premium on bonds payable has **_DECREASED_** by the $676 and the carrying value has **_DECREASED_** by $6768 to $107,4357. Compare this report with Figure 15. 18.

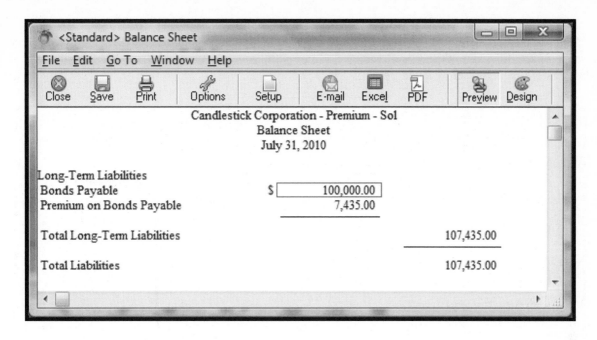

Figure 15. 18 Candlestick's balance sheet showing long-term liabilities after the interest payment of July 1, 2010

The next event associated with the bond is the interest accrued from July 1, 2010, through December 31, 2010, to correctly record and report interest expense, interest payable, and bond carrying value for the fiscal year of 2010. This is done with a general journal entry. Utilizing the general journal entry screen, set the date to December 31, 2010, use a reference of Adj Entry #1, a debit account of 718 – Interest Expense for the sum of the interest to be paid, $5,000, less the amortization of the premium on bonds payable for the SECOND period from Figure 15. 16, $703, totaling $4,297. Credit account of 205 – Interest Payable for the amount the bond holders will receive, $5,000. The descriptions can be seen in Figure 15. 19. Compare your work with Figure 15. 19 and make any necessary adjustments before saving your work.

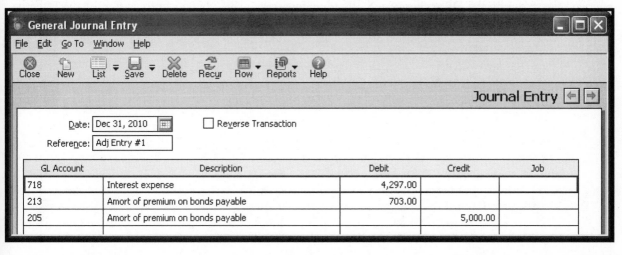

Figure 15. 19 General journal entry to record the interest expense, amortization of premium on bonds payable, and interest payable as of December 31, 2010

On January 1, 2011, the interest obligation incurred on December 31, 2010, is paid with check number 132. Utilize the write check screen and compare your work with Figure 15. 20 and make any necessary adjustments before saving your work.

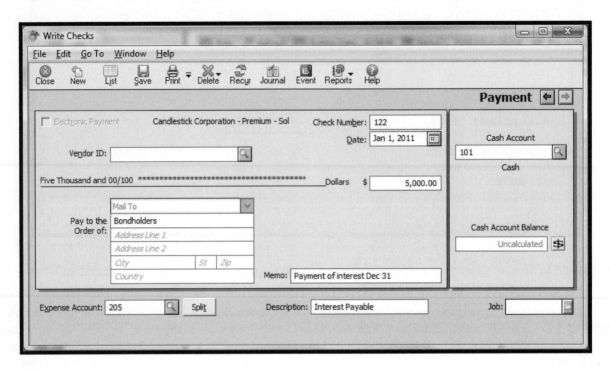

Figure 15. 20 Write checks screen to pay interest incurred on December 31, 2010 and paid on January 1, 2011

And, as shown in Figure 15. 21, the premium on bonds payable and the bond carrying value has changed again due to the December 31, 2010, adjusting entry. This change follows that of the effective interest table of Figure 15. 16.

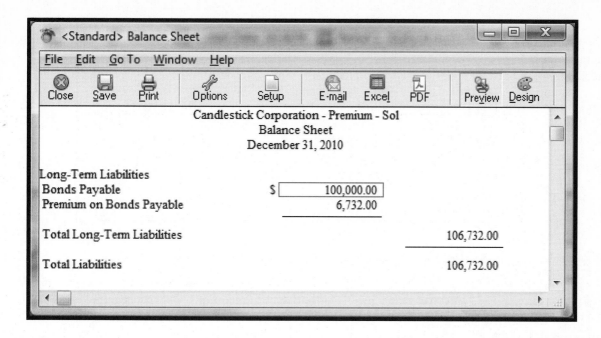

Figure 15. 21 Candlestick's balance sheet showing long-term liabilities as of December 31, 2010

When this bond matures, a check will be written for the last interest payment and another check will be written for the payment of the bond. The check for interest and the amortization of premium on bonds payable will be similar to checks 131 and 132. You would write check number 133 dated January 1, 2015, similar to Figure 15. 5 to accomplish this.

Note: This check is out of Peachtree's accessible accounting periods. Do not attempt to record or save it as it will require Peachtree to initiate the Year-End Wizard and close the preceding fiscal years.

LONG-TERM NOTES PAYABLE

The use of notes payable in long-term debt financing is also common. Long-term notes are similar to short-term interest bearing notes except that the terms will exceed a year. The accounting procedures are similar to accounting for bonds with accounts such as 200 – Note Payable-Long-term, 201 – Notes Payable-Current, 205 – Interest Payable, and 718 – Interest Expense.

The company used in the text, Porter Technology Inc., has been established within the student data set to follow this portion of the text.

Assume that Porter Technology Inc. issues a $500,000, 12%, 20-year mortgage note on January 1, 2011, (to remain within two fiscal years for Peachtree without executing the Year-End Wizard) to obtain needed financing for a new research laboratory. The terms provide for semiannual installment payments of $33,231 (not including real estate taxes and insurance). The installment payment schedule for the first two years is as shown in Figure 15. 22. *Note:* The first date is adjusted due to Peachtree's two fiscal year stipulation.

Semiannual Interest Period	(A) Cash Payment	(B) Interest Expense (D) × 6%	(C) Reduction in Principal (A) - (B)	(D) Principal Balance (D) - (C)
1/1/2011				$500,000
6/30/2011	$33,231	$30,000	$3,231	496,769
12/31/2011	33,231	29,806	3,425	493,344
6/30/2012	33,231	29,601	3,630	489,714
12/31/2012	33,231	29,383	3,848	485,866

Figure 15. 22 Porter Technology's notes payable payment details for two years

Utilize the receipts screen of Porter Technology Inc. to issue the note payable to First National Bank on January 1, 2011. The deposit ticket ID is 11-01-01 and the reference and receipt number is 2011-01-01. The 211 – Mortgage Notes Payable account has been established as a long-term liability account. Remember to use the Journal icon on the task bar to set the accounts. Compare your work with Figure 15. 23 and make any necessary corrections before saving it.

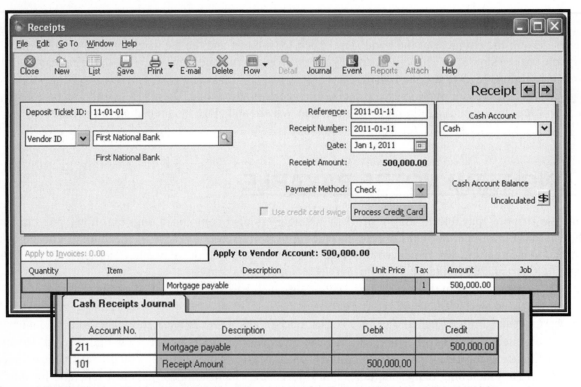

Figure 15. 23 Porter Technology's receipts screen for the mortgage note payable

Utilize the write checks screen on June 30, 2011 to record Porter making the first payment in accordance with the table of Figure 15. 22. All accounts have been set up for you. Check your work with Figure 15. 24 and make any necessary corrections before saving it.

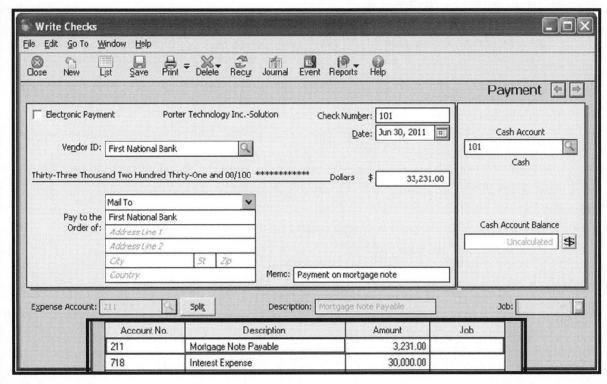

Figure 15. 24 Porter Technology's receipts screen for the mortgage note payable

And, with the recording of the note payable and the first payment due on the note, the balance sheet of Porter will show the current carrying balance of the note, shown in Figure 15. 25.

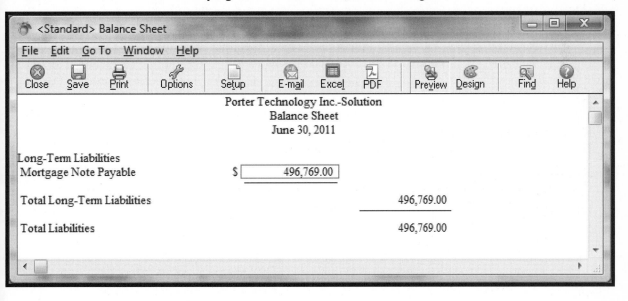

Figure 15. 25 Porter Technology's balance sheet presentation of long-term liabilities after recording the mortgage note payable and one payment

Comprehensive Do It! Problem, Snyder Software Inc., Directory Wey_AP9e_Snyder_Software_Inc

Snyder Software Inc. has successfully developed a new spreadsheet program. To produce and market the program, the company needed $2 million of additional financing. On January 1, 2011, Snyder borrowed money as follows.

1. Snyder issued $500,000, 11%, 10-year convertible bonds. The bonds sold at face value and pay semiannual interest on January 1 and July 1. Each $1,000 bond is convertible into 30 shares of Snyder's $20 par value common stock.
2. Snyder issued $1 million, 10%, 10-year bonds at face value. Interest is payable semiannually on January 1 and July 1.
3. Snyder also issued a $500,000, 12%, 15-year mortgage note payable. The terms provide for semiannual installment payments of $36,324 on June 30 and December 31.

Instructions

1. For the convertible bonds, prepare general journal entries for:
   (a) The issuance of the bonds on January 1, 2011. Use reference JE #01.
   (b) Interest expense on July 1, 2011. Use reference JE #02.
   (c) Interest expense on December 31, 2011. Use reference JE #03.
   (d) The payment of interest on January 1, 2012. Use reference JE #04.
   (d) The conversion of all bonds into common stock on January 1, 2012, when the market value of the common stock was $67 per share. Use reference JE #05.
2. For the 10-year, 10% bonds:
   (a) Use the general journal to journalize the issuance of the bonds on January 1, 2011. Use reference JE #06.
   (b) Prepare the general journal entry for interest expense as of July 1, 2011. Assume no accrual of interest on July 1. Use reference JE #07.
   (b) Prepare the general journal entry for interest expense as of December 31, 2011. Use reference JE #08.
   (c) Note: This journal entry as printed in the Weygandt Accounting Principles textbook is outside Peachtree's two year access limitation. Date this journal entry December 31, 2012, and use the reference JE #09-01/01/2014. Prepare the entry for the redemption of the bonds at 101 for January 1, 2014 using date December 31, 2012, assuming that the interest due on December 31, 2014, was paid.
3. For the mortgage note payable:
   (a) Record the general journal entry for the issuance of the note on January 1, 2011. Use reference JE #10.
   (b) Print the general journal report for the range January 1, 2011, through December 31, 2012. See the note following the general journal report screen print.
   (c) Prepare a payment schedule for the first four installment payments.
   (d) Indicate the current and noncurrent amounts for the mortgage note payable at December 31, 2011.

General journal of Snyder Software Inc.

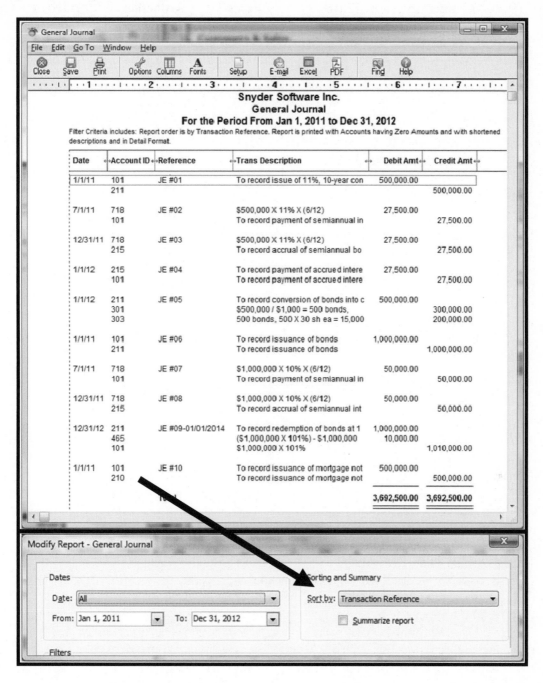

Note: This general journal has had the Sorting and Summary Sort By function set to transaction reference as shown by the arrow in the screen print. This function is located under Options.

(c)

Semiannual Interest Period	Cash Payment	Interest Expense	Reduction of Principal	Principal Balance
Issue date				$500,000
1	$36,324	$30,000	$6,324	493,676
2	36,324	29,621	6,703	486,973
3	36,324	29,218	7,106	479,867
4	36,324	28,792	7,532	472,335

(d)   Current liability $14,638 ($7,106 + $7,532)
Long-term liability $472,335

CHAPTER 16

Investments

OBJECTIVES

- Discuss why corporations invest in debt and stock securities.
- Explain the accounting for debt investments.
- Explain the accounting for stock investments.
- Describe the use of consolidated financial statements.
- Indicate how debt and stock investments are reported in the financial statements.
- Distinguish between short term and long term investments

WHY CORPORATIONS INVEST

There are three reasons why corporations purchase investments in either debt or securities:

1. A corporation may have excess cash that it does not need for the immediate purchase of operating assets or for general operations.
2. Some companies purchase investments to generate investment income. For example, although banks make most of their earnings by lending money, they also generate earnings by investing in debt and equity securities.
3. Strategic reasons are the third basis for investing. A company may purchase an interest in another business in a related industry in which it wishes to establish a presence.

ACCOUNTING FOR DEBT INVESTMENTS

Three types of entries are required for debt investing such as government or corporate bonds:

1. The acquisition
2. The interest revenue
3. The sale

At acquisition, the cost principle applies. The cost will include all expenditures necessary to acquire these investments. For example, the price paid and commissions would be included in the cost. Kuhl Corporation acquires 50 Doan, Inc. 8%, 10-year, $1,000 bonds on January 1, 2010, for $54,000, including brokerage fees of $1,000.

      Step 1:   Open the file "Kuhl Corporation" from within your student data set.

Step 2: Use the write checks screen, as shown, to record the investment in Doan bonds. Use check number 101 on January 1, 2010, and insure that account 165 – Debt Investments, is set as the Expense Account. Check your work with Figure 16. 1 and make any necessary adjustments before saving.

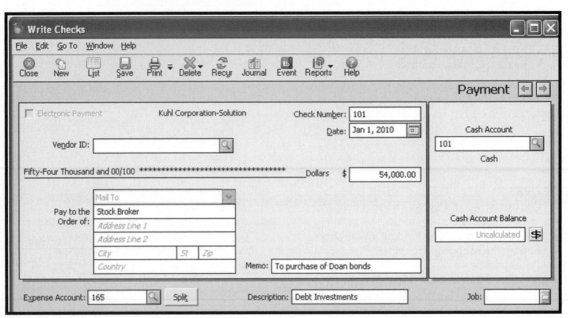

Figure 16. 1 Write checks screen for the acquisition of debt investments

The bonds pay interest of $2,000 ($50,000 × 8% × 1/2) semiannually on July 1 and January 1. Use the receipts screen to record the receipt of the interest on July 1, 2010. Set the deposit ticket ID to 10-07-01 and the reference and receipt number to 2010-07-01. Utilize the "Journal" icon on the task bar to ensure that the GL (General Ledger) account is set to 410 – Interest Revenue. Compare your work with Figure 16. 2 and make any adjustments necessary before saving your work.

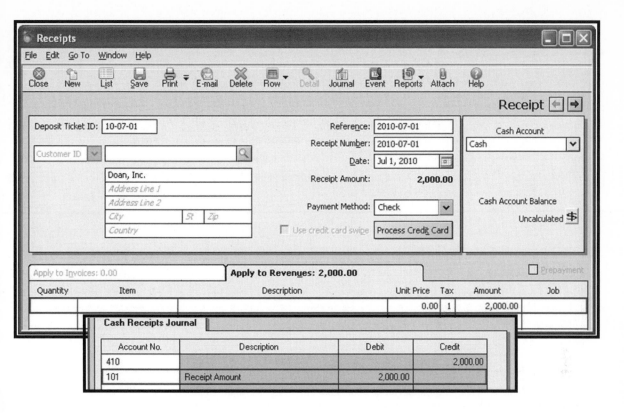

Figure 16. 2   Receipts screen for the receipt of interest on Doan's bonds

If Kuhl's fiscal year ends on December 31, an accrual of the interest of $2,000 earned since July 1 must be recorded. It is an adjusting entry as shown in Figure 16. 3. Use the general journal entry screen to make the adjusting entry as shown in Figure 16. 3.

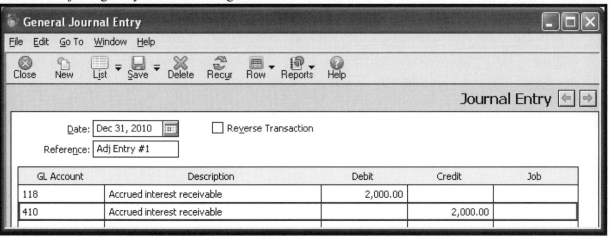

Figure 16. 3   General journal screen for the adjusting entry for accrued interest revenue on bonds

Interest revenue is reported on the income statement while interest receivable is reported on the balance sheet. When the interest is received on January 1, 2011, Figure 16. 4, the entry is:

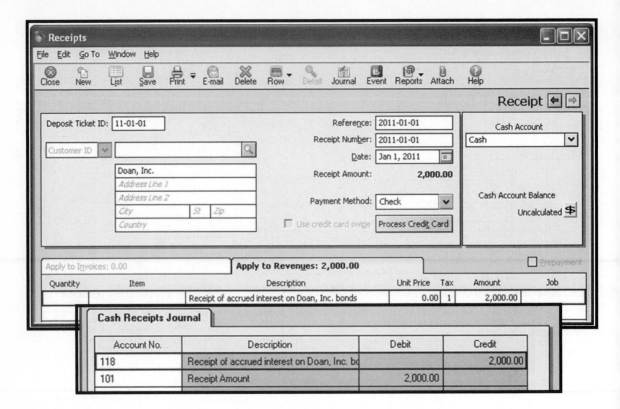

Figure 16. 4 Receipts screen of accrued interest on Doan's bonds.

When the bonds are sold, it is necessary to debit the 101 – Cash account, credit the 165 – Debt Investment account for the cost of the bonds, and recognize any gain or loss on the sale is recorded in the 444/445 – Gain or Loss on Sale of Debt Investments accounts.

For example, Kuhl Corporation receives net proceeds of $58,000 on the sale of the Doan bonds, which they sell on January 1, 2011. Since the securities cost $54,000, a gain of $4,000 will be realized. The interest earned does not come into play here; it has already been received and recorded.

Use the receipts screen and the "Journal" function to receive the $58,000, remove the cost value of the Doan, Inc bonds and realize the gain. This screen is shown in Figure 16. 5.

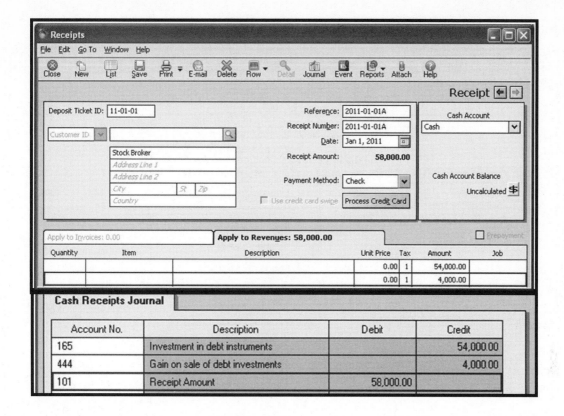

Figure 16. 5   Receipts screen for the sale of Doan's bonds with a gain

View the income statements and the balance sheets for the ranges January 1, 2010 through December 31, 2010, and January 1, 2011 through December 31, 2011, to see the effects on income and the change in assets caused by these recordings.

Appreciate the presentation of Peachtree's general ledger. Looking at the 410 – Interest Revenue account, shown in Figure 16. 6, the balance on January 1, 2010 was zero. Interest revenue was received on July 1, 2010, shown as a credit/negative value while Cash, not shown, was debited, a positive number for presentation. There are no values in the debit or credit columns for the months of August through November 2010, and the account balance is carried through to December 1, 2010, the account's beginning balance for December. On December 31, 2010, the adjusting entry for accrued interest revenue was recorded. This increased the account balance to a credit value of $4,000. Since 410 – Interest Revenue is defined as an income account and the fiscal year is defined within Peachtree as January 1 through December 31, Peachtree does not carry the $4,000 credit balance as of December 31, 2010, to the January 1, 2011, beginning balance as nominal or temporary account values are not carried from fiscal year to fiscal year in their nominal or temporary accounts. These values are carried forward as net income or retained earnings, depending on whether the Year-End Wizard has been utilized or not. And Peachtree does not show zeros to provide a neater presentation.

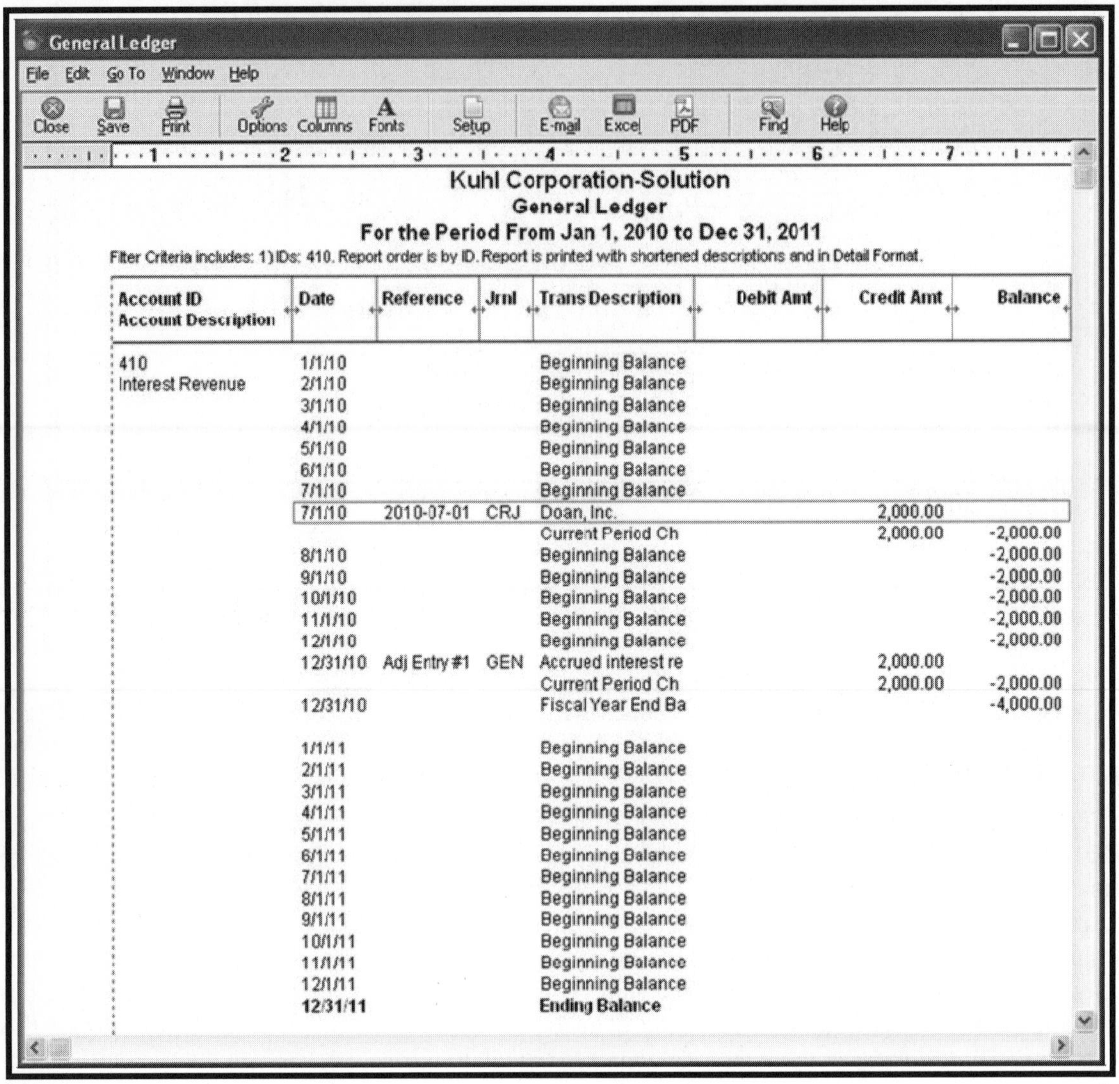

Kuhl Corporation-Solution
General Ledger
For the Period From Jan 1, 2010 to Dec 31, 2011
Filter Criteria includes: 1) IDs: 410. Report order is by ID. Report is printed with shortened descriptions and in Detail Format.

Account ID Account Description	Date	Reference	Jrnl	Trans Description	Debit Amt	Credit Amt	Balance
410	1/1/10			Beginning Balance			
Interest Revenue	2/1/10			Beginning Balance			
	3/1/10			Beginning Balance			
	4/1/10			Beginning Balance			
	5/1/10			Beginning Balance			
	6/1/10			Beginning Balance			
	7/1/10			Beginning Balance			
	7/1/10	2010-07-01	CRJ	Doan, Inc.		2,000.00	
				Current Period Ch		2,000.00	-2,000.00
	8/1/10			Beginning Balance			-2,000.00
	9/1/10			Beginning Balance			-2,000.00
	10/1/10			Beginning Balance			-2,000.00
	11/1/10			Beginning Balance			-2,000.00
	12/1/10			Beginning Balance			-2,000.00
	12/31/10	Adj Entry #1	GEN	Accrued interest re		2,000.00	
				Current Period Ch		2,000.00	-2,000.00
	12/31/10			Fiscal Year End Ba			-4,000.00
	1/1/11			Beginning Balance			
	2/1/11			Beginning Balance			
	3/1/11			Beginning Balance			
	4/1/11			Beginning Balance			
	5/1/11			Beginning Balance			
	6/1/11			Beginning Balance			
	7/1/11			Beginning Balance			
	8/1/11			Beginning Balance			
	9/1/11			Beginning Balance			
	10/1/11			Beginning Balance			
	11/1/11			Beginning Balance			
	12/1/11			Beginning Balance			
	12/31/11			**Ending Balance**			

Figure 16. 6 General ledger interest receivable account for Kuhl Corporation

P16-2A, Noble Company, Directory Wey_AP9e_P16_2A_Noble_Co

In January 2010, the management of Noble Company concludes that it has sufficient cash to permit some short-term investments in debt and stock securities. During the year, the following transactions occurred:

Feb	1	Purchased 600 shares of Hiens common stock for $31,800, plus brokerage fees of $600.
Mar	1	Purchased 800 shares Pryce common stock for $20,000, plus brokerage fees of $400.
Apr	1	Purchased 50 $1,000, 7% Roy bonds for $50,000, plus $1,000 brokerage fees. Interest is payable semiannually on April 1 and October 1.
Jul	1	Received a cash dividend of $0.60 per share on the Hiens common stock.
Aug	1	Sold 200 shares of Hiens common stock at $58 per share less brokerage fees of $200.
Sept	1	Received a $1 per share cash dividend on the Pryce common stock.
Oct	1	Received the semiannual interest on the Roy bonds.
Oct	1	Sold the Roy bonds for $50,000 less $1,000 brokerage fees.

At December 31, the fair value of the Hiens common stock was $55 per share. The fair value of the Pryce common stock was $24 per share.

Instructions:
(a) Open the Noble Company from within your student data set and familiarize yourself with the chart of accounts.

(b) Using the general journal entry screen, journalize the provided transactions.

(c) Using the general journal entry screen, journalize the adjusting entry for the fair value at the end of the year.

(d) Print the general journal report, general ledger, and the income statement for the year ended December 31, 2010.

(e) Print the balance sheet as of December 31, 2010.

(f) Identity the income statement accounts and statement classification of each account.

CHAPTER 17

The Statement of Cash Flow

OBJECTIVES

- Indicate the usefulness of the statement of cash flows.
- Distinguish among operating, investing, and financing activities.

- Prepare a statement of cash flows using Peachtree Complete Accounting.
- Analyze the statement of cash flows.

THE PURPOSE OF A STATEMENT OF CASH FLOWS

The three basic financial statements presented thus far provide very little information concerning a company's cash flow. An analyst would like to know more about the cash receipts and cash payments of the business. For example, balance sheets generated by Peachtree show the increases (or decreases) in property, plant, and equipment during the year, but they do not show how the additions were paid for or financed.

The income statement shows revenues and expenses under the accrual accounting concepts but the statement does not show the amount of cash that was generated by operating activities. The statement of retained earnings shows net income added to beginning balance of retained earnings and dividends declared deducted from that amount but not the statement does not show the cash dividends that were paid during the year. The balance sheet shows the values of many accounts such as cash, accounts receivable, accounts payable and inventory but only the cash accounts usually directly relate to actual cash dollars.

The primary purpose of the statement of cash flow is to provide information about cash receipts and cash payments during a fiscal period. A secondary objective is to provide information about operating, investing, and financing activities. Reporting the causes of changes in cash helps managers, investors, creditors, and other interested parties understand what is happening to a company's most liquid resource – cash.

Open the Peachtree Complete Accounting sample company for Bellwether Garden Supply. Under reports, select financial reports and then <Standard> Cash Flows. The period the report opens to should be for the first three months ending March 31, 2007. If this is not the case, reset the date range through the "Options" icon on the report. A segment of this report is provided as Figure 17. 1. This statement of cash flows is an indirect statement since it starts with net income. Familiarize yourself with the report. It contains the three critical areas – operations, investments, and finance. To ensure that information is conveyed or presented, the default is to show accounts or processes that would influence the report even if their current value is zero. Options has been used to not show zero balance accounts to minimize display size.

Bellwether Garden Supply
Statement of Cash Flow
For the three Months Ended March 31, 2007

	Current Month	Year to Date
Cash Flows from operating activities		
Net Income	$ 3,824.75	$ 31,927.18
Adjustments to reconcile net income to net cash provided by operating activities		
Accum. Depreciation-Furniture	420.80	1,262.40
Accum. Depreciation-Equipment	385.05	1,265.25
Accum. Depreciation-Vehicles	1,437.89	4,313.67
Accum. Depreciation-Other	64.57	193.71
Accum. Depreciation-Buildings	396.37	1,189.11
Accum. Depreciation-Bldg Imp	56.63	169.87
Accounts Receivable	(9,748.64)	(171,590.87)
Other Receivables	0.00	(3,672.24)
Inventory	13,695.07	6,256.43
Accounts Payable	9,516.43	75,968.31
Sales Tax Payable	4,281.25	15,518.07
401 K Deductions Payable	654.95	1,964.85
Health Insurance Payable	(530.64)	(530.64)
Federal Payroll Taxes Payable	13,088.92	39,266.76
State Payroll Taxes Payable	1,911.17	5,733.51
Other Taxes Payable	50.00	50.00
Other Current Liabilities	150.00	150.00
Total Adjustments	35,829.82	(22,491.81)
Net Cash provided by Operations	39,654.57	9,435.37
Cash Flows from investing activities Used For		
Net cash used in investing	0.00	0.00
Cash Flows from financing activities Proceeds From Used For		
Net cash used in financing	0.00	0.00
Net increase <decrease> in cash	$ 39,654.57	$ 9,435.37
Summary		
Cash Balance at End of Period	$ 36,778.92	$ 36,778.92
Cash Balance at Beg of Period	2,875.54	(27,343.66)
Net Increase <Decrease> in Cash	$ 39,654.46	$ 9,435.26

Figure 17. 1 The statement of cash flows for Bellwether Garden Supply for the three months ending March 31, 2007

The period of the statement of cash flows can be changed through the "Options" icon on the report screen. The report details the cash flows of operations in the first section, the details of Investing in the second section, and the details of finance in the third section. In the final and fourth section the tie to cash is accomplished. This details the cash generated or consumed for the period, the beginning balance of cash and the ending balance of cash. This complies with the GAAP and SEC presentation requirements.

As a general statement, the printing and presentation of financials is normally the income statement then the retained earnings statement. This is because net income, the final line of the income statement, is an element of the retained earnings statement. The retained earnings statement is followed by the balance sheet since the ending capital values generated by the retained earnings statement are elements of the balance sheet. Lastly the statement of cash flows is generated. This is because of the "string" of the first three reports and the requirement for net income as a starting point of the (indirect) statement of cash flows as presented by Peachtree Complete Accounting.

Chapters 18 ~ 26

There are no other academic challenges within the textbook for Peachtree Complete Accounting. There are no additional issues that need to be addressed to continue your use of Peachtree Complete Accounting as a tool in both the academic and professional environment.

APPENDIX A

Using the General Journal

OBJECTIVES

- Be able to understand how to generate and read the basic financial statements in Peachtree Accounting
- Be able to enter transactions into Peachtree's general journal system

- Be able to check for errors in entries made into the general journal

- Be able to edit a general journal entry

PEACHTREE VS. THE GENERAL LEDGER PACKAGE

Entering data into Peachtree's general journal entry screen is comparable to the General Ledger Software provided by John Wiley and Sons as a supplement to accounting textbooks. Peachtree Complete Accounting however, is a total accounting software package that is much more robust than the General Ledger Software. Peachtree Complete Accounting is a commercial software application used by many businesses as their sole accounting software package.

In this workbook, many of the sections or modules of the Peachtree software correlates with the Weygandt text. The subject matter is explained in the workbook and demonstration problems and "translated problems" from the text, ones that are marked with the Peachtree logo are introduced. When we discuss "translated problems", remember that the problems appearing in the textbook were created and written for a manual entry accounting system and *not* for an automated or integrated system. Each problem in the workbook has been edited somewhat from the Weygandt text for ease in making entries in an automated system. That is why the wording and the deliverables are different.

In any case, the various Peachtree modules *do not* have to be used along with the text in the classroom. The instructor may elect to use only the general journal entry system (without special ledgers and journals) and arrive at the basic financial statements.

This appendix walks you through the use of the general journal entry system employed by Peachtree Complete Accounting using the ten provided examples.

This section uses "*App A - Softbyte Computer*" from within your student data set.

GENERAL JOURNAL TRANSACTIONS

Transaction (1) Investment by Owner. Ray Neal decides to open a computer programming service. On January 1, 2010, he invests $15,000 cash in the business, which he names Softbyte Computer. This transaction results in an equal increase in assets and owner's equity. The asset cash increases by $15,000 and the owner's equity, R. Neal, Capital increases by the same amount. Using Peachtree Complete Accounting, step through this initial entry.

Step 1:   Using the menu bar from the main Peachtree window, click on "Tasks."

Step 2:   On the pull down menu, as shown in Figure A. 1, click on "General Journal Entry."

Figure A. 1   Pull down menu from Tasks on menu bar

Step 3:   Make sure that your window looks like that shown in Figure A. 2.

Figure A. 2   Blank screen for general journal entry

Step 4:   Set the date to January 1, 2010. This can be entered a number of ways but 01/01/10 is probably the quickest and easiest.

Step 5:   As a reference, type in "Trans #1" in the blank reference Box, just under the date of January 1, 2010.

Step 6:   Click on the magnifying glass that appears next to the account number column to get a pull down menu that lists the available accounts for Softbyte, the chart of accounts, as shown in Figure A. 3.

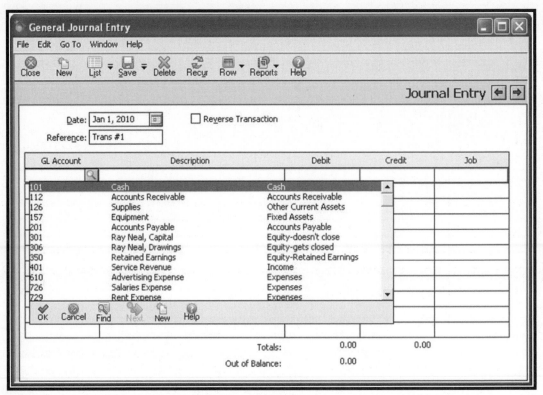

Figure A. 3   Chart of accounts within a journal entry

Step 7:   Double-click on GL (General Ledger) account number 101 – Cash. In the description column type in "Ray Neal, Initial investment." And, in the debit column, type in "1-5-0-0-0-decimal point-0-0" (Do not type in the dash – they represent the separation between the numerals.)

Be careful in Peachtree Accounting how you enter numbers requiring decimal points. The "system" may *automatically* insert a decimal point two places to the left of the last numeral entered number. For example, if you entered "1-5-0-0", Peachtree may recognize it as $15.00 not $1,500.00, a capital mistake. Make sure your screen looks like Figure A. 4.

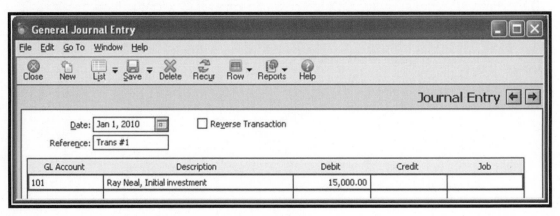

Figure A. 4   First entry line for the first transaction

Step 8: Press the enter key (or tab key) three times to get your insertion point to the next line, as shown in Figure A. 5.

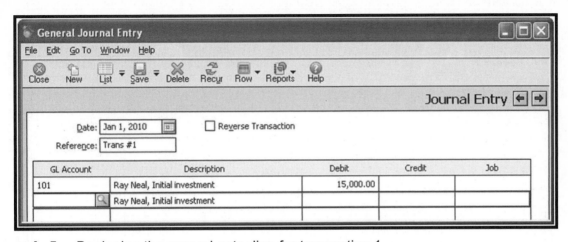

Figure A. 5   Beginning the second entry line for transaction 1

Using the illustrated examples above, enter the amount for owner's equity by:

Step 9: Clicking on the magnifying glass in the Account No. column.

Step 10: Double-clicking the GL (General Ledger) account number 301 – Ray Neal, Capital.

Step 11: In the credit column, entering the amount, $15,000.00 – the dollar sign is not necessary, but the decimal point should be entered manually. Your entry should look like Figure A. 6.

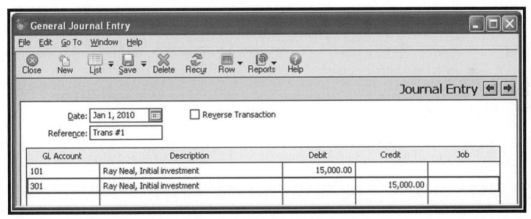

Figure A. 6   Entry for owner's investment of cash in the business.

Look at the window in Figure A. 7. Notice the amounts at the bottom of the window, in the gray area outside the entry area. They indicate whether or not your entry is in balance. In Figure A. 7, $15,000 appears under the debit column <u>and</u> under the credit column. The figure next to "Out of Balance" is zero. Therefore, your entry is in balance.

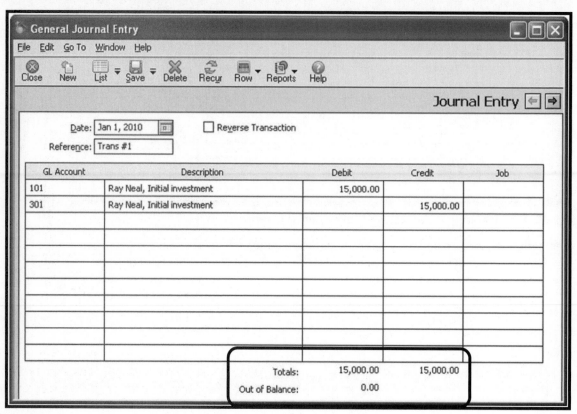

Figure A. 7 In balance journal entries

If we had mistakenly entered both amounts in the debit column, as shown in Figure A. 8, or both amounts in the credit column, we would be "Out of Balance."

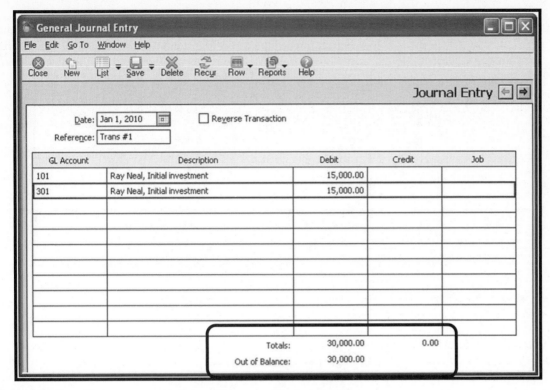

Figure A. 8   Entry error as shown by out of balance tally

Always double-check your entries before continuing. Just because the system indicates you are "in balance" does not necessarily mean your transaction is correct. It just means what you have entered is "in balance." However, as shown in Figure A. 9, the system will not let you continue if you are "Out of Balance" and will return an error message.

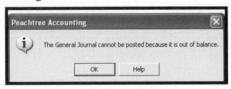

Figure A. 9   The system will not let you continue if you are "out of balance" on your entry

Step 12: To post the transaction (enter it into the system) click on the "Save" icon (see Figure A. 10) in the tool bar section toward the top of the window.

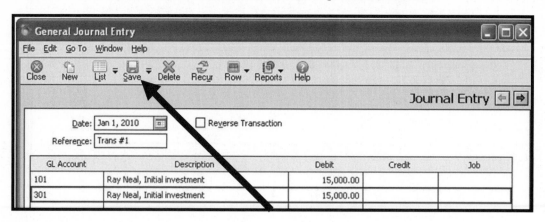

Figure A. 10 Click on the "Save" icon to post or enter your transaction

Step 13: The general journal entry screen clears all that has been previously entered and is now ready for the second transaction. Notice that the reference window now reads Trans #2" as it automatically advances.

You are now ready for the next transaction.

Transaction (2). Purchase of Equipment for Cash. Softbyte purchases computer equipment for $7,000 cash on January 1, 2010.
Using the process you learned in Transaction 1 make this general journal entry.

Step 1: The date should have remained January 1, 2010. You can change the date by clicking into the date window and using the Plus/+ and Minus/- keys to make small changes if needed. Tabbing out of or clicking into another window on the screen sets the date.

Step 2: Type in "Trans #2" in the reference box, if it is different.

Step 3: Click on the magnifying glass to get the pull down menu of the chart of accounts. Highlight 157 – Equipment" and double-click (you may also press the <ENTER> key).

Step 4: Press the <TAB> key to move your insertion point over to the description column and type in "Paid cash for equipment."

Step 5: Press the <TAB> key to move your insertion point to the next column, the debit column and enter, in error the amount $8,000.00. This amount is in error because in the second part of this exercise you will learn how to edit a general journal entry, after it has been posted. Remember you do not enter the "$," but you should enter the decimal point.

Step 6: Press the <ENTER> key three times so that your insertion point is in the Account No. column of the next line. Click on the magnifying glass to get the pull down menu of the chart of accounts. Highlight "101 – Cash" and double-click (you may also press the <ENTER> key).

Step 7: Press the <TAB> key to move your insertion point over to the description column and type in "Paid cash for equipment." (The system may have already generated this for you.)

Step 8: Press the <TAB> key twice to move your insertion point to the credit column and enter the amount, purposely in error $8,000.00. We enter this amount in error for our books to balance. This will be edited in the next part of this exercise. Again, remember you do not enter the "$," but you should enter the decimal point.

Step 9: Make sure your screen looks like Figure A. 11 before continuing. If there are no errors (besides the intentional ones you typed in) go ahead and post your transaction. Notice that even though we know there is an error, the system will let you post because technically your books are in balance.

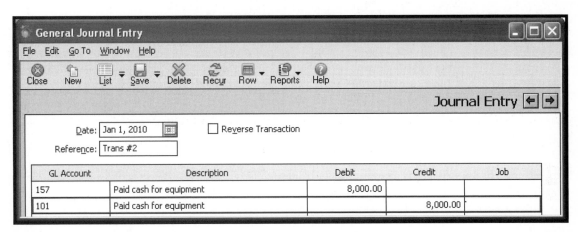

Figure A. 11 General journal entry shown in error

EDITING A GENERAL JOURNAL ENTRY

Editing a general journal entry is just as simple as making the original entry.

Step 1: Make sure you have a blank general journal entry screen. If not, create one by clicking on "Tasks," then "General Journal Entry."

Step 2: On the task bar menu, illustrated in Figure A. 12, click on the "List" icon.

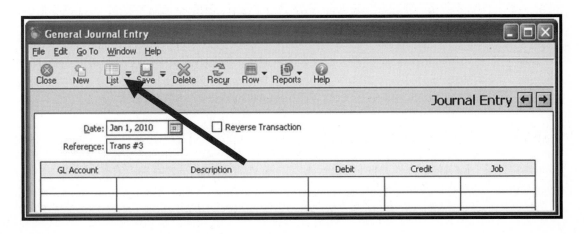

Figure A. 12 Open on the general journal entry tool bar

Step 3:   You will be presented with a general journal list menu listing all of the general journal entries you have entered in this accounting period. Do not worry about accounting periods at this time. Figure A. 13 below shows only two entries for demonstration purposes. The first transaction, for $15,000 is the first entry you made and the second one, for $8,000 is the one with the error, which you are going to correct. Double-click on the second entry.

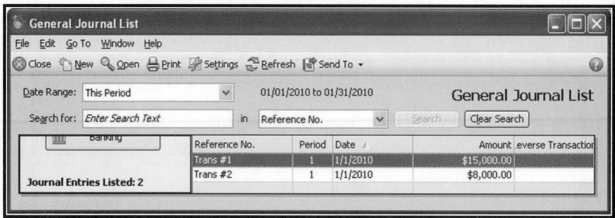

Figure A. 13   Select general list menu

Step 4:   You will be returned to the general journal entry screen like the one you had when you made the earlier entry. Your screen should look like Figure A. 14.

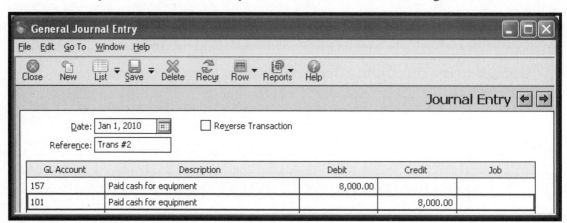

Figure A. 14   General journal entry screen showing second transaction in error

Step 5:   Any field on the screen can be changed and saved. However, we are only interested in changing the amounts, $8,000 to $7,000. Place the insertion point in the first amount field, the debit value, highlight the $8,000, and change it to $7,000.

Step 6:   Do the same with the second amount, the credit value. Your screen should match the one shown in Figure A. 15.

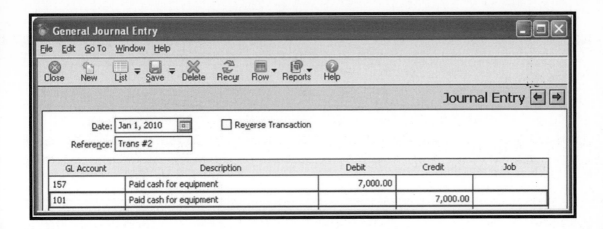

Figure A. 15 Corrected general journal entry for Transaction 2

Step 7: Click on "Save" on the general journal entry task bar. Peachtree will ensure that you want to record the changes before it saves or records the journal entry.

Transaction (3). Purchase of Supplies on Credit. On January 1, 2010, Softbyte purchases computer paper and other supplies expected to last several months for $1,600.00 from Acme Supply Company. Using the process you learned in Transaction 1 make this general journal entry on your own.

Step 1: Ensure the Date window is set to January 1, 2010. If not correct it.

Step 2: Type in "Trans #3" in the reference box, if it is different. Leave the date as it is, January 1, 2010.

Step 3: Click on the magnifying glass to get the pull down menu of the chart of accounts. Highlight "126 - Supplies" and double-click (you may also press the <ENTER> key).

Step 4: Press the <TAB> key to move your insertion point over to the description column and type in "Purchased supplies on account."

Step 5: Press the <TAB> key to move your insertion point to the next column, the debit column and enter $1,600.

Step 6: Press the <ENTER> key three times so that your insertion point is in the account number column of the next line. Click on the magnifying glass to get the pull-down menu of the chart of accounts. Highlight "201 - Accounts Payable" and double-click (you may also press the <ENTER> key).

Step 7: Press the <TAB> key to move your insertion point over to the description column "Purchased supplies on account" should have automatically been generated for you; if not go ahead and enter it.

Step 8: Press the <TAB> key twice to move your insertion point to the credit column and enter the amount $1,600.

Step 9: Make sure your screen looks like Figure A. 16 and correct any errors before continuing.

Before you save your entry, again double-check what you have entered.

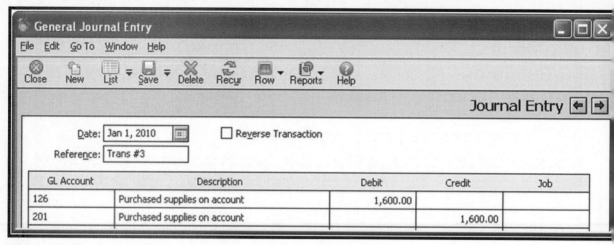

Figure A. 16 Journal entry for a credit (on account) purchase

Step 9: Click on the "Save" icon on the task bar to post your transaction into the general journal.

Transaction (4). Services Rendered for Cash. Softbyte receives $1,200 cash from customers for programming services it has provided on January 1, 2010. This transaction represents the company's principal revenue producing activity. Remember that revenue will increase owner's equity. However, revenue does have its own separate account under "Equity."

Make the general journal entry:

Step 1: The account 101 – Cash should be increased by $1,200 (a debit entry).

Step 2: The account 401 – Service Revenue should be increased by $1,200 (a credit entry).

Step 3: Before posting, make sure your entry matches the one below in Figure A. 17.

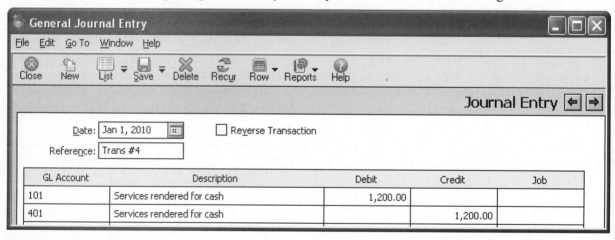

Figure A. 17 General journal entry for service revenue

Step 4: If there are no errors, "Save" the entry.

Transaction (5). Purchase of Advertising on Credit. Transaction #5, on January 2, 2010, Softbyte receives a bill for $250 from the *Daily News* for advertising. Softbyte decides to postpone payment of the bill until a later date. This transaction results in an increase in liabilities and an increase in expenses which is a decrease in equity.

Step 1: The account 610 – Advertising Expense, is increased (debited) by $250.

Step 2: The account 201 – Accounts Payable is also increased (credited) by $250.

The entry is shown in Figure A. 18.

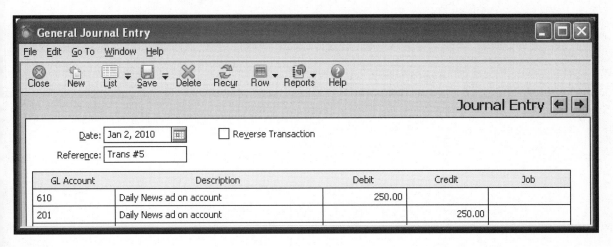

Figure A. 18 Advertising expense to be paid later

Step 3: If your entries are correct, save the general journal entry.

Transaction (6). Services Rendered for Cash and Credit. Softbyte provides $3,500 of programming services for customers. On January 7, 2010, Cash, $1,500 is received from customers and the balance of $2,000 is billed on account. This transaction results in an equal increase in assets and owner's equity.

Three specific accounts are affected:

- 101 – Cash is increased by $1,500
- 112 – Accounts Receivable is increased by $2,000
- 401 – Service Revenues is increased by $3,500.

Cash and Accounts Receivable, both assets, will be increased (debited). Cash increases by $1,500 whereas Accounts Receivable increases by $2,000. The third entry will increase the revenue account by $3,500.

Step 1: Change the date from January 1 to January 7. You may enter the date directly in the date box or by clicking on the calendar icon; you will be able to click the appropriate date for entry directly from a pull-down calendar.

Step 2: Change the transaction number under the date to "Trans #6".

Step 3: Using the magnifying glass, find account 101 – Cash and press <ENTER>. In the description column type in "Received cash from customers for services rendered" and enter the amount, $1,500 in the debit column.

Step 4: Using the magnifying glass, find account 112 – Accounts Receivable and press <ENTER>. In the description column type in "Rendered services on account" and enter the amount, $2,000, in the debit column.

Step 5: And again, using the magnifying glass, find account 401 – Service Revenues and press <ENTER>. In the description column type in "Rendered services for cash and on account." Tab over to the credit column and enter the amount, $3,500.

Step 6: Notice that all three entries will increase the appropriate accounts and that glancing at the bottom of the window, you should be in balance at $3,500.

Step 7: Your entry should match Figure A. 19. Make any necessary changes before posting your entry.

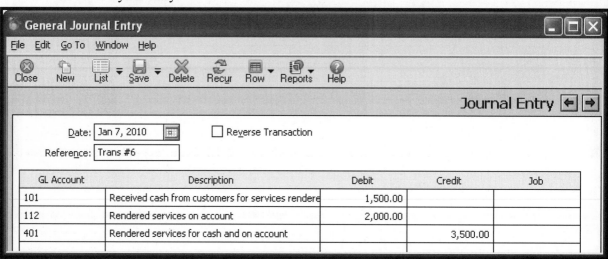

Figure A. 19 General journal entry showing date change and account entries

Transaction (7) Payment of Expenses. Expenses paid in cash on January 15 include the store rent of $600; salaries of employees of $900; and utilities of $200. These payments will result in an equal decrease in assets (cash) and owner's equity (the individual expense items).

Step 1: Change the date to January 15, 2010.

Step 2: Change the transaction number to "Trans #7".

Step 3: Identify the 729 – Rent Expense, highlight it and press <ENTER> (or click) to place it the GL (General Ledger) account window. Type in "Paid store rent" in the description window and enter $600 in the debit window.

Step 4: On the next line identify 726 – Salaries Expense, making sure it appears in the GL (General Ledger) account window on the second line. Type in "Paid salaries of employees" on the description window and enter in $900 in the debit window.

Step 5: On the third line, identify 732 – Utilities Expense make sure it appears in the GL (General Ledger) account window on the third line. In the description window enter "Paid utilities expense." In the debit window enter $200.

Step 6: Cash will be decreased by the total amount of the above expenses, $1,700. The cash account is 101. You may type that in directly or search for it using the magnifying glass. Type in a description of each of the expenses paid in the description column along with the corresponding debit amount – the amount paid on the expense. The total credit amount (we are decreasing an asset) is $1,700 that is credited to cash.

Step 7: Check to see that your entries are in balance before posting. Your entry should match the one in Figure A. 20.

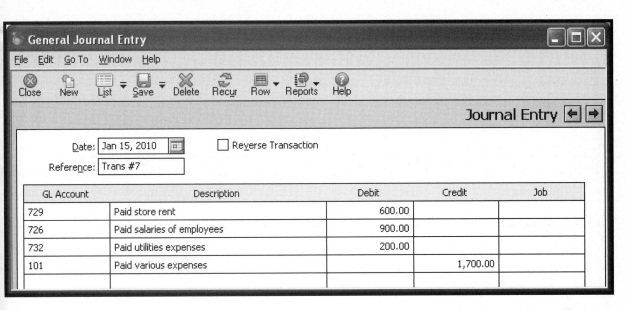

Figure A. 20 Paid cash for monthly expenses

Transaction (8). Payment of Accounts Payable. Softbyte pays its *Daily News* advertising bill of $250 in cash. The bill had been previously recorded in Transaction 5 as an increase in Accounts Payable and an increase in expenses (a decrease in owner's equity). This payment "on account" will decrease the asset cash (a credit) and will also decrease the liability accounts payable (a debit) – both by $250.

Step 1: Keep the date, January 15, 2010 as is, but change the transaction number to "Trans #8".

Step 1: Entering the debit amount first, 201 – Accounts Payable.

Step 3: Type in "Paid Daily News for ads on account" in the description window. And enter $250 in the debit window to complete the first line.

Step 4: 101 is the account number for the Cash account which goes in the first window of the second line.

Step 5: "Paid Daily News for ads on account" should have been automatically generated by the system in the description window of the second row. If so, press the <TAB> key twice to move to the credit window and enter $250.

Step 6: Check to make sure your entry is in balance and matches Figure A. 21.

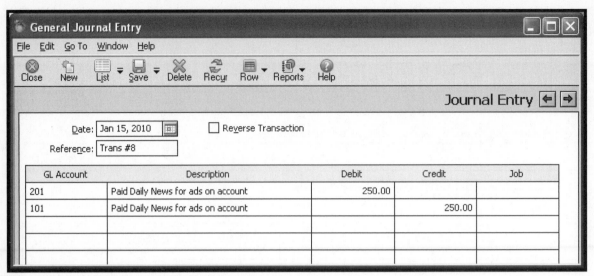

Figure A. 21 Paid Daily News account due

Transaction (9). Receipt of Cash on Account. The sum of $600 in cash is received from those customers who have previously been billed for services in Transaction 6. This transaction does not change any of the totals in assets, but it will change the composition of those accounts. Cash is increased by $600 and accounts receivable is decreased by $600.

Step 1: If you went directly to Transaction 9 from Transaction 8, you will notice that the reference has automatically changed to "Trans #9". If that change did not occur, enter "Trans #9" in the reference box. Leave the date at January 15.

Step 2: Enter 101 – Cash in the first line's GL (General Ledger) account window. Enter "Received cash from customers on account" in the description window. In the debit column enter $600.

Step 3: On the second line, enter 112 – Accounts Receivable as the account. "Received cash from customers on account" should have been automatically entered by the system. Enter $600 in the Credit window of line two so that your entry will balance.

Step 4: Check your entry with the one in Figure A. 22 before posting. Make any necessary changes.

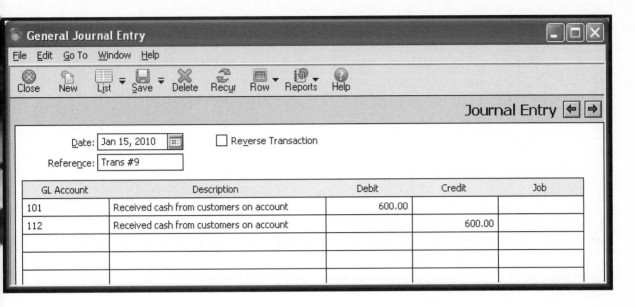

Figure A. 22 Received cash from customers on account

> *Transaction (10). Withdrawal of Cash By Owner.* On January 31, Ray Neal withdraws $1,300 in cash from the business for his personal use. This transaction results in an equal decrease in assets (cash) and owner's equity (drawing).

Step 1: Change the date to January 31. Also, make sure that Transaction 10 is in the reference window.

Step 2: Account number 306 is the Ray Neal, Drawings account that will be debited. Enter "306" as the account number. In the description window type in "Ray Neal, drawing" and in the Debit window (a decrease to capital) enter $1,300.

Step 3: Because Ray wants cash for his withdrawal, the asset Cash must be decreased (a credit). Enter 101 for the Cash account in the GL (General Ledger) account window. "Ray Neal, drawing" will most likely have been defaulted in the description window; if not, make the appropriate entry. And, in the Credit window, enter $1,300.

Step 4: Check your entry with Figure A. 23 and make any corrections before posting your entry.

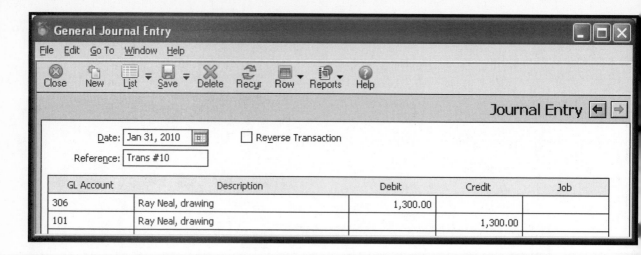

Figure A. 23 Owner drawings cash from the business for personal use

FINANCIAL STATEMENTS

After all of the transactions have been identified, analyzed, and entered into Peachtree, the, four financial statements can be prepared from your data. In reality, when you made your first entry each of the appropriate statements were automatically updated, and kept up to date as you went along.

Those statements are:

- An income statement presents the revenues and expenses and resulting net income or net loss for a specific period of time.
- An owner's equity statement (also known as the change in capital or equity) summarizes the changes in owner's equity for a specific period of time.
- A balance sheet reports the assets, liabilities, and owner's equity at a specific date.
- A statement of cash flow is a summary of information about the cash inflows (receipts) and outflows (payments) for a specific period of time.

Each Peachtree financial statement provides owners, management, and other interested parties with relevant financial data. The statements are interrelated. For example, Net income of $2,750 shown on the income statement is added to the beginning balance of retained earnings (equity) in the retained earnings statement. Retained earnings of $2,750 through net income is reduced by the $1,300 in owner's drawings resulting in an ending balance to retained earnings of $1,450. Until the Year-End Wizard is run the Capital section of the balance sheet will show net income for the period, $2,750, and drawings, $1,300, as separate values. The balance sheet will also show detailed asset and liability values.

The reports used throughout this workbook are provided already preset for each of your assignments. The Peachtree assignments in the textbook have a "Peach" icon in the margin. Other than adding your name, as shown in the appendices, the customizing of the appearance and information appearing on the reports is outside the scope of this text.

In addition to the four statements mentioned previously, several other reports also deserve attention. They are included, under the general ledger heading:

- The chart of accounts which is a listing of all of the accounts for the company. This will change as controlled by the company which is open.
- The general journal is a chronological listing of the journal entries.
- The general ledger which is a listing of the accounts and is a grouping of all of the influences on each specific account.

GENERATING THE INCOME STATEMENT

Step 1: On the main menu bar, Figure A. 24, click on "Reports & Forms" to get the drop-down menu shown here:

Figure A. 24 Main menu bar and reports drop-down menu

Step 2: Click on "Financial Statements" to get the financial statements menu of shown in Figure A. 25.

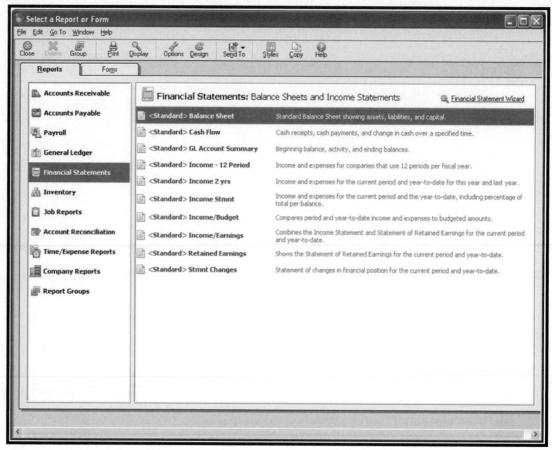

Figure A. 25   Select a financial report menu

Double-click on <Standard> Income Stmnt (Statement).

Step 3:   The dialog box, shown in Figure A. 26, gives several option choices including the choice of financial periods, the margins for the printer, whether or not we want to show accounts that have a zero balance, whether or not we want page numbers, and so on.

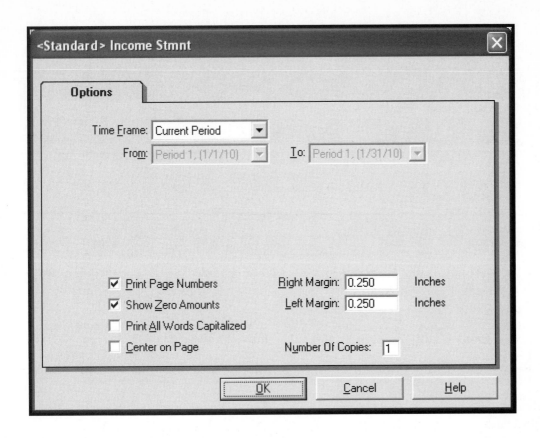

Figure A. 26   Dialog box to prepare the income statement for display

Step 4:   Click "OK" to show the income statement, Figure A. 27, on your computer screen.

The <Standard> Income Statement is a complete income statement already set up by the Peachtree system during the original company set up.

Figure A. 27 Full screen display of the income statement for Softbyte

The revenues and expenses are reported for a specific period of time, the month ending on January 31, 2010. The statement was generated from all of the data you entered since the beginning of the chapter. Make sure your data matches what is shown in Figure A. 27. Go back and correct any errors if your figures do not match.

On the income statement the revenues are listed first, followed by expenses. Finally, net income (or net loss) is determined. Although practice sometimes varies in the "real world", the expenses in our example have been generated based on account number. In some cases, expenses appear in order of financial magnitude.

Investment and withdrawal transactions between the owner and the business are not included in the measurement of net income. Remember, Ray Neal's withdrawal of cash from Softbyte was not regarded as an expense of the business.

To print the report you click on the "Print" icon once the report is open and viewed.

GENERATING THE STATEMENT OF OWNER'S EQUITY/RETAINED EARNINGS

In Peachtree Accounting, changes in owner's equity due to revenues, expenses, and withdrawals or dividends are presented in the retained earnings report and statement of changes in financial position. This data, again, was obtained from the entries you made in the earlier transactions.

When learning accounting principles, retained earnings, is usually covered as a part of corporate accounting and not while learning about sole proprietorships. We will look at retained earnings more in depth in our section on corporate accounting. However, the Peachtree Complete Accounting system, when setting up the original company, requires the creation of a retained earnings account in the set up procedure.

By definition, retained earnings are the net income retained in a corporation. Net income is recorded and added to retained earnings by a closing entry in which income summary is debited and retained earnings is credited. Closing entries are covered elsewhere in the textbook. Ray Neal's Capital account would contain all of the paid-in contributions by the sole proprietor (Ray Neal).

To generate the retained earnings statement:

Step 1:   On the main menu bar, click on "Reports & Forms" to get the pull down menu.

Step 2:   Click on "Financial Statements" to get the "Select a Report or Form" menu of shown in Figure A. 28.

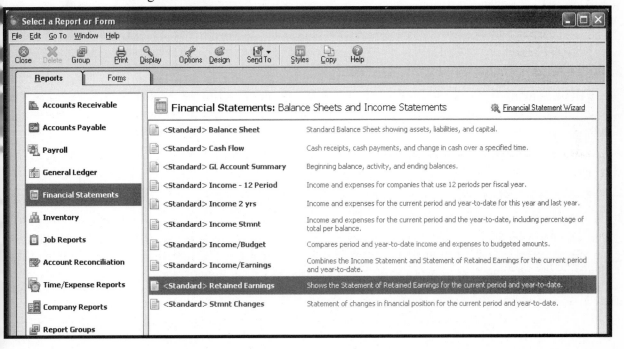

Figure A. 28   Select a report or form menu

Step 3:   Double-click on <Standard> Retained Earnings.

Step 4:   Again, a dialog box such as that for the income statement appears which gives you several choices including fiscal period. Make your selections and click on "OK" to advance and see the retained earnings statement. As with the income statement, page setup, printer selection, and printing is done through the "Setup" and "Print" icons on the report's menu bar.

Step 5: The retained earnings statement, Figure A. 29, should be on your computer screen.

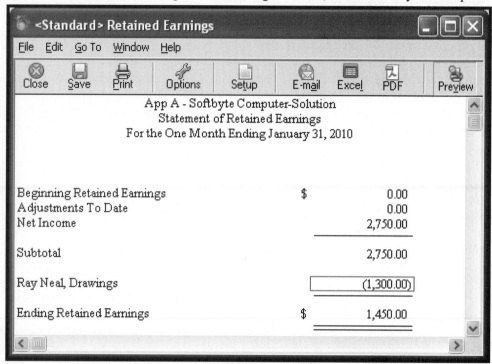

Figure A. 29 Retained earnings statement

The beginning retained earnings balance is shown on the first line of the statement. The balance is zero since this is a startup company with no previous earned income. Next month, the amount should equal (for the beginning balance) the ending balance, $1,450 as of January 31, 2010.

GENERATING THE BALANCE SHEET

The balance sheet is also prepared from all of the data you previously entered. The assets will appear at the top of the balance sheet, followed by liabilities, then owner's equity. Recall from the beginning of the chapter that assets must equal the total of the liabilities plus (in addition to) the owner's equity. Peachtree Complete Accounting will make sure this balances for you. The system will let you know if it does not balance.

The balance sheet is obtained in a similar manner as the income statement and retained earnings statement were obtained.

Step 1: On the task bar click on "Reports & Forms" to get the pull-down menu.

Step 2: Click on Financial Statements to get the "Select a Report or Form" menu.

Step 3: Double-click on "<Standard> Balance Sheet."

Again, the dialog box gives us several choices discussed earlier.

Step 4: Click "OK" to show the Softbyte balance sheet, Figure A. 30, on your computer screen. It is shown below in full screen.

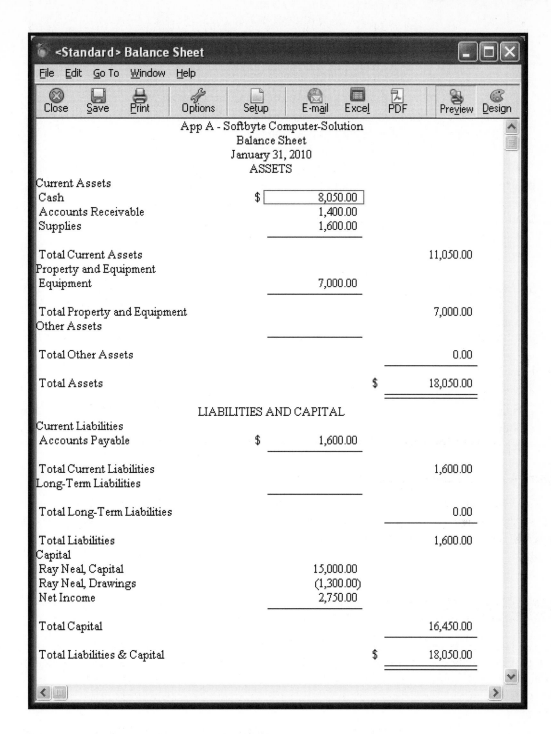

Figure A. 30 Full screen balance sheet for Softbyte

GENERATING THE STATEMENT OF CASH FLOWS

The statement of cash flows reports:
- The cash effects of a company's operations during a period.
- The cash effects of investing transactions.
- The cash effects of financing transactions.
- The net increase or decrease in cash during the period.
- The cash amount at the end of the period.

Reporting the sources, uses, and net increase or decrease in cash is useful because investors, creditors, and others want to know what is happening to a company's most liquid resource. Thus the statement of cash flows provides answers to the following simple but important questions:
- Where did the cash come from during the period?
- What was the cash used for during the period?
- What was the change in the cash balance during the period?

The statement of cash flows for Softbyte is shown in Figure A. 31. Cash increased by $8,050 during the period (January). Net cash flow provided from operating activities increased cash $1,350. Cash flow from investing transactions decreased cash $7,000 and cash flow from financing transactions increased cash $13,700. Do not be concerned at this point with how these amounts were determined, but, be aware that they are based on your earlier entries.

Step 1: On the main menu bar click on "Reports" to get the pull down menu.

Step 2: Click on "Financial Statements" to get the "Select a Report or Form" menu.

Step 3: Double-click on \<Standard> Cash Flow.

Again, the dialog box gives you several choices as addressed earlier.

Step 4: Click "OK" to show the cash flows statement for Softbyte, Figure A. 31, on your computer screen. It is shown full screen below.

<Standard> Cash Flow

File   Edit   Go To   Window   Help

Close   Save   Print   Options   Setup   E-mail   Excel   PDF   Preview   Design   Find

App A - Softbyte Computer-Solution
Statement of Cash Flow
For the one Month Ended January 31, 2010

	Current Month	Year to Date
Cash Flows from operating activities		
Net Income	$ 2,750.00	$ 2,750.00
Adjustments to reconcile net income to net cash provided by operating activities		
Accounts Receivable	(1,400.00)	(1,400.00)
Supplies	(1,600.00)	(1,600.00)
Accounts Payable	1,600.00	1,600.00
Total Adjustments	(1,400.00)	(1,400.00)
Net Cash provided by Operations	1,350.00	1,350.00
Cash Flows from investing activities		
Used For		
Equipment	(7,000.00)	(7,000.00)
Net cash used in investing	(7,000.00)	(7,000.00)
Cash Flows from financing activities		
Proceeds From		
Ray Neal, Capital	15,000.00	15,000.00
Ray Neal, Drawings	0.00	0.00
Used For		
Ray Neal, Capital	0.00	0.00
Ray Neal, Drawings	(1,300.00)	(1,300.00)
Net cash used in financing	13,700.00	13,700.00
Net increase <decrease> in cash	$ 8,050.00	$ 8,050.00
Summary		
Cash Balance at End of Period	$ 8,050.00	$ 8,050.00
Cash Balance at Beg of Period	0.00	0.00
Net Increase <Decrease> in Cash	$ 8,050.00	$ 8,050.00

Figure A. 31   Statement of cash flows

INDEX

NOTES

NOTES

NOTES

NOTES

NOTES

NOTES

NOTES

NOTES

NOTES

NOTES

NOTES

NOTES

NOTES